Political Economy of Contemporary India

The first generation of studies on political economy were efforts at explaining India's modest economic performance in the initial post-independence decades, especially the industrial stagnation since the mid-1960s, despite successful completion of import substitution, and the Green Revolution. Speeding up of growth under a more liberal policy regime, and deepening of democracy seem to have given rise to many new questions that may be considered under the second generation of political economy.

More recent developments have given rise to new concerns. The fiscal role of the state has changed, and changes in the role of the state seem discernible from being a provider to a facilitator. Food security and land acquisition have emerged as major policy dilemmas today, involving government, civil society, the private sector and the judiciary. The differential performance of various sectors, particularly the unimpressive performance of manufacturing, has also emerged as a question of interest.

The need to understand regional variation in politics and political economy, and how these have contributed to different developmental outcomes across various parts of India, remains pressing. It was suggested in the early 1960s that in India the central government was largely under the control of national capitalist class, while the states were dominated by landed interests. Does such a formulation hold ground today? With increasing political mobilization among lower classes and castes and the diffusion of economic power to the state level after the reforms, how can variation in regional development be characterized?

This volume aims to answer these questions by studying aspects of macro-economy, land, labour and employment from a variety of analytical and disciplinary perspectives. It offers rich analyses of economic growth viewed through the lenses of caste, regional politics and public investment, while also looking at long term trends in employment and wages in the public sector, and consequences of legal and policy reform.

R. Nagaraj is Professor at Indira Gandhi Institute of Development Research, Mumbai. He has worked on India's economic growth and industrialization, public sector performance and industrial labour market. He has taught a variety of courses on Indian economy, comparative economic development of India and China, and development economics.

Sripad Motiram is Associate Professor at the University of Massachusetts, Boston, and Professor at Indira Gandhi Institute of Development Research, Mumbai. His research interests are development economics, welfare economics, political economy and applied econometrics.

Political Economy of Contemporary India

Edited by

R. Nagaraj
Sripad Motiram

CAMBRIDGE
UNIVERSITY PRESS

CAMBRIDGE
UNIVERSITY PRESS

University Printing House, Cambridge CB2 8BS, United Kingdom
One Liberty Plaza, 20th Floor, New York, NY 10006, USA
477 Williamstown Road, Port Melbourne, vic 3207, Australia
4843/24, 2nd Floor, Ansari Road, Daryaganj, Delhi – 110002, India
79 Anson Road, #06–04/06, Singapore 079906

Cambridge University Press is part of the University of Cambridge.

It furthers the University's mission by disseminating knowledge in the pursuit of education, learning and research at the highest international levels of excellence.

www.cambridge.org
Information on this title: www.cambridge.org/9781107164956

First published 2017

Printed in India by Shree Maitrey Printech Pvt. Ltd., Noida

A catalogue record for this publication is available from the British Library

Library of Congress Cataloging-in-Publication Data
Names: Nagaraj, R., editor. | Motiram, Sripad, editor.
Title: Political economy of contemporary India / edited by R. Nagaraj, Sripad Motiram.
Description: New York : Cambridge University Press, 2016. | "Papers included in this volume were presented at a conference on "Political Economy of Contemporary India" held at Indira Gandhi Institute of Development Research, Mumbai (IGIDR) in November 2014." | Includes bibliographical references and index.
Identifiers: LCCN 2016049745 | ISBN 9781107164956 (hardback)
Subjects: LCSH: India--Economic policy--Congresses. | Economic development--India--Congresses. | Social classes--India--Congresses. | Democracy--India--Congresses. | India--Politics and government--Congresses/
Classification: LCC HC435.3 .P656 2017 | DDC 330.954--dc23 LC record available at https://lccn.loc.gov/2016049745

ISBN 978-1-107-16495-6 Hardback

Contents

List of Tables and Maps

Maps

List of Figures and Pictures

Figures

Pictures

Preface

The papers included in this volume were presented at a conference held at the Indira Gandhi Institute of Development Research, Mumbai (IGIDR) in November 2014. The conference, in a sense, was the culmination of a collaborative academic effort of three institutions – University of California Berkeley, King's India Institute at King's College London, and IGIDR. This conference was financed by the UK-India Education and Research Initiative (UKIERI) to bring together scholars from various academic disciplines and analytical perspectives interested in understanding the political economy of contemporary India. More details of the activities that formed a part of this initiative are available at the following web site: http://www.igidr.ac.in/indiapolecon.

We place on record our thanks to UKIERI which financed the research initiative, and scholars from the three institutions who shaped it: Pranab Bardhan and Sanchita Saxena from University of California Berkeley, Sunil Khilnani and Louise Tillin from King's India Institute, and P. G. Babu and S. Mahendra Dev from IGIDR.

While there is considerable interest in bringing together scholarship from diverse perspectives on problems and issues confronting contemporary India, doing so posed several challenges. However, it turned out to be a rewarding experience for us largely due to the enthusiasm of those who presented papers at the conference. We made an effort to look for fresh scholarship, and we were lucky that several scholars obliged, turning in fine papers. We are grateful to all those who presented papers. Three anonymous referees provided valuable feedback on the papers submitted to the volume, and we thank them. We also organized two panel discussions, which considerably enhanced the vibrancy of the conference. We thank all the panelists – C. Ram Manohar Reddy, Siddharth Varadarajan, Gautam Mody, Bernard D'Mello and Aseem Shrivastava.

The conference and the volume would not have seen the light of the day without the support of IGIDR administration and accounts, in particular the registrar Jai Mohan Pandit and conference assistant Jayshree Borkar. We are grateful for their assistance. Many scholars from Mumbai took time away from their busy schedules and participated in the conference, enriching the discussions. Given the long list, we cannot name them, but thank all of them.

Last, but not the least, we gratefully acknowledge the support of Cambridge University Press and its staff. Dhiraj Pandey was involved with the project since its inception and took it through the process of external review and revisions. Qudsiya Ahmed, Jayati Das, Anurupa Sen, Suvadip Bhattacharjee and Anwesha Rana helped see the project through.

1

Introduction

From 'Intermediate Regime' to Crony Capitalism

R. Nagaraj and Sripad Motiram

Introduction

This volume brings a selection of papers which were presented at a conference on "Political Economy of Contemporary India" at Indira Gandhi Institute of Development Research, Mumbai (IGIDR) in November 2014.[1] The conference was organised by the desire to re-focus academic attention on issues which have enormous significance for understanding the recent developments in the economy and polity of India, and that often seem to fall between the increasingly narrow disciplinary boundaries in social sciences. It also sought to revive the academic culture that looked at contemporary problems in a more holistic fashion in the classical traditions of political economy.

The papers were rich and varied, and were presented from diverse disciplinary and analytical perspectives, but clearly focused on illuminating many recent concerns. This introduction seeks to locate these papers in the context of the ongoing discourse on India's political economy. However, considering the voluminous and multi-disciplinary nature of this discourse, the introduction would necessarily have to be selective in choosing only the pieces that in our view have shaped the contours of the literature and have set the research agenda. Such an attempt would inevitably involve the authors' professional (or other) biases, which, we believe, readers will appreciate.

I India's Political Economy: An Overview

1.1 For a long time in post-independent India, economists, who occupied a pre-eminent position in the national development discourse, had agonized over the nation's modest (or mediocre) economic performance. Though it represented a distinct break from the colonial stagnation, and has accelerated in recent decades, the output growth per capita has remained modest relative to its potential (both natural and economic), and compared to the achievements of its peers in Asia. This was especially true during the first three decades after independence, when despite a variety of development plans and programmes, the economy refused to budge from the trend growth rate of about 3.5 per cent per year. Professor Raj Krishna disparagingly termed this "changelessness" in performance as "the Hindu growth rate".[2] Raj Krishna's somewhat less-acknowledged, short essay titled, "Stagnant Parameters" in *Seminar* in 1984, provided copious evidence to substantiate "his popular imagery".

In the early 1970s, while economists and planners were still grappling with refining their plan models to find quantitative "solutions" to augment growth, K. N. Raj, in his seminal paper – an application of Michal Kalecki's concept of "intermediate regimes" – offered a class theoretic explanation for the modest performance which was different from the classical Marxian analysis – in a society committed to electoral democracy. In Raj's view, the economic policy was largely circumscribed by the interests of organized working class, middle peasantry, small entrepreneurs and urban poor. In other words, this loose coalition of class interests used state power or state capitalism to enhance their class interests by limiting the power of big and foreign capital, and big landlords. In other words, these 'intermediate classes' are the ones which gained the most from state-led development as practiced in India. Hence, the state's limited resources were being frittered away in concessions and subsidies, not enough economic surplus was being re-invested to realize the economy's long term potential.

Raj's explanation drew a sharp response from the orthodox Marxist theoretician, E. M. S. Namboodiripad (1973), who reiterated the correctness of the official line of the domination of the propertied classes in India, namely, big bourgeois, landlords and foreign capital. In such a formulation, implied political change will come about only by the alliance of workers and peasants to bring about a 'people's revolution'.

About a decade later, in the context of industrial stagnation (from the mid-sixties to the late 1970s) – despite rising saving and investment rates, growing food stocks, and improved external balance – Pranab Bardhan's (1984) thesis of lack of collective action in a large, heterogeneous economy as the primary cause of the economic stagnation made its appealing presence. Positing the problem in the theoretical framework of new institutional economics, Bardhan contended that India's politics was dominated by the interests of big business, large land-owning classes and the organized working class. The inability of these classes to come together on a common policy agenda was the principal reason for lack of adequate long-term investment, and the frittering away of the meager public resources in subsidies and handouts for (mostly) undeserved.

Writing in 1993 (honouring K. N. Raj), Bardhan revisited the question: Has India graduated from the intermediate regime? There was some objective basis to believe it to be the case. Economic growth had accelerated to about 5.5 per cent per year, industry was not stagnating any longer and exports were on the upswing. However, fiscal and external balances had deteriorated. Nevertheless, Bardhan reiterated the lack of collective action by the dominant classes and ever proliferating subsidies draining away the meager public resources to be the perennial problems. Further, in 1998, in the second edition of the justly celebrated book, Bardhan dwelled on the complexity of the Indian situation, in the context of growing political and economic uncertainties caused by the 3Ms – 'Mandal, 'Masjid' and 'Market' (not necessarily in that order of significance). Bardhan reiterated the validity of his earlier thesis of collective action problem in realizing India's growth potential.

While economists were still debating the secular stagnation in industry, the economy got on to a higher growth path, from the Hindu growth rate of 3.5 per cent per year to about 5.5–6 per cent in the 1980s and the 1990s. Then, the last decade witnessed a boom that boosted India growth rate to over 8 per cent per year – being counted among the world's fastest growing economies, and snipping at China's heels – until the boom was busted by the global financial crisis (Nagaraj, 2013). Now with three decades of growth acceleration, many of Raj Krishna's stagnant parameters have turned into variables. Perhaps, most significantly, absolute poverty seems to have declined.[3] Although experts debate and question the methodology for poverty estimation, and consequently the precise numbers of the poor and the pace of poverty reduction, there is less disagreement about the direction of change.[4] There is, however, considerable debate about welfare implications of growth since it has not been translated into a proportionate improvement in health and nutrition indicators of the poor (See articles in the *Economic and Political Weekly*; Deaton and Dreze, 2009).

The national elites and vocal international interests (regardless of their political affiliation) who probably gained the most from rising growth, have celebrated the growth acceleration as a vindication of market-friendly or, free-market reforms. Critics have, however, highlighted 'costs' of growth as being borne disproportionately by the most vulnerable. They have further contended that the two-dimensional metric of growth and poverty reduction to assess economic performance could hide more than what it reveals in an unequal and diverse society. This is held to be true especially with respect to growing inequality, however measured, and widespread displacement and dispossession of the poor. Moreover, with the collapse of service exports, growth deceleration since 2011–12 and the overhang of private corporate debt on the banking system, it is perhaps time to re-think, or at a minimum re-calibrate, the liberal model.

1.2 During the last three decades, Indian politics has witnessed a diffusion of democratic power, for reasons such as (i) lowering of the age of voting from 21 to 18, thus bringing in younger citizens into the political mainstream, and (ii) passage of 73rd and 74th amendments, giving constitutional status to village panchayats and urban local bodies. Moreover, enactment of reservation for Other Backward Classes (OBCs) in government jobs and in higher education (that is, implementation of the Mandal Commission), and the demolition of Babri Masjid have deepened the politics of caste, religion and regional identities. Interestingly, these enlargements of democratic identities have significantly eroded class identities, as the size of the organized working class has shrunk, from about 10 per cent of the workforce to about 8 per cent (NCEUS, 2009). Above all, dismantling of the state-led development model and the embrace of market-friendly policies has had profound effects on the political economy. In other words, what is needed for India is class-analysis significantly supplemented by in-depth study of caste and regional dimensions.

These aspects are perhaps better captured in the narratives of political scientists, who have been keen observers of Indian development. Francine Frankel, and Llyod and Susanne Rudolph are perhaps the best representatives of this line of inquiry. Frankel's (2005) detailed account traces the interaction between politics and economics in shaping public policy and performance since independence to declare India as a case of 'Gradual Revolution' (which is in fact the sub-title of her magnum opus). Rudolph and Rudolph (1987) titled their book imaginatively as *In Pursuit of Lakshmi* using the goddess as a metaphor for aspirations in a highly complex economy and polity. In this rich narrative, the authors seem to suggest that India defies easy generalizations although they also suggest the limitations of class-theoretic analysis.

There is a widespread perception that with growing complexity, the political economy of India cannot be adequately viewed in the aggregate and mainly in economic terms; we need disaggregated regional explanations with caste composition of political forces at work. In one sense, this perhaps represents a fusion of the discourses of economists and other social scientists in understanding India's political economy.

For the economy as a whole, caste continues to play a big role. Caste-based loyalties still constitute a big axis of power in rural and urban India (even given the feeling of "castelessness" among the upper castes, as Satish Deshpande (2013) has argued). This means that there is still the need to analyze how changes in the power structure and ruling coalitions are mediated by the interface between caste, social position and control over resources. There could also be interesting regional patterns of caste configuration which could explain political economy at the sub-regional level, as will be illustrated in one of the chapters of this collection.

Many social movements in India have been responsible for significant changes in the alignment of social groups and control over resources. The clear case is that of Dalit/OBC assertion through identity-based movements. Strong farmer organizations have become powerful interest groups and lobbies around minimum support prices, public procurement, fertilizer and input subsidies and free power supply. In addition, there have also been struggles against construction of big dams (like the Narmada Bachao Andolan – Save Narmada Movement), resistance to the inroads made by corporate capital, rights-based movements for information, food, work and education, resistance movements of tribal communities for forest rights, 'left-wing extremist' movements etc. The combined effect of these movements has been to constantly reconfigure the regional political and economic contexts in many ways. Social movements unleash forces of change even when they apparently fail.

1.3 The market-oriented reforms since 1991 have been gradual, compared to reforms in most other countries, but very rapid in the context of India's historical experience. It could not have been otherwise, considering the enormous resistance to change and intense public debate on almost all aspects of the reform agenda. But, the last decade has witnessed an intense resistance and organized response to the liberal agenda, in the form of rights-based movements to protect the poor and the vulnerable against the adverse effects of the reforms. Some of these have led to the enactment of laws that are at the heart of current discourse on political economy.

In the 2000s, to further the cause of liberal reforms, abolition of urban ceiling act, formation of Special Economic Zones (SEZs) by private enterprises to promote industrialization, and acquisition of agricultural land by private enterprises for infrastructure have dramatically affected the land market. It is worth reminding that given the adverse land-man ratio, its unequal distribution and its centrality in the rural economy, the land market remained suppressed. Under the planning regime, acquisition of land by private agencies and financing of its purchase by bank credit were highly restricted to prevent accentuation of rural inequality and speculative investment in land. While the pre-existing laws were far from just or optimal, the changes brought about by the policy reform seem to have worsened the situation for the following reasons: (i) private agents could not only acquire land but government acquired the land from poor farmers on behalf of private agents (ostensibly for public purpose), (ii) Not just domestic credit even foreign capital was allowed to invest (indirectly) in land via corporate entities, leading to the creation of large land banks by private corporate entities for speculative purposes. These changes have apparently transformed the land market, adversely affecting the rural poor.

While the liberal reforms were being pursued, deepening electoral democracy seems to have put pressure from below to counter them by bringing in rights-based demands for equity and social inclusion. Since 2004, India has witnessed a series of progressive legislations to protect the poor from the vicissitudes of market forces. Though these progressive legislations have not materially changed the resources spent on social programmes as a proportion of domestic output (given the binding self-imposed fiscal austerity), they have nevertheless helped mobilize the poor and disenfranchised to redress their grievances (Nagaraj, 2012).

The above mentioned reforms have very quickly unleashed a new set of conflicts. This is amply demonstrated in growing left-wing extremism in eastern India, nation-wide protests against land acquisition favouring the corporate sector, or the revulsion in urban India against unprecedented scale of corruption that makes Bofors scandal – that toppled the Rajiv Gandhi government look like a quibble over small change. Scholars and critics have characterized the new regime as pro-business state (Kohli, 2012), or predatory capitalism (Bhaduri, 2008), or crony capitalism.

If any of these characterizations ring true, then India has surely moved away from an 'intermediate regime'. What is the economic and social composition of the ascending coalition that sustains the new regime, and how different and durable is it compared to the earlier configuration? Can the new coalition sustain, in the light of deepening democracy and in an open economy?

Kohli (2006) ascribes the faster economic growth to the abandoning of the rhetoric of socialism that sought to placate private business, giving rise to the popular term 'India incorporated'. In theory, the reforms were expected to be market friendly, implying greater competition to bring out the virtues of a competitive economy. Instead the reforms in India have been business friendly, leading to allegations of crony capitalism.

Bhaduri (2008) describes the present phase of growth as predatory capitalism, where the state supports big business against the weak and vulnerable, leading to growing economic inequality. Therefore, it is a case of growth acceleration with polarization.[5] This can be supported by evidence on growth of private corporate infrastructure companies, most of which are new entrepreneurial groups, which have expanded enormously during the last decade. These groups have accumulated enormous debt, including external commercial debt, which they are finding hard to service as the market conditions have changed. Most of these companies, in the name of infrastructure have acquired enormous land banks, often supported by the state, which is at the heart of many on-going conflicts (Nagaraj, 2013). Prabhat Patnaik (2012) locates these trends in the context of neo-liberalism. He argues that neo-liberalism has been understood only with reference to the economy (particularly in terms of the subservience of the economy to finance capital) and this understanding is incomplete since neo-liberalism also relies on an appropriate polity. He identifies the rise of sub-national and divisive identity politics and corruption as two important features of the neoliberal polity.[6]

As mentioned earlier, the last decade witnessed the enactment of many rights-based entitlements for the citizens that have come into direct confrontation with the liberal (or neo-liberal) economic agenda spearheaded since the early 1990s. This conflict is best exemplified by the issues of right to food, right to work and land acquisition.

Since 1991, governments at the centre (regardless of the coalition in power) have made various attempts to shrink access to subsidized food grains under the Public Distribution System (PDS) by targeting the subsidies to the poor in order to reduce the outflow of subsidy, and thereby the fiscal deficit. Despite apprehensions of mis-targeting, leaving out the poorest and vulnerable, a shift to a Targeted Public Distribution System (TPDS) was made in 1997. Since then, the debate has moved on to cash vs. kind transfers and the provisions of the National Food Security Act, which came into effect in 2013. Different states have also taken various steps and measures towards the implementation of PDS (e.g. changes in entitlements, universalization, expanded coverage, etc.) and this has given rise to debate and controversy.[7]

The Mahatma Gandhi National Rural Employment Guarantee Act (MNREGA, also referred to as NREGA), passed in 2005, remains a highly contested legislation. While supporters of the act have seen it as contributing to increases in wages, creating productive assets and providing employment to the poor and other marginalized groups (women, Dalits and Adivasis), the opponents have seen it as a 'policy barrier' that prevents the economic benefits from migration to be captured (World Bank, 2009) and as an inefficient programme, characterized by design flaws, that fritters away scarce public resources in populist (and political) give away.[8]

Perhaps the most contentious of all has been the Right to Fair Compensation and Transparency in Land Acquisition, Rehabilitation and Resettlement Act (LARRA) of 2013. Land acquisition, which has sharpened the economic conflicts in India (particularly in rural areas) and LARRA are the focus of several papers in this volume which are summarized in the next section. While the architects of the act (Ramesh and Khan, 2015) make a case for the act and take credit for its progressive content, others including private land acquirers have criticized that with such a stringent law, it has become impossible to acquire land for industrialization and urbanization.

To sum it up, while the liberal reforms have apparently given rise to crony capitalism (moving away from a broad coalition of state capitalism in support of the intermediate regime), the foregoing progressive legislations have seemingly blunted such a movement of the political forces. Or have they? Probably not, given that government final consumption expenditure as a proportion of domestic output has not gone up after these legislations were enacted.

If the foregoing stylized account of the studies on India's political economy holds adequate water, then what are the questions that will either contest the above narratives to offer new perspectives, or 'fill-in the picture' with detailed narratives, or qualify or modify to add nuances to it? The conference was motivated by the above questions. The papers presented at the conference can be broadly categorized into four themes: (i) macroeconomic considerations, (ii) politics of regional development, (iii) organised and urban labour markets, and (iv) the politically contentious issues surrounding land and its acquisition. While the themes may appear diverse, the underlying thread of these contributions is the focus on questions of contemporary relevance. The volume self-consciously brings together contributions from scholars with different disciplinary backgrounds (e.g. economics, political science, and social anthropology), who have used different methodologies (e.g. statistical analysis of secondary data, and ethnography). While a strong case for such an academic enterprise has been made in understanding the process of development and in framing policies,[9] attempts in the Indian context have been limited.[10] Hence, through this endeavour, we hope to encourage the intellectual tradition of broad social enquiry, cutting across narrow disciplinary and methodological boundaries. The next section will present an overview of the issues explored, locating them in their broader context.

II A Synoptic View of the Contributions

2.1 While many accounts of political economy of public institutions are available (such as the agricultural prices commission (Mitra, 1977)), none to our knowledge exists on understanding the politics of the functioning of the nation's Central Bank (Reserve Bank of India (RBI)). Partha Ray's paper has sought to fill this gap. It has attempted to capture the durable tensions in monetary policy formulation between the central bank and the union government, and the central bank and the financial markets. While the paper details many such conflicts, we will mention here two telling examples, in different policy regimes.

Nationalization of the major commercial banks in 1969 was one such instance, which even to this day draws strong opinions for and against it. In order to acquire supremacy of the Congress Party, Indira Gandhi sought to move the political agenda towards the left, by proposing populist economic policies like Garibi Hatao (abolish poverty). To achieve this goal, she sought to get control of the credit system by nationalizing the banks. Given its legally subservient status, RBI was simply made to accept the political dictate. In fact, the central bank's principal role after the nationalization became one of mobilizing the financial savings to meet the fiscal expansion and to supply credit to the 'priority sector' (agriculture and small industry) at less than market interest rates. While such a move increased financial repression, expansion of the bank branch network did lead to a rise in the domestic savings rate, and with a lag, made a dent in absolute poverty (Burgess and Pande, 2005).

More recently, foreign capital has acquired a significant stake in the monetary policy, as it now finances a substantial share of the current account deficit and seeks to influence the central bank via the finance ministry. Partha Ray's paper offers a rare insight into the conflicting interests at work during the economic boom last decade. RBI, under Y. V. Reddy's governorship, sought to highlight the potential risks of an open capital account, in a situation of fiscal dominance, whereas the finance ministry was seeking further financial liberalization (egged on perhaps by external interests) to take advantage of the international inflows, and to make Mumbai an international financial centre. Though the financial crisis in 2008 vindicated the central bank's cautious stance, the episode brought to the fore the conflicts of interest in pursuing a reasonably independent monetary policy stance.

By definition, infrastructure investments have a long-gestation period, and are capital-intensive with low rates of return spread over a long period. Given the public good nature of many of their outputs, infrastructure pricing has effectively become a public policy issue. Many of these characteristics make such industries more suitable for public ownership, or as heavily regulated private industries. Since independence, electricity was reserved for the public sector precisely for these considerations. State Electricity Boards (SEBs), as autonomous bodies, were created by an act of the parliament to grant them autonomy from government. But the reality turned out to be different. SEBs became emblematic of all the ills of public sector that is widely discussed in the contributions by Raj and Bardhan referred to earlier. After the economic reforms in 1991, entry of private and foreign capital in this sector was mooted. The enactment of the Electricity Act, 2003 (allowing entry of private capital) replacing the 1949 act was a major landmark. What are the outcomes of this legal change?

This is the question Elizabeth Chatterjee seeks to inquire in her chapter. In the electricity sector reforms, Chatterjee finds an open tilt towards big business, without any demonstrable difference in output performance. The reform has not meant a clear replacement of public sector with private enterprises, but creation of 'a dysfunctional state-market hybrid', via 'institutional multi-layering'. Public sector got undermined despite the resilience of its performance. If in the earlier state-dominated system, agriculture was the principal recipient of subsidies, in the changed hybrid, there are many more claimants to it. To quote Chatterjee: '… the political economy of power today is not reducible only to "rural bias", … a wider set of elites also contribute, including elite domestic consumers, well-connected firms, (both domestic and private), and politicians.' (p. 68).

2.2 Understanding contemporary India seems increasingly inadequate as a national narrative, though such narratives are nevertheless needed. The developments at the regional level seem to offer a much more nuanced (and granular) picture of the complexities of the nation. Marathas, who once prided themselves as the dominant caste challenging the supremacy of Brahmins in Maharashtra, are now desperately seeking the status of a backward caste (to secure a better representation in public employment and in higher education).

Why are they doing so? Rajeswari Deshpande and Suhas Pulshikar's paper offers an answer in terms of the changing political fortunes of the dominant caste, and the changing economic structure and performance of the state of Maharashtra.

Marathas are a numerically dominant and economically differentiated caste spread across the state. In the initial post-independence decades, they aligned themselves closely with the Congress party, and used the sugar cooperatives as the institutional mechanism for economic mobility. Congress Party, perceiving its dependence on the dominant caste and its ambitious caste leaders, at some point during the last three decades, encouraged non-Marathas to come into its fold. This change, slowly but surely, undermined Marathas' political dominance.

As the state's economy has become increasingly urban and service oriented, sugar industry's dominance got eclipsed with economic liberalization. As Marathas are numerically large, the poor among them seem unable to find adequate avenues for self-advancement, which perhaps explains the crisis of the dominant caste.

The earlier papers on political economy of development were written against the background of industrial stagnation after the mid-1960s. Interestingly, regional dimensions of the stagnation were mostly absent in the discourse. More recent studies have sought to explain the regional variations in much more detail. A. Kalaiyarasan's paper is an exercise in comparing the economic performance of two large Indian states, and offering a political and historical explanation for their divergent outcomes. Tamil Nadu (TN) is counted among the richer states, and West Bengal (WB) stands around the average. As is widely known, modern industry has been declining in West Bengal since the early 1970s and improvement in agricultural performance was discernible since the 1980s (Saha and Swaminathan, 1994). The paper first demonstrates that by most economic and social indicators, Tamil Nadu has outperformed West Bengal. Why is this so, despite TN's much chastised 'populist' policies draining scarce public resources away from productive investment, as against the radical political agenda of the Left Front government which ruled uninterrupted for over three decades? Kalaiyarasan seeks to address this question through the prism of 'political milieu and policy regimes in the two states in terms of populism and party-society'.

Historically, the two states were under different land tenurial systems: TN was under ryotwari, and WB under zamindari. As is well known, zamindari land tenure did not provide incentives to the tiller for productivity enhancing investment, whereas ryotwari land tenure did. Further, the author claims that the zamindari system in Bengal benefited not just the British but also the absentee landlords belonging to the upper castes, who used the surplus not for productive purposes but for other worldly pursuits. The historical legacy of the dominance of this class, the author contends, has persisted even to this day, regardless of the party in power.

In contrast, the political ethos in TN right from the colonial period was 'productivist': that is, characterized by the eagerness of rich farmers to invest in industry and technical education – seeking to emulate the Parsis of Bombay. After the Dravidian parties came to power in the 1960s, the backward castes witnessed political ascendancy, and along with it came 'assertive populism' leading to finer and finer gradations of reservations in employment and higher education. This was followed by 'paternalistic populism' where the political leader ruling the state is perceived as the benevolent ruler (*mai-baap*) protecting the weak – women, children, socially most backward. The author contends that the redistributive policies that such a regime followed – instead of being the proverbial leaky bucket of public provisioning – turned out to encourage industrialization.

In comparison, WB 'could not break the path set by the history, though under the left rule for three decades. The regional elites, despite being of left of some kind, lacked ethos needed for industrialization and redistribution'.

P. S. Vijay Shankar's paper in some sense complements Kalaiyarasan's above-mentioned contribution as it looks at agricultural performance across states. It is also well-known that green revolution technologies (that is, HYV seeds, combination of water and fertilizer) in wheat and rice gradually spread across the country. Vijay Shankar builds on the well-known Bhalla-Alagh dataset of district-wise crop production to examine the variations in agricultural performance across 300-odd districts over four decades. The districts covered account for 35 major crops and 90–95 per cent of cropped area in these districts. Interestingly, measured in terms of land productivity, the ranks of districts and states have remained roughly the same over the past four decades. In other words, despite diffusion of modern agricultural practices, the relative position of districts and states remain the same. Further, there seems to be some correlation between the ranking of land productivity and overall economic well-being (as measured by monthly per capita consumption expenditure).

To demonstrate the diffusion of modern practices, the study then offers detailed accounts of improved agricultural performance at the sub-state level in many part of the country: Malwa region of Madhya Pradesh and Telangana state (until recently part of Andhra Pradesh), just to name a few. The main finding of the paper is that the surge in the use of groundwater with the spread of electricity, and state level initiatives like procurement of food grains has expanded opportunities in agriculture. Further, the study contends that regions that have been left behind are those with sizable tribal populations, and concludes with a plea for disaggregated studies to understand their patterns of development.

2.3 Two papers deal with labour, one on public sector employment, and the other on the urban unorganized sector. Public sector workers – as part of the organized sector – form a vital constituency in many an account of India's political economy. How has this segment fared after the reforms? Has it lost its relevance under the changed policy regime? R. Nagaraj's paper seeks to report the changes in the size and structure of public employment using official statistics over a long period and NSS survey data for 2000s, and then offers a political economic explanation for the observed changes (or lack of it).

Contrary to the widely held view, the size of public employment, as a proportion of total workforce in India is distinctly smaller than in developed economies. Official figures show a 10 percentage point fall in public sector employment since 1997. But NSS estimates (based on the 5-yearly employment and unemployment surveys) show a boom in public employment in the last decade. How does one reconcile these divergent trends? The study contends that the employment boom is on account of contracting out of routine low-skilled services such as maintenance, security and transport. As these services are provided by small private agencies, it has meant informalisation of formal employment, mostly with short-term job contracts.

Though official employment has declined by 10 percentage points, one suspects that much of it is on account of natural attrition (that is retirement) of those who had joined service in the boom period of the 1960s and the 1970s. However, there does not seem to have been much reorganization of employment towards skill-intensive professions. The structure of public employment continues to be highly pyramidal with most of the employees belonging to semi and unskilled jobs in the class 3 and class 4 categories.

Why does such a dysfunctional bureaucracy persist? Why has the much discussed office automation and e-governance barely touched public services, despite India being the leader in providing back-office services globally? The study has suggested two political reasons for it. First, given the critical role of the lower-level bureaucracy in conducting elections (which can subtly influence the electoral outcomes) no political party would like to antagonize these public servants. Second, bureaucracy forms a crucial cog that not just greases the wheel of administration, but also finances the electoral system. Perhaps, it is for these reasons that even when faced with the hard budget constraint of fiscal deficit, state governments have cut back on public investment rather than on public sector employment.

Economic reforms, it is widely believed, have been a setback for organized labour, with the ascendancy of private capital, withdrawal of the state from economic activity, and the dilution of labour laws. However, some scholars, such as Rina Agarwala and Emmanuel Teitelbaum, have argued against such a simplistic view, claiming that many of the concerns of labour have moved out of capital-labour contestation, on to the broader political arena in the guise of social or citizens' rights; thus political parties have judiciously balanced business interests with workers' rights.

Supriya Roy Choudhury's paper, using recent survey data of construction workers in Bangalore, contests such a benign view. Her main findings are: (i) nearly half of the workers did not receive the minimum wage, (ii) availability of work is inadequate and irregular, (iii) awareness of social welfare board was minimal among the workers, and (iv) the social welfare provisions (that is, accident insurance, pension and scholarships) existed just in name, with pathetic quality of implementation.[11] These findings are consistent with many surveys of unorganized workers across the country.[12] The reasons for it, in economic terms, are simply the lack of political agency to implement the minimum wages act and the welfare provisions in a situation of excess supply of labour.

2.4 Land has become, as discussed in the previous section, a central issue in India's political economy and conflicts around acquisition of land for the corporate sector in various parts of India have attracted a lot of attention. It is fair to say that these conflicts have affected millions of people and influenced political outcomes in at least some states, e.g. West Bengal. Two important pieces of legislation – the Special Economic Zone (SEZ) Act and the Right to Fair Compensation and Transparency in Land Acquisition, Rehabilitation and Resettlement Act (LARRA) came into being during the United Progressive Alliance governments. After coming to power in the general election of 2014, the National Democratic Alliance (NDA) government led by the Bharatiya Janata Party (BJP) has sought to amend LARRA, leading to further debate, protest and controversy.[13] Given this, several papers in the volume focus on the issue of land.

Amit Bhadhuri's (2014), paper is not included in this volume, but presented at the conference, and captures certain important features of India's recent growth.[14] Although India has grown rapidly in the past two decades, jobs have been created mostly in un-remunerative sectors (e.g. construction). As estimated by the National Commission for Enterprises in the Unorganized Sector (NCEUS), the informal sector is large and characterized by extreme poverty and vulnerability. Bhaduri conceptualizes the process that India has been going through in the past two decades as 'development by dispossession', and formalizes it using a three-sector (corporate, informal and agricultural/natural resource) model.

The corporate sector is characterized by higher labor productivity and natural resource intensity as compared to the agricultural sector. Government acquires land on behalf of the corporate sector, which results in an increase of output in this sector and a less than proportionate decrease of output in the agricultural sector. Employment increases in the corporate sector, but decreases by a more than proportionate extent in the agricultural sector. Some of those thrown out of the agricultural sector find employment in the corporate sector or the informal sector – the rest are truly destitute. The informal sector lowers the productivity of the corporate sector (e.g. through congestion). There are two outcomes consistent with this framework: a small formal sector with high labor productivity and a large informal sector with low labor productivity.

M. Vijaybaskar and Ajit Menon analyze the land market and sales of land in peri-urban India, based upon their fieldwork in four Panchayats in Kancheepuram district, about 50 km from Chennai. They argue that changes in the way land is used have to be understood as arising from both exogenous and endogenous (e.g. ecological) factors, and the interaction between these two. Moreover, the endogenous factors could themselves be products of policies – in this case, neglect of the agricultural sector in Tamil Nadu. Although Tamil Nadu has grown faster than the country and achieved considerable progress on various development indicators, the performance of the agricultural sector has been poor. The crisis in Tamil Nadu agriculture has been more severe than in some other parts of India, agricultural incomes have declined and levels of indebtedness are high. Land markets have to be understood in this context.

Vijaybhaskar and Menon find the land market to be quite active. There is considerable difference in bargaining power among sellers; while distress-induced marginal farmers have low bargaining power, better-off farmers can wait for the right time to exploit market conditions. The buyers, who view land as an investment, mostly belong to Chennai, although from diverse backgrounds – developers, real-estate agencies, educational institutions and individuals. They operate through brokers, many of who are economically well off or politically connected farmers or residents. A key insight that emerges from this analysis is that land markets could be driven by motives of speculation and expansion by firms, and not for better agriculture. Land markets bear a complex relationship with inequality – on the one hand inequality provides an impetus to land transactions, these in turn exacerbate pre-existing disparities and iniquities (e.g. between those with information and connections and those who do not, between marginal farmers and larger farmers etc.).

Preeti Sampat provides an analysis of the evolution of Special Economic Zone (SEZ) law and policy in India. She examines the role and influence of both formal processes and 'soft law' ("non-binding coercions") on SEZ policy. While the former involved different ministries and departments, the latter comprised of meetings of industry representatives and bureaucrats, reports of industry etc. She argues that through SEZs, Indian capital aided by the Ministry of Commerce, tried to wrest control of valuable resources like land and cheap labor. However, this attempt ran into resistance from not only grassroots movements, but also surprisingly from the Ministry of Finance. The Ministry of Finance created hurdles through measures like the Minimum Alternate Tax (MAT) and Direct Taxes Code (DTC). Sampat provides a fascinating description of the conflict between the Ministries of Finance and Commerce over SEZs, discussing various explanations – clash of personalities (ministers), turf war, loss of revenue to Finance from SEZs etc.

Sampat argues that the case of SEZs illustrates an important insight into the Indian state (and states in general) that rather than being monolithic, it comprises of different and contesting ideologies and interests. The SEZ case also brings home the fact that ministerial personalities, turf wars etc. play an important role in shaping infrastructural policies that impact the lives of millions of people. Sampat therefore argues (correctly, in our opinion) for greater accountability and transparency in these policies.

Sai Balakrishnan's study focuses on the issue of Land Based Financing (LBF), which she defines as a way of monetizing land, i.e. converting it into money. She argues that there are two diametrically opposite perspectives on LBF in India. On the one hand are those on the critical left who see it as yet another instance of land grabbing/accumulation by dispossession with the state acting on behalf of private capital, whereas on the other hand are those who see it as a departure from mechanisms used in the past with enormous positive potential. Balakrishnan argues that reality is more nuanced and complex, not exactly conforming to either of these perspectives. LBF in India does have a long history, going back to the late nineteenth century when the British set up City Improvement Trust Boards (CITB) to build suburbs by acquiring agricultural lands outside cities. However, in its recent avatar, LBF is characterized by some important breaks from the past. She identifies three of these – a new price regime of land, privatization and decentralization of surpluses.

She presents a case study of the new Bangalore Airport – a particular instance of LBF. The Bangalore Airport, like some other airports around the world (e.g. Heathrow), has been envisaged so that a large part of the revenue can be derived from non-aviation activities, e.g. real estate. The advantage of this strategy is that market forces can be exploited to a greater extent since non-aviation activities (unlike aviation) are outside the purview of pricing controls. Using this and other examples, she illustrates how recent land policies have given rise to new actors ('real estate politician') and tensions and conflicts centering on firms which are financially powerful and agrarian propertied classes which are powerful in the electoral domain. She argues that LBF has accentuated spatial inequities and depoliticized the choice among various types of infrastructure (e.g. rural roads vs. airports).

Shashi R. Singh's paper presents a detailed description of land acquisition and resource development policies discussing the various theoretical perspectives that have informed them. He presents a critical evaluation of LARRA. Rob Jenkins' paper examines two issues – how the new central government has attempted to revise/reform LARRA and how different states have responded to it. He highlights four key features of LARRA that are also shared by other rights-based legislations under UPA (e.g. MNREGA) – a recognition of the disruptive role of state-led development on the lives of people; a circumscribing of public purpose, under which the state can acquire land; specification of the mechanisms through which rights can be ensured; creation of institutions to carry out functions enshrined. These allow us to characterize LARRA under the rubric of 'governance rights' – 'a combination of specific entitlements with precise procedural mechanisms to ensure their fulfillment'.

Jenkins presents a comprehensive overview of how different kinds of states (BJP-led, Congress-led etc.) have responded to LARRA and discusses case studies of particular states to argue that considerable 'path dependence' (influence of past policies) exists. Based upon his analysis, he makes two arguments. First, centre-state relations have influenced policies on issues related to land, including LARRA. Second, LARRA gives 'flexibility' to the states – which would be higher after the changes proposed by the NDA government. This flexibility, coupled with the animosity of the present NDA government towards NGOs (perceived as 'anti-development') is likely to make the states as sites for activism on land-related issues.

Nandini Nayak's paper focuses on another rights-based legislation, viz. NREGA, and is based upon ethnographic fieldwork in Barwani district in south-west Madhya Pradesh. She draws upon letters and memoranda submitted by Jagrut Adivasi Dalit Sangathan (JADS, a collective of indigenous people) to the state and civil society groups on the implementation of NREGA. Letters were used by JADS as 'tools of contention' against the local power structures.

Barwani was one of the 200 districts in which NREGA was first implemented in 2006. Prior to NREGA, owing to its proneness to drought and the vulnerability of livelihoods, Barwani saw the implementation of other such programmes – Sampoorna Gramin Rozgar Yojana (SGRY) and the National Food for Work Programme (NFWP).

Nayak provides a detailed description and analysis of the content of some of the letters submitted by JADS, throwing light on conflicts and tensions that have ensued in the implementation of NREGA. She describes various processes that are unfolding in the implementation of NREGA, some of which (e.g. self-employment as a part of NREGA) have the potential to undermine the rights enshrined in the act. She provides a mixed picture regarding the radical and emancipatory potential of rights-based legislations. With respect to NREGA, she concludes that: '… different actors engaged in the process of NREGA implementation draw on the law in vastly different ways. Not all engage in counter-hegemonic claim making, and some actors engage with the rhetoric of rights in a manner does not necessarily disturb the status quo ante, and, in fact perpetuates it, in questionable ways.'

III

The first generation studies on India's political economy in the 1970s and the 1980s were concerned with the lack of adequate growth, despite steadily improving economic fundamentals, like saving, investment, and so on. The second generation studies focused on explaining the character of faster economic growth in the recent decades, which determines the distribution of the fruits of growth. Applauding the decline in absolute poverty, policy makers have emphasized the virtues of growth acceleration, whereas political economists have sought to explain growing inequality (however measured), poor human development and growing political discontent with the pattern of growth that has been unleashed. Increasing conflicts over natural resources, political consequences of the abdication of state's responsibilities are highlighted in some of the micro pictures of political economy.

We locate this volume in this broader context. We see something of value in our attempt at methodological and disciplinary pluralism, but the question of the proverbial pudding remains. Readers will be the ultimate judges of how successful we have been in shedding light on contemporary India. Neverthless, we have endeavored to offer some insights that have been missed or underemphasized in previous analyses, particularly those emanating from within particular disciplines. The Indian state and the policies that it enacts have to be viewed in a sophisticated manner – while theoretical constructs like 'neoliberal', 'predatory', 'developmental' etc. are undoubtedly needed, they have to be unpacked rigorously. Rights and rights-based approaches are not merely 'wasteful,' or 'beneficial', or 'protective', or 'emancipatory' – they are results of particular kinds of politics, and in turn have the potential to unfold in multiple/ contradictory directions.[15] Processes of accumulation and dispossession have to be grounded in particular micro-contexts, so that the concrete mechanisms through which they operate are better understood. Finally, we need to move beyond national narratives and focus on state/regional level and comparative analyses since these smaller units could emerge as the main sites for activism, protest and the articulation of demands.

Endnotes

1. For more details of the conference and the project of which it is a part of, see http://www.igidr.ac.in/indiapolecon.
2. Among economists, there used to be a joke that each plan document was a new version of the previous plan.
3. The official estimates are present in the reports of various expert groups and committees, including the most recent one chaired by C. Rangarajan (http://planningcommission.nic.in/reports/genrep/pov_rep0707.pdf). These estimates put the figure around 50 per cent in the late seventies and around 30 per cent in 2011–12.
4. On controversies involved in the setting of poverty lines in India, see Subramanian (2012) and several articles published in the *Economic and Political Weekly* in response to the reports of the committee chaired by C. Rangarajan and its predecessor, chaired by Suresh Tendulkar.
5. For various conceptualizations of polarization and evidence that inequality and polarization have increased in India since the early 1990s, see Motiram and Sarma (2014).
6. See Patnaik (2006) which contains a more theoretically oriented discussion about the neoliberal state.
7. In the interests of space refer to Swaminathan (2000), Khera (2011), Himanshu and Sen (2013 a, b), Rahman (2014) and Narayanan (2014).

8. See the debate between a group of economists who wrote an open letter to the Prime Minister in support of NREGA (*NDTV*, 2014; *TOI*, 2014 and the references therein) and the responses by critics (Bhagwati and Panagariya (2014a, b) and the references therein). Also see Bhaduri (2007).
9. See Harriss (2002), Kanbur and Schaeffer (2007), Vakulabharanam and Motiram (2012) and the references therein.
10. Ruparelia *et al.* (2011) is an exception in this regard.
11. Reading the details of wages and working conditions reported in this study showed how little the ground reality has changed from what one of the authors of the introduction had observed in his field survey of workers in a small manufacturing enterprise in Bangalore in 1983 (Nagaraj, 1989).
12. See Naraparaju (2015) from Mumbai and Breman (2015a,b) from Ahmedabad.
13. There was therefore widespread coverage in the news media. Some examples of op-ed pieces in national newspapers are Sampat (2015) and Chakravorty (2015).
14. This paper is available on the conference web page: http://www.igidr.ac.in/indiapolecon/conference.php.
15. Such a nuanced understanding was lacking in several debates leading up to the general elections in 2014.

References

2014. 'Full Text of Leading Economists' Letter to PM Modi on NREGA.' NDTV, October 14. Available at, http://www.ndtv.com/india-news/full-text-of-leading-economists-letter-to-pm-modi-on-nrega-679089.

2014. 'Wrong Numbers: Attack on NREGA is Misleading.' *The Times of India*, November 9. Available at, http://timesofindia.indiatimes.com/home/ sunday-times/all-that-matters/Wrong-numbers-Attack-on-NREGA-is-misleading/ articleshow/45085301.cms?.

Bardhan, Pranab. 1984. *Political Economy of India*. Oxford: Clarendon Press.

Bhaduri, Amit. 2007. *Development with Dignity: A Case for Full Employment*. New Delhi: National Book Trust.

________. 2008. 'Predatory Growth.' *Economic and Political Weekly* 43 (16): 10-14. April 19.

________. 2014. 'A Study in Development by Dispossession.' Paper presented at the conference the on Political Economy of Contemporary India, held at the Indira Gandhi Institute of Development Research, Mumbai. Available at, http://www.igidr.ac.in/indiapolecon/conference.php.

Bhagwati, Jagdish and Arvind Panagariya. 2014a. 'Rural Inefficiency Act: Despite Protests About Diluting NREGA, the PM is Right to Confine it to 200 Poorest Districts.' *The Times of India* Blog, October 23. Available at, http://blogs.timesofindia.indiatimes.com/toi-edit-page/rural-inefficiency-act-despite-protests-about-diluting-nrega-the-pm-is-right-to-confine-it-to-200-poorest-districts/.

________. 2014b. 'Rejoinder on NREGA.' *The Times of India*, November 19. Available at, http://blogs.timesofindia.indiatimes.com/toi-edit-page/rejoinder-on-nrega/.

Breman, Jan. 2015a. 'The Coming and Going of Labourers in the Building Industry.' Paper presented in the Indira Gandhi Institute of Development Research Seminar Series, Mumbai, March 9.

________ . 2015b. 'Down and Out in Ahmedabad.' *Economic and Political Weekly* 50 (12): 70–71.

Burgess, Robin and Rohini Pande. 2005. 'Can Rural Banks Reduce Poverty? Evidence from the Indian Social Banking Experiment.' *American Economic Review* 95 (3): 780–795.

Chakravorty, Sanjoy. 2015. 'Whose Land?' *Indian Express*, March 10.

Deaton, Angus, and Jean Dreze. 2009. 'Food and Nutrition in India: Facts and Interpretations.' *Economic and Political Weekly* 44 (7): 42-65.

Deshpande, Satish. 2013. 'Towards a Biography of the General Category.' *Economic and Political Weekly* 48 (15): 32-39.

Frankel, Francine. 2005. *India's Political Economy 1947–2004*. New Delhi: Oxford University Press.

Harriss, J. 2003. 'The Case for Cross-Disciplinary Approaches in International Development.' *World Development* 39 (3): 487–496.

Himanshu and Abhijit Sen. 2013a. 'In-Kind Food Transfers – I.' *Economic and Political Weekly* 47 (45–46): 46-54.

________ . 'In-Kind Food Transfers – II.' *Economic and Political Weekly* 47 (47): 60-73.

Kanbur, Ravi and Paul Shaffer. 2007. 'Epistemology, Normative Theory and Poverty Analysis: Implications for Q-Squared in Practice.' *World Development* 35 (2): 183–196.

Khera, Reetika. 2011. 'India's Public Distribution System: Utilisation and Impact.' *Journal of Development Studies* 47 (7): 1038–1060.

Kohli, Atul. 2006. 'Politics of Economic Growth in India, 1980–2005.' *Economic and Political Weekly* (in two parts) 41 (13 and 14), April 1 and April 8.

________ . 2012. *Poverty amid Plenty in the New India*. Cambridge University Press.

Mitra, Ashok. 1977. *Terms of Trade and Class Relations*. London: Frank Cass.

Motiram, Sripad and Nayantara Sarma. 2014. 'Polarization, Inequality and Growth: The Indian Experience.' *Oxford Development Studies* 42 (3): 297–318.

Nagaraj, R. 1989. *Sub-Contracting in Manufacturing Industries: The Bangalore Experience*. Unpublished doctoral dissertation submitted to Jawaharlal Nehru University, New Delhi. Available at, http://shodhganga.inflibnet.ac.in/simple-search?query=Nagaraj+Rayaprolu&submit=Go.

________ . 2012. 'Development Strategies and Poverty Reduction'. In *Growth, Inequality and Social Development in India: Is Inclusive Growth Possible?*, edited by R. Nagaraj. Geneva: Palgrave Macmillan for United Nations Research Institute for Social Development.

________ . 2013. 'India's Dream Run: Understanding the Boom and its Aftermath.' *Economic and Political Weekly* 48 (20): 39-51, May 18.

Namboodiripad, E. M. S. 1973. 'On Intermediate Regimes.' *Economic and Political Weekly* 8 (48): 2133-2140, December 1.

Naraparaju, Karthikeya. 2015. *Essays on Labour Markets and Inclusive Growth in India*. Unpublished Ph.D. dissertation, Indira Gandhi Institute of Development Research, Mumbai.

National Commission for Enterprises in the Unorganised Sector. 2009. *The Main Report, Volume 1.* Available at, http://nceuis.nic.in/The_Challenge_of_Employment_in_India.pdf.

Narayanan, Sudha. 2014. 'Food Security in India: A Review of Current Debates.' *In India Development Report 2015*, edited by S. Mahendra Dev. New Delhi: Oxford University Press.

Patnaik, Prabhat. 2006. 'The State Under Neoliberalism.' *Macroscan*, October 31. Available at, http://www.macroscan.org/fet/oct06/fet311006Neo-liberalism.htm.

________. 2012. 'The Ways of Neoliberalism.' *Frontline* 29 (25), December 15–28. Available at, http://www.frontline.in/navigation/?type=static& page=archive.

Rahman, Andaleeb. 2014. 'Revival of Rural Public Distribution System.' *Economic and Political Weekly* 49 (20): 62-68.

Raj, K. N. 1973. 'The Politics and Economics of 'Intermediate Regimes.' *Economic and Political Weekly* 8 (27): 1189-1198, July 7.

Ramesh, Jairam, and Muhammad Ali Khan. 2015. *Legislating for Justice: The Making of the 2013 Land Acquisition Law.* Delhi: Oxford University Press.

Rudolph, Llyod and Susan Hoeber Rudolph. 1987. *In Pursuit of Lakshmi: The Political Economy of the Indian State.* Hyderabad: Orient Longman.

Ruparelia, Sanjay, Sanjay Reddy, John Harriss and Stuart Corbridge. 2011. eds. *Understanding India's New Political Economy: A Great Transformation?.* London: Routledge.

Saha, Anamitra and Madura Swaminathan. 1994. 'Agricultural Growth in West Bengal in the 1980s-A Disaggregation by Districts and Crops.' *Economic and Political Weekly* 29 (13): A-2 - A-11 (Review of Agriculture), March 26.

Sampat, Preeti. 2015. 'Growth for a Few, Loss for Many.' *The Hindu*, March 28.

Swaminathan, Madura. 2000. *Weakening Welfare: The Public Distribution of Food in India.* New Delhi: Left Word Books.

Subramanian, S. 2010. *The Poverty Line.* New Delhi: Oxford University Press.

Vakulabharanam, Vamsi and Sripad Motiram. 2012. 'Understanding Poverty and Inequality in Urban India since Reforms: Bringing Quantitative and Qualitative Approaches Together.' *Economic and Political Weekly* 48 (47-48): 44–52.

Economy-wide Considerations

2

The Relationship between the Reserve Bank and the Government of India

Political Economy of Central Banking in India[1]

Partha Ray

Introduction

Can the political economy of an economic institution be captured solely in terms of the political economy of the aggregate economy? If a confluence of elite interest groups such as professionals, big business, and big farmers dictates the Indian economic policy configuration, do the same groups not define the political economy of central banking in India?[2] If answers to such questions are in the affirmative, then looking into the political economy of a Central Bank could be somewhat superfluous. However, it has been noted, 'The paradox is that while the state in India has been powerful (and often heavy-handed) in its regulatory and interventionist role, it will not be described as what the political economy literature calls a "strong state"' (Bardhan, undated).[3] Thus, in presence of a not-so-strong state in an emerging economy like India, various institutions can come up and assert their influence on the policy of their mandate. It is in this context that the political economy of Central Banking in India deserves special attention.

Admittedly, to a large extent, in mainstream economics, Central Banks have been widely seen as technocratic institutions handling monetary policy (and banking supervision in many cases), essentially enjoying a monopoly over monetary policy. Then the obvious question is: why can't a Central Bank perform as a specialised government department? After all, in a representative democracy, at a level of broad generalization, peoples' aspirations are expected to be reflected in the elected government's functioning. Can then existence of Central Banks be explained solely in terms of the intricacies of financial markets (through which monetary policy operates) and the need for associated technical knowledge? Or, are there issues relating to objectives of the government and the Central Bank?

There is now a large literature in mainstream economics to the effect that a democratically elected government may have a tendency to utilize the trade-off implicit in short run Philips curve that generates an inflationary bias, which could be avoided by employing an independent Central Banker.[4] This tension between the Central Bank and the government is, however, one angle to the story. In any market economy, the Central Banks operate through financial markets; also they often regulate financial institutions. What is the relationship between the Central Bank (both as a monetary policy maker as well as a financial regulator) and the financial institutions then? Recent research have revealed that the financial regulator (often the Central Bank but not necessarily so) being part of the financial / banking sector tends to have an in-built social bias in favour of the regulated entities.[5] Moreover, in the financially advanced Western world (the US and the UK in particular), there is a large intersecting subset between the bankers and the regulators so much so that there is a 'swinging door syndrome' whereby a financial market player of today becomes a financial markets regulator tomorrow and back to the financial market the day after. In this tri-party game between the Central Bank, the government and the financial market players, are the Central Banks more tilted towards the interest of the financial market players? Or, is it the case that over time, financial market players have emerged as a significant pressure group that can influence government?

Thus, to a large extent, the functioning of a Central Bank may be couched primarily in terms of two kinds of tensions: (a) between the Central Bank (CB) and the government; and (b) between the CB and the financial market players.[6] The present paper tries to capture the evolution of political economy of Central Banking in India broadly in terms of these two general forces.

However, within these forces, the interaction between the government and the Central Bank has been of paramount importance in India. This has been buttressed by the adoption of overall macro planning in the economy in which the Central Bank was largely seen as a supplier of resources via deficit financing. Additionally, after the nationalisation of banking in 1969, channelization of saving via the banking sector and the related paradigm of 'financial repression' got in-built into the economy-wide model of resource mobilization/allocation.

In this context, three traits of the Indian Central Bank (the Reserve Bank of India (RBI)) can be noted.

First, as elsewhere, Central Bank governors in India are appointed by the government and mostly from outside and rarely from the cadre of career Central Bankers. Thus, the Central Bank governors could be seen as government emissaries to implement monetary and banking policy. This happens all over the world and India is no exception to this general trend. But what is unique in India is that the RBI Governor perhaps is more powerful and that in all practical sense all the powers of the Central Board of Directors of the RBI (the body that governs the RBI) are also vested with the Governor. Furthermore, till very recently India did not follow a committee approach to monetary policy.

Second, at the same time, it may be noted at the very outset that *de jure* RBI does not seem to be an independent institution. This is reflected in Section 30 and Section 58 of the Reserve Bank of India Act 1934. While section 30 deals with 'Powers of Central Government to supersede Central Board'[7], section 58 is devoted to 'Power of the Central Board to make regulations'. This has invited comments like, '(The RBI is) a faithful implementer of the wishes of the Finance Ministry...almost all its practices can be traced to the orders of the Finance Ministry' (Desai, 1994).

Third, as in the Indian case, most of the times, Governor is a bureaucrat / technocrat or an academic of repute and rarely a financial market professional, likelihood of the "swinging door syndrome" between the financial sector and the Central Bank could be low (Annex 1 gives a list of RBI Governors).

As the current paper tries to capture the evolution of political economy of Central Banking in India since independence, the historical chronicle is divided into three distinct phases (covering three distinct sections of the paper).[8]

The first phase would cover the first three and half decades since independence (1951 – 1985) when forces of planning were very strong. Thus, it would also cover issues like subsuming of monetary policy under credit planning of the general planning imperatives as well as bank nationalisation in 1969.

The second phase would cover the period between 1985 and 1997 that demanded reduction of net RBI credit to Central government to begin with and ultimately ending at stoppage of automatic monetization. The starting point has been taken as adoption of monetary targeting in India in sync with the recommendations of the Committee to Review the Working of the Monetary System (Chairman: Sukhamoy Chakravarty, 1985). With the cessation of *ad hoc* Treasury bills in 1997, the practice of automatic monetization was brought to a close.

The third phase would cover the period from 1997 till date. During this period, Indian monetary regime moved from 'monetary targeting' to a 'multiple indicator approach', and moved to a system of market based monetary policy *via* Liquidity Adjustment Facility (LAF) introduced in June 2000. Thus, this period would illustrate much more interesting interaction of the Central Bank not only with the government but also with financial markets and with the foreign portfolio investors. In particular, it would cover issues like perceived difference of opinion between the RBI and the Central Government in terms of extent of opening up of the economy with special reference to capital account liberalization.

Central Banking till 1985: A Hindu Marriage

To begin at the beginning, it is interesting to note that, on the eve of setting up the RBI, Montague Norman, the then Governor of Bank of England, contemplated 'a Hindoo marriage' between the Bank of England (the dominant spouse) and the RBI (the subservient wife), 'whereby in return for formal advisory services, the RBI was, to yield to the Bank of England the right to determine the disposition of its funds and generally cooperate with it in matters affecting the good management of sterling' (Chandavarkar, 2005). Retrospectively, it seems obvious that during the heyday of planning, the functioning of a Central Bank can essentially be captured in terms of objectives of planning. Former RBI Governor, P. C. Bhattacharya noted categorically, 'Monetary Policy is as much as an aspect of the State's intervention in the economic process and must naturally be attuned to the larger economic objective of the State' (Bhattacharya, 1966). A few comments are in order.

First, purely in terms of personalities, this period witnessed the resignation of RBI Governor, Sir Benegal Rama Rau in January 1957 before his second extended term of office expired, due to differences with the then Finance Minister, T. T. Krishnamachari. In fact, the Official RBI History is quite candid on the episode:

> Events in 1956–57 underlined with startling clarity that it was possible for a powerful Finance Minister to transform levers of influence that had largely

> lain dormant for many years into instruments with which to subordinate the will of the Bank to his own. These events culminated in Rama Rau's resignation as Governor directly as a result of disagreements with Finance Minister T. T. Krishnamachari, which erupted into barely concealed conflict late in 1956, and Prime Minister Jawaharlal Nehru's refusal to distance himself from TTK's efforts to undermine the independence of the Bank. The Rama Rau resignation episode was a defining moment in the Bank's history... (RBI, 1998).

Second, there cannot be any denial that Central Banking and monetary policy was subservient to fiscal policy during this period. The Second Five Year Plan (1956–67 to 1960–61) was candid in this regard and commented, 'In a developing economy the basic trend of governmental operations in the fiscal and monetary field is inevitably expansionist'. While from the vantage point of twenty-first century, this inclination of treating monetary policy as an arm of economic planning could seem inappropriate, in the context of the 1950s and the 1960s it may not be that misplaced. After all, in the early years after independence, with either low inflation or structural inflation when the problem was one of financing development, it was quite natural that monetary policy was seen as a financing source.[9] However, such a tendency of monetary policy in a *dirigisme* regime has invited comments such as, 'Indian monetary policy ...has been operated as an adjunct of an overall economic policy which remained throughout as strongly interventionist. In actual practice, it has come to be only penumbra of a fiscal policy, with much greater accent on direct methods of control' (Khatkhate, 1990).

Third, despite this, one should be careful not to compare the role of Indian monetary policy with Soviet Style command economy and infer that a submissive Central Bank acted as an agent of the government in India during this period. On the contrary, Bhattacharya (1966) hinted that the role of Indian monetary policy within the overall approach to planning was in some way comparable to French type indicative planning. More recent research on French indicative planning reveals the association between banking / finance and the golden age of European growth during 1954 – 1974, as Monnet (2013) observed:

> The discrepancies between the high growth of credit and output and the many distortions in financial markets have led many economists to conclude that the Golden Age of European growth occurred despite the numerous financial restraints. ...They discuss the effects of financial restraints but do not study the financial institutions and mechanisms that - as imperfect as they were -

> have been associated with growth. They assume that the fast development of credit and real balances has been pulled by growth rather than the contrary. On the other hand, political scientists working on the French economy ...have highlighted the strong relationships between industrial policy and credit policy. They argued that these links benefitted growth and agreed that the French state's characteristic ability to promote investment through control over the supply of credit enabled the French to achieve rapid industrial development and industrialization in the 1950s and 1960s ...Historians who have studied some specific industries and banks over this period also underlined the role of the state in credit development (pp. 2–3).

Indian Central Banking experience of this period looked remarkably similar to the French experience, wherein the Central Bank played a crucial role in credit allocation through banking supervision, rediscounting and various types of credit control.[10] Thus, the model followed in India was essentially one of 'development Central Banking' whereby the RBI had built a three-pronged strategy of providing finance through: (a) developing an institutional framework of industrial financing; (b) extending the role of rural credit; and (c) designing concessional financing schemes for economic development (Singh, Shetty and Venkatachalam, 1982).[11]

Forth, did the Indian economists commenting on the Central Banking of this period suffer from the French-kind of myopia? This is most critically revealed in Indian experience of bank nationalisation. Bank nationalisation is often seen in the larger context of left-leaning of Mrs. Indira Gandhi's (occupying both the positions of the Prime Minister and the Finance Minister at that point of time) who favoured the young-Turks in the party, comprising leaders like Chandra Sekhar or Mohan Dharia and tried to assert herself through strategic moves against the Congress Syndicate (comprising important regional leaders like Kamaraj, Nijalingappa, Atulya Ghosh and SK Patil).[12] Within such differences of opinion, it was the young Turks who finally won in terms of policy outcome and in tune with Mrs. Gandhi's tilt towards socialist economic policies, the Indian government decided to nationalise fourteen private sector banks on 20 July 1969 (Torri, 1975).

Economists' community was divided in their support of bank nationalisation. In terms of polar opposites (somewhat caricatured), two views emerged – the conservative opinion was in favour of introducing elements of social banking within the existing structure while the radicals wanted a newer banking structure in the form of bank nationalisation. While K. N. Raj was the major exponent of bank nationalisation, P. R. Brahamananda spoke out against it

(Brahamanda, 2000; Raj, 1974). Senior bureaucrats (like P. N. Haksar or P. N. Dhar) of the day also had their views either for or against bank nationalisation.[13]

While the debate from the present-day vantage point does have the possibility of getting caricatured into left versus right ideologies, taking a more holistic framework, Nayyar (1998) described the period 1967–1980 as one of co-option and mediation. The salient features of the period have been captured succinctly by Nayyar (1998):

> The crisis in the economy and the political setback to the Congress Party, at the very beginning of the first period in this phase, led to rethinking in economics and politics. There was recognition of two realities. For one, the rich peasantry had emerged as a new force demanding its due share in benefits derived from economic policies and seeking an upward mobility in the political process. For another, the poor, who had not seen any improvement in their living conditions, did exercise their right to vote in a political democracy. ...In the sphere of economics, the response was twofold. First, there was a strong, new, emphasis on agriculture. ...Second, poverty alleviation programmes began life in independent India, albeit on a modest scale...The slogan of *garibi hatao*, even if it was mere words, captured the popular imagination. But the rhetoric went further to the nationalisation of banks and the abolition of privy purses. It was these steps which gave Indira Gandhi, who dominated politics in this period through the democratic, populist and authoritarian phases of her rule, a stranglehold on the political process.

There is, however, another contrarian view that in the late 1960s, Indira Gandhi's left turn was, 'accompanied by concrete anti-capitalist – rather than pro-poor – policy measurers, like the Monopolies and Restrictive Trade Practices (MRTP) Act, and the nationalisation of banks in 1969, the nationalisation of coal and oil products in 1973, the Foreign Exchange Regulation Act (FERA) in 1974, and a set of other measures which further tightened the grip of the state over the economy, contributing to the creation of 'one of the most comprehensive systems of control and regulation of the private sector of the non-communist world' (Maiorano, 2014). In particular, a precursor to bank nationalisation was adoption of the principle of 'social control over banks' in Jabalpur session of the All India Congress Committee (AICC) in 1967 (Frankel, 2004). Thus, whatever be the interpretation, nationalisation of banks appeared to be a part of a grand strategy of a left leaning Mrs. Gandhi.

In July 1967, L. K. Jha became RBI Governor, who as a Principal Secretary to the Prime Minister had a close working relationship with Mrs. Gandhi.[14] It was during the Governorship of L. K. Jha that bank nationalisation took place. In fact, I. G. Patel, the then Secretary, Economic Affairs (and later Governor of the RBI) in his autobiography mentions,

> It was, I think, later in July 1969 that I was sent for once again. No one else was present. Without any fanfare, she (the Late Mrs. Indira Gandhi, the then Prime Minister) asked me whether banking was under my charge. On my telling that it was, she simply said: 'For political reasons, it has been decided to nationalise the banks....' There was no pretence that this was a political decision (Patel, 2002).

Patel is said to have offered two suggestions to Mrs Gandhi: (a) foreign banks should not be nationalized; and (b) instead of nationalizing all banks, it would be better if only the major banks, which accounted for 85–90 per cent of the total banking business, were nationalized; both these suggestions were accepted.[15]

What was the nature of Central Banking during this period? Joshi and Little (1994) summed it as, 'India does not have an independent Central Bank. Responsibility for major decisions on monetary policy rests with the Finance Ministry, although the Reserve Bank is closely involved. ... For some years after independence the Reserve Bank had a lot of *de facto* power and influence, but this was severely eroded after bank nationalisation' (p. 244).

The Phase of Monetary Targeting (1986–1998): Emergence of a Joint Family System

This period witnessed shifting of the RBI's framework of monetary policy, the economic foundation of which was, no doubt, provided in the Chakravarty Committee Report. As far as the framework of the monetary policy of India is concerned, Chakravarty committee advocated a simple 'monetary targeting rule with feedback'. Monetary targeting was adopted as an operational strategy of monetary policy since the mid-1980s. For the first time, the Central government budget for 1987–88 set out the target of net RBI credit to government as an integral part of the targeting exercise. What is the performance of the regime of monetary targeting? In pure numerical terms, the answer is 'unequivocally bad' – in fact, out of the 15 years span of monetary targeting, it is for only four years during which the targets were achieved (Mohanty, 2010; Ray, 2013; Table 2.1).

Table 2.1 Nature of Monetary Expansion: 1968–1985 (as % of M3)

	Bank Credit to Government			*Bank Credit to Commercial Sector*	*Net Forex Assets*	*Other Items (Net)*	*M3*
	RBI	*Commercial Banks*	*Total*				
1967–68	43.5	13.5	57.0	47.8	2.2	7.0	100.0
1968–69	43.2	13.3	56.5	49.0	3.9	9.5	100.0
1969–70	36.3	13.0	49.3	56.1	6.1	11.5	100.0
1970–71	36.3	13.2	49.5	59.2	5.0	13.7	100.0
1971–72	38.4	13.8	52.2	58.0	4.9	15.1	100.0
1972–73	37.9	15.2	53.1	58.4	3.9	15.4	100.0
1973–74	36.7	14.1	50.7	61.2	3.8	15.7	100.0
1974–75	36.4	14.7	51.1	65.1	2.1	18.4	100.0
1975–76	30.8	16.5	47.3	69.5	4.2	20.9	100.0
1976–77	24.9	14.5	42.5	67.9	9.1	19.4	100.0
1977–78	23.2	18.5	41.7	64.5	13.5	19.7	100.0
1978–79	23.5	16.2	39.7	63.7	13.3	16.7	100.0
1979–80	26.3	16.1	42.4	65.7	11.3	19.4	100.0
1980–81	29.5	16.6	46.1	65.7	8.5	20.3	100.0
1981–82	32.6	16.2	48.8	69.3	4.4	22.5	100.0
1982–83	31.2	17.0	48.2	69.9	2.5	20.6	100.0
1983–84	31.0	16.0	47.0	70.2	1.9	19.1	100.0
1984–85	33.4	15.5	48.9	68.9	3.0	20.9	100.0

Source: Ray, 2013.

A key personality in this experimentation of monetary targeting in India has been C. Rangarajan. Unlike a career bureaucrat who normally tends to be much more eclectic, Rangarajan came from academia and his economic ideology was tilted towards monetarism in the sense that perhaps he tended to believe that inflation is ultimately a monetary phenomenon. He served as a Deputy Governor of the RBI (in charge of monetary policy, research, statistics and external investment) from 1982 to 1991 and after a brief stint at the Planning Commission he came back to the RBI as Governor and was there in that capacity during December 1992 to December 1997.

But why is the performance of monetary targeting dismal in India? It is well known that a monetary targeting strategy comprises three elements: (1) reliance on information conveyed by a monetary aggregate to conduct monetary policy; (2) announcement of targets for monetary aggregates; and (3) some accountability mechanism to preclude large and systematic deviations from the monetary targets (Mishkin, 2000).[16] Empirically, a standard way for assessment of such a regime would be to do a before-after analysis. A comparison of the key macro indicators indicates that there has been a marginal reduction in average M3 growth; while growth was higher, inflation too turned out to be higher (Mohanty, 2010). The most striking feature was the presence of higher fiscal deficit, which was the main factor responsible for the dismal performance of monetary targeting. In fact, it has been observed that: 'The latter half of the 1980s have been rather unheroic years for monetary policy in India. The phase of explicit monetary targeting unfortunately coincided with a period of fiscal profligacy with the result that the credibility of monetary planning has been seriously eroded' (Mujumdar, 1989).

There are perhaps two distinct ways in which one can view adoption of monetary targeting in India.

First, it can be seen as following an old dogma which by the late 1980s had already been discredited in a number of countries and whose theoretical foundation has been questioned. Illustratively, it has been observed that, 'Monetary targeting of the type recommended will not lead us anywhere except the quagmire of stagnation; Milton Friedman is not a suitable seer for India' (Ghosh, 1987). Contrary opinions of course existed, e.g., Rangarajan himself noted that, "the scheme of fixing monetary targets based on expected increase in output and the tolerable level of inflation is far removed from the Friedmanite or any other version of monetarism" (Rangarajan, 2001).

Second, from a political economy angle (may be from a strategic consideration from the Central Bank) it may be seen as an expression of a somewhat feeble protest on the part of the Central Bank against the Central Government's rampant usage of deficit financing *via* the practice of *ad-hoc* Treasury bills. This could be a charitable explanation of this phase of monetary targeting. After all, during this period, the Central Bank tried to communicate different aspects of monetary-fiscal nexus.

The monetary-fiscal nexus of the Indian economy during this period is amply illustrated in the increasing trends in net RBI credit to Central Government till at least 1994. The way this used to be operated was through a system of *ad hoc* Treasury bills. As the name indicates, under the system of *ad hoc* Treasury bills, there was no limit of deficit financing and money was created against the backing of *ad hoc* Treasury bills with a fixed coupon of 4.6 per cent. It is as though a constant tap of monetary flows was available for the Central Government from the RBI at 4.6 per cent per annum – no matter what the situation in the financial markets was. Furthermore, due to

Government's inability to redeem these *ad hoc* Treasury bills, the Treasury bills were periodically funded into long-term securities. This system made the monetary policy completely subservient to the needs of the fisc. There was constant discomfort about this system and it was repeatedly emphasized in the writings of the senior officials of the RBI. Illustratively, Rangarajan in his Presidential address to the Indian Economic Association at Calcutta in December 1988 went on to say:

> '...The essence of coordination between fiscal policy and monetary policy lies in reaching an agreement on the extent of expansion in Reserve Bank credit to Government, year to year. This will set a limit on the extent of fiscal deficit and its monetization and thereby provide greater manoeuvrability to the monetary authorities to regulate the volume of money. It is in this context the introduction of a system of monetary targeting mutually agreed upon between the Government and the Central Bank assumes significance.'

This period also witnessed the crisis of 1991 and subsequent initiation of an all around pro-market liberalization strategy. While the initial years of liberalization witnessed the beginning of dismantling of a *dirigisme* regime, to begin with these were concentrated in industrial and trade areas. The process of financial sector liberalisation was initiated with acceptance of many of the recommendations of the Committee on the Financial System (Chairman: M. Narasimham), constituted by the RBI in 1991. While in general, this Committee initiated measures for market-driven monetary and financial policies, in specific terms it recommended measures like removal of the duality of control of banks between the RBI (who is the regulator and the supervisor of the banking system) and the Banking Division of the Ministry of Finance (who own the public sector banks). Implicitly, the issue of crowding out of private investment as a result of unbridled automatic monetization was also very much in the air.

A series of measures towards stoppage of automatic monetization were initiated. An Agreement was signed between the RBI and the Central Government on September 9, 1994 to put in place a system of limiting the creation of *ad hoc* Treasury bills during the three-year period ending 1996–97. It was mutually agreed that the *ad hoc* Treasury bills would be completely eliminated by April 1997. Subsequently, a second Agreement was signed between the RBI and the Central Government in April 1997 and the *ad hoc* Treasury Bills were completely phased out by funding *ad hoc* Treasury Bills (as on end-March 1997) into special undated securities at an interest rate of 4.6

per cent on April 1997. This marked a new beginning of the fiscal-monetary interface in India. A new system of Way and Means Advances (WMA) for the Central Government was introduced in place of the *ad hoc* Treasury bills from April 1, 1997. These new arrangements and the declining trend in deficit financing were noticeable since the early 1990s in the monetary data.

Was monetary targeting a technocratic solution to a political bias of the fiscal authorities to run a deficit perennially? There is a minority view that perhaps it was not. It may be instructive to turn to Lohmann (2006), who went on to say:

> 'In the 1960 and 1970s, monetarists proposed monetary targeting rules arguing that monetary policy matters rather than fiscal policy (their Keynesian opponents argued the opposite) and that stabilizing the money supply would serve to stabilize employment and output (ditto) .... In other words, monetary targeting rules were celebrated for their economic properties and not their political properties. The reason why policy-makers adopted monetary targeting regimes in the 1970s, however, was because in the oil price shock era monetary targeting rules turned out to be a useful political device to fend off political pressures to inflate. In the political implementation of monetary targeting rules, their political properties prevailed.'

More Recent Period: Cracks in the Joint Family or Adulthood of the RBI

The influence of personalities in central banking was perhaps evident in RBI's abandonment of monetary targeting in 1998.[17] After Rangarajan's term was over, Bimal Jalan became RBI Governor on 22 November 1997 and the RBI switched over to a more broad-based 'multiple indicators approach' since 1998–99.[18]

While the earlier issue of difference of opinion between the RBI and Government about the Centrality of RBI credit to Central government in monetary expansion got reasonably settled during this period with the agreements signed between the RBI and the Government and gradual withdrawal of the RBI from primary market of government securities, a newer dimension was added. This related to the opening up of the Indian economy in general and to the extent of capital account convertibility in particular.

When Jalan took over the RBI, the East-Asian crisis hit India and the situation became extremely volatile with heavy withdrawals of foreign funds pulling out, bringing the currency under pressure. To stabilize the exchange rate he used a variety of measures – market, monetary and administrative.

There is an influential view that, 'He challenged the received wisdom on exchange-rate management, especially the corner solutions' (Thorat, 2010).

The pattern of Indian's Balance of Payments since 2000 is well-known. In most of the years, India experienced a deficit in its current account, which was primarily financed through capital inflows – emanating from foreign direct investment (FDI), foreign portfolio investment (FPI) and external commercial borrowing (ECB). While the restriction on the flows from FDI and ECB was less controversial – over the years significant difference of opinion between the government and the RBI emerged insofar as FPI is concerned. At the risk of caricaturing RBI's position on this issue, perhaps the RBI's stance can be summed up as follows. The milestones mentioned by Tarapore Committee II were three: low inflation, low non-performing assets of the banking sector and low government deficit. Of these, the most important lacuna around early 2000 was on account of Government Deficit. Thus, till the time some semblance of order is restored in the Government's budgetary operations, exposing the country's debt to foreign players could be risky and would expose India to the 'original sin' of floating debt in a currency that was not its own. This is particularly true for Sovereign debt. Equity could be different as it would entail risk sharing by the foreign investor as well. This apart, a difference of opinion was reflected regarding the huge flow of foreign inflows through participatory notes (PNs).[19]

Liberalising capital account of the BoP

The difference of viewpoint between the RBI and the Central Government was most clearly observed in the context of the 2005 Report of the 'Expert Group on Encouraging FII Flows and Checking the Vulnerability of Capital Markets to Speculative flows' (Chairman: Ashok Lahiri)[20] to which the RBI attached a dissent note. An instance of adding a dissent note to a Government (actually Ministry of Finance) appointed committee was almost unheard of. The difference of opinion occurred along various dimensions. First, 'in view of macroeconomic implications, impact on financial stability, especially on exchange rate, and fiscal vulnerability, apart from monetary management', the RBI wanted a special group to be constituted to study measures to contain large volatility in FII flows. Second, the RBI differed on the threshold limits of different caps to be imposed on FDI and FII. Third, the RBI wanted the PNs to be wound up. Fourth, there was also difference of opinion regarding treatment of hedge funds, ceiling on holding of shares by FII and sub-accounts, operational flexibility to impart stability to the markets. To the popular press, the stance was caricatured as a debate of pro-market and anti-market and was often interpreted as, 'RBI's yearning for more capital controls' (Shah, 2006).

This difference of opinion seemed to have prolonged further. Subsequent attempts to liberalize India's capital accounts did not have much RBI involvement. This was reflected in the reports of the 2007 High Powered Expert Committee on Making Mumbai an International Financial Centre (Chairman: Percy Mistry) and the 2009 Committee on Financial Sector Reforms (Chairman: Raghuram Rajan). In fact, both these committees did not have any RBI representatives; in view of the fact that both these committees were to do with the financial sector, it was indeed surprising.

Can there be any political economy angle to this difference of opinion between the government and the RBI? This is perhaps best illustrated through the following incident. The then RBI Governor Y. V. Reddy gave a speech on the "Current Status of the Indian Economy" on February 9, 2005 at the release function of the IGIDR *India Development Report 2004–05* in Mumbai. In that speech, he dealt at length with various issues on capital account management and went on to say:

> First, a view needs to be taken on the quantity and quality of FII flows. While quotas or ceilings, as practiced by certain countries, may not be desirable at this stage, there is merit in our keeping such an option open and exercising it selectively as needed, after due notice to the FIIs. Second, there is scope for enhancing quality of flows through a review of policies relating to eligibility for registration as FIIs, and assessment of risks involved in flows through hedge funds, participatory notes, sub-accounts, etc. Strict adherence to 'Know Your Investor' principle, especially in regard to flows from tax-havens, including beneficial ownership would enhance quality. Third, price-based measures such as taxes could be examined though their effectiveness is arguable and hence may not be desirable (Reddy, 2005).

Apprehending that the RBI is contemplating some Tobin-type tax on FII inflows, select FIIS made a hue and cry and, if press reports are to be believed, they effectively conveyed that feeling to the Ministry of Finance.

The then Finance Minister, P. Chidambaram (after discussing with Reddy) appeared on TV channels to clarify that there was no proposal to cap portfolio inflows or tax them.[21] The rest of the evening's happenings is summarized in the *Business Standard* as: 'At an unscheduled press conference late that same evening at RBI headquarters on Mint Road, Reddy had to say that personally he was 'not in favour' of a ceiling on foreign fund inflows. By that time, minor changes had been made to his IGIDR speech on the Indian Central Bank's website.'

Is the incident indicative of the fact that in the political economy of the monetary policy there is now a new pressure group called foreign portfolio investors, who can be amply influential, given India's dependence on FII inflows? Does it mean that given the tensions of impossible trinity and India's fragility on the capital account front, monetary policy is now a hostage to FII influence? In absence of any further research one can only speculate. It is, however, instructive to refer to D. N. Ghosh, who, in reviewing a recent book of Reddy commented:

> First, liberalisation of the financial markets was a critical area where Reddy had been consistently advocating caution even as private financial market participants, egged on by the major Wall Street operators, had turned into strong lobbyists calling for rapid liberalisation on the plea that India was being denied the benefits of many new financial instruments that promoted efficiency in the markets. They were joined by operators in the real sector whose argument was that a cautionary policy was depriving them of the benefits of different types of financial instruments that could enable them to manage costs and risks better. The RBI and the government were both committed to a healthy development of the financial market, but Reddy, as governor, had been stressing, and quite often at that, on the need to maintain a proper balance between the different components of what goes on in the name of liberalisation. He was of the view that unless development of the domestic bond market was put on a firm footing, it would be premature to open it up to foreign investors. His particular concern was that, in the matter of the development of the bond market, the RBI, as the Central Bank of the country, had a stake, given its importance in the transmission of monetary policy and financing of infrastructure. In several areas, such as capital flows, the fiscal deficit and current account gap, there are well-known vulnerabilities in emerging market economies and the RBI was greatly concerned that we could be swept off our feet. It stuck to its conviction, even in the face of intense pressure from the political government to liberalise fast and thereby push up the growth rate. In hindsight, it is not difficult to visualise how pitiable a condition we would have found ourselves in if Reddy had succumbed! (Ghosh, 2009).

Public debt and the RBI

The difference of opinion between the RBI and the Central Government was not confined to issues relating to liberalizing capital account of the balance of payments alone. An area where the RBI and the Central Government differed significantly was debt management of the Central Government. There is an influential view that there could be conflicting objectives between RBI's pursuit of monetary policy instruments and public debt management – after all, while the objective of Debt management is minimization of cost of borrowing, monetary policy would aim at price stability and employment generation *via* tinkering with interest rates. A number of committees since 1997 have emphasized the setting up of an independent debt management office (Kanagasabapathy and Singh, 2013). The argument is succinctly summed up in a 2011 Working Group (of the Financial Sector Legislative Reforms Commission) report on debt management office (NIPFP, 2011), which said:

> While monetary management has become increasingly market oriented, there are questions in regard to RBI's operations and functional independence. Given that RBI is a major investor in government securities, its market interventions through open market operations, liquidity management operations through cash reserve ratio (CRR) and liquidity adjustment facility (LAF) can be clouded by debt management objectives. There is a possibility of a renewed fiscal-monetary nexus coming about through these channels. Additionally, RBI is also the banking regulator, and exercises control over investment proportions of banks in form of statutory liquidity ratio.

The view in the RBI till 2008 was that such a separation between debt management and monetary policy is unwarranted on practical grounds. This was reflected in a speech of RBI Deputy Governor Rakesh Mohan delivered in 2006:

> In theory, separation between the two functions would perhaps enhance the efficiency in monetary policy formulation and debt management, but the debate in the Indian context needs to recognize certain key dynamics of the fiscal-monetary nexus. First, in India, the joint policy initiatives by the Government and the RBI have facilitated good co-ordination between public debt management and monetary policy formulation. .... Second, the RBI's experience in managing public debt over the years has equipped it with the requisite technicalcapacity of efficiently fulfilling the twin responsibilities of debt and monetarymanagement in tune with requirements of the Government and market conditions. ... With all of these changes taking place in the monetary fiscal environment in the near future, there will be great need for a continued high degree of coordination in debt management between RBI and the Government. In fact, in the US, even though debt management is formally

done by the Treasury, the close co-operation that actually exists between the Federal Reserve Bank of New York and the Treasury is not very different in function from the relationship between the RBI and the Government in its debt management function (Mohan, 2006).

With the change of guard in the RBI since 2008, the views on this matter have perhaps changed in the RBI, and initially a middle office on debt management was established in the Ministry of Finance. Eventually in his Budget speech of 2015–16, Finance Minister declared his intention to establish a Public Debt Management Agency (PDMA) which would bring both India's external borrowings and domestic debt under one roof.

To reduce or not to reduce (repo rate): the Hamletian dilemma of Central Banking

In the caricatured world of opposites, the Central Bank is often seen as an "inflation nutter", while the government is believed to be primarily concerned with growth. Assuming a Phillips curve or its modern variant of a New-Keynesian non-vertical short run aggregate supply function (derived from some wage-price rigidity), a trade-off is believed and seen to exist between inflation and employment. In such a situation a central bank is expected to be more concerned with inflation and the government will be more concerned with output. Though it rarely comes out in the open in public policy pronouncements, in reality there are often plural diagnoses on the state of the economy – one from the central bank (often emphasizing the view that inflation is enemy number 1 and adopts a contractionary monetary policy) and the other from the government (articulating the view that growth is subdued and hence Central bank should make credit cheaper). This is the starting point of the Hamletian dilemma of whether to reduce the repo rate or not.

This was best illustrated in recent period in terms of a difference of opinion between D. Subbarao, the then RBI Governor and P. Chidambaram, the then Finance Minister on the issue of a necessity of a repo rate cut in 2012. To get a sense of perspective, it may be noted here that in the second quarter review of monetary policy for 2012–13, the RBI made the following evaluation of the existing growth and inflationary situation:

> In response to rising inflation pressures in the period January 2010 - October 2011, the Reserve Bank started monetary tightening. This helped in moderating inflation from its peak of 10.9 per cent in April 2010 to an average

> level of 7.5 per cent over the period January-August 2012. Over this period, however, growth slowed down and is currently below trend. *This slowdown is due to a host of factors, including monetary tightening.* … Since April 2012, the monetary policy stance has sought to balance the growth–inflation dynamic through calibrated easing. The transmission of these policy impulses through the economy is underway, and in conjunction with the fiscal and other measures recently announced, should work towards arresting the loss of growth momentum over the next few months. As inflation eases further, there will be an opportunity for monetary policy to act in conjunction with fiscal and other measures to mitigate the growth risks and take the economy to a sustained higher growth trajectory. …*It is important, however, to note that inflation turned up again in September.* To some extent, this reflected the partial pass-through of revisions of diesel and electricity prices which, notwithstanding their contribution to inflation, were absolutely necessary. Besides, underlying inflationary pressures reflected in non-food manufactured products inflation has remained stubbornly above comfort levels. *Accordingly, it is critical that even as the monetary policy stance shifts further towards addressing growth risks, the objective of containing inflation and anchoring inflation expectations is not de-emphasised* (emphasis added).

Accordingly, while reducing the CRR, the RBI decided to keep repo rate and other policy rates unchanged. Finance Minister Chidambaram expressed unhappiness over this decision of the RBI and reportedly went on to say, 'Growth is as much a concern as inflation. The government has to walk alone to face the challenge of growth... Sometimes it is best to speak and sometimes it is best to be silent. I think this is a time for silence.'[22]

Perhaps this prompted Subbarao to comment in his last lecture as RBI Governor, 'There has been a lot of media coverage on policy differences between the government and the Reserve Bank. Gerard Schroeder, the former German Chancellor, once said, "I am often frustrated by the Bundesbank. But thank God, it exists." I do hope Finance Minister Chidambaram will one day say, I am often frustrated by the Reserve Bank, so frustrated that I want to go for a walk, even if I have to walk alone. But thank God, the Reserve Bank exists.'[23]

Shape of things to come

Before concluding this paper, it may be worthwhile to speculate on the shape of things to come in the immediate future.

First, the recommendation of the Financial Sector Legislative Reforms Commission (FSLRC) of creating a unified financial regulator is largely seen as curbing the powers of the Central Bank.[24] RBI Governor Raghuram Rajan went on record to say:

> The FSLRC also seems to be inconsistent in its emphasis on synergies and regulatory uniformity. It proposes all regulation of trading should move under one roof, all regulation of consumer protection should move under another roof, but the regulation of credit should be balkanised – banks should continue to be regulated by the RBI but the regulation of the quasi-bank NBFCs should move to the Unified Financial Agency, a regulatory behemoth that would combine supervision of trading as well as credit. This balkanisation would hamper regulatory uniformity, the supervision of credit growth, and the conduct of monetary policy. ....(W)hile negotiations and cooperation between regulators can overcome organisational barriers, it is not wise to give a regulator a responsibility and leave the tools for exercising that responsibility in other hands. The RBI has responsibility for managing the internal and external value of the rupee, and more broadly, for macroeconomic stability. As a number of multilateral agencies and academics have recognised, the ability to shape capital inflows is now a recognised part of the macro-prudential tool kit. But by taking away control over internal capital inflows from the RBI, isn't the FSLRC taking away an important tool from the RBI? (Rajan, 2014).

Does it mean going forward unless such recommendations of FSLRC are rationalized there will be serious issues of co-ordination between the RBI and the Government?

Second, there is the issue of adoption of inflation targeting as a strategy of monetary policy. A large body of literature on inflation targeting emphasises that an independent Central Banker is responsible for delivering a low and stable inflation and is often accountable directly to the legislature.[25] Over the last two decades, in a large number of countries inflation targeting has emerged as a monetary policy paradigm giving birth to a new dimension in the political economy of Central Banking. What started with New Zealand in 1989 soon spread to the United Kingdom and a host of Asian countries like Thailand and the Philippines.

At the current juncture, two caveats on inflation targeting are in order. First, the idea of Central Bank independence and associated inflation targeting paradigm received a big jolt during the recent global financial crisis which showed that a country may suffer from financial instability even with a stable inflation rate. Second, even with clamour for (and also with reasonable attainment of) Central Bank independence, political economy of Central

Banking remains a live issue. Japan is a case in point. Japan adopted Central Bank independence over a decade ago, but there are ample evidence that Japanese politicians have tried to influence monetary policy through the power of appointments, threats of legal reform, and public suasion (Dwyer, 2012). Interestingly, in India, both the 2008 Report of the Committee on Financial Sector Reform (Chairman: Raghuram Rajan) as well as FSLRC spoke in favour of it and more recently the Report of a RBI appointed Expert Committee to Revise and Strengthen the Monetary Policy Framework (Chairman: Urjit Patel) recommended, 'inflation should be the nominal anchor for the monetary policy framework'.

While a single-minded focus on inflation control may not be appropriate for a country like India (Subbarao, 2011), as long as a short-run trade-off between inflation and unemployment is a reality, recent research on political economy of inflation targeting also points out to adverse distributional consequence arising out of inflation targeting (Jayadev, 2008). The recent signing of a contract between '(the) President of India acting through the Ministry of Finance and (the) Reserve Bank of India' wherein it was explicitly mentioned that, (a) the RBI will aim to bring inflation below 6 per cent by January 2016; and (b) the target for 2016–17 and for all subsequent years shall be 4 per cent with a band of plus or minus 2 per cent is an interesting development in this arena.

Conclusion

The paper has made an attempt to gauge various dimensions of political economy of Central Banking primarily in terms of its interaction with the Government. In doing so and in an effort towards summarizing trends of Central Banking since 1950s, various bends and swings were detected in the relationship between the Central Bank and Government in India. In fact, while stating the obvious without being necessarily informative, it may not be an exaggeration to say that the political economy of the Central Banking in India followed the *zeitgeist* of the Indian economy. Admittedly, the clamour for independence of the RBI so far can essentially be couched in terms of 'increasing independence within government'. As far as the recent period is concerned, one can see the emergence of foreign investors as a distinct interest group in this context. Finally, going forward the details of implementation of inflation targeting could define the contours of the relationship between the RBI and Government in India.

Annex 1: list of RBI Governors

1. Osborne Smith (1 April 1935 – 30 June 1937)
2. James Braid Taylor (1 July 1937 – 17 February 1943)
3. C. D. Deshmukh (11 August 1943 – 30 June 1949)
4. Benegal Rama Rau (1 July 1949 – 14 January 1957)
5. K. G. Ambegaonkar (14 February 1957 –28 February 1957)
6. H. V. R. Iyengar (1 March 1957 – 28 February 1962)
7. P. C. Bhattacharya (1 March 1962 – 30 June 1967)
8. L. K. Jha (1 July 1967 – 3 May 1970)
9. B. N. Adarkar (4 May 1970 – 15 June 1970)
10. S. Jagannathan (16 June 1970 – 19 May 1975)
11. N. C. Sen Gupta (19 May 1975 – 19 August 1975)
12. K. R. Puri (20 August 1975 – 2 May 1977)
13. M. Narasimham (2 May 1977 – 30 November 1977)
14. I. G. Patel (1 December 1977 – 15 September 1982)
15. Manmohan Singh (16 September 1982 – 14 January 1985)
16. A. Ghosh (15 January 1985 – 4 February 1985)
17. R. N. Malhotra (4 February 1985 – 22 December 1990)
18. S. Venkitaramanan (22 December 1990 – 21 December 1992)
19. C. Rangarajan (22 December 1992 – 21 November 1997)
20. Bimal Jalan (22 November 1997 – 6 September 2003)
21. Y. V. Reddy (6 September 2003 – 5 September 2008)
22. D. Subbarao (6 September 2008 – 4th September 2013)
23. Raghuram Rajan (4 September 2013 – 4 September 2016)
24. Urjit R. Patel (4 September 2016 – Present)

Endnotes

1. Apart from the participants of the Conference, I am grateful to S. L. Shetty, K. Kanagasabapathy, Biju Paul Abraham, Runa Sarkar, Soumyen Sikdar, R. Nagaraj and Alok Sheel for their comments on an earlier version of the paper. The usual disclaimer applies.
2. See Bardhan (1984) for a discussion on influence of these interest groups on Indian political economy.
3. 'Political Economy of India.' Accessed March 2015. Available at, http://eml.berkeley.edu/~webfac/bardhan/papers/ BardhanPoliticalEconomy.pdf.
4. See Cukierman (1992) for a snapshot of this literature.
5. This tendency among the regulators has been examined in detail in Barth, Caprio and Levine (2012), who argue that, "...regulatory bias has a natural human manifestation of the current institutional structure of financial regulation in which the financial services industry enjoys a decisive home field advantage".

6. There can still be another player in this context. Given the pace of globalization and clamour for international coordination for economic policies in recent years one can add a third dimension of international financial institution like the International Monetary Fund (IMF), the Bank for International Settlement (BIS) or the Financial Stability Board (FSB) as well as various standard setting bodies like International Organization of Securities Commissions (IOSCO) to this menu of tensions. This issue has, by and large, not been touched upon in the present paper.
7. The provisions under this section are as follows:
(1) If in the opinion of the Central Government the Bank fails to carry out any of the obligations imposed on it by or under this Act the Central Government may, by notification in the Gazette of India, declare the Central Board to be superseded, and thereafter the general superintendence and direction of the affairs of the Bank shall be entrusted to such agency as the Central Government may determine, and such agency may exercise the powers and do all acts and things which may be exercised or done by the Central Board under this Act.
(2) When action is taken under this section the Central Government shall cause a full report of the circumstances leading to such action and of the action taken to be laid before Parliament at the earliest possible opportunity and in any case within three months from the issue of the notification superseding the Board.
8. See Ray (2013), Goyal (2014) and Shetty and Ray (2015) for an account of Indian monetary policy.
9. In fact, till the 8th Five Year Plan (1992–1997), deficit financing was mentioned as sources of financing the Plan expenditure.
10. In fact, Monnet's comment on economists' myopia on French Central Banking looks prophetic in view of the following observation of Bell and Rousseau (2001), who for India noted: "Financial development can promote economic growth and structural change even in an environment in which both industrial investment and financial activities are highly regulated. …For India, at least, it appears that a particular form of financial development, whatever its flaws, has played an important role in the industrialization process".
11. The RBI played a key role in establishment of a number of industrial finance institutions like, the Industrial Finance Corporation of India (1948); Refinance Corporation of India (1958), Industrial Development Bank of India (1964; which also took over the Refinance Corporation) and the Industrial Reconstruction Corporation of India (1971). The RBI had also subscribed 50 per cent of the initial capital of the Unit Trust of India. Such developmental activities by a Central Bank have a long history in the West; see Epstein (2005) for a discussion on the developmental activities of the Central Banks across the globe.
12. There was, however, lack of ideological homogeneity among the Syndicate members: while Patil and Morarji Desai (who was seen as a member of a great syndicate later) were well-known rightists and spokesmen for the business community, Kamaraj and Chavan were in a slightly left-of-center position.

13. P. N. Dhar, the then Principal Secretary to the Prime Minister's office (during 1973–1977) recollects in his memoir:
'I had several meetings with him (P. N. Haksar) on the nationalisation of banks. I particularly remember two such meetings. In one, Mr. Krishna Menon made the startling point that if we nationalise banks we do not have to bother about mobilising resources! The other meeting, along with Mr. K. N. Raj, was at Mr. Haksar's house. I learnt later that the second meeting was at the suggestion of the Prime Minister, who was keen to know Dr. Raj's views on the subject. Dr. Raj was wholeheartedly for nationalisation and said it would take at least six months to prepare for it and that it should be done as an elaborate but clandestine exercise. Three days later banks were nationalized' (Dhar, 2000). Also see Ghosh (2015).
14. Interestingly, an offer of Governorship was made to B. K. Nehru in 1967. He declined and made the following comment in his autobiography, 'The reason why I had so far refused was the lack of independence of the Governor. I explained to him that the great battle between TTK and Rama Rao, which the latter lost, had made it clear that the Governor was a subordinate of the Ministry of Finance. Even as Joint Secretary, I used to issue orders to the Reserve Bank. I did not cherish the idea of my juniors ordering me about' (Nehru, 1997).
15. What was the impact of bank nationalization on the Indian economy? Various views emerged. Illustratively, Ketkar & Ketkar (1992) noted, 'The aggressive bank branch expansion program under the auspices of bank nationalization has increased financial savings, but the credit allocation program associated with it has had a negative effect on deposit mobilization and capital accumulation'. Athukorala and Sen (2004), on the other hand, went on to comment: '… Bank density stands out to be a highly significant variable in explaining variations in the private saving rate. A 10% decline in population per bank branch seems to increase the private saving rate by 0.4 percentage points'.
16. While monetary targeting is shown to be a failure in the US, Canada and the UK, illustrations of successful monetary targeters would include Germany and Switzerland.
17. Interestingly, Friedman (1962) argued that Central Banks are hostage to the individuals who head them.
18. While presenting the 'Monetary and Credit Policy for the First Half of 1998–99' on 29 April 1998, Jalan went on to say: 'Monetary policy in the past has been fashioned largely on the lines of specification of the desirable rate of expansion in broad money (M3) which is worked out on the basis of the response of demand for real money to income growth and the tolerable rate of inflation. Most studies in India have shown that money demand functions have so far been fairly stable. However, the financial innovations that have recently emerged in the economy provide some evidence that the dominant effect on the demand for money in near future need not necessarily be real income, as in the past. Interest rates too seem to exercise some influence on the decisions to hold money. It is not easy to evolve, in the present circumstances, a monetary conditions index or a clear-cut interest rate channel of transmission of effects of monetary policy. The information base required for such an exercise is substantial. …

As a first step to move in this direction, it is necessary to adopt a multiple indicator approach wherein interest rates or rates of return in different markets (money, capital and government securities markets) along with such data as on currency, credit extended by banks and financial institutions, fiscal position, trade, capital flows, inflation rate, exchange rate, refinancing and transactions in foreign exchange available on high frequency basis are juxtaposed with output data for drawing policy perspectives (emphasis added).'

19. Participatory Notes (PN) is a general name used for the investment by Foreign Institutional Investors (FIIs) through Offshore Derivative Instruments (ODIs) such as Participatory Notes, Equity-Linked Notes, Capped Return Notes and Participating Return Notes.
20. Available at, http://finmin.nic.in/theministry/deptecoaffairs/capitalmarketdiv/ReportEGFII.pdf.
21. In fact, in a leading business news channel, one of the spokespersons of the FII community used abusive language against Reddy on the issue of taxing FII outflows. The Channel has distanced itself from the comment of the individual next day.
22. Reported in http://www.businesstoday.in/current/economy-politics/p-chidambaram-unhappy-as-rbi-holds-back-on-cutting-rates/story/189479.html.
23. D Subbarao, 'Five Years of Leading the Reserve Bank - Looking Ahead by Looking Back' Tenth Nani A. Palkhivala Memorial Lecture delivered by on August 29, 2013, available at https://www.rbi.org.in. Also see Subbarao (2016).
24. Meanwhile, consequent to the amendment of the RBI Act in 2012, there are now two representatives from the Ministry of Finance in the RBI Board since 2012.
25. See, for example, Walsh (2009).

References

(All the URLs have been accessed during February/March 2015)

Athukorala, Prema-Chandra and Kunal Sen. 2004. 'The Determinants of Private Saving in India.' *World Development* 32 (3): 491–503.

Bardhan, Pranab. 1984. *The Political Economy of Development in India*. Delhi: Oxford University Press.

Barth, James, Gerard Caprio and Ross Levine. 2012. *Guardian of Finance: Making Regulators Work for Us*. Cambridge, Massachusetts: MIT Press.

Bell, Clive and Peter L. Rousseau. 2001. 'Post-independence India: a Case of Finance-led Industrialization?.' *Journal of Development Economics* 65 (1): 153–175.

Bernhard, William, J. Lawrence Broz and William Roberts Clark. 2002. 'The Political Economy of Monetary Institutions.' *International Organization* 56 (4): 693–723.

Bhattacharya, P. C. 1966. 'Monetary Policy and Economic Development.' B. F. Madan Memorial Lecture, reprinted in Reserve Bank of India in 2010. *Perspectives on Central Banking: Governors Speak*. Mumbai: RBI.

Brahmananda, P. R. 2000. 'Bank Nationalisation: Story of Ad Hocism and Arbitrariness.' *Hindu Business Line*, July 26. Available at, http://hindu.com/businessline/2000/07/26/stories/042608bn.htm.

Chandavarkar, Anand. 2005. 'Towards an Independent Federal Reserve Bank of India: A Political Economy Agenda for Reconstitution.' *Economic and Political Weekly* 40 (35): 3837–3845.

Cukierman, A. S. 1992. *Central Bank Strategy, Credibility, and Independence: Theory and Evidence*. Cambridge, Massachusetts: MIT Press.

Desai, Ashok. 1994. *My Economic Affair, 2nd Edition*. New York: Wiley Eastern.

Desai, Meghnad. 2009. *The Rediscovery of India*. New Delhi: Penguin Books.

Dhar, P. N. 2000. *Indira Gandhi, the 'Emergency', and Indian Democracy*. Delhi: Oxford University Press.

Dwyer, Jennifer Holt. 2012. 'Explaining the Politicization of Monetary Policy in Japan.' *Social Science Japan Journal* 15 (Summer): 179–200.

Epstein, Gerald. 2005. 'Central Banks as Agents of Economic Development.' *PERI Working Paper No. 104*. University of Massachusetts Amherst.

Frankel, Francine R. 2004. *India's Political Economy: 1947–2004*. Delhi: Oxford University Press.

Friedman, Milton. 1962. 'Should there be an Independent Monetary Authority.' In *In Search of a Monetary Constitution*, edited by L. B. Yeager. Cambridge Massachusetts: Harvard University Press.

Ghosh, Arun. 1987. 'Monetary Targeting and the Banking Sector.' *Economic and Political Weekly* 22 (1–2): 13–16.

Ghosh, D. N. 2009. 'An Inconvenient but Wise Governor of a Central Bank.' Review of *India and the Global Financial Crisis Managing Money and Finance*, by Y. V. Reddy. *Economic and Political Weekly* 44 (37): 32–34.

Ghosh, D. N. 2015. *No Regrets*. New Delhi: Rupa Publications.

Goyal, Ashima. 2014. *History of Monetary Policy in India since Independence*. Delhi: Springer.

Jayadev, A. 2008. 'The Class Content of Preferences towards Anti-Inflation and Anti-Unemployment Policies.' *International Review of Applied Economics* 22: 161–172.

Joshi, Vijay and I. M. D. Little. 1994. *India: Macroeconomics and Political Economy*. Delhi: Oxford University Press.

Kanagasabapathy, K. and Charan Singh. 2013. 'Independent Debt Management Office: Rationale, Scope and Structure.' *IIM Bangalore Working Paper No. 431*.

Ketkar, Kusum W. and Suhas L. Ketkar. 1992. 'Bank Nationalisation, Financial Savings, and Economic Development: A Case Study of India.' *Journal of Developing Areas* 27 (1): 69–84.

Khatkhate, Deena. 1990. 'Monetary Policy in India: A Command Approach.' *Economic and Political Weekly* 25 (33): 1856–1858.

Lohmann, Susanne. 2006. 'The Non-Politics of Monetary Policy.' In *Oxford Handbook of Political Economy*, edited by Barry R. Weingast and Donald A. Wittman. Oxford: Oxford University Press.

Maiorano, Diego. 2014. 'Continuity amid Change in India's Political Economy from 1980 to 2004.' *Economic and Political Weekly* 69 (9): 44–54.

Mishkin, Frederic S. 2000. From Monetary Targeting To Inflation Targeting: Lessons from the Industrialized Countries.' *Columbia University Working Paper*. Available at, https://www.gsb.columbia.edu/faculty/fmishkin/PDFpapers/00BOMEX.pdf.

Mohan, Rakesh. 2006. 'Evolution of Central Banking in India.' Lecture delivered by the Deputy Governor, RBI at the seminar organized by the London School of Economics and the National Institute of Bank Management at Mumbai on January 24. Available at, http://www.rakeshmohan.com/docs/RBIBulletinJune2006–1.pdf.

Mohanty, Deepak. 2010. 'Monetary Policy Framework in India: Experience with Multiple-Indicators Approach.' *RBI Bulletin*, April. Available at, https://www.rbi.org.in/scripts/BS_ViewBulletin.aspx?Id=11115.

Monnet, Eric. 2013. 'Financing a Planned Economy: Institutions and Credit Allocation in the French Golden Age of Growth, 1954–1974.' *Berkeley Economic History Laboratory Working Paper No. 2013–02.*

Mujumdar, N. A. 1989. 'Monetary Targeting-Objectives and Appropriate Indicators.' *Economic and Political Weekly* 24 (34).

Nayyar, Deepak. 1998. 'Economic Development and Political Democracy-Interaction of Economics and Politics in Independent India.' *Economic and Political Weekly* 33 (49): 3121–3131.

Nehru, B. K. 1997. *Nice Guys Finish Second: An Autobiography*. New Delhi: Viking Penguin India.

NIPFP. 2011. *Report of the Working Group on Debt Management Office*. Chairman: Govinda Rao. Delhi: National Institute of Public Finance and Policy (NIPFP). Available at, https://macrofinance.nipfp.org.in/fslrc/documents/wgdmoreport.pdf.

Patel I. G. 2002. *Glimpses of Indian Economic Policy: An Insider's View,* 135. New Delhi: Oxford University Press.

Raj, K. N. 1974. 'Monetary Management and Nationalisation of Banking in India.' In *Economic Theory and Planning: Essays in Honour of A. K. Das Gupta*, edited by Ashok Mitra, 302–329. Calcutta: Oxford University Press.

Rajan, Raghuram. 2014. 'Financial Sector Legislative Reforms Committee Report (FSLRC): What to do and When?.' Available at, http://rbi.org.in/Scripts/BSViewBulletin.aspx?Id =15008.

Rangarajan, C. 2001. 'Some Critical Issues in Monetary Policy.' *Economic and Political Weekly* 36 (24): 2139–2146.

Ray, Partha. 2013. *Monetary Policy (Oxford India Short Introductions)*. New Delhi: Oxford University Press.

Reddy, Y. V. 2005. 'Indian Economy: Current Status and Select Issues.' Remarks by Governor of the Reserve Bank of India, at the release of the India Development Report 2004–05, Mumbai. Available at, rbidocs.rbi.org.in/rdocs/Bulletin/PDFs/60812.pdf.

Reserve Bank of India. 1970. *History of the Reserve Bank of India. 1935–51, Volume 1.* Mumbai: Reserve Bank of India.

Balachandran, G. 1998. *The Reserve Bank of India: 1951–1967.* New Delhi: Oxford University Press (On behalf of the Reserve Bank of India).

Reserve Bank of India. 2005. *History of the Reserve Bank of India, 1967–81, Volume 3.* Mumbai: Reserve Bank of India.

Shah, Ajay. 2006. 'RBI's Yearning for More Capital Controls.' Available at, http://ajayshahblog.blogspot.in.

Shetty, S. L. and Partha Ray. 2015. 'The Evolving Contours of Monetary Policy and Commercial Banking in India.' In *Macroeconomics (ICSSR Research Surveys and Explorations, Volume 3)*, edited by Prabhat Patnaik. Delhi: Oxford University Press.

Singh, Anoop, S. L. Shetty and T. R. Venkatachalam. 1982. 'Monetary Policy in India: Issues and Evidence.' *Occasional Papers*. Mumbai: Reserve Bank of India.

Subbarao, D. 2011. 'Central Bank Governance Issues: Some RBI Perspectives.' Comments by RBI Governor at the meeting of the Central Bank Governance Group in Basel. Available at, https://www.rbi.org.in/Scripts/BS_SpeechesView.aspx?Id=563.

Subbarao, D. 2016. *Who Moved My Interest Rate? Leading the Reserve Bank of India through Five Turbulent Years*. New Delhi: Penguin Random House India.

Thorat, Usha. 2010. 'Sound Banks Needed to Protect Customers.' *Mint*, November 10. Available at, http://www.livemint.com/Politics/CKMrlRB1C2CsbZggeeTFsL/Sound-banks-needed-to-protect-customers.html.

Torri, Michelguglielmo. 1975. 'Factional Politics and Economic Policy: The Case of India's Bank Nationalisation.' *Asian Survey* 15 (12): 1077–1096.

Walsh, Carl. 2009. 'Inflation Targeting: What Have We Learned?.' *International Finance* 12 (2): 195–233.

3

The Limits of Liberalization

The Power Sector

Elizabeth Chatterjee[1]

Introduction

Alongside capital, land, and labour, energy – and especially electricity – is *the* key input for contemporary capital accumulation. Electricity is fundamental to distributive conflicts and the politics of natural resource mobilization. It has also been inextricably bound up with the Indian state project and regional modes of governance for over a century (Kale, 2014b). Reflecting this importance, power was the first major sector opened to private investors in 1991. Since then it has witnessed almost a quarter-century of institutional restructuring to recalibrate the state's role. By 2014, it was taken to provide evidence of both catchphrases of the general election, 'crony capitalism' and 'policy paralysis'. For all these reasons, Arvind Subramanian (2012) compared it to the Dandi Salt March of 1930: 'Is power, or rather the power sector, today's salt – emblematic of both the pessimistic outlook and promise of India?'

The power sector therefore provides a crucial lens on Indian political economy. This chapter assesses the light that developments in the sector cast on contemporary Indian political economy from two related angles: the changing balance of power between dominant socioeconomic groups and the country's distinctive trajectory of institutional change as it has been shaped by these constraints. It shows that power sector evidence unsettles two key analytical frames that are commonly applied to liberalization-era India.

First, and most obviously, the sector's continually poor performance casts doubt on the extent of the state's 'pro-business tilt', seen by many as the hallmark of the era of economic reforms from the 1980s onwards.[2] A survey of contemporary power subsidies for consumers and producers instead reveals an admixture of continuity and change in India's 'basic political equilibrium' (Bardhan, 1998). Despite almost a quarter-century of putative liberalization, in many States consumer-side electricity subsidies persist, most notoriously those which go to wealthy farmers. Meanwhile, poor-quality supply continues to damage industrial and commercial interests, aside from a narrow subset of well-connected energy producers. This pattern of subsidies and rents suggests that the pro-business tilt has in practice been limited, painful, and regionally uneven.

Second, this persistent inter-elite competition has fostered a distinctive dynamic of institutional change in the sector, a dynamic which troubles conventional accounts of liberalization as a single global process of displacing the statist system. The process of reform has instead been *accretive*, quite different to the institutional displacement that is associated with the archetypical, Anglo-American mode of 'deregulatory' liberalization.[3] Market institutions and producer subsidies have not displaced the statist system, but have been grafted onto it. The result is a form of liberalization as segmentation: the twin sets of subsidies – for politically important consumer groups on one side, and politically connected producers on the other – are institutionalized in a segmented 'dual-track economy, whereby state-run and market-run production exist side-by-side' (Joseph, 2010). Just as interest-group competition constrains the potential for sweeping institutional change, the new politics of the reform era are in turn informed by this segmented system.

That India's reform process has been characterized by a 'very special type of gradualism'[4] is well known. This type of incremental, partial reform has often been seen as strategic 'reform by stealth' (Jenkins, 1999); or, especially in the electricity sector, as a pathway toward second-best 'reform without losers' analogous to that taken by China (Joseph, 2010; Victor and Heller, 2007). Instead this chapter suggests that, at least in the power sector, the state-market hybrid system is neither stable nor coherent. Not only is it failing virtually all categories of consumers; it is financed through the short-term exploitation of natural resources and state-owned enterprises, and through the suppression of demand. Rather than stealthy gradualism, then, the ad hoc compromises of the reform process have so far institutionalized a system which is technically, financially, and environmentally dysfunctional.

The first half of the chapter explores the lessons from power sector evidence about the relative influence of competing dominant socioeconomic groups since 1991. It surveys major subsidies in the power sector today, providing a snapshot of its regionally varied political economy after more than two decades of putative reforms. The second half examines the constrained trajectory of institutional reform that this has helped to shape and through which these multiple subsidies are institutionalized, before examining the sustainability of this emergent system.

Electricity Subsidies: Continuity and Change in the 'Basic Political Equilibrium'

This section provides a review of contemporary electricity subsidies, both consumer- and producer-side. The utility of electricity subsidies – and the informal subsidy that is politically condoned and systematic power theft – as an indicator of wider trends is well established, both as an indicator of the relative power of different socioeconomic groups (Golden and Min, 2013) and a proxy for governance quality (Kochhar et al., 2006; Smith, 2004; Subramanian, 2012).

Across South Asia, inadequate electricity supply is *the* biggest problem businessmen report facing (Ahmed and Ghani, 2007). Improved power has become a major target of industrial lobbying. We might thus expect that a state undergoing a 'pro-business tilt' would alter policy to favour big business consumers hit by both internationally uncompetitive electricity costs and, more importantly, low quality of supply.[5] As large consumer subsidies for non-industrial and non-commercial users are widely recognized as a key cause of the sector's problems, we would expect a reduction in these subsidies.

Instead, while the proximate causes of the sector's poor performance have somewhat shifted over time, the persistence of consumer subsidies and the incompleteness of reforms continue to harm most categories of industrial and commercial consumers. Evidence from the contemporary power sector thus suggests that the pro-business tilt has been painful, incomplete, and geographically uneven.

Agricultural power

The most notorious set of consumer-side subsidies in India go to agricultural consumers. In the first decade after independence, many State governments subsidized power for industrial users.[6] From the 1960s, as Green Revolution policies helped to spread irrigated agriculture, this pattern began to be reversed.

The power sector came to be characterized by increasingly large subsidies for agricultural users, an 'energy–irrigation nexus' subsidized by higher tariffs for industrial and commercial consumers. Electricity consumption by the agricultural sector grew at an annual average compound rate of over 14 per cent between 1960/61 and 1970/71. This locked farmers into irrigation-dependent agricultural systems, creating a burgeoning environmental crisis and leading to a cycle of persistent underinvestment and low performance for many State utilities.

The beneficiaries of these subsidies tended to be wealthier farmers, able to afford to install and maintain tube wells. The subsidies have thus been read as 'widely representative of the distortions associated with the political economy of reform in India' (Sen and Jamasb, 2012). Analysts of independent India's 'first-generation' political economy used them as archetypical evidence of the influence of the dominant proprietary class of wealthy agriculturalists (Bardhan, 1998 [1984]; Varshney, 1995). State-level evidence supports this emphasis on rural influence. The pro-agriculture shift in tariff subsidies was not regionally even, but was especially pronounced in States with powerful agricultural lobbies.[7] In mirror image, public-choice theorists considered them a typical example of patronage politics. Increasingly, intense party-political competition led to downward pressure on agricultural tariffs as politicians competed to offer sops to wealthy farmers, who came to use power subsidies 'as a litmus test to judge whether politicians will serve their interests' (Golden and Min, 2013; Tongia, 2007; Victor, 2009; Wilkinson, 2006).

Moreover, often these subsidies pitted large farmers' interests against their industrial rivals directly, both through cross-subsidization and the allocation of scarce supply. In Andhra Pradesh, for example, rural electrification led to government-mandated power cuts for industrial consumers (Kale, 2014a). As a result large businesses increasingly exercised their option to exit the state-owned system. Industrial consumers, who accounted for almost two-thirds of total SEB sales in 1960, increasingly resorted to captive power plants. By 1991 the industrial share of public power usage had diminished to only 40 per cent. The rise of captive generation was particularly pronounced in states with poor utility performance and high transmission and distribution losses – and even more strongly linked to higher consumption from electrical pump sets in the agricultural sector (Joseph, 2010).

Has economic liberalization substantively changed this scenario? The initiation of power sector reforms in 1991 – with the advent of independent power producers (IPPs) in the generation segment – brought no sharp break.

Regional political economies of power appeared path-dependent in the medium term. Kale (2014a) forcefully argues that states with powerful farmer lobbies and high levels of 'wet' agriculture were *both* early rural electrifiers *and* found it difficult to reform their power sectors in the early years after 1991. Such states, even those which are otherwise considered comparatively industry- and FDI-friendly, struggled to raise electricity tariffs and thus with a cycle of underinvestment and power cuts. Faced with elections immediately after the passage of the 'watershed' Electricity Act of 2003, Andhra Pradesh, Punjab, Maharashtra, and Tamil Nadu all promised free power to farmers, while the reformist chief minister Chandrababu Naidu's 2004 election loss was widely regarded as a response to his push for power reform in Andhra Pradesh. In contrast, states with less dominant farmer lobbies appeared better placed: Odisha, with low levels of rural electrification and irrigated agriculture, became the unlikely pioneer of power reforms in the 1990s. Delhi, the only other province to privatize distribution, was also precociously urban (Kale, 2007).

By the early 2000s, industrial and commercial tariffs remained double those for domestic consumers, and more than 10 times those for agriculture (Tongia, 2007). Agriculture has accounted for around 25 per cent of total electricity consumption since 1990, but 4 per cent of total revenue – and only 7 per cent as late as 2011 (Table 3.1). The gap between subsidies booked by State utilities and the amount actually received from governments has continued to grow, between 2003 and 2011 reaching a cumulative total of $10 billion (Pargal and Banerjee, 2014).

Table 3.1 Changing Consumer Mix Over Time

	Share of consumption (%)			*Share of revenue (%)*		
	1991	2001	2011	1991	2001	2011
Agriculture	26	26	23	4	4	7
Domestic	17	25	24	11	16	20
Industrial, commercial and others	57	49	53	83	79	72

Source: From Figure 4.13 in Pargal and Banerjee (2014, 85), using Planning Commission data.

More than two decades after 1991, electricity subsidies remain a pillar of the 'subsidy syndrome' in Indian agriculture and the sector continues to be plagued by endemic load-shedding and financial turmoil. Power sector evidence thus provides some support for the notion that larger agriculturalists remain a dominant socioeconomic grouping, especially in certain states.

Plural elites

Nonetheless, the 'basic political equilibrium' has not remained static. Nor are agricultural consumers a monolithic class or the only group with an interest in the maintenance of the unreformed status quo. The political economy of power subsidies today is more complex than the classic emphasis on agriculture versus industry or 'rural bias' might suggest.

First, agriculturalists are a diverse group. The benefits of rural electrification and subsidies have historically not only been concentrated among larger landholders, but have often favoured those cultivating specific water-intensive crops: the wheat and rice farmers of Punjab and the 'sugar barons' of western Maharashtra with their links to urban politics, for example (Kale, 2014a). This has only become more apparent as the liberalization era has progressed. Evidence is mounting that virtually *all* categories of consumer would be willing to pay more for a higher quality of service (Santhakumar, 2008) – including large 'progressive farmers' oriented to export markets (Kale, 2007). In the Bharatiya Janata Party's 2014 general election campaign, consistent rather than free power appeared to become the political promise of choice.

As this suggests, regional political economies are not frozen landscapes; path dependence is not fate. There are indications of a shift in power or the willingness of politicians and regulators to take on rural interests: in recent years, all-India average agricultural tariffs have risen faster than those for other groups, although they remain low (Planning Commission, 2014). Several states with historically powerful agricultural lobbies have partially restored the financial health of their utilities. Most famously, Gujarat took administrative action to recalibrate the subsidy regime by separating out rural feeder lines into (cheap but unreliable) farm- and (more expensive but higher-quality) non-farm supplies, an idea recently imitated in seven other states.[8] Several of the worst loss-making states have embarked upon reforms, including Madhya Pradesh and Rajasthan, while Andhra Pradesh and Maharashtra both score highly for power governance reforms.[9]

The pace of change should not be exaggerated. In many states agricultural subsidies and power theft are declining only slowly. Tamil Nadu, Punjab, Andhra Pradesh, and Haryana continue with agricultural tariffs well below the all-India average (Planning Commission, 2014). Today the most dramatic losses – and debts – are concentrated in a small number of States, including Madhya Pradesh, Tamil Nadu, Jharkhand, Rajasthan, and Uttar Pradesh (Pargal and Banerjee, 2014). In 2011, only Kerala, Delhi, and West Bengal had tariffs that covered costs and made profits without requiring a subsidy. Nationally, the gap between cost and revenue has virtually doubled since 2003: across India the ratio of sales revenue to cost was only 66 per cent in 2011–12 (Planning Commission, 2014). This is due not to any major expansion of subsidies and theft, but rather rising interest costs and the soaring cost of purchased power, thanks to increasing fuel prices and poor power procurement planning (Bhattacharya and Patel, 2011; Pargal and Banerjee, 2014). Nonetheless, the sector's older political settlement constrains utilities' ability to raise tariffs enough to compensate for these rising costs.

The responsibility of agricultural subsidies for the financial plight of the power sector has often been exaggerated, however.[10] Other interests are also implicated in the proliferation of subsidies and blocking reforms. Domestic consumption remains extensively subsidized, if less heavily than agriculture in most states.[11] Again, these subsidies largely go to elites: in 21 states fixed or minimum consumption charges mean that low-consumption households pay more than higher-consumption households (Pargal and Banerjee, 2014). Farmer lobbies are not the only interests to mobilize to block tariff rises, as demonstrated by urban activism in Delhi – for example, through the middle-class United Residents' Joint Action (URJA) and the Aam Admi Party's stance towards tariff revision.

For many years, too, agricultural subsidies were calculated as a residual, masking poor utility productivity and power theft, and systematically underestimating consumption by domestic and industrial consumers (Gulati and Narayanan, 2000). The all-India average aggregate technical and commercial losses had dropped by 12 per cent since 2003, but still stood at 26 per cent of power generated in 2011 – five times the estimate for China (Pargal and Banerjee, 2014). Again, there is wide regional variation in this figure. States which have succeeded in reducing transmission and distribution (T&D) losses include Andhra Pradesh, Tamil Nadu, and Punjab. In contrast, states with extremely high levels of T&D losses, and correspondingly poor-quality supply, include Jammu & Kashmir, Bihar, Madhya Pradesh, Jharkhand, Uttar Pradesh, and much of the Northeast. In such states theft is not simply a matter of micro-level corruption, but is a tacitly condoned informal subsidy (Golden and Min, 2014) demonstrate that in UP tolerating power theft became 'part of deliberate political strategy', rising around elections. There appears to be a distinction, then, between regimes with influential farmer lobbies and a well-institutionalized tradition of 'electric populism' (Kale, 2014a), and less well-institutionalized systems in which clientelism is associated with weak rule of law and corruption (Smith, 2004).

Who steals all this power? While much theft is undoubtedly rural,[12] the extremely high levels of T&D losses in Delhi before privatization – almost 60 per cent – suggest that urban constituencies are also often implicated, and on a scale that cannot be blamed on theft in urban slums. The then power secretary argued in 2000 that the sector's problems had been misdiagnosed throughout the first decade of reforms: 'the reality is in a very organized manner electricity is pilfered by large consumers in industrial groups and high-income residential and commercial groups' (Shahi, 2005). In 1998, for example, news broke of a set of mini-steel plants in Maharashtra that had systematically stolen power worth Rs. 20 crore (Smith, 2004). Like the exit of business consumers to captive options, such high levels of theft have trapped some utilities in a spiral of weak revenues and underinvestment.

There therefore exists a wide, if incoherent, coalition of interests with an interest in retaining elements of the consumer subsidy regime – thereby damaging wider business interests. There *has* been a set of business interests that has benefited from reforms since 1991, however, albeit inconsistently: large, politically connected domestic energy players who receive producer-side subsidies.[13] Most notorious were the lavishly attractive terms offered to independent power producers (IPPs) in the 1990s, including the public shouldering of default risk, as 'attracting capital became an end in itself, rather than a considered means' (Dubash, 2011).

Even after mitigating the excesses of the first decade after 1991, privileged firms still receive generous terms from the state. These include subsidies, tax holidays, guaranteed rates of return, soft loans, and the discretionary allocation of natural resources such as coal blocks, land, and land-based financing, as the breaking of the 'Coalgate' coal block allocation scandal in 2012 revealed. A study of 19 'average' thermal projects (i.e. excluding the excesses of some early projects like Enron's Dabhol plant in Maharashtra) by the World Institute for Sustainable Energy found that cumulative subsidies amounted to 150 per cent of the original investment (WISE, 2008). Furthermore, while overly generous power purchase agreements are mostly a thing of the past thanks to competitive bidding, large corporations have made sustained efforts to renegotiate agreements where they have become less than favourable, a persistent problem in Indian infrastructure sectors (Pratap, 2013).

These benefits do not apply equally to all firms. For example, companies not awarded captive coal blocks struggle to compete when fuel supplies tighten. Unsurprisingly, given the rent-intensive nature of utilities sectors, the beneficiaries of the pro-business tilt in the power sector have so far comprised not 'business' as a whole but only a narrow subset of industrial interests. In practice policymakers often favour well-connected 'powerbroker' firms with particularistic closed deals rather than fostering open competition (Sen and Kar, 2014). Some of these benefits – such as favourable access to natural resources and the very generous rates of return built into many contracts – also apply to central public sector undertakings (CPSUs) like NTPC.[14] For their shared combination of political connections and adequate technical management, some scholars bracket both privileged state and private enterprises together as 'dual firms' (Tongia, 2007; Victor and Heller, 2007).[15] These incumbents form a new constituency that favours reforms of a particular type: gradual, opaque, and particularistic (*ibid*).

Such particularistic rents have proved unstable, however. As in the wider economy, the 'closed deal' world of the era of high mineral prices and high economic growth gradually brought about 'negative feedback effects' as the national regime's legitimacy fell (Sen and Kar, 2014). Closed deals upstream in the power sector proved especially difficult to legitimize in the longer term because the sector's performance remains poor in many areas. Many private projects have become stranded or financially unviable after changes in coal availability and regulation.

This brief survey of power sector subsidies confirms the resilience of agricultural influence in some states. It thus suggests that the fragmentation of de facto political power among interest groups continues, with large industrial and commercial interests remaining the most obvious losers from the continuing underperformance that this engenders. In an updated epilogue to his 1984 work which considered the early years of liberalization, Pranab Bardhan thus singled out electricity subsidies as evidence that 'one should not exaggerate the extent of shift in the basic political equilibrium' (1998). Writing from the alternative perspective of Kalecki's 'intermediate regime', Barbara Harriss-White agreed that '[i]n practice, control of the economy is being wrenched with the greatest difficulty from the "intermediate classes"', with 'considerable inertia and indecision in tackling the very largest state transfers' like power subsidies (2003). That these interests are *elite* is clear, and such elite pluralism has led to fundamentally unequal outcomes. Three-quarters of Indians lack regular access to commercial energy for household use – 300 million people still lack power altogether – yet in 2010 only 13 per cent of subsidy payments went to households below the poverty line (Pargal and Banerjee, 2014).

Nonetheless, the reform era has brought changes in this pattern of subsidies. First, there is some evidence that virtually all categories of consumer would be willing to pay more for higher-quality supply – though middle-class activism in Delhi despite the city's improved supply suggests that mistrust of politicians and private firms may subvert this. Second, the shift from a state-centred to a partially reformed system has created new, if unstable, rents for some producer firms. The coexistence of both older consumer subsidies and new producer subsidies raises crucial questions about the institutional trajectory of reform, to which we turn now.

Forging a Dual-Track System: India's Distinctive Dynamic of Institutional Change

The presence of a broad coalition of interests with some stake in maintaining the status quo constrains the direction of reform. As the then chairman of the Central Electricity Regulatory Commission stated in 2012: 'The political economy of the sector is crucial. Utilities are nothing but extension of government in developing countries… Solutions must lie within the existing political settlement.'[16] This section examines the distinctive trajectory of institutional reform that has resulted from these political-economic constraints.

Since 1991, the power sector has witnessed broadly three phases of reform. The first phase amended the 1948 Electricity (Supply) Act to permit private players to enter the sector as independent power producers (IPPs) with long-term contracts to supply state utilities. The second phase of reform involved a period of State-level experiments with SEB restructuring, independent regulators, and the privatization of distribution, informed by the World Bank's so-called 'global template' for power reforms (World Bank, 1993). Both of these phases were regarded as comparative failures for their high costs and lack of success in attracting sustained private investor interest. The policy fiascos of the 1990s and the arrival of a more stable national regime in 1999 together provided fuel for more thoroughgoing reform. In the third phase, the centre took up the initiative through the drafting and (attempted) enactment of the Electricity Act of 2003, in which competition superseded the thornier issue of privatization as a silver bullet.

While on paper the Electricity Act was in many ways a radical piece of pro-market legislation, in practice the striking facts have been institutional continuity and institutional proliferation alongside the changes prescribed by the 'global template'. Given the political-economic constraints that policymakers face – as well as serious intellectual and ideological challenges to the continued relevance of the global template – the sector has witnessed not a process of liberalization as deregulation but something far more segmented and dualistic.

Deregulatory liberalization involves the explicit dismantling of older institutions through direct assault (Thelen, 2012). In contrast, the mode of liberalization in the Indian power sector amounts to a form of dualization:[17] it 'do[es] not necessarily imply any direct and comprehensive attack on organized interests, but only the enlargement of certain areas of the economy within which market forces and associated relations of authority and control are able to operate more freely than in others' (Goldthorpe, 1984; Thelen, 2012). The process of institutional change that this type of liberalization brings is necessarily more marked by compromise and continuities than the more familiar deregulatory model, because it is shaped by distinct political dynamics: the persistent inter-elite competition outlined in the first section. The practical result in the power sector has been the creation of a layered and improvised state-market hybrid that institutionalizes the uneven involvement of the private sector alongside the continuation of older subsidies and statist instruments.

The segmented policy process

The broad political-economy changes introduced in the previous section are mediated through institutions. With constitutional responsibility for power policy shared between the centre and states, and with energy policy strewn across different ministries until 2014, the fragmentary nature of the state and the fragmentary character of the political settlement prove mutually reinforcing. They facilitate the creation of a segmented policy process in which particular groups are differentially able to influence various policymaking activities.

Today there is widespread agreement among influential Indian scholars that federalism has facilitated reform by fragmenting opposition (Jenkins, 1999). Yet the same proliferation also fragments the spread of reforms. The Indian state's organizational structure – multi-tiered and increasingly complex – provides multiple points of entry for new rent-seeking strategies and multiple veto points at which these strategies can be resisted. To stylize, residential and agricultural elites rely upon their influence on state governments through the ballot box, regulators, and the courts, and typically seek to influence particular policy implementation decisions, such as tariff rises. Private firms instead rely not upon electoral weight but on high-level lobbying, seeking to influence earlier stages of the policy process – agenda setting and policy formulation – as well as ad hoc renegotiation attempts behind closed doors. The fragmented state system enables both sets of groups to exercise influence upon different levels of the state. In this way 'reform by stealth' also produces unreformed zones outside its heartlands: it produces *segmentation*.

As the regionally differentiated subsidy patterns discussed above suggest, the federal division of responsibility for electricity has often facilitated resistance to power reforms at the state level. In this context, attempts at liberalization amount to form of discreet centralization, providing the newly 'fiscal disciplinarian' central government with instruments to reorient the sector away from the older subsidy regime (Rudolph and Rudolph, 2001). The centre uses its not considerable financial sway as both carrot and stick to incentivize reform compliance, both rewarding restructuring and disciplining states for underperformance. The centre's ability to harden budget constraints is limited in practice, however. States can circumvent controls, for example through underpayments to central generation firms, market borrowing, or using capital allocations to cover operating costs.[18]

The state's fissures are not only vertical. Horizontal competition between state agencies and ministries also until recently undermined comprehensive energy planning by institutionalizing representation for naturally opposed interests – like the power and coal sectors – in different bodies at the apex of the state. In such a 'byzantine and fragmented' bureaucracy, India has had virtually no coordinated energy planning (Dubash, 2011). Federalism and institutional proliferation thus together act to compartmentalize and concentrate societal influence while weakening state coordination, so interest-group competition does not simply facilitate state autonomy. Whether the current trend of centralization under the new national administration bears fruit remains to be seen.

The dual-track power sector

This fragmentation of political power between different elites, institutionalized through a vertically and horizontally fragmented state, leads to a reform process marked by unevenness and compromise. The result has not been sweeping privatization or a simple state transition from provider to facilitator. It is instead 'more accurate to describe the market as grafted on to rather than replacing the state sector, and with decidedly mixed results' (Dubash, 2011). By 2014 around 36 per cent of installed generation capacity was owned and financed by the private sector, compared with 27 per cent for the centre and 37 per cent for the States.[19] More than this, thanks to the political inability to tackle older consumer subsidies head-on, competing interests dominate in almost parallel domains of the power sector. Change has been introduced at the margins or in parallel, while the state system continues to drift into financial unviability.

The system's financial problems are primarily down to distribution. Yet the first phase of reform, the IPP policy, did not deal directly with the politicization of the distribution segment. It focused narrowly on increasing generation capacity and mobilizing scarce capital, thereby 'promising to support rather than dismantle the existing [political-economic] matrix' (Kale, 2014a). The emphasis was not on privatization, but the introduction of new greenfield projects in parallel with the public system. This continues with the ultra mega power plants of the twenty-first century, partnerships which fuse the private sector with renewed state activism.

Even after distribution was recognized as a gaping hole in the reform process, politicians and technocrats have struggled to reform the segment – it is simply too politically unpalatable. As a result, reform has often taken the form of unsuccessful backdoor initiatives, which layer new institutions atop or alongside the sediment of the state-owned system rather than displacing it. Independent regulatory agencies were imported 'through the back door' as part of the World Bank's global template, in order to depoliticize tariff-setting and encourage private investment (Dubash, 2013). This was no strategic reform by stealth, however. Instead, the uncritical fashion in which the agencies were transplanted meant that they were swiftly forced to creatively accommodate 'populist pressures' and moderate tariff hikes (*ibid*).

Backdoor reform continued with open access, the pillar of the Electricity Act, 2003. Increasing numbers of industrial and commercial consumers opted for captive generation from the 1980s on, despite its greater cost. (Others have illegally exited through meter tampering and other forms of theft, as above.) This offered an opportunity to leverage reform, increase private investment, and bring in competition. The open access provisions of the Electricity Act thus amounted to a pragmatic attempt to institutionalize the exit option, putting pressure on SEBs as their most lucrative customers abandoned them. For Joseph (2010), this marks an attempt to reform distribution by the back door while avoiding directly antagonizing agriculturalists or state governments. In practice, however, many states have remained reluctant to cede control over such lucrative customers, resorting to high charges to discourage exit and thereby stymieing distribution reform from above.[20]

Today private participation is still concentrated in generation and (to a lesser extent) transmission, but remains limited in the sector's more troubled segments. Only Odisha and Delhi, both of which lack strong farmer lobbies (as above), have privatized distribution, both before the Electricity Act, 2003. Attempts to award franchises for ring-fenced urban networks have enjoyed mixed success in attracting bidders, while the private sector has so far largely stayed away from making large-scale investments in rural electrification (Mukherjee, 2014). In this context, the large rents that some private firms receive for their involvement amounts to a form of state compensation for the risks that they run in becoming embroiled in this most politicized of sectors.

Similar policy initiatives resemble attempts to institutionalize a segmented, dualistic system more explicitly. Increasing attention to urban distribution franchises, the rise of short-term market power purchases alongside long-term contracts, and special economic zones with dedicated power plants again attempt to create parallel systems. Without decent regulation, such a solution risks ceding 'all the family silver (big cities, industrial areas, and SEZs)' to private players (Kumar and Chatterjee, 2012). Lower-revenue consumer categories, such as rural areas and small, poorer consumers, will be left to increasingly decrepit state utilities. In this way, 'financially viable units (generally privately owned) and insolvent systems (generally state-owned) can co-exist' (Victor and Heller, 2007).

Other elements of reform have more closely cleaved to the state-centred model. From the mid-1970s, power CPSUs were created to permit greater central control and to provide examples of techno-managerial efficiency in the public sector. In parallel with the constitution of market organizations, this use of public 'national champions' continues, reworked in line with the market transition to give them a veneer of corporate governance. Such firms place pressure on state-level utilities, threatening to deny supplies to defaulting states and forcing reforms on sectors and provinces – rural areas, 'neo-patrimonial' states, perhaps even the coal industry – that have hitherto proved slow to change. In this light, reform in part appears a recalibration of the system to favour energy firms and CPSUs over 'mass' users. So Surya Sethi complains:

> The tariff increases and efficiency gains at the state utilities primarily guarantee the protected returns of bloated CPSUs and the private sector both of whom have gradually raised their stake in the sector and are, today, the dominant force because of being rewarded selectively with the highest regulated returns in the world. All this is at the cost of the state utilities… (2014, 19).

Nor are these firms mere relicts. Statism's resilience is bolstered by fears about energy security and the irrelevance of the global template outside its 1990s developed-world heartlands, a debate which raises the prospect of worldwide convergence between the extremes of liberalized power markets and central planning (Sen, 2014).

The result of these piecemeal reforms is a segmented system, a 'hybrid market, where public and private investment coexist' as the result of confused waves of change rather than coordinated policy choices (Gratwick and Eberhard, 2008). As state agencies and older subsidies have proved difficult to demolish, reforms have simply overlaid new organizational structures atop the sediment of older organizations. This process has been far more haphazard, piecemeal, and faltering than the concept of stealthy, strategic 'gradualism' suggests.

The sustainability of the state-market hybrid

How sustainable and stable is this system, then? If segmentation and not institutional displacement has been the order of the game, is this process creating a durable alternative to the global standard of market-dominated 'deregulatory' power liberalization?

India is not unique in its continued state intervention in the energy sector and heavy consumer subsidies for electricity: 40 per cent of global energy subsidies are found in developing countries (Lockwood, 2014). Hybrid state-market power systems are also found in a number of other large emerging economies. Reviewing the evidence across five countries, utility regulation specialists conclude that such hybrid systems are 'not a brief waypoint on the road to some Shangri-la textbook market organization' (Victor and Heller, 2007). Instead, they offer a distinct and stable alternative to the 'global template':

> a 'dual market', combining attributes of the state-and market-based systems... While not the most economically efficiency outcome, the dual market arises and is held in place by strong political forces that favour a system in which parts of power generation and delivery are profitable even as other parts are plagued by non-payment, inadequate investment, and economically inefficient operation (*ibid*, 30).

In this vein, Joseph (2010) likens the Indian power sector to the 'dual-track economy' argued to be China's successful reform strategy. Its gradual and backdoor reforms, she suggests, may permit 'reform without losers'.

Such an assessment appears complacent in the current scenario. As late as 2011/12, India was the fourth largest provider of consumer-side fossil fuel subsidies in the world. Those above it – Saudi Arabia, Iran, Russia – enjoy far greater natural resource endowments. In contrast to many other subsidy-heavy countries, India is not fossil fuel-rich. Its 'dual-track' system has instead been funded through short-term means.

India's natural resources are directly passed on to both private power players, as well as through persistent coal theft (often with the collaboration of party politicians and bureaucrats). Profitable power and energy central state-owned enterprises are milked for resources through dividends, divestment (including cosmetic divestment – share buybacks and cross-holdings among SOEs – when private demand has been weak), underpricing, non-payment by state utilities, and the transfer of assets to private firms. SOE divestment thus appears less a consistent project of 'vacating the commanding heights of the economy' than an attempt to mobilize resources, as the government remains the majority owner in such successful firms.[21] The result has been to undermine public sector enterprises despite their improved financial performance (Khanna, 2015; Nagaraj, 2015).

In addition, public sector banks and term-lending institutions have bolstered investments in the power sector, providing loans at below-market rates. New infrastructure finance corporations have developed bonds and partial credit guarantees to push up ratings and thereby encourage long-term investments by pension funds and insurance companies, while State Bank of India and the Life Insurance Corporation have also been used to prop up share sales. This direction of investment helped to bring about the impressive capacity additions of the Eleventh Five-Year Plan, based on target-beating private investment. As growth slowed and the fuel crisis worsened, though, the banking sector was left overexposed to 'subprime lending' in the stagnating power sector. Non-performing assets went up almost ten times between September 2011 and September 2012, leading commentators to speculate about the risk of financial contagion (Bhattacharya and Patel, 2011; Pargal and Banerjee, 2014).

The centre's incentives for improved performance have also been weakened by political exigencies and the need to avoid financial contagion from overexposure to non-performing assets in the power sector, creating moral hazard. This led to the second large-scale central bailout in a decade. Again, as when the Dabhol power plant formerly owned by Enron was handed over to state-owned GAIL and NTPC, it appeared that the state had stepped in to socialize private sector losses.

In the end, the system is funded through the suppression of demand: through load-shedding, especially at peak times. The two-tier strategy thus has obvious limits. It harms consumers and concentrates vast financial liabilities in the hands of the state (Victor and Heller, 2007), while many private firms have been burned by the fuel supply crisis and the sector's overall financial and regulatory uncertainty (Mukherjee, 2014). Further reform therefore appears inevitable, but the process of institutional change and the ultimate fate of state intervention in the sector are, I submit, likely to remain distinct from the global template for 'liberalization'.

Conclusion

The spectre of the blind men and the elephant always looms over such a study. It is dangerous to extrapolate from the allocation of subsidies for a single good or service.[22] Nonetheless, the importance of electricity for capitalist accumulation, distributive politics, the state, and the environment make it a critical lens through which to understand India's contemporary political economy.

With this caveat, this chapter has sought to draw out two troublesome sets of ideas that post-1991 developments in the power sector offer for theories of liberalization in India. First, continuities in consumer subsidies show the limits of the state's pro-business turn and the resilience of agricultural power. Nonetheless, the political economy of power today is not reducible only 'rural bias': a wider set of elites also contribute, including elite domestic consumers, well-connected firms (both domestic and private), and politicians. More broadly, the sector's deep failings have created a situation that is increasingly recognized as a low-level equilibrium, which even some sets of agricultural elites admit might benefit from policy change.

These plural and competing elites tug power policy in different directions, magnified by state fragmentation on both vertical and horizontal lines. Such fraught political dynamics have created a distinctive trajectory of institutional change in the sector. Power reform has proceeded not through displacement of older statist organizations, but through ad hoc institutional layering. The result is a dysfunctional state-market hybrid, with market institutions and private participation grafted onto a loss-making state sector. This system is financed through short-term exploitation of natural resources and the state-owned enterprises that dominate them. Unlike its equivalents in resource-rich emerging economies, then, this hybrid system is neither stable nor coherent.

If it does not amount to a coherent model for the power sector, the dualistic dynamic of institutional change that has emerged from dominant class competition may indeed be a hallmark of Indian liberalization. It captures the surprising resilience, and neglect, of the public sector (Khanna, 2015; Nagaraj, 2015), even as valuable segments of the economy are 'cherry-picked' for private players.

Endnotes

1. I am very grateful to Barbara Harriss-White and to conference participants at the Indira Gandhi Institute of Development Research, Mumbai, for useful comments on an earlier version of this chapter.
2. The phrase is Atul Kohli's (Kohli, 2006, 2012; see also Rodrik and Subramanian, 2004). Subsequently the notion that 'industrial capitalists are now the dominant group within the state apparatus' (Gupta and Sivaramakrishnan, 2011, 6), systematically favoured by government policy, has since received wide credence. See, for example, Chatterjee (2008, 61) and the consensus presented in Tillin (2013).
3. On Anglo-American 'deregulatory' liberalization and institutional displacement, see Thelen (2012, 146–7). Of course, even in the United States and Britain liberalization has had limits, as is revealed by Paul Pierson's celebrated work on the resilience of welfare state institutions (Pierson, 1994).
4. Montek Singh Ahluwalia, quoted in Jenkins (2004, 348).
5. As had been suggested as early as a World Bank survey in 1962 (King, 1967, 229–231), industrial consumers appear to prioritize *quality* rather price concerns (see also Joseph 2010, 509).
6. Constitutional responsibility for electricity is shared between the centre and States, although the latter have responsibility for distribution (the all-important 'last mile' of delivery to individual consumers). The crucial institutions were the State electricity boards (SEBs), vertically integrated monopolies formed under the 1948 Electricity (Supply) Act. In most cases they came to operate as extensions of State energy ministries, relying on inconsistent payments from State governments.
7. This is clearly demonstrated by Kale (2014a). Tamil Nadu, for example, enjoyed relatively high levels of rural electrification even before 1947, and turned early to cross-subsidization of rural electrification by industrialists. As a result it suffered from power shortages by the 1970s (*ibid*, 170). As early as 1968, Punjab turned to flat metering of agricultural power as did Maharashtra in 1977; in the latter, although Mumbai remained an enclave of private ownership, the power sector accounted for 40 per cent of planned allocations by 1978 (*ibid*, 62–99). The relationship was iterative, Kale shows: States in which farmers mobilized or gained influence within government enjoyed higher levels of rural electrification; rural electrification in turn reinforced the growing power of these groups.
8. For a review of varying State experiences with the separation of rural feeders, see ASTAE (2014). While Gujarat has successfully controlled financial losses from the agricultural sector, evidence from Rajasthan is more mixed. Since the original time of writing, feeder separation has been institutionalized at the national level through the Deendayal Upadhyaya Gram Jyoti Yojana.
9. As measured by a 2013 reform implementation scorecard by Deloitte and the World Bank (see Pargal and Banerjee 2014, 97–104).
10. Indeed, Gulati and Narayanan (2003) argued that policy in general is biased against agricultural interests.

11. In 2011–12, the all-India average tariff for domestic consumers was 313.72 paise/kwh, compared to 143.64 for agricultural, 513.92 for industrial, and 689.88 for commercial consumers (Planning Commission, 2014, 195). Domestic subsidies were estimated to cost Rs. 37,047 crore nationwide, compared to Rs. 57,901 crore for agricultural subsidies (*ibid*, 211, 208).
12. Again drawing on evidence from UP, Golden and Min (2013) suggest that the beneficiaries of theft may also be wealthy farmers, as their supply is unmetered and so easy to expand (though the same may be true when meters are tampered with). They find evidence *both* that wealthy farmers benefit regardless of the party elected, *and* that parties reward domestic voters in their 'core' strongholds (rather than those in swing constituencies).
13. Labour interests, implicated in the literature as a common obstacle to reforms, have more often been outmanoeuvred. The number of utility employees has dropped from 977,000 in 1998–99 to 660,000 in 2011–12, and the number of employees per thousand customers from 9.89 to 0.36 over the same period (Planning Commission, 2014, 150). It is telling, though, that Gujarat's successful power reforms involved patiently working *with* utility staff rather than tackling them directly.
14. Formerly the National Thermal Power Corporation.
15. Their examples include NTPC on one hand and Reliance and Tata on the other. The discussion of the system's sustainability below clarifies the difference between public and private players on this front, however, arguing that public sector enterprises are open to other forms of short-term exploitation by the state to help fund the subsidy economy.
16. At a CRISIL power sector seminar in New Delhi on May 7, 2012.
17. 'Dualization' is typically associated with developments in labour markets: the segmentation of the labour force between a core of privileged, unionized 'insiders' and the growing mass of 'outsiders' denied many of the benefits and stability that accrue to the core. Here I am more interested in a similar dynamic of *institutional* change to that pinpointed by Thelen (2012). The practical dynamic is reversed: rather than leaving intact a set of state-supported elites, power sector reform has left the state-owned residual to decay, though again a new market-oriented zone profits. I prefer the term 'segmentation' to 'dualization' because it more accurately captures the organizational incoherence and complexity that has accompanied this dynamic.
18. It remains to be seen whether the centre's most recent bailout scheme, the Ujwal Discom Assurance Yojana (UDAY), will prove any more successful than similar previous attempts.
19. Central Electricity Authority data, August 31, 2014.
20. While several states comply on paper, Pargal and Banerjee (2014, 8) found that only one had specified a route to reduce the cross-subsidization surcharge and so facilitate open access in practice.
21. CPSU prospectuses make it clear that the state sets their direction and could require the enterprises to act in ways counter to the interests of profit-minded minority shareholders.

22. Studying five different goods and services across three African countries, Kramon and Posner (2013) found that 'the outcome one studies affects the answer one gets': politicians and officials may compensate groups for higher tariffs in one area with subsidies in another.

References

Ahmed, Sadiq and Ejaz Ghani. 2007. *South Asia: Growth and Regional Integration*. Washington, DC: World Bank.

Asia Sustainable and Alternative Energy Program (ASTAE). 2014. *Lighting Rural India: Load Segregation Experience in Selected States*. Washington, DC: World Bank.

Bardhan, Pranab. 1998. *The Political Economy of Development in India* (Expanded edition). Delhi: Oxford University Press.

Bhattacharya, Saugata and Urjit R. Patel. 2011. 'Does the Exuberance in the Indian Power Sector Have Legs?' *Global Economy and Development, Brookings Institution Working Paper No. 45*.

Chatterjee, Partha. 2008. 'Democracy and Economic Transformation in India.' *Economic and Political Weekly* 43 (16): 53–62.

Dubash, Navroz K. 2011. 'From Norm Taker to Norm Maker? Indian Energy Governance in Global Context.' *Global Policy* 2 (2): 66–79.

Dubash, Navroz K. 2013. 'Regulating Through the Back Door: Understanding the Implications of Institutional Transfer.' In *The Rise of the Regulatory State of the South: Infrastructure and Development in Emerging Economies*, edited by Navroz K. Dubash and Bronwen Morgan, 98–114. Oxford: Oxford University Press.

Golden, Miriam, and Brian Min. 2013. 'Distributive Politics Around the World.' *Annual Review of Political Science* 16 (1): 73–99.

Goldthorpe, John H. 1984. 'The End of Convergence: Corporatist and Dualist Tendencies in Modern Western Societies.' In *Order and Conflict in Contemporary Capitalism*, edited by John H. Goldthorpe, 315–343. Oxford: Clarendon Press.

Gratwick, Katharine Nawaal and Anton Eberhard. 2008. 'Demise of the Standard Model for Power Sector Reform and the Emergence of Hybrid Power Markets.' *Energy Policy* 36 (10): 3948–3960.

Gulati, Ashok and Sudha Narayanan. 2000. 'Demystifying Fertiliser and Power Subsidies in India.' *Economic and Political Weekly* 35 (10): 784–794.

———. 2003. *The Subsidy Syndrome in Indian Agriculture*. New Delhi: Oxford University Press.

Gupta, Akhil and K. Sivaramakrishnan. 2011. 'Introduction: The State in India After Liberalization.' In *The State in India after Liberalization: Interdisciplinary Perspectives*, edited by Akhil Gupta and K. Sivaramakrishnan, 1–27. London: New York: Routledge.

Harriss-White, Barbara. 2003. *India Working: Essays on Society and Economy*. Cambridge: Cambridge University Press.

Jenkins, Rob. 1999. *Democratic Politics and Economic Reform in India*. Cambridge: Cambridge University Press.

Jenkins, Rob. 2004. 'Labor Policy and the Second Generation of Economic Reform in India.' *India Review* 3 (4): 333–363.

Joseph, Kelli L. 2010. 'The Politics of Power: Electricity Reform in India.' *Energy Policy* 38 (1): 503–511.

Kale, Sunila S. 2007. *Power Steering: The Politics of Utility Privatization in India*. PhD thesis, University of Texas, Austin.

———. 2014a. *Electrifying India: Regional Political Economies of Development*. Stanford, California: Stanford University Press.

———. 2014b. 'Structures of Power: Electrification in Colonial India.' *Comparative Studies of South Asia, Africa and the Middle East* 34 (3): 454–475.

Khanna, Sushil. 2015. 'The Transformation of India's Public Sector.' *Economic and Political Weekly* 50 (5): 47–60.

King, John Andrews. 1967. *Economic Development Projects and Their Appraisal: Cases and Principles from the Experience of the World Bank*. Baltimore: Johns Hopkins University Press, Economic Development Institute.

Kochhar, Kalpana, Utsav Kumar, Raghuram Rajan, Arvind Subramanian and Ioannis Tokatlidis. 2006. 'India's Pattern of Development: What Happened, What Follows?.' *Journal of Monetary Economics* 53 (5): 981–1019.

Kohli, Atul. 2006. 'Politics of Economic Growth in India, 1980–2005, Parts I and II.' *Economic and Political Weekly* 41 (13): 1251–1259 and 41 (14): 1361–1370.

———. 2012. *Poverty Amid Plenty in the New India*. Cambridge: Cambridge University Press.

Kramon, Eric and Daniel N. Posner. 2013. 'Who Benefits from Distributive Politics? How the Outcome One Studies Affects the Answer One Gets.' *Perspectives on Politics* 11 (2): 461–474.

Kumar, Alok and Sushanta K. Chatterjee. 2012. *Electricity Sector in India: Policy and Regulation*. New Delhi, Oxford: Oxford University Press.

Lockwood, Matthew. 2014. 'Fossil Fuel Subsidy Reform, Rent Management and Political Fragmentation in Developing Countries.' *New Political Economy* 20 (4): 1–20.

Min, Brian and Miriam Golden. 2014. 'Electoral Cycles in Electricity Losses in India.' *Energy Policy* 65: 619–625.

Mukherjee, Mohua. 2014. *Private Participation in the Indian Power Sector: Lessons from Two Decades of Experience*. Washington, D. C.: World Bank.

Nagaraj, R. 2015. 'Can the Public Sector Revive the Economy?' *Economic and Political Weekly* 50 (5): 41–46.

Pargal, Sheoli and Sudeshna Ghosh Banerjee. 2014. *More Power to India: The Challenge of Electricity Distribution*. Washington, D. C.: World Bank.

Pierson, Paul. 1994. *Dismantling the Welfare State? Reagan, Thatcher, and the Politics of Retrenchment*. Cambridge: Cambridge University Press.

Planning Commission. 2011. *Annual Report on the Working of State Power Utilities and Electricity Departments*. New Delhi: Government of India.

———. 2014. *Annual Report (2013–14) on the Working of State Power Utilities and Electricity Departments.* New Delhi: Government of India.

Pratap, Kumar V. 2013. 'Renegotiations in Long-term Infrastructure Contracts.' *Economic and Political Weekly* 48 (37): 14–16.

Rodrik, Dani, and Arvind Subramanian. 2004. 'From "Hindu Growth" to Productivity Surge: The Mystery of the Indian Growth Transition.' *IMF Working Paper 04/77.* Washington, DC: International Monetary Fund.

Rudolph, Lloyd I. and Susanne Hoeber Rudolph. 2001. 'Iconisation of Chandrababu: Sharing Sovereignty in India's Federal Market Economy.' *Economic and Political Weekly* 36 (18): 1541–1552.

Santhakumar, V. 2008. *Analysing Social Opposition to Reforms: The Electricity Sector in India.* Los Angeles, California: Sage Publications.

Sen, Anupama. 2014. 'Divergent Paths to a Common Goal? An Overview of Challenges to Electricity Sector Reform in Developing Versus Developed Countries.' *OIES Paper EL No. 10.* Oxford: Oxford Institute for Energy Studies.

Sen, Anupama and Tooraj Jamasb. 2012. 'Diversity in Unity: An Empirical Analysis of Electricity Deregulation in Indian States.' *The Energy Journal* 33 (1): 83–130.

Sen, Kunal and Sabyasachi Kar. 2014. 'Boom and Bust? A Political Economy Reading of India's Growth Experience, 1993–2013.' *Economic and Political Weekly* 49 (50): 40–51.

Sethi, Surya P. 2014. 'Rescue Package for Power Discoms.' *Economic and Political Weekly* 49 (4): 17–19.

Shahi, R. V. 2005. *Indian Power Sector: Challenge and Response: Compilation of Papers Presented during 1991–2001.* New Delhi: Excel Books.

Smith, Thomas B. 2004. 'Electricity Theft: A Comparative Analysis.' *Energy Policy* 32 (18): 2067–2076.

Subramanian, Arvind. 2012. 'Can India's Power Problems Be Solved?' *Business Standard,* August 5.

Thelen, Kathleen. 2012. 'Varieties of Capitalism: Trajectories of Liberalization and the New Politics of Social Solidarity.' *Annual Review of Political Science* 15 (1): 137–159.

Tillin, Louise. 2013. 'Varieties of State-Capital Relations in India.' *Economic and Political Weekly* 48 (39): 19–22.

Tongia, Rahul. 2007. 'The Political Economy of Indian Power Sector Reforms.' In *The Political Economy of Power Sector Reform: The Experiences of Five Major Developing Countries*, edited by David G. Victor and Thomas C. Heller, 109–174. Cambridge: Cambridge University Press.

Varshney, Ashutosh. 1995. *Democracy, Development, and the Countryside: Urban-Rural Struggles in India.* Cambridge: Cambridge University Press.

Victor, David G. 2009. *The Politics of Fossil Fuel Subsidies.* Winnipeg, MB: International Institute for Sustainable Development.

Victor, David G. and Thomas C. Heller, eds. 2007. *The Political Economy of Power Sector Reform: The Experiences of Five Major Developing Countries.* Cambridge: Cambridge University Press.

Wilkinson, Steven I. 2006.'The Politics of Infrastructural Spending in India.' Unpublished manuscript. Chicago: University of Chicago.

WISE. 2008. *Power Drain: Hidden Subsidies to Conventional Power in India.* Pune: World Institute of Sustainable Energy.

World Bank. 1993. *The World Bank's Role in the Electric Power Sector.* Washington, DC: World Bank.

Political Economy by Regions of India

4

Political Economy of a Dominant Caste

Rajeshwari Deshpande and Suhas Palshikar

Introduction

This paper attempts to situate the multiple crises facing the Maratha community of Maharashtra in the context of state's political economy. This may have resonance to the situation of intermediate castes in other parts of India, which too find themselves at the intersection of democracy and development. A dominant, intermediate peasantry caste that assumed control of the state's political apparatus in the fifties, the Marathas ordinarily resided politically within the Congress fold and thus facilitated the continued domination of the Congress party within the state. Maratha politics of dominance and Congress politics in Maharashtra went hand in hand. However, Maratha politics has been in flux since the nineties. The long surviving, complex pattern of Maratha dominance is challenged in several ways. One part of the challenge consisted of the threat of loss of Maratha hegemony and consequent loss of leadership of the non-Maratha backward communities, the OBCs. The other challenge pertained to the inability of different factions of Marathas to negotiate peace and ensure their combined domination through power sharing. And the third was the internal crisis of disconnect between political elite and the Maratha community which further contributes to the loss of hegemony.

The present paper is divided in four parts. First part describes the multiple crises of the Marathas and their political fallout; the second part analyzes the discourse of backwardness and the demand for reservations for the Maratha community; the third part is woven around the issue of stratification within the community and in the fourth part we discuss the larger context in which the crisis of 'dominant castes' in various parts of India might obtain.

Multiple Crises of the Marathas

A conservative estimate of its numerical strength places the Maratha–Kunbi caste cluster at around 31 per cent of the state's population. In terms of status, it is a highly stratified caste cluster centering on peasant cultivators but reaching up to rich farmers, feudal aristocrats and rulers. Earlier studies of Maratha dominance in Maharashtra (Lele, 1982 and 1990; Vora, 1994, 2003 and 2009) have amply documented how Maratha dominance emerged as a combination of numerical preponderance, patterns of landownership and a historically nurtured sense of identity that was systematically appropriated by the Congress party in the pre- and the post-independence period[1]. More recently, an ongoing project by a team of scholars from University of British Columbia has brought out the local level political and economic dominance of the Marathas through a large scale empirical study[2] (Anderson, Francois and Kotwal, 2015 and Anderson et al, 2015).

The formative years of Congress dominance in state politics (1930s to 1950s) saw best use of the absorptive powers of the Maratha-Kunbi caste cluster as the Congress party projected the community as a homogenous group of 'agriculturists' and as cultural as well as political leader of the Marathi community. Of course, as Lele shows, the historical self-consciousness of being a 'ruling' community both at the local village level and at a more general societal level, was a major political asset for the Maratha elite when they began to stake their claims in competitive politics (Lele, 1990). It is during the period from the 1930s that *political* claims were made on the basis of the numerical strength of Marathas and Kunbis. Subsequently, after the formation of the Marathi speaking state of Maharashtra in 1960, Marathas consistently secured nearly forty per cent of the seats in legislative assembly (considering the fact that there are constituencies reserved for Scheduled Castes and Scheduled Tribes in proportion to their population – respectively 29 and 25 – the share of Maratha-Kunbi MLAs among remaining constituencies goes up to more than 50 per cent according to Vora, 2009). Often, this numerical strength has survived vagaries of competitive politics.

Probably the most benign and therefore hegemonic expression of Maratha dominance shaped under the leadership of Y. B. Chavan between mid-fifties and mid-sixties. However, the easy equation between their social dominance and political dominance was disrupted at various junctures throughout its subsequent journey. For a widespread community with political clout, it is only natural to have multiple factions often expressing themselves through competition for greater share in formal political power and control over the (Congress) party to which they belonged. However, this factionalism also subsumed two dimensions: one, among the dominant leaders based in the sugar belt, deriving their power from sugar cooperatives, there were differences partly about the extent of their individual power, but also about how to draw benefits from the state machinery. Already, by the late sixties, the urban/industrial interests had begun asserting their power and the question of balancing the agrarian interests and urban interests had become critical. Under the then Chief Minister, V. P. Naik (a non-Maratha but acceptable to the Maratha elite), the state government had tilted in favour of the industrial interests (Kamat, 1983) and soon, the factional leaders from western Maharashtra began to realize that this was going to curtail their capacity to draw greater benefits from state machinery. This factor assumed more explicit shape during the eighties when the confrontation between Indira Gandhi and state level Maratha leadership became acute.

The factionalism among Maratha elite had another dimension too: it combined the regional and the material aspects. Shankarrao (S. B.) Chavan who hailed from the Marathwada region pointed out the neglect of that region in the overall development of the state and more particularly, contested the share sugar cane and agriculture in western region grabbed. It could be argued that these contestations emanated from his political differences with the other leaders. Yet, the claims he made did have objective resonance and they represented the concrete concerns of sections of Maratha leadership. The early seventies was marked by bad drought, stagnant agriculture and large scale migrations from Marathwada region to Mumbai and western Maharashtra (Desai, 1987). So, S. B. Chavan's claims around 1974 were not without objective bases.

In purely factional terms, Vasant Dada Patil and Sharad Pawar (both from western Maharashtra and having base in the sugar cooperative sector) grew up to become factional leaders during the seventies while S. B. Chavan became rival factional leader against the 'sugar lobby'. The political fallout was setback in the 1977 elections. Though the background of emergency and the national atmosphere did contribute, Congress factions used the occasion to try their respective strengths and in the process, losing 28 of 48 Lok Sabha seats from the state (Vora, Palshikar and Sumant, 1983). The assembly elections of 1978 saw clear divisions among Maratha leaders in the state when Indiraloyalists contested elections against the established Maratha lobby. The two Congress parties however, joined hands after the elections to form a coalition ministry. This was clearly aimed at retaining strongholds of material power in rural Maharashtra. But upsetting the other Maratha leaders, Sharad Pawar engineered a split in the predominantly Maratha faction of the Congress party which was then led by Y. B. Chavan (Vora-Palshikar, 1996).

Indira Gandhi's Congress party emerged as the dominant force in the elections of 1980. Following this, Maratha leadership faced humiliation at the hands of Indira Gandhi during 1980–1984. First, a non-Maratha leader, A. R. Antulay (not acceptable to the Maratha lobby), was appointed as chief minister and subsequently, a string of Maratha leaders occupied the position of chief minister. The faction-ridden Maratha leadership could not effectively counter these humiliations. All through this period, Sharad Pawar was outside the official Congress party and was mobilizing the Maratha factions as an opposition leader. Thus, Maratha leadership within the Congress had lost initiative and its control over the state congress.

Since the early eighties, the Marathas have tried various political vehicles in order to maintain their dominance and also to register their anger against the established Maratha leadership. Sharad Pawar continued to lead a major faction of the Maratha elite through his Congress (S) between 1978 and 1986. During the eighties, Shetkari Sanghatana successfully mobilized the Marathas over agrarian issues (Deshpande, 2004). Subsequently it was the Shiv Sena that recruited Maratha youth from more backward regions like Vidarbha, Marathwada and Konkan (Palshikar, 2004). Since late eighties, sections of Maratha elite were becoming more accommodative of Hindutva politics. Many Hindu outfits emerged in small towns of Maharashtra and were patronized by local congress leaders (Vora-Palshikar, 1990). In 1995, many Congress leaders directly or indirectly helped Shiv Sena and BJP and after Assembly elections joined the new government. But at that point, neither BJP, nor Shiv Sena could become parties exclusively upholding Maratha interests. Such a vehicle articulating Maratha interests, albeit only symbolically, emerged (1999) in the form of Nationalist Congress Party (NCP). Since its inception, NCP acquired the form of a party of the Marathas (Birmal, 1999). Most of the NCP seats in the two subsequent assemblies came from western Maharashtra, a Maratha bastion. As we shall note later, the NCP made efforts to transform the anxieties and expectations of the Maratha community into a set of emotive issues and identity politics. But the long standing factionalism within the community and the increasing inability of the Maratha elite to address material concerns of the non-elite sections had already resulted into erosion of electoral support the Maratha community extended to its elite en mass. Thus, by the time NCP came on the electoral scene, the weaker sections from Maratha community had become more alienated from local Maratha leadership and more assertive leadership pursuing caste-specific demands had arisen among Marathas. This moment, during the 2000s, represents not only electoral upsets for Congress and NCP, it also signifies the rupture between Maratha leaders from Congress-NCP and the ordinary Maratha voters in both Western Maharashtra and Marathwada (Palshikar, Deshpande and Birmal, 2014). Throughout the period of 1999–2014, the two Congress parties and the Shiv Sena and BJP competed for Maratha votes. Only in 2014, we find that the trends stabilize decisively in favour of the Shiv Sena and the BJP (Table 4.1).

Table 4.1 Maratha Vote by Party since 1999 (Lok Sabha and Vidhan Sabha Elections)

	LS 1999	*VS 1999*	*LS 2004*	*VS 2004*	*LS 2009*	*VS 2009*	*LS 2014*	*VS 2014*
Congress + NCP	52	47	30	35	34	35	39	Cong.-11
								NCP-17
BJP + Shiv Sena	44	34	57	38	49	30	51	BJP-24
								SS-29

Source: Palshikar, Deshpande, Birmal, 2014, 440–41 and Palshikar-Birmal, 2014.

Of course, for the most part, the traditional feature that Marathas would win at least forty per cent seats in state legislature, also continued during the period of 1999–2009 in spite of the decline of the Congress and fragmentation of Maratha vote and Maratha elite. Also, as a study of the social and regional profile of the Maharashtra cabinets (Datar and Ghotale, 2013) shows, Maratha leaders from the western Maharashtra region continued to monopolize key positions of power within the cabinet. However, the hegemony of the Maratha leadership came to be overshadowed by various factors.

If factionalism represented the increasing limits of that hegemony, the challenges arising from Vidarbh and Marathwada that have always taken the form of the discourse of regional backwardness, represent another such limitation. Accusing the elite from 'western Maharashtra' the leaders from other two regions have always complained that resources are unjustifiably routed to agrarian interests of the western region only. This has led to formation of two committees to inquire into the issue of regional 'imbalance', one in 1983 under the chairmanship of V.M. Dandekar and another in 2011 under the chairmanship of Vijay Kelkar. The picture of regional backwardness does emerge from both the reports and following the first committee, a prolonged debate on the mechanism to overcome the imbalance took place in the political arena. Its fallout was the formation of 'Development Boards' directly under the supervision of the Governor and thus curtailing the powers of the elected representatives and ministers – seen as a limitation imposed on the (often) Maratha elite from Western Maharashtra.

Thirdly and more importantly, since late eighties and more in the nineties, important political decisions were shaped outside the democratic process and were often influenced by bureaucrats, social technocrats and corporate sector. This was mainly because of the shift in the balance between the rural agrarian interests and the urban non-agrarian interests. Though sections of the Maratha elite have entered the modern urban sectors of construction, hoteling and even in some measure industry, the majority of the Maratha community, engaged traditionally in agriculture, continues to look upon the state apparatus to protect its interests because the elite are co-caste fellows. However, the urban interests dominate decision making. Elsewhere, we have pointed out that this process symbolized the decoupling of political power from material power – i.e., formal political positions are disconnected from the operation of dominant material interests (Palshikar-Deshpande, 2003). This leaves Maratha elite to only control limited local material interests (as discussed in Section III below). At the local level politics was reduced to management and appropriation of limited resources and politicians were reduced to contractors. These changes seriously jeopardised the status of Marathas as a ruling community and a hegemonic force.

This multi-level crisis before Maratha hegemony, has been shaping over a long period since the first split within the Maratha elite in the seventies. That split was characteristic of the inability of the Congress party to accommodate political and material ambitions of the Maratha elite. Since then, Maratha hegemony has been weakening consistently. The unprecedented scale of the rebellion by Maratha leaders in 1995 may be seen as the next critical moment while the defeat of the Congress and NCP in the elections to state Assembly (October 2014) constitutes the third moment that represents further erosion of Maratha hegemony (Palshikar, 2014). Apart from the inability of the Maratha elite to function as a united bloc in the politics of the state, the voting pattern over time also indicates the inability of the Maratha leadership to carry the Maratha vote with it. This was not only because of the internal splits among the elites. This phenomenon indicates the deeper anxieties of the ordinary voters from the community. In response, the Maratha elite resorted to politics of caste associations and took recourse to aggressive politics of caste identity. We discuss this mainly in the next section.

Discourse of Backwardness

The growing distance between Maratha elite and the Maratha community in general gave rise to two types of anxieties. One was related to issues of identity and the other was related to issues of material concerns. These two anxieties expressed themselves in a combined manner during the period after 1990.

Frustrated Maratha youths moved beyond the realm of party politics and began pressurizing party politics through militant caste organizations. Such caste organizations of the Maratha community were not an entirely new phenomenon since the Maratha Mahasangh was active even earlier (Vora-Palshikar, 1990). But their political interventions became more prominent after 1990. The Mahasangh and other Maratha caste organizations began resorting to symbolic gestures since the 2000s. They engaged in aggressive contestations over issues of symbolic cultural pride of the caste (Deshpande, 2006).

The James Laine-Bhandarkar Oriental Research Institute (BORI) controversy over a book on Shivaji in 2004 was perhaps the first major instance of this kind[3]. It was followed by several other minor instances where the Maratha activists resorted to a violent politics of intolerance (Deshpande, 2006). These issues were not simply about cultural chauvinism on the part of militant Maratha organisations. As we try to argue here, these political outbursts over symbolic issues were expressions of the unattended material and political anxieties of the Marathas. Politics of the Maratha community since the early twentieth century has often vacillated between claims to Kshatriya status and claims of being part of the larger 'non-Brahmin' category. This has located the community in a complex relationship with both the Brahmins and the non-Brahmin, non-Maratha castes of Maharashtra. (Vora and Palshikar, 1990) have argued that Marathas had a dual relation with the Brahmin community – that of historic contestation and also of sharing dominance.) Therefore, through the twentieth century, we come across differentiated and nuanced discourse of Marathas articulated initially through the non-Brahmin movement. That prism of non-Brahmin movement facilitated the claims over symbols, over leadership and also over the anti-(upper) caste discourse of affirmative action.

The Marathas used the legacies of the non-Brahmin movement to ensure almost hegemony-like acceptance of their political domination. Firstly, the legacy helped them wrest the political initiative from the Brahmins, once the logic of democracy became operative in the late fifties. Secondly, it contributed to the skilful construction of the caste cluster of Marathas and Kunbis that also operated as a numerically preponderant caste cluster in Maharashtra politics. Thirdly, the non-Brahmin legacy firmly established the Marathas as the natural leader of the s*hudra* masses and led to an ideological construct of the Maratha leadership. It further led to appropriation of the '*Bahujan Samaj*' concept by the post-independence Maratha political leaders like Y. B. Chavan. Finally, the legacy of the non-Brahmin movement was used by the Marathas to evolve non-antagonistic relations with other sections of the society. As a result, the claims of backwardness initially articulated by the non-Brahmin movement in its politics in Maharashtra went missing in the early post-independence politics of the Marathas. Instead, the Marathas asserted the role as a natural ruling community of the Marathi masses – by virtue of their being most numerous and also being the legatees of the non-Brahmin struggles.

This role was underscored by the developments in the regional political economy during the 1950s and the sixties. Institutional networks like the cooperatives and economic policies of the state advocating capitalist growth in agrarian sector protected Maratha interests in this period. At the same time the industrial interests also generally benefited under Maratha political dispensation (Kamat, 1983). With the decline of the congress system and with the rising distortions in the regional political economy the material ascendance of the Maratha community was not necessarily protected or advanced (Palshikar-Deshpande, 2003). It was at this juncture that the Marathas began revisiting the legacies of the non-Brahmin movement once again. This took the expression of caste identity and a claim that Marathas are a backward community[4].

The *Maratha Mahasangh*, a leading caste organization of the Marathas, vehemently opposed the reservation policy till 1985 and took pride in their anti-Dalit rhetoric. The same organization has been a front runner in aggressively articulating the Maratha claims of backwardness in more recent times. The Maratha demand for reservations developed interesting narratives of deprivations of the community. Historically, Marathas have been very proud of their Kshatriya status but the recent writings by leaders of Maratha caste organizations reverse this logic and claim a *shudra* status for the Marathas. It is argued that Marathas and Kunbis are one and the same and that both basically depend on subsistence agriculture. Interestingly, these constructions use the same historical tools that were discarded at one time as *brahminical* interpretations of history. The second reversal is about the celebrations of reservation discourse as an emancipatory discourse. The first congregation of the *Maratha Mahasangh* in Mumbai in early 1980s most vehemently put forward its opposition to Mandal commission recommendations and to caste based reservations. It claimed that it would be suicidal to equate Marathas with *Mahars* and *Matangs*, the two important Dalit communities in Maharashtra (Pawar, 2005). The recent texts of the Maratha leaders however celebrate Dr Ambedkar and also strongly uphold the idea of caste based reservations rather than those based on economic criteria. These claims are accompanied by clever construction of caste majorities and there are several interesting subtexts to these constructions. At one level, there is a revival and reformulation of the Brahmin/non-Brahmin cultural divide in which the Dalits are seen as allies of the Marathas. There are attempts to alleviate the memories of past antagonism between Dalits and Marathas by projecting Brahmins as instigators of these conflicts of the past. At another level, Maratha deprivations are defined in terms of overall indicators of social and economic deprivation of the state and these are invoked to prove the economic, social and educational backwardness of the Marathas. It is argued that since Maharashtra is poor and since Marathas constitute majority in Maharashtra, Marathas too are poor and need benefits of reservations. Intra-community gender disparities strangely intersperse in these narratives as pointers to social backwardness of the community and as justification of the demands for reservations (Khedekar, 2008).

The commission for the backward classes of the state had rejected the claims of the Marathas to be a socially and educationally backward community in its report submitted to the government in 2008. The government overruled the decision of the commission in its appointment of the Rane committee in 2013 (led by cabinet minister and staunch Maratha leader Narayan Rane) that declared the Marathas to be educationally and economically backward. In June 2014 the government of Maharashtra decided to allocate 16 per cent reservations for Marathas and 5 per cent for Muslims in education and employment (over and above reservations under Mandal Commission). The decision came after sustained agitations on the part of the Maratha caste organizations for over 10 years led by the '*Maratha Aarkshan Mahamorcha*' a platform of more than 23 caste organizations of the Marathas. Most of the leaders of these organizations come from the backward regions of Marathwada and are aspirants of formal positions of power.

It was not a coincidence that the demand for Maratha reservations found its main supporters from the Marathwada region. Marathas are regionally concentrated in two regions–Western Maharashtra and Marathwada–and there are significant differences in their economic status across regions. Maharashtra has only around a quarter of its agricultural land under irrigation. The percentage dips further down in Marathwada where only 18 per cent of cultivable land is under irrigation. Per Capita and per hectare availability of water in Marathwada is the lowest in Maharashtra and far below the average availability of Maharashtra (GoM, 2013). Most of the Maratha and Kunbi farmers in Marathwada survive as subsistence farmers. Internal contradictions within Maratha-Kunbi caste cluster are often expressed in terms of the irrigated and drought-prone areas, between aristocratic and non-aristocratic families, or in terms of rich and poor Marathas. At all these levels, the regional locations overlap with their economic inequalities. The economic inequalities and the resulting material anxieties of sections of Marathas became an important push in their politics of reservations, particularly so in the Marathwada region. But irrespective of region, the crisis of identity and challenge of adjusting to the new political economy (wherein politics was controlled by its own elite but material interests of the community were not adequately protected) meant that the issue of community's overall backwardness would catch attention of both the elite and the masses alike.

Internal Stratification and Community Claims

Maratha elites historically always faced the challenge of positing a 'community' among Marathas. Being a large community, Marathas are bound to have internal stratification. The early ethnographic literature on Maharashtra makes a distinction between Marathas proper and Kunbis. The Marathas claimed a *Kshatriya* status and were proud of their Rajput lineages. Kunbis on the other hand were cultivators and remained within *shudra* fold. Sections of Kunbis, especially from western Maharashtra and Marathwada region of the state, sought to blur the traditional distinction often through marriage links and also through political consolidation. In the regions of Vidarbha and Konkan, Kunbis retained their distinct caste identity. Kunbis account for around ten per cent of State's population and are concentrated in the above two regions. Thus, one important internal division within the 'Maratha-Kunbi' caste cluster has been between Marathas and Kunbis. The latter have been included in the list of 'Other Backward Classes' by the Mandal Commission, while the Marathas are not.

The evolution of cooperatives could have been a factor addressing and reducing this stratification. At the least, it was expected to ameliorate the acuteness of stratification. Ironically, the sugar cooperatives led to the rise of a new class of well-off farmers within the community (who may be described as the neo-high Maratha as distinct from the 'high' Marathas in the traditional ritual/hierarchical sense). The islands of relative prosperity, (particularly in western Maharashtra) that cooperatives produced, only made this stratification appear more sharply. As the economy of cash crops penetrated the peasantry, those growing sugar cane, onions, tobacco, grapes and later, those who turned to horticulture, became more prosperous than the farmers dependent on coarse cereals. While the demand for 'reservations' (affirmative action) and the discourse of backwardness, in a sense, conceals/denies this internal stratification, it also very emotively and effectively addresses the issue of stratification among the Maratha community.

Again, while the stratification of the community is not new and the emergence of a new rich class too, is not new, the claims of backwardness of the *community as a whole* have an important context. Maharashtra pursued an aggressive agenda of economic liberalization since 1988 under Sharad Pawar's leadership. It was during this latter phase (1988 onwards) that the precarious balance between interests of the rich farmers and the ordinary peasantry got upset. Policies of state government and the structural spaces that new cash crop economy provided were not available to the ordinary peasantry. Similarly, the balance between agrarian interests and urban, non-agrarian interests was also upset. The new political economy neglected rural and agrarian interests in general and advocated export oriented commercialization of agriculture that could benefit only a section of the agricultural classes. There were attempts to situate further industrial expansion outside of Mumbai. Assistance from financial institutions to the industrial sector increased multi-fold and even the tertiary sector recorded its highest share in state domestic product. Maharashtra has always been an industrially advanced state. However, earlier the political leadership tried to maintain a balance between the agrarian and the industrial sectors. The post-1990 phase saw rapid erosion of the balancing elements as capitalist development in Maharashtra became more skewed both in terms of neglect of the agriculture and in terms of its regional concentration. Apart from adding to rural distress, this new imbalance also meant that the political power holders (mostly coming from Maratha community), lost real power.

Despite the chronicles of political ascendance of the Maratha community, the nature of their material domination has always remained somewhat uncertain and open to examination. It is true that Marathas dominate the agrarian resources; that they had evolved an elaborate institutional mechanism to protect and further their material interests through the network of cooperatives in sugar and cotton; and more importantly, also in the field of rural credit and banking. Nevertheless, this always shaped within the context of industrial capitalism and the latter interests have dominated the Maratha interests (Vora, 1994). In this sense, the Marathas could never effectively dominate the economy of the state fully; on the contrary, they had to take a secondary position vis-à-vis the urban-capitalist interests. Maharashtra's aggressive pursuit of the capitalist agenda during the post-liberalization phase added to this imbalance. Since the late eighties and nineties political dominance of the Maratha elite became more and more devoid of capacity to control the material interests. In this period, there was further erosion of the material role of the Marathas. We have described this development as disjunction between political and material dominance (Palshikar-Deshpande, 2003). As a result, the Maratha elite could no more divert flows of material interests to their followers in the rural areas, effectively endangering their clientelist networks.

A call for expansion of the industrial, urban centres naturally attracted Maratha youths to the urban centres since the eighties. However, these sections could not have adequate access to urban resources for various reasons. One, only a few elite Maratha families could invest in medium and large capitalist projects in urban as well as rural areas. Secondly, the Maratha youths lacked skills and training required for the industrial sector both because of the numerically limited opportunities of technical training till mid-eighties and because of the rather unaffordable costs at least in the initial period of expansion of those opportunities from mid-eighties to mid-nineties. The nineties saw a further distortion in the capitalist development that resulted in disproportionate expansion of the service sector and the IT industry (Bhandari and Kale, 2007)[5]. Brahmins monopolized high profile jobs in these sectors with all their advantages as traditional elites in Marathi society. Maratha youths remained engaged in lower rung jobs or were mostly accommodated in the sundry networks of informal economy that flourishes around these sectors. The public sector opportunities were already shrinking when young Marathas began to aspire for them through State Public Service Commission examinations. The lack of access to urban economic resources developed a deep sense of relative deprivation among sections of Marathas.

A large section of the Marathas still remains trapped in the agricultural sector and does not have enough access to urban resources. There is not much systematic empirical evidence available regarding the current material realities of the Maratha Kunbis (The Report of the Rane committee which recommended reservations for Marathas on grounds of their economic backwardness has not been made public). Data on Maharashtra from National Election Studies (NES) give us some useful inputs in this respect. As per the NES data of 2004, more than 70 per cent of Maratha-Kunbis lived in villages. After ten years, the Maratha- Kunbis in Maharashtra still had a predominantly rural existence, as nearly 80 per cent of our sampled Maratha respondents were from villages. The NES data of 2014 also clearly reveals the internal economic stratification within the Marathas. More than fifty per cent Marathas are engaged in agricultural activities. Around 20 per cent of these are landless labourers whereas around 15per cent possess land under 5 acres. The rural rich Marathas account for hardly three per cent of the sampled Maratha families. These realities point to a possible skew within the community which may strike at the roots of claims for a homogenous existence.

To investigate this problem further, we have undertaken an in-depth study of two villages. A socio-economic household study was conducted in these two villages in 2013. These villages were one each from the Marathwada and western Maharashtra region and in both villages the Maratha community had a significant numerical presence. The study brings out the internal economic divisions among Marathas. Nearly 12 per cent of the Maratha families are landless. In addition to this, more than 20 per cent Maratha families own less than 2 acres of land and another 40 per cent have less than five acres of land in their possession. The land ownership patterns suggest that nearly 65 per cent Marathas are poor whereas hardly five per cent own more than 20 acres of land and thus may be classified as rich farmers. More than three quarters of our Maratha respondents in the villages under study, were engaged in agricultural activities. Among them ten per cent are landless agricultural labourers. This pattern underlines the deep threefold division consisting of poor Marathas, well-off Marathas having the capacity to negotiate with the urban environs and the rich Maratha class.

To the extent these micro level studies are representative; these patterns also overlap with the regional disparities. As mentioned earlier, one of the villages, Randhe, is in the Ahmednagar district from the western Maharashtra region. This is one of the most prosperous regions of the state cultivating cash crops and where supportive agrarian infrastructure was put in place long ago. The other village, Khuntegaon, is from the Latur district of the Marathwada region and has a somewhat different social as well as economic profile fromRandhe.

As already mentioned, the region of Marathwada is historically known for its poverty, droughts and agrarian backwardness. Expectedly, the Maratha families in Khuntegaon in Marathwada are poorer than those in Randhe although the overall patterns of internal economic stratification within the community are evident in both the villages. Landlessness is witnessed in less than 10 per cent of the Maratha families in Randhe whereas in Khuntegaon incidence of landlessness goes up to 23. The same is true of share of marginal farmers and the landless agricultural workers among the Marathas in two villages. In Randhe, seven per cent of our Maratha respondents were landless agricultural workers whereas in Khuntegaon their share goes up to 22 among the various occupational groups. In addition to this, 26 per cent Maratha respondents in Randhe and 24 per cent in Khuntegaon does not own any land of their own but cultivate their family land and thus become another significant section of the poor Marathas.

While the internal stratification within the community has implications for both homogenization strategies and leadership patterns, it is also important in the short run in connection with vote-choice of the different sections of the community. Fragmentation of the Maratha vote has been a big story of Maharashtra elections throughout the past decade (as we reported in Section I above).

While the fragmentation of Maratha vote and a turn towards BJP and Shiv Sena is becoming more and more evident over the last one decade, it still eludes a clear pattern. No clear picture emerges as to which Maratha sections particularly prefer the non-Congress (and non-NCP) options. As shown in Table 4.2, the class character of the Maratha-Kunbi vote does not operate much at the obvious level of rich and poor Marathas but more in terms of their occupations and location. Marathas having access to urban and non-agricultural resources seem to have favoured the BJP-Shiv Sena alliance more than the rural, agriculturist Marathas. But even among agriculturist Marathas, a large section voted for the BJP-Shiv Sena alliance in the 2014 parliamentary elections. Besides their economic class and occupation, another factor associated with Maratha vote is their regional location. As Table 4.3 shows, each region seems to have evolved a separate dynamic of the community's political preference. This pattern also gels well with the overall nature of social support to the BJP-Shiv Sena alliance from the privileged groups. There is therefore, some possibility of hypothesizing that stratification among the community is closely linked to its political fragmentation.

Table 4.2 Internal Divisions among Maratha Kunbis (Vote in LS Elections 2014)

	Congress NCP+	*BJP Shiv Sena +*
Agriculturists	40	52
Maratha-Kunbis in non-agricultural occupations	33	46
Rich Maratha-Kunbis	44	43
Poor Maratha- Kunbis	40	39
Rural Maratha- Kunbis	42	48
Urban Maratha-Kunbis	25	51

Source: NES data, 2014

Table 4.3 Maratha Vote by Region: 2014 Assembly

	BJP	*SS*	*Cong*	*NCP*
N. Maharashtra	35	21	11	9
Vidarbh	41	23	20	7
Marathwada	23	22	7	32
Mumbai-Thane	18	43	12	5
W. Maharashtra	18	36	11	25
Total	24	29	11	17

Source: Palshikar (2014, 12)

Conclusion

This paper has attempted to map the challenges faced by the dominant caste and its politics. These challenges are related to the economic and socio-political situation in which the dominant community finds itself. It would be evident from the narrative of Maratha politics and predicament that the phenomenon of dominance that many parts of India experienced at some point or the other is somewhat distinct from the famous formulation of 'dominant caste' (see Endnote 1). On the one hand, many parts of India witnessed the political rise of communities that were not necessarily numerically preponderant and on the other hand, the 'unit' of dominance often transcended small localities. The key to this newly emerging dominance (in most parts during the sixties – though some parts experienced this much later) was in the factor of land holding and control over rural agrarian resources within the logic of democracy. This phenomenon of regionally dominant or entrenched caste could be better understood in terms of the aspirations and politics of regionally based middle peasantry castes. Just as their agrarian roots were a common factor, their intermediate position within the traditional caste hierarchy too was a common feature shared by them. This socio-occupational location made it possible for them to stake claims to power, evolve strategies of rulership, discover historical antecedents of power and above all, forge new political alliances both with other communities and with key political parties of the concerned region. Thus, their political rise was an outcome of the interface between caste and modern democratic politics. At the same time, it was an outcome of political economy of each region. Both these, democratic politics and specificities of political economy, led to the entrenchment of (usually) one caste in each region.

The dominance of Maratha-Kunbi caste cluster was not only an outcome of numerical strength of the community. Besides that, the historical memory and practice of rulership in rural Maharashtra helped the community stake claim for political power once democratic politics evolved (like in the case of Reddis of Andhra Pradesh). This claim was further consolidated because of the ability of the leadership to build a larger coalition – first within the community and later across castes but vis-à-vis the upper castes (Brahmins in particular). But in the period after 1960, the dominance of Marathas owed more to the political economy than to these historical factors (as it happened in the case of Patidars of Gujarat). As we discussed in section one, state-protection accorded to agriculture and agro-based industry and rural cooperatives ensured the consolidation of the dominance of Maratha community. Thus, history and political economy facilitated not merely dominance but hegemony of the community.

The demand for reservations and claim that the community is backward indicate erosion of that hegemony. As Maratha hegemony began to crumble, the dominance too began to be challenged. Exactly the same logic of democracy that propelled the Maratha community into a hegemonic position turned against it since the eighties. 'External' factors such as Indira Gandhi's efforts to undermine the Maratha leadership contributed to the crisis; but basically the challenge was about its acceptance outside the community and ability to hold the community politically united. The Maratha leadership could not manage these challenges. There were limits to the skills and space for accommodation within congress system. So, the elite from the community began to disintegrate as seen in section one. As a corollary to that, the capacity of the elite to accommodate interests of other castes too was limited. In the early eighties, the Marathas refused to recognize claims of the OBCs (both about reservations and about share in political power). Subsequently, the elites from the Maratha community were unable to accommodate those claims because on the one hand, state resources at their disposal were shrinking as the urban-capitalist interests wrested the initiative and on the other hand because factionalism within Maratha elite required more resources and political positions to be shared among themselves rather than across castes. This prevarication weakened its hegemonic position both vis-à-vis the OBCs and vis-à-vis ordinary Maratha community as a whole. Politically, the elite have to be hopelessly dependent on the rural Maratha vote. As elite competition grew, new strategies to garner the Maratha vote had to be invented. Emotive appeals to caste identity and attacks on imaginary enemies of Maratha identity had to be resorted to by the elite for that purpose. This move further eroded the hegemony of the Maratha community. In other words, the various bases of entrenchment – hegemonic relation with other castes, internal homogenization despite stratification and a political unity among elite – were either weakened or lost. The entire period from the 1980s is thus a period of gradual displacement of the dominant caste from hegemonic position to that of numeric preponderance. Once the voters from that caste-cluster began to be politically dispersed, even that advantage was lost. This began happening since the 1990s.

These developments led to the decline and then end of congress system in Maharashtra while on the other hand; they also resulted into political fragmentation of the Maratha community. The Assembly elections of 2014 have pushed the crisis of the dominant caste into a more serious predicament because not only did the leadership and the community fragment in this election, but the elite also lost control over state apparatus and key resources (Palshikar, 2014). Needless to say, all these developments are interwoven with developments at the all-India level and have implications for the politics of dominant caste in general. We contend that the trajectory of the Maratha community and its dominance in Maharashtra is thus representative of the multiple challenges faced by a dominant caste.

One way to comprehend these challenges would simply be to say that such challenges to dominance constitute an inevitable part of the dynamic of democracy. However, we have shown that structural factors (material condition of the Marathas and their internal differentiation) along with a sense of *loss of power and entrenchment* produce most of the challenges. In this sense, besides the specificity of society and economy of Maharashtra, we come across a larger and more general question. As we move away from historical construction of dominance, politics of 'dominant caste' confronts challenges both to its homogeneity and its hegemonic practices.

Anderson, Francois and Kotwal (2015) and Anderson et al (2015) bring out interesting details and traverse a somewhat different theoretical space.

In our view, that study has many overlaps with our present argument but of course, the theoretical move to situate the issue in the contexts of functioning of local institutions, the structural boundedness of democratic processes and the overall context of clientelism as an analytical framework differentiates that study from the present argument. Yet, we find the valuable empirical data from that study as an important factor in understanding the larger, state level predicament and political strategies of the elite from Maratha caste. At the micro level, as Anderson et al show, the elite capture of democratic institutions may continue (and even local manifestations of hegemonic relations may obtain), and yet, the resistance to 'political reservations' and attempts to sabotage political reservations by way of claiming 'Kunbi' status indicate the insecurities of the Maratha elites. Similarly, the local clientelist control of vote notwithstanding, survey data from post-election studies shows that Marathas as a community are facing deep fragmentation since the nineties. Third, while Maratha elite manage to appropriate democratic spaces locally, their control over public policy is severely restricted now and as such they have to resort to claiming overall backwardness of the entire community as a tool to retain control over the community. These factors in conjunction with the data from Anderson et al, present a paradoxical picture of dominance and insecurity, control and loss of power.

We can witness this broader trajectory unfolding in many states – at different times and with different details. The demand for reservations and claims of backwardness were not confined only to the Marathas and Maharashtra during the post-Mandal phase. The locally/ regionally dominant castes from different states used claims of backwardness as a successful political strategy during this period. The Marathas initially opposed politics of affirmative action but later on joined that discourse. The Lingayats and Vokkaligas as the two dominant castes in Karnataka diffused the backward caste challenge to their dominance by successfully appropriating the discourse of backwardness for their own benefits (Deshpande, 2014a). In Rajasthan on the other hand, the elite backlash, on behalf of the Jats, preceded the subaltern challenge (Jenkins, 2004). The Patidar agitations in Gujarat in 2015, with the twin demand of either the community's inclusion among the OBCs or a complete reversal of the caste based affirmative action policies, probably completes the cycle that began way back in Karantaka when Lingayats appropriated the reservation discourse. As Shah (2015) notes, the Patidar rage was an outcome of the shrinking economic opportunities for the community in Gujarat's rural, agrarian as well as urban economy. In that sense, the Patidar narrative of backwardness shares a lot in common with the Maratha predicament. These different strategies of claims of backwardness by the dominant castes are rooted in different regional contexts and thus acquire different regional and temporal dimensions.

We argue that this paradoxical picture sums up the contemporary predicament of the politics of dominant caste. 'Dominance' shaped from and in the context of competitive democracy and that same framework of competitive democracy has now posed challenges before dominance. Another impetus to dominance was the welfare oriented state policies within a capitalist framework. That same political economy has now presented the dominant castes with the situation wherein they have to rely on the (poor) masses but have less and less to deliver to them by way of benefits. This contemporary predicament undermines dominant role of the dominant caste and also the political advantage that the congress party could historically draw from its association with the dominant castes in different parts of the country.

Endnotes

1. These factors make the case of Marathas different from the formulation of 'dominant caste' as proposed by Srinivas; 1955 in that the source of dominance is complex and the incidence of dominance more widespread but the case of the Marathas also does not fit easily into Kothari's (1970/2010, 14, 18) 'entrenched caste' as well. We come back to the discussion of the conceptualization of dominant caste again in the last section.
2. We are thankful to Ashok Kotwal for sharing the earlier drafts and for email interaction on related matters.
3. James Laine, in his book, *Shivaji: Hindu King in Islamic India* (2003) at one place alluded to the alleged rumours regarding Shivaji. Many organizations took umbrage to these alleging that the Brahmin academicians associated with the Bhandarkar institute in Pune must have been instrumental in spreading such rumours. The institute was attacked and ransacked. The involvement of a Maratha organization, *Sambhaji Brigade* was reported in this particular case. For details of Sambhaji Brigade's involvement in the issue see Pawar (2009).
4. For a detailed account of the Maratha claims to backwardness see Deshpande (2014a). Deshpande tries to decipher the claims to other backward class (OBC) status made by two dominant castes– Marathas and Lingayats– from the neighbouring regions of Maharashtra and Karnataka in order to revisit the politics of the dominant castes in the post – Mandal context.
5. There is a marked distortion in the development of the state: the share of primary sector in the NSDP is 11.7 per cent as against 25.3 per cent of secondary and 62.8 per cent of tertiary sector. In contrast, 49.3 per cent of the total workforce is engaged in agriculture (GoM, 2014).

References

Anderson, Siwan, Patrick Francois and Ashok Kotwal. 2015. 'Clientelism in Indian Villages.' *American Economic Review* 105 (6): 1780–1816.

Anderson, Siwan, Patrick Francois, Ashok Kotwal and Ashwini Kulkarni. 2015. 'One Kind of Democracy.' *Economic and Political Weekly* 50 (26-27): 44-48, June 27.

Birmal, Nitin. 1999. 'Prabal Jaaticha Pradeshik Paksha: Rashtravadi Congress (Marathi-NCP: Regional Party of the Dominant Caste).' *Samaj Prabodhan Patrika* 221–5, October–December.

Datar, Abhay and Vivek Ghotale. 2013. 'Maharashtra Cabinets: Social and Regional Profile 1960–2010.' *Economic and Political Weekly* 68 (36): 37-42, September 7.

Desai, Datta. 1987. *Maharashtratil Dushkal* (Marathi-Drought in Maharashtra). Pune: Magoa Prakashan.

Deshpande, Prachi. 2007. *Creative Pasts, Historical Memory and Identity in Western India 1700–1960*. New Delhi: Permanent Black.

Deshpande, Rajeshwari. 2004. 'Reservations to Kunbi Marathas: Backward Journey of a Caste.' *Economic and Political Weekly* 39 (14 and 15): 1448–1449, April 3–10.

———. 2006. 'Maharashtra: Politics of Anxieties, Frustrations and Outrage.' *Economic and Political Weekly* 41 (14): 1304–07, April 8–14.

———. 2010. 'Caste Associations in the Post-Mandal Era: Notes from Maharashtra.' *CAS Occasional Paper Series: No. 2, Department of Politics and Public Admn*. Pune: University of Pune

———. 2014. '*Bhagwangadavarun Mala Mumbai DisateAahe*: How Caste Survives Amidst Democratic Politics.' In *Rethinking Western India: The Changing Contexts of Culture, Society and Religion*, edited by Dusan Deak and Daniel Thorner, 91-104. New Delhi: Orient Blackswan.

———. 2014a. 'Seeking OBC Status: Political Strategies of Two Dominant Castes.' *Studies in Indian Politics* 2 (2): 169–183, December.

Govt. of Maharashtra (GoM). 2013. *Report of the High Level Committee on Balanced Regional Development Issues in Maharashtra*. Mumbai: Department of Planning.

———. 2014. *Economic Survey of Maharashtra: 2013–14, Directorate of Economics and Statistics*. Mumbai: Department of Planning.

Jenkins, Rob. 2004. *Reservation politics in Rajasthan. Crisis States Programme Working Paper*. London: LSE.

Kamat, A. R. 1983. *Essays on Social Change in India*. Mumbai: Somaiyya Prakashan

Khedekar, Purushottam, ed. 2008. *Maratha Aarkshan* (Marathi, Maratha Reservations). Pune: Jijai Prakashan.

Kothari, Rajni, ed. 2010 (1970). *Caste in Indian Politics* (Revised by James Manor). New Delhi: Orient Blackswan.

Lele, Jayant. 1982. *Elite Pluralism and Class Rule: Political Development in Maharashtra*. Mumbai: Popular Prakashan.

———. 1990. 'Caste, Class and Dominance: Political Mobilization in Maharashtra.' In *Dominance and State Power in Modern India: Decline of a Social Order* Volume 2, edited by Francine Frankel and M. S. A. Rao, 115–211. Delhi: Oxford University Press.

Palshikar, Suhas. 2004. 'Shiv Sena: A Tiger with Many Faces?.' *Economic and Political Weekly* 39 (12): 1497-1507, April 3-10.

———. 2014. 'Maharashtra Assembly Election: Farewell to Maratha politics?.' *Economic and Political Weekly* 49 (43-44): 10-13, November 1.

Palshikar, Suhas and Nitin Birmal. 2003. 'Fragmented Marathas Retain Power.' In *India's 1999 Elections and Twentieth Century Politics*, edited by P. Wallace and R. Roy, 206-32. New Delhi: Sage Publications.

Palshikar, Suhas and Rajeshwari Deshpande. 2003. 'Maharashtra: Challenges before the Congress System.' *Journal of Indian School of Political Economy* 15 (1-2): 97-122, January–June.

Palshikar, Suhas, Rajeshwari Deshpande and Nitin Birmal. 2014. 'Survival in the Midst of Decline: A Decade of Congress Rule in Maharashtra: 1999–2009.' In *Party Competition in Indian States: Electoral Politics in Post-Congress Polity*, edited by Palshikar Suhas, K. C. Suri and Yogendra Yadav, 416–430. New Delhi: Oxford University Press.

Pawar, Namdeo. 2009. 'Maratha Seva Sangh Pranit Sambhaji Brigade: Ek Chikitsak Abhyas' (Marathi – A Critical Study of the Maratha Seva Sangh's Sambhaji Brigade). Unpublished M. Phil. Dissertation submitted to the Savitribai Phule Pune University, Pune.

Shah, Ghanashyam. 2015. 'The Shrinking, the Rage.' *Indian Express*, August 28. Mumbai.

Srinivas, M. N. 1955. 'The Social System of a Mysore Village.' In *Village India: Studies in the Little Community*, edited by McKim Marriott, 36–52. Chicago: University of Chicago Press.

Vora, Rajendra. 1994. 'An Agenda for the Study of Political Economy of Maharashtra.' *Occasional Paper no 1, SAP, Department of Politics and Public Admn*. Pune: University of Pune.

———. 2009. 'Maharashtra or Maratha Rashtra?.' In *Rise of the Plebeians? The Changing Face of Indian Legislative Assemblies*, edited by Christophe Jaffrelot and Sanjay Kumar, 215-244. New Delhi: Routledge.

Vora, Rajendra and Suhas Palshikar. 1996. *Maharashtratil Sattantar* (Marathi–Power Transfer in Maharashtra). Mumbai: Granthali.

Vora, Rajendra, Suhas Palshikar and Yeshwant Sumant. 1983. 'Sixth Lok Sabha Elections: Maharashtra.' *Research Abstract Quarterly*, ICSSR, January–June.

5

Populism and Party

Society Developmental Regimes in Tamil Nadu and West Bengal

Kalaiyarasan A.

Introduction

It is increasingly recognised that the nature of political mobilization of classes and castes produces specific political regimes; and these regimes, in turn, set the path of policy regimes and developmental outcomes (Kohli, 1987). Owing to specific regional histories and politics, there are variations in such political regimes. According to John Harriss (1999), Kerala, Tamil Nadu, and West Bengal are states with political regimes dominated by lower castes and classes – albeit in different ways.[1] Pranab Bardhan contrasts 'welfare regimes' in West Bengal and Tamil Nadu and attributes the differences between the two to the divergent nature of regional social movements. He argues that regional capital in Tamil Nadu is more indigenised and it has a 'culture of wealth creation as opposed to redistribution' (Tillin, 2013).

Tamil Nadu is home to anti-caste movements and political mobilisation of OBCs and SCs for over a century (Arooran, 1980; Chandrababu, 1993; Pandian, 2006). The DMK came to power in 1967, with a broad social base among the lower castes and classes, had a huge influence on the policy regime in the state. West Bengalwas ruled by the Left Front Government headed by the Communist Party of India – Marxist (CPM) since 1977 till 2011. The left coalition had an uninterrupted electoral triumph for more than three decades.

The state has been credited to have a distinguished record of implementing agrarian reforms in rural Bengal (Bandyapadhyay, 2008; Mishra, 2007).

This paper uses two distinct categories to understand the political milieu and policy regimes Tamil Nadu and West Bengal – populism and party-society respectively. Contrary to common understanding, populism need not be negative but can have positive connotation for the socially and economically disadvantaged sections. Andrew Wyatt (2013), in the specific context of Tamil Nadu, defines populism as 'an ideological construct that celebrates the importance of the ordinary people, asserts these people should not be divided by social hierarchy and justifies improvements in their welfare.' Bardhan argues that populism has indeed produced positive results in Tamil Nadu by taking economic growth and social welfare together (Bardhan, 2014).

In the case of West Bengal, Dwajpayan Bhattacharya (2010), using Partha Chatterjee's (2004) conception of political society, argues that party-society is a specific form of political society operating in rural Bengal. Political society is defined as a society made up of those who are historically disadvantaged and excluded from civil society due to lack of education, wealth and other forms of capital. It provides the scope for the emergence of competing political parties and civil organisations which then articulate their concerns with state and civil society. In a party-society political parties monopolise the social space and stifle the emergence of civil associations. Even if they emerge for historically contingent reasons, they are constrained to play a subsidiary role. Thus, Bhattacharya argues that party-society, by either suppressing these organisations or curbing their relevance to government and polity, weakens the negotiating power of disadvantaged groups. Whereas populist political regimes must respond to recurrent political mobilization by different social groups, party-society does not allow space for such mobilization.

The paper is organised in two parts. Part I provides details of economic growth, development outcomes and social distribution of enterprises in Tamil Nadu and West Bengal. The evidence shows considerable divergence in outcomes between the states. Part II offers possible explanations for the differential outcomes between the two states. The explanations are broadly located in the nature of political regimes in and specific histories of the states.

Dynamics of Economic Growth

Since the 1980s, Tamil Nadu has witnessed a consistently high economic growth rate. This has been attributed to the economic reforms initiated in the early 1990s. The state decisively embraced neo-liberal policies and has, since, heavily subsidised the corporate sector through various tax exemptions (Vijayabaskar, 2010). While West Bengal has also witnessed sustained economic growth since the 1990s, the growth rate has been lower than that of Tamil Nadu. Whether the sustained higher economic growth is due to the policies initiated in the 1990 or not is beyond the purview of this paper. The paper is concerned with explaining the difference in economic growth and developmental outcomes between the two states.

Table 5.1 gives the sector-wise growth rate and the contribution of each sector to the aggregate growth in both states for the last three decades. The overall GDP growth of Tamil Nadu for this period has been 6.7 per cent per annum and that of West Bengal has been 5.7 per cent per annum. Despite an increase in growth rate in West Bengal in the 1990s, the gap persists.

Table 5.1 GSDP Growth Rate by Sectors and their Contribution to Growth

Sector		*Tamil Nadu*				*West Bengal*		
	1980–1990	1990–2000	2000–2010	1980–2010	1980–1990	1990–2000	2000–2010	1980–2010
Agriculture	4.4 (19)	3.5 (11)	2.1 (3)	3.3 (7)	3.8 (28)	4.5 (21)	2.5 (9)	3.6 (15)
Manufacturing	4.7 (21)	4.6 (16)	8.4 (21)	5.9 (20)	2.9 (8)	6.0 (10)	7.0 (12)	5.3 (11)
Construction	7.6 (7)	7.7 (8)	11.2 11)	8.8 (10)	5.6 (7)	6.0 (6)	7.3 (7)	6.3 (6)
Industry	5.6 (33)	5.5 (27	8.0 (30)	6.4 (30)	3.8 (19)	5.8 (19)	6.6 (20)	5.4 (20)
Services	6.3 (48)	8.2 (62)	9.4 (67)	7.9 (63)	4.9 (53)	7.3 (60)	7.9 (71)	6.7 (65)
GSDP	5.6 (100)	6.4 (100)	8.0 (100)	6.7 (100)	4.3 (100)	6.2 (100)	6.5 (100)	5.7 (100)
Per Capita Income	4.1	5.3	6.4	5.3	2.0	4.5	5.1	3.9

Note: GSDP at 1999–00 constant prices. Figures in parenthesis show contribution to GSDP Growth.
Source: Central Statistical Organization.

When disaggregated, the data shows that in both Tamil Nadu and West Bengal the growth rates of the construction and service sectors have been the highest. For instance, the construction and service sectors in Tamil Nadu have grown at 8.8 and 7.9 per cent per annum respectively. The corresponding figures for West Bengal are 6.3 and 6.7 per cent per annum.

Manufacturing has grown at 5.9 per cent per annum in Tamil Nadu, while the corresponding growth rate for West Bengal is just 5.3 per cent. The industrial sectors as a whole has witnessed a growth rate of 6.4 per cent per annum in Tamil Nadu, while the corresponding figure for West Bengal is just 5.4 per annum. Tamil Nadu has consistently outperformed West Bengal in all sectors but agriculture. Agriculture has grown at 3.3 per cent per annum in Tamil Nadu, while the corresponding growth rate for West Bengal is 3.8 per cent per annum.

There is a significant difference between the two states with respect to drivers (contribution of sub-sectors to aggregate growth) of economic growth. The key drivers of economic growth in Tamil Nadu are the service and manufacturing sectors. In West Bengal, the service sector alone has contributed the largest share. The service sector has contributed approximately 63 per cent of the overall economic growth in Tamil Nadu in the last three decades. The corresponding figure for West Bengal is 65 per cent. Unlike West Bengal, industry continues to be a significant driver of economic growth in Tamil. Industry has contributed about 30 per cent of the overall economic growth in Tamil Nadu while the corresponding figure for West Bengal is only 20 per cent. Within industry, manufacturing has contributed approximately 20 per cent to the overall economic growth in Tamil Nadu, while the sector has contributed just 11 per cent to growth in West Bengal. However, what is significant between the two states is the contribution of agriculture to the overall economic growth. While agriculture sector accounts for 15 per cent of growth in West Bengal in the last three decades, Tamil Nadu (7 per cent) has steadily witnessed a decline in the contribution of agriculture to the overall growth.

Distribution of Enterprises

Table 5.2 gives the figures of distribution of enterprises based on Economic Census (2005) and Ministry of Micro Small and Medium Enterprises (MSME) census (2007–08) for Tamil Nadu and West Bengal. The Economic Census shows that the number of enterprises in Tamil Nadu is three time that in West Bengal. This is confirmed by the MSME census as well. As per the MSME census, the number of enterprises in Tamil Nadu in 2007–2008 was about twenty four thousand as compared to six thousand in West Bengal. The data also shows that the social base of entrepreneurship in Tamil Nadu is more diverse than in West Bengal. Certain traditional non-business castes have an appreciable share in entrepreneurships in Tamil Nadu.[2]

Table 5.2 Distribution of Enterprises (More than 10 Workers) Owned by Socio-Religious Groups

	Economic Census (2005)		*MSME Census (2007–08)*	
	Tamil Nadu	*West Bengal*	*Tamil Nadu*	*West Bengal*
SC/ST	1174 (4.1)	968 (9.4)	1240 (5.0)	287 (4.7)
OBC	22980 (77.5)	622 (6.0)	16151 (65.6)	162 (2.6)
General*	5490 (18.5)	8705 (84.6)	4347 (17.7)	4665 (76.0)
Muslim	...		1193 (4.8)	695 (11.3)
Other Minorities	...		1622 (6.6)	333 (5.4)
Total	29644 (100)	10295 (100)	24627 (100)	6142 (100)

*General category in Economic Census refers upper castes while they are Hindu upper castes in MSME census

Source: Unit Level Records from Economic Census (2005) and MSME Census (2007–08)

According to the MSME census SC/ST, OBC and Muslims – who constitute about 65 per cent of West Bengal's population[3] – own just 19 per cent of the enterprises. The corresponding figures for Tamil Nadu are 95 and 75 percents respectively. The General population (upper castes) – while they constitute only 35 per cent of population – own as much as 76 per cent of total enterprises in West Bengal. In Tamil Nadu, they form 5 per cent of the population and own 18 per cent of total enterprises. The Economic census of 2005 also provides similar evidence.

Poverty Incidence 1994–2012

In this paper, the incidence of poverty and inequality has been estimated using the unit record data from three quinquennial rounds of Consumption Expenditure Surveys (CES) conducted by the National Sample Survey Office (NSSO). These surveys have been conducted in 1993–94, 2004–05 and 2011–12. This paper uses the methodology recommended by Suresh Tendulkar committee and the corresponding poverty lines provided by the Planning Commission.[4]

Rural poverty

Table 5.3 gives the estimate of poverty based on Head Count Ratio (HCR) at aggregate level, as well as for social and religious groups in rural Tamil Nadu and West Bengal. Tamil Nadu has seen a drastic reduction in rural poverty in the period under consideration. Whereas in 1993–94 the proportion of population who were poor in rural Tamil Nadu was 51.2 per cent the figure for 2011–12 is considerably lower – 15.8 per cent. The corresponding figures for West Bengal are 42.5 per cent and 22.5 per cent respectively. Though West Bengal was better placed in the 1990s, it compares unfavourably with Tamil Nadu in 2011–2012. Tamil Nadu has gained 34 percentage points in poverty reduction in rural areas during the last two decade, while West Bengal has gained just 20 percentage points – a difference of 14 percentage points.

Table 5.3 The Incidence of Poverty (HCR) and Rate of Poverty Reduction (Per Annum) for Socio-Religious Groups (Rural)

Social Group	*1993–94*		*2004–05*		*2011–12*		*1993–94 to 2004–05*		*2004–05 to 2011–12*		*1993–94 to 2011–12*	
	Tamil Nadu	*West Bengal*	*Tamil Nadu*	*West Bengal*	*Tamil Nadu*	*West Bengal*	*Tamil Nadu*	*West Bengal*	*Tamil Nadu*	*West Bengal*	*Tamil Nadu*	*West Bengal*
SC/ST	65.8	51.6	51.2	40.9	24	27.2	1.3	1	3.9	2	2.3	1.4
OBC	–	–	32.6	28.1	13	17.1	–	–	2.8	1.6	–	
General*	45.6	25.8	22.2	24.3	1.0	15.8	2.1	0.1	3	1.2	2.5	0.6
Hindu	51.3	39.6	38	33.2	16.2	21.9	1.2	0.6	3.1	1.6	1.9	1.0
Muslim	37.3	50.5	18	49.1	1.6	23.9	1.8	0.1	2.3	3.6	2.0	1.5
Other Minorities	57.0	65.3	36.1	50.0	13.9	19.0	1.9	1.4	3.2	4.4	2.4	2.6
All	51.2	42.5	37.5	38.2	15.8	22.5	1.2	0.4	3.1	2.2	2.0	1.1

*General includes OBC population in 1993–94 as the OBC was not counted then, thus can't be compared across time

Source: Calculated by the author's using NSS CES unit record data for the respective years.

In the period between 1993–94 and 2011–12, rural poverty in Tamil Nadu has declined at the rate of 2 percentage points per annum. The rate of decline of rural poverty in West Bengal in the same period is 1.1 percentage points per annum, considerably lower than Tamil Nadu. On this count, Tamil Nadu fares better in the sub-periods as well. In the first sub-period, 1993–94 and 2004–05, the rate of decline in poverty in Tamil Nadu was about 1.2 percentage point per annum while the corresponding figure for West Bengal was just 0.4 percentage point per annum. In the second sub-period between 2004–05 and 2011–12 too Tamil Nadu has outperformed West Bengal in poverty reduction. The rate of decline in rural poverty for Tamil Nadu is 3.1 percentage points per annum, while the decline in West Bengal is just 2.2 percentage points

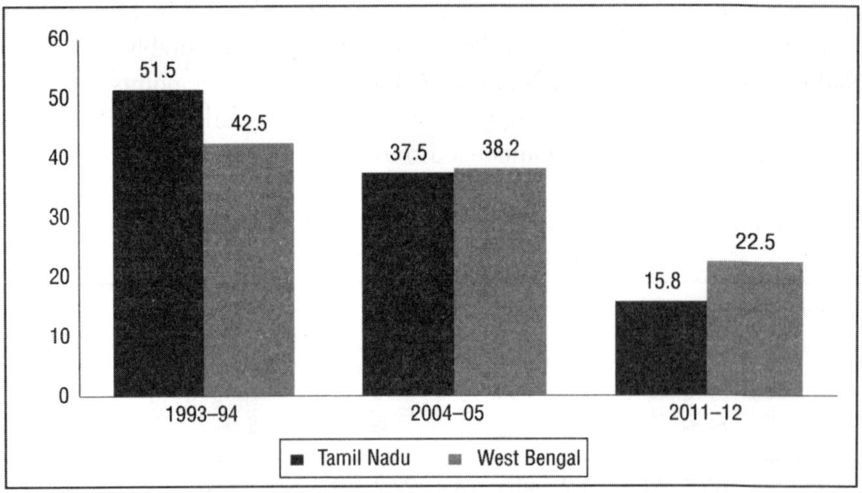

Figure 5.1 Rural Poverty (HCR) for Tamil Nadu and West Bengal (in Percentage)

Source: Calculated by the author's using NSS CES unit record data for the respective years.

Poverty reduction across social and religious groups in the countryside

In respect of poverty reduction across social and religious groups in rural areas Tamil Nadu has done better than West Bengal. The incidence of poverty among SC/STs in rural Tamil Nadu has come down from 66 per cent in 1993–94 to 24 per cent in 2011–12 (Table 5.3). The corresponding figures for SC/STs in West Bengal are 51.6 and 27.2 per cent respectively. The SC/STs gained about 42 percentage points in poverty reduction in Tamil Nadu during this period. The corresponding gain for SC/STs in terms of poverty reduction in West Bengal is just 24.4 percentage points. This is only about half of what Tamil Nadu has achieved. If we look at the rate of decline in poverty among SC/STs in rural areas between 1993–94 and 2011–12, it is about 2.3 percentage points per annum in Tamil Nadu. This is higher than Tamil Nadu's state average of 2 percentage points per annum for the same period. The comparative figure for

West Bengal is just 1.4 percentage points per annum. Clearly, poverty reduction among SC/STs in rural Tamil Nadu has been greater than in West Bengal.

In the sub-periods too, SC/STs have been better off in rural Tamil Nadu than in rural West Bengal. The rate of decline in poverty among them in Tamil Nadu between 1993–94 and 2004–05 was 1.3 percentage points per annum; and the rate increased to 3.9 percentage points between 2004–05 and 2011–12. In rural West Bengal, the rate of decline in poverty was 1.0 percentage point per annum among SC/STs in the first period, while the second period witnessed a decline at the rate of 2.0 percentage points per annum. This is much lower than that of Tamil Nadu. Though we do not have comparable figures over time for the OBCs, the incidence of poverty among the OBCs in 2011–12 is 13 per cent in Tamil Nadu and the corresponding figure for the OBCs in West Bengal is 17.1 per cent.

Poverty reduction among religious minorities such as Muslims has also been higher in rural Tamil Nadu than in rural West Bengal. The incidence of poverty among Muslims in rural Tamil Nadu decreased from 37.3 per cent in 1993–94 to 1.6 per cent in 2011–12. The corresponding figures for Muslims in rural West Bengal are 50.5 and 23.9 respectively. The gain that Muslims have made in poverty reduction in this period is about 35 percentage points in rural Tamil Nadu and only 26.6 percentage points in rural West Bengal. The rate of decline in poverty among Muslims in rural Tamil Nadu was 2 percentage points per annum between 1993–94 and 2011–12, while the corresponding figure for Muslims in West Bengal was 1.5 percentage points per annum. In the first sub-period between 1993–94 to 2004–05, the rate of decline of poverty among Muslims was 1.8 percentage points per annum in rural Tamil Nadu and the corresponding rate in West Bengal was a mere 0.1 percentage point. In the second period of 2004–05 to 2011–12, however, Muslims in West Bengal have fared better. The rate of decline of poverty among Muslims in West Bengal is 3.6 percentage points per annum; and the corresponding figure for in Tamil Nadu is about 2.3 percentage points per annum.

Overall, poverty reduction among the historically disadvantaged and marginalised in rural areas is much higher in Tamil Nadu than in West Bengal.

Incidence of urban poverty, 1994–2012

The data on incidence of urban poverty and its rate of decline is given in Table 5.4. Tamil Nadu has done better than West Bengal on both counts. In the period 1993–94 and 2011–12, the incidence of urban poverty has come down from 33.8 per cent to 6.6 per cent in Tamil Nadu. The corresponding figures for West Bengal are 31.2 per cent and 14.7 per cent respectively. The gain that Tamil Nadu made in poverty reduction in urban areas during the period of 1993–94 to 2011–12 was about 27 percentage points, while West Bengal gained just about 16.5 percentage points. While West Bengal was in a better position at the beginning of the period mentioned, it has clearly lost to Tamil Nadu.

The rate of decline of urban poverty has been higher in Tamil Nadu than in West Bengal. The rate of decline in urban poverty in Tamil Nadu during 1993–94 to 2011–12 is about 1.5 percentage points per annum and the corresponding rate for West Bengal is just 0.9 percentage point per annum. In the sub-periods too, Tamil Nadu has consistently performed better than West Bengal. In the first sub-period of 1993–94 to 2004–10, the rate of decline in urban poverty in Tamil Nadu was 1.3 percentage points per annum. During the sub-period 2004–05 to 2011–12, this increased to 1.9 percentage points per annum. The corresponding figures for West Bengal are 0.6 and 1.4 percentage point per annum respectively.

Table 5.4 The Incidence of Poverty (HCR) and Rate of Poverty Reduction (Per Annum) for Social-Religious Groups (Urban)

Social Group	*1993–94*		*2004–05*		*2011–12*		*1993–94 to 2004–05*		*2004–05 to 2011–12*		*1993–94 to 2011–12*	
	Tamil Nadu	*West Bengal*	*Tamil Nadu*	*West Bengal*	*Tamil Nadu*	*West Bengal*	*Tamil Nadu*	*West Bengal*	*Tamil Nadu*	*West Bengal*	*Tamil Nadu*	*West Bengal*
SC/ST	54	48.5	40.5	41.7	9	18.9	1.2	0.6	4.5	3.3	2.5	1.6
OBC	–	–	17.3	23.6	6.4	17.1	–		1.6	0.9	–	
General*	30	22	6.5	13.2	1.8	7.2	2.1	0.8	0.7	0.9	1.6	0.8
Hindu	33.6	27.5	20.1	20.9	7.0	10.9	1.2	0.6	1.9	1.4	1.5	0.9
Muslim	35.4	56.4	19.1	45.7	3.7	35.5	1.5	1	2.2	1.5	1.8	1.2
Other Minorities	32.9	29.5	16.0	21.4	5.9	1.2	1.5	0.7	1.4	2.9	1.5	1.6
All	33.8	31.2	19.7	24.4	6.6	14.7	1.3	0.6	1.9	1.4	1.5	0.9

*General includes OBC population in 1993–94 as the OBC was not counted then, thus can't be compared across time.

Source: Calculated by the author's using NSS CES unit record data for the respective years.

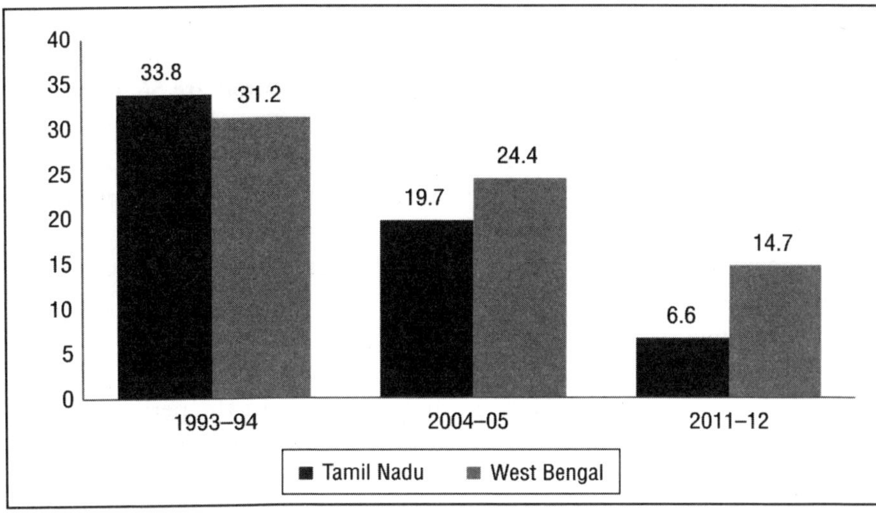

Figure 5.2 Urban Poverty (HCR) for Tamil Nadu and West Bengal (in Percentage)

Source: Calculated by the author's using NSS CES unit record data for the respective years.

Poverty reduction across urban social and religious groups

Tamil Nadu has outperformed West Bengal in reducing urban poverty among the marginalised and disadvantaged social groups. The incidence of poverty among SC/STs in urban Tamil Nadu has come down from 54 per cent in 1993–94 to 9 per cent in 2011–12 (Table 5.4). The corresponding figures for West Bengal are 48.5 and 18.9 per cent respectively. In the period from 1993–94 to 2011–12, SC/STs in urban Tamil Nadu have gained about 45 percentage points in terms of poverty reduction, while their counterparts in West Bengal gained just 29.6 percentage points. The rate of decline of urban poverty among SC/STs for this period is about 2.5 percentage point per annum in Tamil Nadu and just 1.6 percentage point per annum in West Bengal.

In the first sub-period (1993–94 to 2004–05), SC/STs did better in Tamil Nadu than in West Bengal. The rate of poverty decline among SC/ST in urban Tamil Nadu was 1.2 percentage points per annum while the corresponding figure for urban West Bengal was just 0.6 percentage points. In the second sub-period (2004–05 to 2011–12) too SC/STs did better in Tamil Nadu than in West Bengal. The rate of decline of poverty among SC/STs between 2004–05 and 2011–12 in urban Tamil Nadu was about 4.5 percentage points per annum and that in urban West Bengal was 3.3 percentage points.

The incidence of poverty among Muslims in urban Tamil Nadu has reduced dramatically from 35.3 per cent in 1993–94 to 3.7 per cent in 2011–12. The corresponding figures for Muslims in Urban West Bengal are 56.4 and 35.5 per cent respectively. Poverty reduction among Muslims between 1993–94 and 2011–12 amounts to 31 percentage points in urban Tamil Nadu while the corresponding figure for urban West Bengal is 20.9 percentage points. The rate of poverty decline among Muslims in urban areas in this period was 1.8 percentage points per annum in Tamil Nadu 1.2 percentage points per annum in West Bengal. By both measures, Muslims in Tamil Nadu are far better off than their counter parts in West Bengal.

Muslims have fared better in Tamil Nadu in sub-periods as well. The rate of decline in poverty among Muslims in Tamil Nadu in the period between 1993–94 and 2004–05, was 1.5 percentage points per annum. The rate increased to 2.2 percentage points in the period between 2004–05 and 2011–12. The corresponding figures for West Bengal are 1.0 and 1.5 percentage points per annum respectively. Muslim in Tamil Nadu outperformed Muslims in West Bengal in both the measures of poverty However, it needs to be noted that population of Muslims is substantial in West Bengal as compared to Tamil Nadu.

Education and Health Indicators

Literacy rate

Literacy rate (measured for those in the age of 6 years and above) is a key indicator of educational outcomes. As is clear from Table 5.5, Tamil Nadu has performed better than West Bengal on this count. The literacy rate in Tamil Nadu is 81 per cent for 2011–12 and 76 per cent in West Bengal. Literacy rate of Male in Tamil Nadu is 87.5 per cent and about 82 per cent in West Bengal. Female literacy is also higher in Tamil Nadu than in West Bengal. Female literacy is about 75 per cent in Tamil Nadu and about 70 per cent in West Bengal.

The literacy rate among SC/STs and OBCs is about the same in both states. In Tamil Nadu, the literacy rate is 74.8 per cent among SC/STs and 82.4 per cent among OBCs. The corresponding figures for West Bengal are 74.3 and 82.1 per cent respectively. On this count, Muslims in Tamil Nadu are better off than in West Bengal. The literacy rate among Muslims in Tamil Nadu for 2011–12 is about 87 per cent as compared to 67 per cent in West Bengal. Tamil Nadu is better placed in literacy rate as compared to West Bengal.

Table 5.5 Literacy Rate by Caste and Gender (6 Years and above)

Caste/ Gender	*2011–12*	
	Tamil Nadu	*West Bengal*
Male	87.5	81.9
Female	74.8	70.4
SC/ST	74.8	74.3
OBC	82.4	82.1
GEN	94.2	94.1
Hindu	80.3	79.4
Muslim	86.7	67.0
Other Minorities	86.8	87.3
All	81.1	76.3

Source: Calculated by the authors using NSS Employment and Unemployment unit record data.

Educational status of the workforce

An educated workforce is a key factor for productivity in any economy. In this respect, Tamil Nadu has performed better than West Bengal. The percentage of workforce which is illiterate in Tamil Nadu is about 20 per cent for 2011–12 (Table 5.6). The corresponding figure for West Bengal is 26 per cent. Percentage of the workforce who is graduates or above in Tamil Nadu is about 14 per cent. The corresponding figure for West Bengal is 9 per cent. The percentage of the workforce with secondary and higher secondary education is also comparatively higher in Tamil Nadu. The figure for Tamil Nadu is about 38 per cent, as compared to about 30 per cent in West Bengal. Clearly, the workforce in Tamil Nadu is more educated than in West Bengal.

Table 5.6 provides the distribution of workforce by education across caste groups. The gains of deprived castes in education have been greater than in Tamil Nadu than in West Bengal. In 2011–12 about 29 per cent of SC/ST workers in Tamil Nadu were illiterates, as compared to 33 per cent in West Bengal. The percentage of the SC/ST workforce being graduates and above is 7.3 per cent in Tamil Nadu and only 3.8 per cent in West Bengal. The percentage of workers among SC/STs with a secondary and higher secondary education is also higher in Tamil Nadu as compared to West Bengal.

Table 5.6 Percentage Distribution of Usual Status Workers (Principle + Subsidiary) by Level of Education across Social Groups (15 to 59 age)

Socio-Religious Group	*Tamil Nadu*				*West Bengal*			
	Illiterate	*Up to Primary*	*Secondary & Higher Secondary*	*Graduate and Above*	*Illiterate*	*Up to Primary*	*Secondary & Higher Secondary*	*Graduate and Above*
SC/ST	29.5	29.6	33.6	7.3	33.1	38.6	24.5	3.8
OBC	18.2	27.4	39.0	15.4	15.0	37.2	39.6	8.3
General	3.2	12.2	34.4	50.3	11.0	27.0	42.2	19.8
Hindu	21.3	27.5	37.7	13.4	21.7	33.4	33.6	11.3
Muslim	12.3	32.9	38.3	16.6	39	39.7	18.3	2.9
Other Minorities	13.4	23.4	36.2	27.0	12.6	27.0	46.8	13.5
All	20.5	27.6	37.7	14.3	26.2	35	29.7	9.1

Source: Calculated by the authors using NSS Employment and Unemployment unit record data

The level of education of the workforce among the OBCs is also much higher in Tamil Nadu than in West Bengal. The percentage of workforce in the category of graduates and above among OBCs in Tamil Nadu in 2011–12 is 15.4 per cent as compared to 8.3 per cent in West Bengal. Religious minorities too performed better in Tamil Nadu than in West Bengal. The percentage of workforce who is illiterate among Muslims in Tamil Nadu is 12.3 per cent as compared to 39 per cent in West Bengal.[5] The percentage of workforce in the category graduate and above among Muslims is about 17 per cent. This is about five times higher than the percentage of graduates among Muslims in West Bengal. Overall, the level of education of workforce among the deprived castes and religious minority groups is much higher in Tamil Nadu than in West Bengal.

Health indicators

Table 5.7 provides details of basic health indicators including health infrastructure for Tamil Nadu and West Bengal for 2005–06. Tamil Nadu has outperformed West Bengal in respect of key health indicators. Infant Mortality Ratio (IMR) for Tamil Nadu stands at 22 as against 32 for West Bengal. The Maternal Mortality Ratio (MMR) and under 5 mortality ratios (U5MR) for

Tamil Nadu are comparatively more favourable. The MMR in Tamil Nadu stands at 97 as compared to 145 in West Bengal. The U5MR is 25 in Tamil Nadu against 38 of West Bengal. Life Expectancy Rates are comparable for both states – 67 for male and 71 for female in 2005–06.

Table 5.7 Basic Health Indicators (2005–06)

Indicators	*TN*	*WB*	*All India*
IMR (2011)	22	32	44
U5MR (2011)	25	38	55
MMR (2011)	97	145	212
Life Expectancy-Male	67	67	64
Life Expectancy-Female	71	71	67
TFR (2011)	1.7	1.7	2.4
Weight for Age	29.8	38.7	42.5
Height for Age	30.9	44.6	48
Full Immunisation of Child	80.9	64.3	43.5
Safe Delivery	89	54	47.6
Institutional Delivery	88	42	38
Proportioned of births assisted by Skilled Health personnel	90.6	47.6	46.6
ANC Visits	98.6	91.7	76.4
Post- Natal Check-up	91.3	44.3	41.2
Health Infrastructure			
Population for PHC (000)	32.1	37.9	49
PHC with Medical Officer	85.3	80.3	75.8
PHC with Pharmacist	93.9	76.9	69.2
PHC with Functional OT	90.1	25.2	61.3
PHC with Essential Drugs	97.9	43.1	69.6
% of villages with any health facility	61.8	40.1	46.2

Source: Select Socio Indicators, NFHS-3, (2005–06), IIPS and Sample Registration System (SRS), Population Census.

Tamil Nadu has performed better in reducing the percentage of children who are undernourished. Thirty one per cent of children were undernourished in Tamil Nadu in 2005–06 as compared to about 45 per cent in West Bengal.

In terms of key Reproductive and Child Health (RCH) Indicators as well, Tamil Nadu has performed better. The following are considered that topmost priorities of a reproductive and child health programme in India: (i) ensuring safe motherhood and improved child health and (ii) raising contraceptive prevalence rates. Studies (Sen and Dreze, 2013) show that Tamil Nadu has performed better on both counts. Table 5.7 provides some details on the status of RCH indicators for Tamil Nadu and West Bengal. In Tamil Nadu, antenatal check up is done in 99 per cent cases as compared to 91 per cent in West Bengal. The rate of safe delivery in Tamil Nadu is about 89 per cent, while the corresponding figure for West Bengal stands at a lowly 54 per cent. The rate of institutional delivery in Tamil Nadu is 88 per cent; much higher than the 42 per cent in West Bengal. The child immunisation coverage for Tamil Nadu stands at 80.9 per cent whereas it is a meagrely 64.3 per cent for West Bengal.

In the provision of health infrastructure too, Tamil Nadu stands much better than West Bengal. Population per Primary Health Centre (PHC) is 32,000 in Tamil Nadu as compared to 38,000 in West Bengal. The facilities in PHCs are also better in Tamil Nadu than in West Bengal. For instance, the percentages of PHCs with medical officer and pharmacist in Tamil Nadu are 85 and 95 respectively. The corresponding figures for West Bengal are 80 and 77. Similarly, the PHCs with functional operational theatre (OT) in Tamil Nadu are 90 per cent as compared to an abysmal 25 per cent in West Bengal. The PHCs with the provision of essential drugs in Tamil Nadu is 99 per cent as compared to just 43 per cent in West Bengal.[6]

Possible Explanations

As shown in the earlier sections, there are significant differences in economic growth and developmental outcomes between Tamil Nadu and West Bengal. Tamil Nadu has outperformed Bengal. This section tries to locate the difference in the historical setting of the respective states. To begin with, let me take up the history of land tenurial system and its impact on the political regime and economic development in each of these states.

History of land tenure and incentive structure

As well-known, there were broadly two set of land tenurial system that the British administration introduced in India. One that had intermediaries between the tenant and the state was known as the Zamindari system, and the second one that had no such intermediaries was the Ryotwari system. The colonial Government took less interest in investing in Zamindari areas as the land revenue was fixed and did not depend directly on the prosperity of the cultivator. The Zamindars too took little interest in the productivity of land or the condition of cultivators. Banerjee and Iyer (2005) demonstrate that areas in which property rights to land were given to Zamindars systematically exhibit lower agricultural investment and productivity as compared to Ryotwari areas where individual cultivators owned the land. According to the authors, the differential effects of land tenurial system continue to persist even in the post-independence period. They further argue that infrastructural provisions too have differed based on the land tenurial patterns. The areas that were under Ryotwari have better infrastructures as compared to Zamindari areas. While Tamil Nadu was historically under the Ryotwari system, West Bengal was under the Zamindari system.[7]

It is argued that the history of land tenure in West Bengal had a negative impact on the incentive structure for economic activities (Banerjee and Iyer, 2005; Gupta, 2012). Thus the poor economic performance of the region is generally attributed to the colonial land tenure policy. However, what is usually not stated is that the beneficiaries of the system were not only the British, but the Bengali bhadraloks too. As Zamindars, they formed a rentier class and a large section of them were absentee landlords, living far away from the site of production.

Given their rentier status, they hardly partook in productivist ethos. As Saibal Gupta argues, 'instead of occupying themselves with the question of production, [they] trekked to Ramkrishna Paramahansa, a spiritual head, who seemed to represent the very opposite...' (Gupta, 2012). Significantly, the Bengali bhadraloks were drawn from upper castes and continue to dominate the social and political life of the state. Prabhat Patnaik, a known sympathiser of the parliamentary left, notes, 'One reality in Bengal, one of great importance, scarcely ever gets talked about. This relates to the domination of the Brahmin "Boddi", Kayastha castes in the intellectual, social, political and cultural life of the state' (Patnaik, 2013). He laments that such domination of castes elite continues to persist even 'after 65 years after the country's independence' and 'three decades of the left rule in the state' (*ibid*).[8]

As Partha Chatterjee sums it up,

> ...the continued and unchallenged dominance of upper-caste hindus in virtually every public institution, whether political or cultural. In fact, the two features are connected. That is to say, caste appears to be insignificant in West Bengal's politics precisely because public political life is thoroughly dominated by the upper castes (Chatterjee 2012, 69).

In short, the ruling elite in Bengal neither entertained productivist ethos nor were they sensitive to caste-based discrimination. For instance, as Sekhar Bandyopadhyay notes, 'In 1980s when the Mandal Commission first recommended the extension of affirmative action policies to the OBCs, CPI (M) strongly asserted that there were no OBCs in West Bengal and in their province "backwardness" should be defined in terms of class rather caste, because caste did not matter in Bengal' (Bandyopadhyay, 2014). This leaves us with the question of why the left took up the question of land reform, despite lacking in productivist ethos.

Land reform in West Bengal is generally attributed to the CPI (M) (Mishra 2007). However, it could be argued that given the history of peasant movement in the region independent of the left, the land question assumed centrality in political and policy regimes. The political elite in the state had no option but to respond to the land question. As Bardhan and Mookherjee (2003) suggests, the electoral competitiveness is the main driver of land reform in the state. They further point out, as the CPI (M) assumed complete electoral control, there was slack in implementation of the programme.[9]

Gupta (2005) argues that in Ryotwari regions, the social movements were occupied in addressing the operational aspect of development and production since the incentive structure of production has been embedded in their cognitive world. He further argues that anti-caste and anti-Brahmin moments have focussed on development and industrialization. In the process, they also developed a sense of sub-national identity. According to him, the sub-national identity and incentive structure for production together contributed to the development of these regions.

The Justice Party which emerged in the early twentieth century and countered the Brahmin domination in the socio-economic life of the Tamil region, was informed, for instance, by productivist ethos. For instance, Thegaraya Chetti, a founding member of the Justice Party, wrote,

> We all know that Bombay is the premier of city of India! What was the cause of this greatness? It is not the Sanskrit literature, it is not the world-admired Shankara's philosophy, and it is not the political greatness that we are hankering after, which has Bombay so great. It is enterprise – the enterprise of a small community of settlers, the Parsees (cited in Pandian 2006, 163).

The party also gave importance of industry oriented education. For instance, Thegaraya Chetti argued that the colonial education system was only fitted to make 'automatic quill-drivers, indifferent school-masters and petty-fogging lawyers... there is no such thing as education suitable to the development of industries' (*ibid*).

In addition, Tamil Nadu aligned its lower caste politics with a sub-national identity based on developmentalism. For instance, C. N. Annadurai, a founding member of the DMK, speaking in the Rajya Sabha in 1962, invoked the Southern Question in Italy to seek economic advancement of the Tamil region:

> For the information of the house I may say, that the very same problem arose in Italy. Southern Italy was industrially very backward compared to Northern Italy and then the Italian Government took very intelligent, very bold and very radical steps formulating a special scheme for Southern Italy. They offered tax concessions for new industries to be started in Southern Italy. They gave loans and other aids for this purpose in order to improve this part of Italy (Ramachandran 1975, 103–104).

Further, unlike in West Bengal where the village and rural development has been romanticised, in Tamil Nadu, the village was ideologically seen as the site of oppression and the urban as liberative. E. V. Ramasamy a.k.a Periyar, the founder of the non-Brahmin Self-Respect Movement and Dravidar Kazhagam, saw the village reconstruction of Gandhi as a political strategy to arrest the masses within traditional, caste-bound geographical spaces (Aloysius, 2013). As Aloysius sums up,

> Periyar sees the village as a sort of geographical lower caste destined to serve the 'upper caste towns'. The call for the renewal of traditional occupation, Periyar pointed out, is closely linked to Gandhi's articulated bias towards *Varnasramic*, that is non-egalitarian social order (Aloysius 2013, 7).

This understanding continues to inform lower caste aspirations in Tamil Nadu.

Political regimes

Populism in Tamil Nadu

As Narendra Subramanian argues, populism took two forms in Tamil Nadu from the 1960s onwards, i.e. with the Dravidian parties gaining political power in the state. The first one is called 'assertive populism', and it is defined as:

> Assertive populism urges supporters towards militant action to open up hitherto restricted spheres; and creates entitlements to education, jobs, loans,

> subsidized producer goods and sometimes small pieces of property. Due to the scarcity of such goods, they are usually rationed (perhaps through preferential policies) but not granted freely to all. Groups with some social power, albeit modest, are best able to compete for these entitlements… (Subramanian 1999, 376).

Primarily, assertive populism was practiced by the DMK and it took the form of (a) extending admission to higher education and government jobs to the OBCs and SCs, and (b) expanding the number of castes eligible for the same. In short, it took the form of expanding the scope of affirmative action. This has socio-economic consequences for the lower castes.

The second form that populism took in Tamil Nadu is characterized as 'paternalistic populism', and it is defined as follows:

> Paternalist populism promises that a benevolent leader, party or state will provide the poor and powerless with subsidized wage goods and protection from repressive elites. The lower strata and women, often unable to assert themselves independently or compete for the more substantial benefits assertive populism provides, are its main supporters (*ibid*).

Such populism was primarily practiced by the political rival of the DMK, i.e., the AIADMK under the leadership of the charismatic M. G. Ramachandran. A good example of paternalist populism was the Noon Meal Scheme introduced by the AIADMK in 1982. According to Andrew Wyatt, 'The noon meals enhanced MGR's image as the protector of children, women and the poor.' In addition, the AIADMK government also expanded food subsidies and increased the number of ration shops so that the rural poor got better access to this benefits'. (Wyatt, 2013).

While paternalist populism is primarily part of the politics and policies of the AIADMK, the DMK too did not fully avoid such populism in formulating and implementing policies. Giving an account of the DMK's policy regime in the late 1960s, Wyatt writes: 'Slum clearance was accelerated, subsidised rice was provided in selected urban areas', and not only this 'college fees were waived for poorer students and prohibition' were' introduced to protect women from the consequences of over-consumption of alcohol by male members of the household' (*ibid*, p. 5). Competing with the AIADMK, the DMK shifted over time its emphasis from assertive populism to paternalist populism.

The significance of such persistence of paternalist populism (even in the context of neo-liberalism) points to the fact that when state paternalism becomes the dominant expectation of the electorate, it becomes difficult for competing political regimes to deviate from such policies. In other words, paternalistic policies acquire path dependency over time.

The competitive populism between the two rival parties has yielded a space for independent social movements to make specific demands. Different socially disadvantaged groups could ask for their share of resources from the state. The parties in the power have to respond to such demands. For example, the Pattali Makka Katchi (PMK), a party of Vanniars, an intermediate backward caste faced with socio-economic stagnancy, hit the streets in September 1987 seeking 20 per cent exclusive reservation in Government jobs and education (Pandian, 1994). The DMK, which was in power then, had to yield to the demands of the PMK. It introduced the compartmental reservation by setting apart a substantial 20 per cent for the most backwards and de-notified communities out of the overall BC reservation of 50 per cent.

To give another example, in 1997, based on the recommendation of the central Government, the Government of Tamil introduced the policy of targeted PDS and made it available only to those families identified as living below the poverty line. The policy was withdrawn within a week due to wide spread protest across the state and the Government had to reintroduce the policy of universal coverage PDS (Srinivasan, 2010).

Party-society of West Bengal

The possibility of such mobilisation from below by multiple social groups was more or less absent in West Bengal. As stated earlier, Dwajpayan Bhattacharya (2010) argues that party-society is a specific form of political society operating in rural Bengal. Party-society has its roots in the peasant movements of rural West Bengal. Historically, the peasants in the region, given the Zamindari system, offered militant struggles against landlords. Given the specific historical and socio-economic condition in the state, the left parties offered the leadership to such struggles. The peasants were also in need of a strong and coherent "vanguard" party to counter the brutality of landlords. In this context, the left led by CPI (M) gained ascendancy in rural West Bengal and was elected to power in 1977. In addition to the land question, the party intervened in local issues faced by the poor and underprivileged. In the process, the party started playing an active role in every aspect of social life ranging from the panchayat to the school, from the sports clubs to the family. In essence, the party monopolised the social space of rural West Bengal.

However, the party did not attempt to end the extant exploitative social and cultural practices but accommodated them carefully in its structure. Rather than attempting to address different identities such as caste and religion, the party rendered them invisible in the organised domain of politics.

However, Dwajpayan Bhattacharya argues that the party-society as a category is not applicable to urban West Bengal. He argues that unlike in rural areas, where political parties monopolise the social space and other competing channels of public transaction are virtually non-existent, the urban West Bengal has the wide presence of competing civil society organisations. This claim may not be true. For instance, Raka Ray (2000) through intensive field work convincingly shows that independent of civil society organisations occupy a marginal space in Kolkata and are in great difficulties to function without the political party's patronage. Her work compares two metropolitan cities, namely, Kolkata and Mumbai, and compares the functioning of women's organisations there. Ray characterises Kolkata city as a 'hegemonic political field' with long and strong hold of CPI (M) where power is concentrated and culturally hegemonic. Mumbai is seen as a 'fragmented political field' where power is fragmented and culture is pluralistic. She attributes that the absence of independent women's movement in Kolkata to the hegemonic political field of CPI (M). On the other hand, she finds vibrant independent women's movement in Mumbai where the political field is fragmented and pluralistic. She also argues that the political field sets the limits to the demands that an independent movement can make in Kolkata. In other words, the demands of independent women's movements have to be in congruent with that the politics of political field.

To understand how populism in Tamil Nadu and party-society in West Bengal works on the ground, I provide the case study of public distribution system (PDS). The PDS is seen as an important achievement of populism in Tamil Nadu. On the contrary, in West Bengal, the functioning PDS is said to have unravelled the fault lines in party-society.

A case study of PDS

The PDS is considered to be a source of income support and social protection in India. The functioning of the PDS in Tamil Nadu has been acknowledged for its efficiency and inclusiveness (Dreze and Sen, 2011). The state has been maintaining universal PDS while most other states including West Bengal have gone for targeted PDS since 1997. A recent study by Khera (2011b) shows that the PDS in Tamil Nadu, as compared to other states, has performed better or even topped in terms of degree of inclusiveness, integrity of the system, quality of PDS grain, physical access (distance and time), predictability, reliability, record-keeping and institutional arrangements. The PDS in Tamil Nadu provides 35 kg rice per month for Antyodaya Anna Yojana card holders and 20 kg rice per month for other call holders free of cost since 2011 (Alamu, 2011).

In contrast to Tamil Nadu, PDS in West Bengal is exclusionary and functionally inefficient (Khera, 2011a). According to Reetika Khera, West Bengal falls under the category of languishing states which does not meet average per capita purchase of even 1 kg a month. The per capita purchase of PDS grain in West Bengal is low. Tamil Nadu, on the other hand, has a higher per capita PDS consumption and highest per capita rice purchase from PDS by consumers. For instance, in 2007–08, the per capita rich purchased per month from the PDS in West Bengal is 0.4 kg in rural and 0.14 kg in urban areas. The corresponding figures for Tamil Nadu are 4.84 kg and 3.19 kg (Khera, 2011a).

Further, Tamil Nadu has a diversion rate (the proportion of grain that does not reach beneficiary households) of 4.4 per cent; one of the lowest among the states compared. The diversion rate in West Bengal is as high as 75 per cent, a sign of the party-society at work (figure 5.3). The study further shows that large percentage of the poorest in West Bengal do not get any subsidised grain due to poor coverage and the exclusionary nature of targeted PDS.

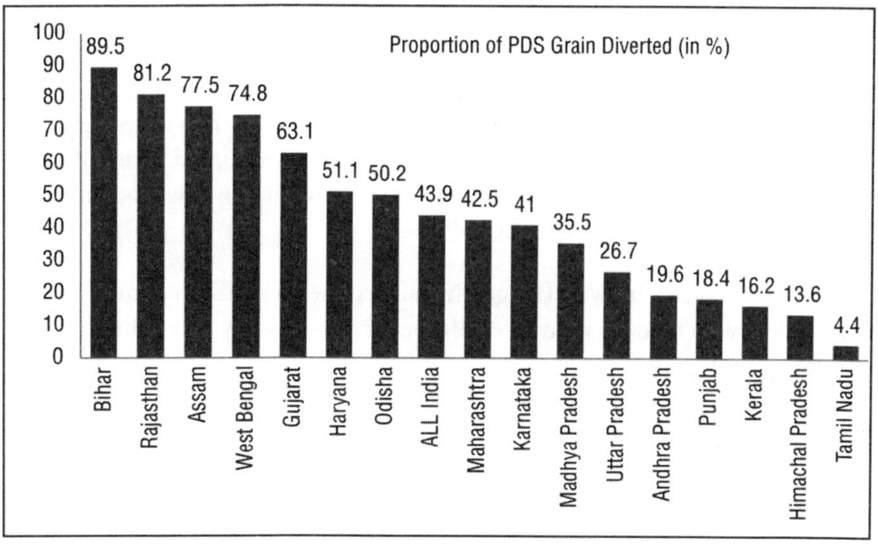

Figure 5.3 Estimated Diversion of Food Grain

Source: Khera, Reetika, 2011.

The political commitment nurtured through paternalist populism coupled with public pressure from below ensures effective and transparent functioning of PDS without much leakage or corruption in Tamil Nadu (Srinivasan, 2010). In contrast to the populism of Tamil Nadu, the party-society provides little scope for challenging the corruption and ensuring the effective functioning of PDS in rural West Bengal.

In congruence with macro data, the field studies too show wide spread prevalence of corruption and ineffective delivery of PDS in West Bengal (Bhattacharya and Rana, 2008). It is argued that the protest against the malfunctioning of PDS was the precursor to the massive violence that took place across rural West Bengal in 2007. Bhattacharya and Rana (2008) provide detailed field-based evidence as to how the ration dealers allegedly misbehave with the poor; cheat them in weight and quality of food grains. Unlike Tamil Nadu, the fair price shops are run by private dealers in West Bengal. The dealers work in close nexus with the local panchayat bodies, most often controlled by the left. For instance, when villagers in Bhankura, a district dominated by CPI (M), mobilised themselves against corruption in the PDS, the protest became violent; villagers assaulted the dealers and ransacked their property and houses. Similarly, in 2007, in a village in Swarupnagar block, North 24-Paraganas district, villagers gathered front of the fair price shop confronting the dealer for missing ration stocks. A filed report sums up the incident thus,

> The villagers' anger and resentment at perceived manipulation by the dealers spills out as they talk about how they have often been overcharged for ration cards and food grains, had irregular access to PDS provisions, and been bullied by dealers who, once poor like them, are now living in big concrete houses and driving around in cars (Mitra, 2007).

The party-society in West Bengal thus stifled the possibilities of mobilisation from below which could guarantee efficiency, a necessary condition to reach developmental goals.

Conclusion

This paper shows that Tamil Nadu has outperformed West Bengal in terms of both economic growth and distributive measures. Growth in Tamil Nadu has been more socially inclusive than growth in West Bengal. The legacy of land tenurial systems introduced by the colonial Government has been a factor in setting the path for development in these regions. As the infrastructural provisions and incentive structure in production differed on the basis of tenurial system, the paths for political regime also differed. The political regime that came into being in Tamil Nadu was distinctly influenced by productivist ethos and lower caste/class leadership. Its populism installed a complementary policy structure, such as public provision of certain basic services, which in turn facilitated the process of industrialisation in Tamil Nadu.

West Bengal, on the other hand, could not break the path set by the history, though under the left rule for three decades. The regional elite, despite being left of some kind, lacked productivist ethos needed for industrialisation and redistribution. Half hearted land reform is the best that Bengal's predominantly upper-caste political elite could do. Disconnected from production and organised in a strong vanguard structure, Bengal's political elite erected a 'party-society' which hardly allowed space for independent mobilization of direct producers.

Thus, history and political regimes together produced a specific policy structures that set the paths of differential development of these two states.

(This is the revised version of the paper presented at the conference on 'the Political Economy of Contemporary India' held at Indira Gandhi Institute of Development Research, Mumbai, November 20–21, 2014. The initial ideas for the paper emerged from my conversations with M. S. S. Pandian. The discussions with Vijaya Baskar, Shantanu Chakravarty, Vanessa Chishti, Santosh Mehrotra, and, Atul Sood were useful in formulating arguments. Incisive comments by Prof. Pranab Bardhan and others in the conference were great help in revising the paper. Manjoj Jatav took time off in helping to produce maps. I am thankful to all of them).

Endnotes

1. Kerala is often stated as a state ruled by the left and its economic performance in the social sector is attributed to the left. However, if the left held power for seven times in Kerala since 1956 (when the state was formed), the Congress did so for six times. The history of social development in Kerala goes beyond the left regime. The social reform movements, including the role of Christianity and specific nature of colonial intervention, have to be accounted for the better social indicators. Rammohan (2000) rightly argues, 'The modernity project in Kerala, it may be remembered, was realised, among others, through robust caste-based social movements, especially the movements of the 'lower' castes and "out"castes. The part played by such democratisation in Kerala's social development was unique, as evidenced by West Bengal, also marked by a project of modernity and strong left movement, but failing to attain similar social development (*ibid*, p. 1234).'
2. Certain agricultural castes such as Gounder and Nadar have indeed become successful entrepreneurial communities in Tamil Nadu. This transition took place by social

mobilization in the form of caste and kinship through a system of networks. Such transition didn't take place in West Bengal. Business in West Bengal continues to be dominated cultural outsiders such as Marwaris and Gujaratis. For further details see Mahadevan (2012) and Damodaran (2008).

3. As per population census 2001, the percentage of SCs, STs and Muslims in West Bengal are 24, 6 and 25 respectively. The corresponding figures for Tamil Nadu are 19, 1 and 6 per cent respectively. As per NSS0 2011–12, the OBCs in Tamil Nadu are 75 per cent and 9 per cent in West Bengal. The Hindu upper castes are 4 per cent in Tamil Nadu and about 36 per cent in West Bengal.
4. Tendulkar methodology needs Mixed Reference Period (MRP) series of expenditure to calculate incidence of poverty. Since the 1993–94 data sets do not have MRP series, the author constructed MRP series. The method used to construct the MRP series is the following: MRP = 30 days reference period data for all other items + 365 days reference period for low frequency items (cloth, footwear, durable goods, education and medical) – 30 days reference period for low frequency items.
5. The Sachar Committee (2006) report too has shown the precarious condition of Muslims in West Bengal. The report places the state in the worst performing category of states in the country in terms of representation of Muslims in employment and education. An another report, *Status of the Muslims in Bengal 2014*, prepared by Social Network for Assistance to People (SNAP) and Guidance Guild too shows that Muslims have seen no improvement in the state despite the Sachar committee recommendations and they are still caught in petty, low-income and livelihoods options in West Bengal.
6. The better health outcome in the state is attributed to such provision of free essential drugs in the PHCs. In order to ensure the availability of essential drugs, Tamil Nadu Medical Services Corporation Ltd., (TNMSC) was set up adopting a streamlined procedure for their procurement, storage and distribution.
7. The study by Banerjee and Iyer (2005) shows that of the 11 districts in Tamil Nadu, 9 were under ryotwari system, whereas in Bengal all the 11 districts were under the zamindari system. What is not said is fact that there is substantial difference in trajectory of development within areas which were under ryotwari. Therefore, the differences in economic outcome cannot merely be attributed to the history of land tenurial system.
8. Arild Ruud (1994) who studied rural West Bengal in detail notes that the left rule in the state did not lead to any deeper changes in perceptions of power and influence. The caste-based inequality, hierarchy and separateness continue to persist in rural West Bengal.
9. Contrary to the popular perception that Tamil Nadu has large holdings and land reform had little effect in the state, the state has seen the disappearance of large land holdings in the last four decades. For instance, in 1971–72, large land holdings account for 10 per cent of the total area and it has come down to nil in 2003. However, what is persisting in Tamil Nadu is medium size holding which accounted for 23 per cent of the area in 1971–72 and continue to be 20 per cent in 2003. In West Bengal, since 1971–72, the land ownership has gradually shifted from medium size holdings to

marginal holdings. For instance, the medium size holdings accounted for about 19 per cent of area in 1971–72 and it has come down to 4 per cent in 2003. The corresponding figures for marginal holdings are 27 and 58 percents respectively. For further details see the NSSO (2003) report no. 491.

Reference

Alamu. 2011. 'It Just Works in TN.' *The Hindu*, September 24.

Aloysius, G. 2013. *Village Reconstruction*. New Delhi: Critical Quest.

Arooran, Nambi K. 1980. *Tamil Renaissance and Dravidian Nationalism, 1905–1944*. Madurai: Koodal Publishers.

Bandyopadhyay, Sekhar. 2014. 'Does Caste Matter in Bengal? Examining the Myth of Bengali Externalism.' In *Being Bengali: At Home and in the World*, edited by Mridula Nath Chakraborty. New York: Routledge.

Banerjee, Abhijit and Lakshmi Iyer. 2005. 'History, Institutions, and Economic Performance: The Legacy of Colonial Land Tenure Systems in India.' *The American Economic Review* 95 (4): 1190–1213.

Bardhan, Pranab and Dilip Mookherjee. 2005. 'Political Economy of Land Reforms in West Bengal 1978–98.' Boston: Institute for Economic Development, Boston University.

Bhattacharyya, Dwaipayan and Kumar Rana. 2008. 'Politics of PDS Anger in West Bengal'. *Economic and Political Weekly*, 63-69, February 2.

Bhattacharyya, Dwaipayan. 2010. 'Left in the Lurch: The Demise of the World's Longest Elected Regime?.' *Economic and Political Weekly*, 45 (3): 51–59, January 28.

Chandrababu, B. S. 1993. *Social Protest and its Impact in Tamil Nadu*. Madras: Emerald Publishers.

Chatterjee, Partha. 2004. *The Politics of the Governed: Reflections on Popular Politics in Most of the World*. Delhi: Permanent Black.

———. 2012. 'Historicising Caste in Bengal Politics.' *Economic and Political Weekly* 47 (50): 69–70, December 15.

Damodaran, Harish. 2008. *India's New Capitalists: Caste, Business and Industry in a Modern Nation*. New Delhi: Palgrave Macmillan.

Dreze, Jean and Amartya Sen. 2011. 'Putting Growth in its Place.' *Outlook*, November 14.

———. 2013. '*Uncertain Glory: India and its Contradictions*.' Princeton, New Jersey: Princeton University Press.

Gupta, Shaibal. 2013. 'Economic History of Bengal Presidency.' Patna: Asian Development Research Institute ADRI .

Harriss, John. 1999. 'Comparing Political Regimes across Indian States.' *Economic and Political Weekly*, 3367–3377, November 27.

Khera, Reetika. 2011a. 'Trends in Diversion of Grain from the Public Distribution System.' *Economic and Political Weekly* 46 (21): 106–114, May 21.

———. 2011b. 'Revival of the Public Distribution System: Evidence and Explanations.' *Economic and Political Weekly* 46 (45): 36–50, November 5.

Kohli, Atul. 1987. *The State and Poverty in India: The Politics of Reform*. India: Cambridge University Press.

Mahadevan, Raman. 2012. 'Everyone is a Vaishya.' *Outlook*, October 1.

Mishra, K. Surjya. 2007. 'On Agrarian Transition in West Bengal.' *The Marxist* 23 (2).

Mitra Nandini, Maureen. 2011. 'PDS protests in West Bengal.' *Down to Earth*, November 30.

Patnaik, Prabhat. 2013. 'In the long Run- the Social Divide in Bengal.' *The Telegraph*, July 30.

Planning Commission. 2009. 'Report of the Expert Group to Review the Methodology for Estimation of Poverty.' New Delhi: Government of India.

———. 2013. 'Poverty Estimates for 2011–12.' New Delhi: Government of India.

Ramachandran, S. 1975. *Anna Speaks: At the Rajya Sabha 1962–66*. New Delhi: Orient Longman.

Ray, Raka. 2000. *Fields of Protest: Women's Movements in India*. New Delhi: Kali for Women.

Ruud, Arild E. 2003. *Poetics of Village Politics: The Making of West Bengal's Rural Communism*. New Delhi: Oxford University Press.

Srinivasan, Vivek. 2010. 'Understanding Public Services in Tamil Nadu: An Institutional Perspective.' Ph.D dissertation, University of Syracuse, New York.

Subramanian, Narendra. 1999. *Ethnicity and Populist Mobilization: Political Parties, Citizens and Democracy in South India*. New Delhi: Oxford University Press.

Tillin, Louise. 2013. 'Varieties of State-Capital Relations in India.' *Economic and Political Weekly* 48 (39): 19–22, September 28.

Vijayabaskar, M. 2010. 'Saving Agricultural Labour from Agriculture: SEZs and Politics of Silence in Tamil Nadu.' *Economic and Political Weekly* 45 (6): 36–43.

Wyatt, Andrew. 2013. 'Combining Clientelist and Programmatic Politics in Tamil Nadu, South India.' *Commonwealth and Comparative Politics* 51 (1): 27–55.

6

India's Agricultural Development

A Regional Perspective

P. S. Vijayshankar

Introduction

Regional differences in growth performance have always attracted considerable attention in academic writing as well as in popular imagination. The fact that different regions and nations have followed different growth trajectories is a stylised fact in development economics. What is perhaps more serious is the consideration that such diverse trajectories has resulted in widening the gap between regions in terms of economic and social opportunity of their people. Hence, we need to look closely at how regional differences shape *regional inequalities* and result in growth processes that are polarising, exploitative and undesirable. While some regions have seen substantial improvements in living standards, backwardness is still concentrated in a few regions. While the indicators of the levels of living in some southern states like Kerala and Tamil Nadu are comparable to many developed countries, those in large, densely populated, northern states like Uttar Pradesh, Rajasthan, Odisha and Madhya Pradesh are closer to that of the poorest parts of the world, such as sub-Saharan Africa (Shankar and Shah, 2012). The concern is also often expressed in scholarly literature that regional inequality in India (in fact, all over the world) has been increasing in recent years and that regions which are already unequal in terms of poverty, income levels, consumption expenditure and access to basic services have further drifted apart over time. To bridge this gap, governments have periodically formulated various policies and direct public investment as an instrument to remedy the situation.

This paper seeks to provide an overview of the regional differences in agricultural growth during the last four decades (1962–2008). It also examines what are the key drivers of regional differentiation in India, the question often asked by many development economists in India (Bharadwaj, 1982). Re-opening this classical question has immense contemporary relevance. The persistence of regional identities and old geographies in spite of the efforts of the nation state towards homogenisation renders a 'spectral quality' to their existence (Ludden, 2002). Moreover, one can also argue that the national politics is increasingly getting regionalised (Palshikar, 2006). Regionalisation not only means increasing prominence of regional issues in electoral politics, but also the changing *regional composition* of the coalition of ruling classes itself.

The paper is divided into four sections. The first section provides a few general considerations to show how regional differences go way back into history. The second section offers an overview of the contrasting experiences of agricultural growth across regions. The third section follows a few selected regions in detail to understand the dynamics of change within the rural economy. The fourth and concluding section brings together some of the results of the previous section to bear upon analysis of and policy on regional inequalities in India.

Regions in Indian History

Regional identities were already fairly formed in different parts of what we now know as India even before colonialism. These regions were defined by their territoriality, geographical boundaries, agro-ecological settings and administrative control by the state. Through the interaction between the physiography and social processes, regional identities got crystallised towards the end of 18th century. Within each region, unique configuration of social classes, caste groups, production technology, commodity movement, labour circulation, state formations and cultural exchanges developed. For example, in some regions, crops such as cotton, tobacco and sugarcane were grown fairly extensively even before the advent of British rule, since they commanded a higher price compared to that of foodgrains (Raj, 1985). As Dharma Kumar has shown, the system of wage labour existed even before the colonial rule, with the big peasants cultivating their holdings based on wage labour drawn from the "menial castes", estimated at between a fifth to a quarter of the rural population at that time (Kumar, 1965). Various forms of agricultural labour prevailed in South India ranging from free wage labour to absolute and complete slavery. Clearly, there were sharp differences between regions in these key features.

The colonial state encountered these and selectively conquered and integrated regions into its fold. While doing so, the structure of the society that underlay the regional systems were also largely reconstituted. The changes were brought in through (a) changes in land tenure and creation of private property on land; (b) introduction of new technologies such as railways; (c) opening up new markets; and (d) public investment in irrigation. The impact of these varied across regions and different social classes responded to it differently. For instance, the regional distribution of public investment in irrigation was markedly uneven, with the "canal colonies" of Punjab receiving substantially higher amounts compared to the Eastern UP (Bharadwaj, 1982). Ludden describes that from here onwards two contradictory movements are visible, especially in the rural areas: first, that which selectively integrates different regions to the global economy through commodity chains and markets (what has been termed as the 'commercialisation of agriculture'), thereby strengthening regional identities; and second, that integrates these by drawing them together into one national fabric and national identity, thereby breaking down regionalism.

This dual process is also visible in the snapshot picture of regions around 1930, developed by Daniel Thorner (Thorner, 1996). Thorner's atlas of the ecological and agrarian regions of India could be the starting point of the study of agrarian regions in India. Though he primarily demarcated agrarian regions in terms of 'topography, water supply, crop system, land system and general economic development', Thorner was quick to point out that the relationships among people, resources, the market and the state are at the core of the 'agrarian problem'. Physical space provides the *terra firma* in which these relationships are built and changed over time. Thorner also insightfully points out that by comparing these regions, defined as physical spaces, over time with the original snapshot, we could get an idea how the dynamics of change has operated within each region. In Section 3, this comparative method has been adopted.

In the post independence period, the developmental state undertook the mission of balanced regional development. Public investment was seen as one of the principal vehicle for homogenisation of regions and transforming the rural areas. The state also passed legislations for changing outmoded rural institutions such as land tenurial relations (land reforms) and committed itself to re-structuring rural society on new principles ("community development"). The growing consolidation of the national market and the rising power of the national capitalist class were the key drivers in homogenisation.

Processes of democratisation and social movements from the margins for equality and rights overturned old hierarchies and thus also strived towards a more inclusive society. But, interestingly, the same set of factors can also be seen in specific regional contexts, working in the opposite direction, contributing creating more regional differentiation. It is well-known that public investment flows often accentuated pre-existing regional differences by discriminating between regions. For example, the "tribal areas" of the North East consolidated as a region with this differential flow of public investment. Public investments in irrigation discriminated between hills and valleys, rain-fed and irrigated agriculture and hilly, rain-fed regions again emerged as pockets of backwardness. Democratisation led to identity politics and consolidation of regions around identities created on the basis of caste and community. This created region-specific dynamics of inclusion and exclusion.

The need to speak of typology of regions follows from this. First, regional identities seem to survive homogenisation efforts of the developmental state. They also at times re-assert strongly in the form of demand for a separate nationhood (North East) or statehood (Jharkhand, Chhattisgarh, Telangana, Vidarbha) (Tillin, 2014). Second, the pace of rural transformation is uneven across regions and the same set of factors produce different results depending on the initial conditions. Regional differences are closely linked to the processes of accumulation within each region, its natural resource endowments and the social relationships of power, domination and resistance. For policy, it is important to be tuned to these regional typologies for the obvious reason that the approach of 'one-size-fits-all' will not work. However, the reason perhaps not so obvious is that as much as policies make regions, regions make policies as well. Emergence and consolidation of new regions requires changes in policy to accommodate their needs and aspirations. New regions also force old policies to be imagined in different ways. For example, when public procurement and price support policies are extended outside the Green Revolution areas (Punjab) to rainfed areas (Madhya Pradesh), this necessarily implies that the policy has to be re-imagined to suit the new context. Moreover, the dynamics of transformation of regional typologies show operation of the underlying power structure and social relations which contribute to making and unmaking of policies. Hence, policy change can be seen as an outcome of these forces acting together and acquiring strong political articulation.

Agrarian Regions: A Comparative Picture

We now compare the performance of different regions within India in terms of agricultural development. We have the long period dataset compiled by GS Bhalla and Gurmail Singh (2012). In this dataset, the original district boundaries as at early 1960s are kept constant and the current districts are re-configured to these original districts. The dataset estimates triennium averages of crop area, irrigated area, value of production, agricultural workers and inputs (fertilisers, pumpsets and tractors) over the period spanning 1962–65 to 2005–08. The value output calculations are made taking into account the area and production of 35 major crops at constant 1990–93 prices. This methodology has the advantage of allowing overtime comparisons in agricultural growth across districts and states in India. However, it has several limitations. First, it takes into account only 35 major field crops (covering roughly 90–95 per cent of the gross cropped area) and hence is likely to be biased against districts which have sizeable area under tree crops and plantations. Second, this dataset excludes some districts, most notable being the north east states other than Assam. Third, it does not take into account the value of livestock production, which is increasingly becoming an important source of value in rural India. Fourth, the use of constant price ignores the effect of relative price movements, which again could be a major contributor to growth in many parts of India. Even with all these limitations, this dataset still remains an important source for over time comparison of agricultural growth in India.

In this paper, we have tried to identify agrarian regions, broadly defined as groups of districts sharing common topographic, agro-climatic, social and economic characteristics. For the purpose of identifying regions, we have made use of the classification of states into NSS regions (NSSO, 2012), without strictly adhering to the NSS grouping of districts[1]. This breaking up the states into 54 relatively homogenous groups of districts helps arrive at some aggregate features of the development process at a considerably higher level than that of the district. Annexure 1 gives the details of the regions with region codes (derived from not strictly comparable to the NSS region codes) and the current districts included in each region.

The analysis of agricultural productivity, value of production and other variables was carried out at three time points, 1962–65, 1980–83 and 2005–08. Table 6.1 presents the list of regions with relatively high agricultural land productivity[2] at three time-points.

Table 6.1 Comparative Productivity Levels (Rs./HA) of Agrarian Regions

A. Ranking of Regions, 1962–65			
Rank	*Region Code*	*State-Region*	*Productivity (Rs./Ha)*
1	322	Kerala – South	11462
2	321	Kerala – North	10352
3	181	Assam – East	8289
4	331	TN – Coastal	6880
5	291	Karnataka – Coastal	6857
6	332	TN – South	6532
7	333	TN – Inland	6392
8	182	Assam – Barak Valley	6085
9	281	AP – Coastal	5548
10	32	Punjab – South	5490
B. Ranking of Regions, 1980–83			
Rank	*Region Code*	*State-Region*	*Productivity (Rs./Ha)*
1	322	Kerala – South	12074
2	321	Kerala - North	10930
3	291	Karnataka – Coastal	10302
4	32	Punjab- South	10009
5	181	Assam - East	9684
6	333	TN – Inland	9633
7	31	Punjab- North	9227
8	331	TN – Coastal	8661
9	95	UP - Himalayan	8471
10	12	J&K Valley	8461
C. Ranking Of Regions, 2005–08			
Rank	*Region Code*	*State-Region*	*Productivity (Rs./Ha)*
1	322	Kerala – South	21911
2	333	TN – Inland	21793

Contd.

Contd.

C. Ranking Of Regions, 2005–08			
Rank	*Region Code*	*State-Region*	*Productivity (Rs./Ha)*
3	321	Kerala – North	21214
4	244	GUJ – Saurashtra	15795
5	291	Karnataka – Coastal	15786
6	331	TN – Coastal	15630
7	32	Punjab – South	15262
8	332	TN – South	14329
9	281	AP – Coastal	13726
10	31	Punjab - North	13542

Source: Calculated from Bhalla and Singh, 2012.

What is striking about the above table is that many region names seem to be repeating at the top of the productivity ranking table. In fact, there are at least 6–7 regions out of 10 regularly seem to appear among the top 20 per cent of high productivity districts during the 45 year period under consideration. The same holds true at the bottom of the hierarchy as well.

Table 6.2 Best- and Worst-Performing Agricultural Regions in Terms of Agricultural Productivity

Agricultural Productivity – Best-Performing Regions (Top 20%)				
	State	*1962–65*	*1980–83*	*2005–08*
1	Kerala	Kerala – South	Kerala – South	Kerala – South
		Kerala – North	Kerala – North	Kerala – North
2	Tamil Nadu	TN – Coastal	TN – Coastal	TN – Coastal
		TN – Inland	TN – Inland	TN – Inland
		TN - South		TN - South
3	Andhra Pradesh	AP – Coastal	AP – Coastal	AP – Coastal
4	Karnataka	Karnataka - Coastal	Karnataka - Coastal	Karnataka – Coastal
5	Maharashtra	Mah – Konkan		

Contd.

Contd.

Agricultural Productivity – Best-Performing Regions (Top 20%)				
	State	*1962–65*	*1980–83*	*2005–08*
6	Assam	Assam – East	Assam – East	
		Assam - Barak Valley		
7	Punjab		Punjab – North	Punjab – North
			Punjab – South	Punjab – South
8	UP		UP – Himalayan	
9	Gujarat			Gujarat – Saurashtra
Agricultural Productivity – Worst-Performing Regions (Bottom 20%)				
		1962–65	*1980–83*	*2005–08*
1	Rajasthan	Raj – West	Raj - West	Raj – West
		Raj – North	Raj - North	Raj – North
		Raj - North East		
2	Gujarat	Guj - Dry Areas		
3	Maharashtra	Mah - Marathwada	Mah - Marathwada	Mah - Marathwada
		Mah – Vidarbha	Mah - Vidarbha	
4	Madhya Pradesh	MP - Madhya Bharat	MP - Madhya Bharat	MP - Madhya Bharat
		MP - Vindhyachal	MP - Vindhyachal	MP – Vindhyachal
			MP - Malwa	
			MP - Narmada	
			MP - Mahakoshal	MP – Mahakoshal
			Mp - Chhattisgarh	MP – Chhattisgarh
5	Karnataka	Karnataka - North		
6	J&K	J&K – Hills		J&K – Hills
7	Bihar			Bihar – North
				Bihar – South

Source: Calculated from Bhalla and Singh, 2012.

The shaded cells in the above table shows regions which are repeated across time points selected. At the bottom of the productivity chart, again, as many as 6–7 regions out of 10 are common between the different time points. The relatively unchanging (or slow-changing) ranking of regions in terms of their land productivity probably shows the effect of the initial conditions of the region on its future growth prospects. What this would mean is that the higher the level you are at the starting point, the more likely that you will perform well and vice versa.[3] This, however, needs more careful analysis.

This, by no means, is the whole story. What is even more interesting is that there is another group of regions which have been in the low productivity category for a long time but which have now managed to break out of that group. They have managed to raise levels of both the value of production as well as productivity per hectare of land cultivated. Along with them, there are also regions which have grown consistently slowly. Not surprisingly, most of these slow-growing regions still figure in the list of 'Worst-performing Regions' given above. The list of both sets of regions is given in Table 6.3.

Table 6.3 Rate of Growth of Production and Productivity in Agrarian Regions, 1962–2008

1. Relatively Fast Growing Regions				
State	*Region Code*	*Region*	*Rate of Growth % p.a.*	
			Value of Production	*Productivity (Rs./Ha)*
Gujarat	243	Dry Areas	4.23	3.99
Andhra Pradesh	282	Telangana	3.53	3.47
Gujarat	244	Saurashtra	3.84	3.43
Rajasthan	84	North	3.96	3.13
Tamil Nadu	333	Inland	2.32	2.89
Haryana	62	West	3.67	2.79
Rajasthan	81	West	3.76	2.79
Haryana	61	East	3.67	2.53
Rajasthan	82	North East	3.12	2.49
Punjab	32	South	3.69	2.41

Contd.

Contd.

2. Relatively Slow Growing Regions				
State	*Region Code*	*Region*	*Rate of Growth % p.a.*	
			Value of Production	*Productivity (Rs./Ha)*
Bihar	102	Central	0.93	1.40
Odisha	211	Coastal	1.12	1.29
Assam	182	West	1.66	1.28
Bihar	103	South	0.77	1.20
Uttar Pradesh	94	South	1.75	1.14
Madhya Pradesh	231	Vindhyachal	1.89	1.03
Odisha	212	South	1.59	0.98
Assam	182	Barak Valley	1.44	0.91
Bihar	101	North	0.97	0.88
J&K	12	Jk Valley	(-) 0.55	0.81

Source: Calculated from Bhalla and Singh, 2012.

This list of fast growing regions is interesting not only because it includes many of the hither-to backward regions but also because most of these regions have exhibited dynamism only in recent years, especially after 1990. The strong push given by the state governments could have been one of the major reasons behind their growth. This would apply especially to regions located in states with significant share of rainfed agriculture, such as Rajasthan, Gujarat, Andhra Pradesh and Tamil Nadu (Planning Commission, 2013).

Before moving further, it is instructive to compare the above ranking of regions on the basis of agricultural productivity alone with the rankings in terms of the level of Monthly Per Capita Expenditure (MPCE) and rates of poverty, derived from other studies (Dubey and Srivastava, 2007; Jha, Gaiha and Sharma, 2006; Mishra, 2014). The results are summarised in Table 6.4.

The shaded cells are regions which repeat in the top and bottom 20 per cent on these variables. Since there are many regions which are repeated, these results show that there is some correspondence between ranking of regions on different indicators. However, we cannot assume a complete overlap between these three groups. The conclusions drawn only on the basis of a comparison of agricultural productivity should be treated with caution. They should be read along with other indicators of rural well-being and rural incomes, especially since non-farm incomes have been contributing a rising share of household incomes in rural areas (IHDS, 2010). In fact, the separation of the 'rural' and the 'agricultural' is particularly visible in the more advanced of the agrarian regions rather than in the backward ones.

Table 6.4 Cross-Classification of Agrarian Regions on the Basis of Land Productivity, MPCE and Rural Poverty Ratio

	Best-Performing Regions (Top 20%)			
	State	*Land Productivty 2005–08*	*Rural MPCE 60Th Round (2004)*	*Rural Poverty 2004–05*
1	Kerala	Kerala – South	Kerala – South	Kerala – South
		Kerala – North	Kerala – North	
2	Tamil Nadu	TN – Coastal	TN – Coastal	TN – Coastal
		TN – Inland		
		TN – South		
3	Andhra Pradesh	AP – Coastal		AP – Coastal
4	Karnataka	Karntaka – Coastal		Karntaka – Coastal
5	Maharashtra		Mah-Konkan	
			Mah – West	Mah – West
6	Punjab	Punjab – North	Punjab – North	Punjab – North
		Punjab – South	Punjab – South	
7	Haryana		Haryana – East	Haryana - East
8	Gujarat	Guj – Saurashtra	Guj – Saurashtra	Guj – Saurashtra
			Gujarat – South	
	Worst-Performing Regions (Bottom 20%)			
		Land Productivty 2005–08	*Rural MPCE 60Th Round (2004)*	*Rural Poverty 2004–05*
1	Rajasthan	Raasthan – West		
		Rajasthan – North		
				Rajasthan - South

Contd.

Contd.

		Worst-Performing Regions (Bottom 20%)		
		Land Productivty 2005–08	*Rural MPCE 60Th Round (2004)*	*Rural Poverty 2004–05*
2	Gujarat			
3	Maharashtra	Mah - Marathwada		Mah - Marathwada
4	Madhya Pradesh	MP – Madhya Bharat	MP – Madhya Bharat	MP – Madhya Bharat
		MP – Vindhyachal	MP – Vindhyachal	MP – Vindhyachal
		MP – Mahakoshal	MP – Mahakoshal	MP – Mahakoshal
		MP – Chhattisgarh	MP – Chhattisgarh	MP – Chhattisgarh
5	J&K	J&K – Hills		
6	Odisha		Odisha – South	Odisha – South
			Odisha – North	Odisha – North
7	Bihar	Bihar – North	Bihar – North	Bihar – North
		Bihar – South	Bihar – South	

Source: Land Productivity computed from Bhalla and Singh, 2012; Rural MPCE estimates from Jha, Gaiha and Sharma, 2006; and Rural Poverty Estimates from Mishra, 2014.

To understand the dynamic factors contributing to agricultural growth and structural changes (or the lack of them) in these regions, we need to carefully follow each specific region and understand their growth trajectory. We intend to take up this question in the following section.

Agrarian Regions: Pathways of Change

Telangana

Within Andhra Pradesh, the Coastal Andhra region was much more prosperous than Telangana at the time of the formation of the state in 1956. Canal irrigation has historically been concentrated in the Coastal Andhra region. This had led to severe irrigation inequality within the state. For instance, in 1962–65, 60 per cent of Andhra Pradesh's irrigated area was in Coastal

Andhra, compared to 27 per cent in Telangana (Vakulabharanam, 2004). The merger of Telangana with politically dominant Coastal Andhra gave rise to new tensions and universal discontent among the people of Telangana (Rao, 2014). However, the picture of relative backwardness of Telangana seems to have changed with the growth of groundwater irrigation in that region since 1984–85. By 2008–09, 50.4 per cent of the cropped area in Telangana was irrigated compared to 60.6 per cent of Coastal Andhra.

Table 6.5 Regionwise and Sourcewise Net Irrigated Area in Andhra Pradesh

	1964–65	*1984–85*	*1994–95*	*2008–09*
Net Irrigated Area/Net Sown Area by Region (%)				
Telangana	20.9	27.0	36.5	50.4
Rayalaseema	20.4	21.7	22.6	25.3
Coastal Andhra	46.5	54.8	53.7	60.6
Share of Canals in Net Irrigated Area (%)				
Telangana	18.6	31.4	18.5	14.5
Rayalaseema	22.2	31.1	23.1	22.1
Coastal Andhra	55.1	64.7	57.7	54.5
Share of Wells in Net Irrigated Area (%)				
Telangana	16.8	35.0	59.3	69.5
Rayalaseema	28.0	46.3	64.5	68.7
Coastal Andhra	7.1	13.4	18.3	25.1

Source: Indian Agricultural Statistics, MoA, various issues.

More than two third of this irrigation in Telangana was sourced from groundwater. By 2008–09, the share of Telangana in total irrigated area of Andhra Pradesh went up to 40 per cent. Along with this, there was a shift in the cropping pattern away from millets and pulses towards paddy, cotton and other high value crops. In 2005–08, Telangana contributed nearly 40 per cent of the total value of output of Andhra Pradesh, compared to 27 per cent in 1962–65 (Bhalla and Singh, 2012). The comparative rates of growth of productivity of important crops are shown in the table below.

Table 6.6 Comparative Productivity Growth of Important Crops in AP, Regionwise

Crop	*Period*	*Telangana*	*RoG (%)*	*Rayalaseema*	*RoG (%)*	*Coastal Andhra*	*RoG (%)*
A. Rice	1964–75	1326	–	1562	–	1392	–
	1984–95	2219	2.48	2353	1.97	2419	2.67
	2006–07	2980	1.75	3040	1.52	3219	1.69
B. Groundnut	1964–75	644	–	849	–	972	–
	1984–95	850	1.33	850	0.01	1130	0.72
	2006–07	1293	2.50	763	(-) 0.63	1383	1.20
C. Cotton	1964–75	310	–	170	–	1436	–
	1984–95	1033	5.90	1251	9.97	2098	1.82
	2006–07	2057	4.13	1234	(-) 0.08	3045	2.22

Source: GoI, 2010.

What led to this dramatic turnaround in Telangana? It is clear that groundwater irrigation and adoption of the new seed and fertiliser technologies have played a significant role in reducing inter-regional disparities in levels of agricultural productivity. Recent studies show that the adoption of new agricultural technologies such as seeds and irrigation equipment had a strong caste base in Telangana (Motiram and Vakulabharanam, 2014). They argue that the exodus of traditional upper caste elite from rural Telangana, emergence of the TDP and creation of mandal administrative structures led to a strong OBC consolidation in the Telangana rural areas. This consolidation, forming a strong electoral coalition[4], was able to influence government policies and improve agricultural growth significantly. The caste composition of this community of groundwater irrigators (middle peasants who were mainly OBC) in Telangana is different from that in Coastal Andhra (traditional dominant castes). While groundwater thus raised agricultural growth in Telangana and contributed to further strengthening the regional identity (finally leading to the formation of a separate state in 2014), this growth has also been 'immiserising' in nature. Telangana witnessed enormous agrarian distress, manifested in a large number of farmer suicides that started in the late 1990s and continuing even now. The distress is associated on the one hand with the dominance of informal credit in the rural economy and, on the other, with increasing market orientation of agriculture. It is also remarkable that in spite of its agricultural growth, the MPCE of Telangana (excluding Hyderabad) is relatively low compared to Coastal Andhra. There is also considerable divergence between the MPCE of social groups within each region (Table 6.7). Clearly, the implication of the agricultural turnaround in Telangana is not the same for all social groups within the region.

Table 6.7 Per Capita MPCE, Regionwise and Social Groups, Andhra Pradesh, 2007–08

	All Groups	*SC*	*ST*	*OBC*	*Others*
Telangana (with Hyd)	1025	734	734	889	1846
Telangana (without Hyd)	895	710	726	836	1450
Rayalaseema	788	590	803	707	1099
Coastal Andhra	1003	759	570	902	1427
Total AP	971	719	680	860	1484

Source: GoI, 2010.

Saurashtra, Gujarat

Saurashtra receives an annual rainfall of 550 mm. For many years, Saurashtra in Gujarat was one of the poorest regions of India. The region was ruled by 200 odd princely states till independence. The rule of regressive institutions continued even afterwards, with much of the region being under zamindari land tenure system with myriad intermediaries between the government and peasants (Shah, 2014). Only about 15 per cent of the cropped area of the region was under irrigation in 1990. As late as 1991, Saurashtra has been described as part of the Poor Periphery surrounding the rich heartland in Gujarat (Patel, 1991). However, within a decade, agricultural growth picked up in the region and it has become one of the main agricultural growth centres of Gujarat. The average value of production per cropped area went up by three times between 1990–93 and 2005–08. Compared to other agrarian regions of Gujarat, both the level and the rate of growth of value of output from crops and milk in Saurashtra have been high in recent years.

This change has been brought about by several factors. Being a semi-arid region, agriculture in the area is possible only with considerable state support to irrigation and infrastructure development. In contrast to South Gujarat, north Gujarat, Saurashtra and Kachchh have very poor surface water endowment and the rivers and rivulets there have only limited seasonal flows. The numerous major and medium irrigation schemes built in Saurashtra during 1970s and 1980s impound the monsoon runoff from around 91 basins in Saurashtra (Kumar, 2010). The region also had one of the largest water conservation programmes in India, with considerable state support. The Sardar Patel Sahbhagi Jal Sanchay Yojana reportedly liberally helped village communities in constructing hundreds of thousands of community-managed groundwater recharge structures for recharge of groundwater. Extensive tapping of groundwater seems to have been at the base of rapid agricultural growth in Saurashtra. Energised open wells accounted for about 80 per cent of the irrigated area in Saurashtra in 2007–08. Moreover, Saurasthtra accounted for 55 per cent of irrigation from open wells in the whole state.

Table 6.8 Regionwise Level and Rate of Growth of Value of Output from Agriculture and Allied Sectors

Regions	*Value of Output per Hectare of Crops and Milk, (Rs./Ha), 1999–2000 prices*			*CAGR of Value of Output of Crops & Milk (%)*	
	TE 1999–2000	*TE 2005–06*	*% Growth*	*1991–92 to 1998–99*	*1999–00 to 2005–06*
Canal Districts	30967	38368	23.9	3.7	5.2
Saurashtra & Kutch	23898	35321	47.8	13.3	21.4
North Gujarat	24913	34031	36.6	5.5	8.7
Tribal Districts	21297	25918	21.7	8.1	10.7

Source: Shah, et.al., 2009.

Table 6.9 Regionwise Gross Irrigated Area by Source, 2007-08 (%)

Regionwise Gross Irrigated Area by Source, 2007–08 (%)						
	Canals	*Tank*	*Tubewells*	*Other Wells*	*Others*	*Total*
Dry Areas	6	0	48	46	0	100
North Gujarat	17	1	51	28	2	100
Saurashtra	8	0	10	79	2	100
South Gujarat	41	2	13	39	6	100
TOTAL	18	1	27	52	3	100
Share of Regions in Gross Irrigated Area, 2007–08 (%)						
Dry Areas	4	5	24	12	1	13
North Gujarat	24	31	50	14	22	26
Saurashtra	16	16	14	55	26	36
South Gujarat	56	48	12	19	51	25
Total	100	100	100	100	100	100

Source: Indian Agricultural Statistics, MoA, various issues.

Equally important, the region seems to have also benefited from the electricity reforms under Jyotirgram Yojana, where feeders supplying power to borewells and domestic use have been separated. Between 2000–01 and 2007–08, though the number of groundwater wells and tubewells in Saurashtra registered no major increase, the gross area irrigated by groundwater wells increased nearly three times (Shah, 2014). Active state support is also visible in the promotion of cash crops like cotton, chillis, cumin and vegetables. Price support to cotton and other crops and increased market access due to APMC reforms seem to have shifted the terms of trade in favour of agriculture, giving a further boost to the agrarian economy.

While these claims are yet to be validated through rigorous and systematic research, it is indisputable that that there has been a significant improvement in agricultural growth in Saurashtra in recent years. Increased public support in terms of improved market access, technology, extension and credit as well as improvements in infrastructure – all these seems to have contributed to this growth (Shah, 2014). Just as in the case of Telangana, electoral coalitions centred on the middle peasantry (Patels, Patidars and Ahirs) seems to have been able to influence public policy and bring about a major agrarian transformation of this semi-arid and hither-to backward agrarian region.

North and North East Rajasthan

Rajasthan has been part of the BIMARU category of states. Over two-third of the state is desert and 60 per cent of India's desert blocks are in Rajasthan. Agriculture in the state comprises crop-livestock mixed farming system for livelihoods. But even with such a harsh and arid-semi arid landscape, many parts of Rajasthan, especially the north and north east regions, have moved into a vibrant agrarian economy based on food grains, oilseeds and dairying, between 1995 and 2010. Irrigation expansion has played a key role here also. Region-wise irrigated area by source and regional shares are shown in the table below (Table 6.10). Canal irrigation is mainly concentrated in North Rajasthan (accounting for 59 per cent of the area under irrigation) whereas the rest of the state is predominantly groundwater-irrigated.

Surface water irrigated expanded in the northern region (comprising Ganganagar, Hanumanthgarh and Sikar districts) mainly on account of the Indira Gandhi Nahar Project (IGNP). In North-East Rajasthan as well as in the rest of the state, the key driver behind rapid agricultural growth seems to be an aggressive exploitation of groundwater. In 2013, groundwater accounted for over 70 per cent of the gross irrigated area in Rajasthan as a whole. The rapid growth of groundwater irrigation in Rajasthan is shown in the figure below

Table 6.10 Regionwise Gross Irrigated Area by Source, 2008 (%)

Regionwise Gross Irrigated Area by Source, 2008 (%)						
Region	*Canal*	*Tank*	*Tubewell*	*Other Wells*	*Other Sources*	*Total*
North	59	0	23	19	0	100
North East	6	0	62	30	1	100
South	23	1	36	35	4	100
West	18	0	52	30	0	100
Total	29	0	43	27	1	100
Share of Regions in Gross Irrigated Area, 2008 (%)						
North	67	0	18	22	0	33
North East	7	16	44	33	38	30
South	13	84	14	22	62	17
West	13	0	25	23	0	20
Total	100	100	100	100	100	100

Source: Indian Agricultural Statistics, MoA, various issues.

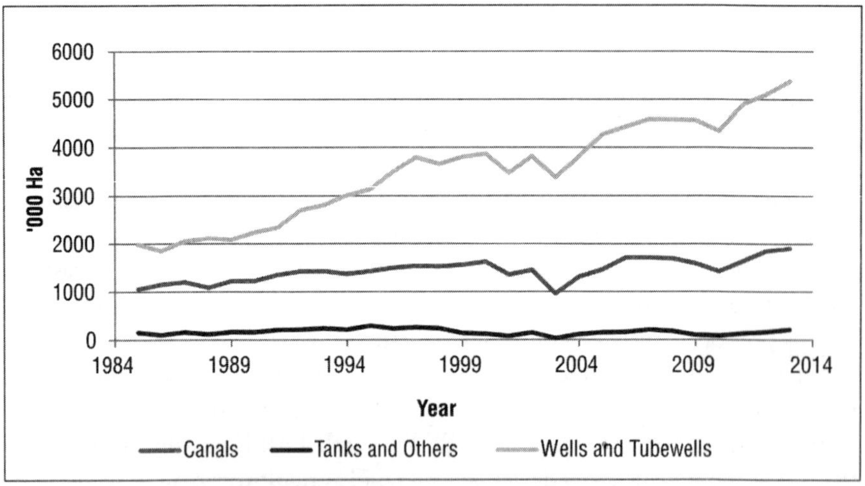

Figure 6.1 Net Irrigated Area by Source

Source: Indian Agricultural Statistics, various issues.

Such irrigation expansion would not have been possible without substantial state support and public investment. Hence, like in other regions discussed above, the combination of middle peasantry forming a strong electoral coalition and demanding state support seems to have been operative in Rajasthan as well. However, given Rajasthan's arid, semi-arid bio-climate and water-stressed environment, rapid agricultural growth based on irrigation expansion seems to be encountering constraints imposed by the eco-system. This is true in the case of both surface water (IGNP) as well as groundwater. While IGNP has contributed to agricultural growth in North Rajasthan, several studies have brought out the negative environmental impact of the project in terms of water-logging and land degradation (Sharma, 2001). The data periodically compiled by the Central Groundwater Board (CGWB) provides information on the annual recharge of groundwater and annual extraction rates. A comparison of the CGWB estimates from 1995 to 2009 show that the groundwater balance has alarmingly worsened in Rajasthan (CGWB, 2009). The Stage of Groundwater Development (ratio of annual groundwater extraction to annual replenishment) fell alarmingly from 59 per cent in 1995 to 135 per cent in 2009, indicating that the state is in the "overexploited" category. Of the 236 blocks in the state, 164 (69 per cent) were in this category in 2009 (Table 4 and Map 6.1). From the map we can see that excepting the north region (irrigated from surface water) and the extremely arid western region, rest of the state is intensively exploiting its water resources leading to severe sustainability issues. Rajasthan is, thus, a clear case of state-sponsored agricultural growth causing considerable environmental destruction. The dramatic change in groundwater balance in the state between 1995 and 2004 is a clear indicator of the damage such mindless and aggressive growth strategy can create in an arid region.[5]

Table 6.11 Estimated Volume of Groundwater Resource (BCM), CGWB Data

	Rajasthan	*1995*	*2004*	*2009*
1	Gross Groundwater Recharge	13.16	11.56	11 86
2	Irrigation	9.09	11.60	12.86
3	Domestic and Industrial	0.70	1.39	1.65
4	Gross Draft (2+3)	9.78	12.99	14.52
5	Groundwater Balance (1–4)	3.38	(-) 1.43	(-) 2.66
6	Level of GW Development (4/1)	59	125	135

Source: CGWB, 1996, 2006 and 2014.

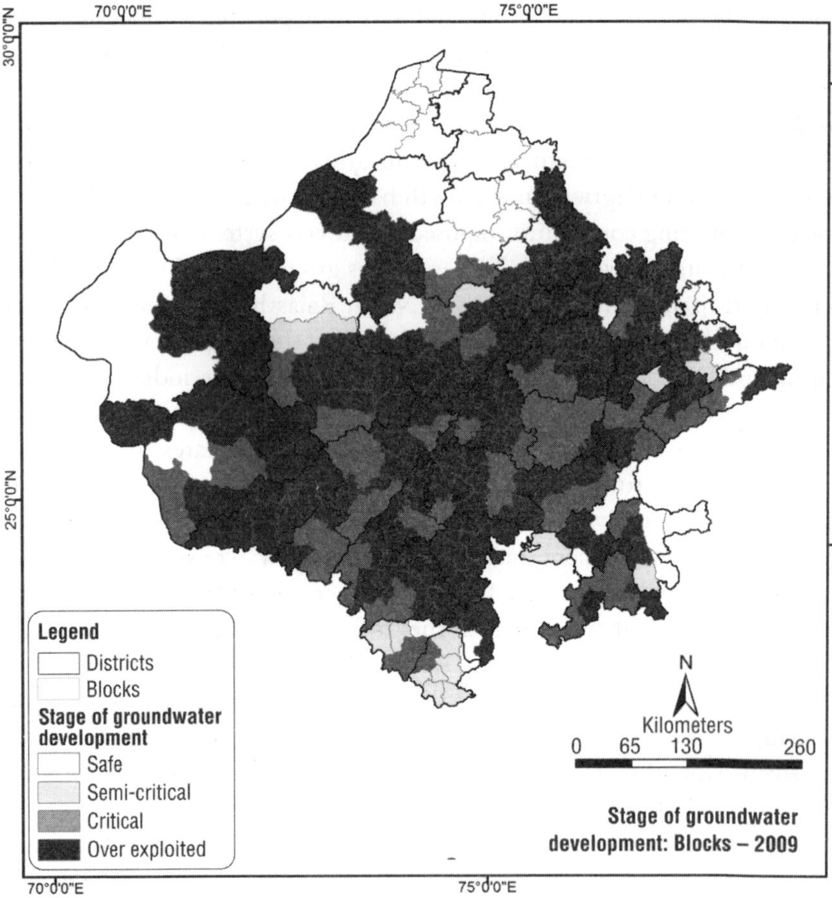

Map 6.1 Over-exploited Blocks of Rajasthan

Source: CGWB, GoI, 2014.

Malwa region, Madhya Pradesh

The Malwa region in Western Madhya Pradesh is located in a comparatively low rainfall regime, with an annual rainfall of 800 mm. Since this region has hardly any large perennial streams, groundwater is the backbone of Malwa's agrarian economy, accounting for 85 per cent of the gross irrigated area. Open dugwells and tanks have traditionally been the modes of irrigation in this area. In 1970–71, the cropping pattern of this area was dominated by rainfed crops with only 6 per cent of the gross cropped area under irrigation. It was largely millet and pulses-growing area, with jowar, red gram and cotton as the main crops. The region has deep black soils which allowed raising an unirrigated wheat crop after keeping the land fallow in kharif. Compared to traditionally wheat-growing areas of Narmada valley, the productivity of agriculture on the whole was low. Agriculture in Malwa region underwent a dramatic transformation with the introduction of tube wells in early 1980s. The growth of groundwater structures (dugwells and tubewells) over successive Minor Irrigation censuses is given in the table below.

Table 6.12 Number of Groundwater Structures ('000) Used in Irrigation in Malwa, 1986–2011

MI Census	*Year*	*Dugwell*	*Shallow Tubewell*	*Deep Tubewell*	*Total*	*Annual Rate of Growth %*
1st Census	1986–87	272.93	11.84	2.06	286.82	–
2nd Census	1993–94	386.10	65.04	8.30	459.44	6.06
3rd Census	2000–01	438.84	129.50	15.47	583.80	3.48
4th Census	2006–07	445.37	134.77	26.65	606.79	0.65

Source: MoWR, Report of Minor Irrigation Census, various years.

There are, on an average, 18 groundwater structures per 100 hectare of net sown area in Malwa in 2010–11. As the table shows, the most remarkable fact to be noted is the expansion in the number of tubewells. In 1986–87, the whole of Malwa region had about 13000 tubewells used for irrigation purposes, which went up to 75000 by 1994 (2nd MI Census) and stood at 1.61 lakh tube wells in 2010–11 (4th MI Census). With such intensive tapping of groundwater, cropping intensity (Gross Cropped Area/Net Sown Area) in the region rose from 109 in 1970–71 to 166 in 2010–11 and area under irrigation recorded a nine-fold increase. Nearly 33 per cent of the gross cropped area is currently irrigated, mostly from groundwater. There has also been a substitution of un-irrigated and low irrigation-intensive varieties with high irrigation-intensive varieties in wheat and chickpea, the two main irrigated crops. Nearly all of the wheat in Malwa is irrigated and half the area under chickpea also needs irrigation. Therefore, the expansion in irrigated area has been accompanied by a rise in the "irrigated delta" or depth of irrigation. The combined result has been a larger scale of groundwater withdrawal[6].

Along with expansion of irrigation, the land use pattern of the area underwent a radical change. Soybean was introduced in the area as a new crop in early 1980s and was heavily promoted with state support in the area. The mechanism of minimum support price was utilised to promote the crop and industries were encouraged to set up processing facilities in towns like Indore, which created a ready market for the crop. Though soybean is a kharif crop grown without irrigation, its introduction coincided with the irrigation revolution in Malwa region. This is because as a short-duration crop it facilitated cultivation of wheat as second crop even on soils which were otherwise kept fallow earlier. Due to the coincidence of these circumstances, Malwa region's diverse cropping system was replaced with an annual crop cycle of soybean-wheat. There is no doubt that rapid expansion of groundwater irrigation has raised agricultural productivity of Malwa in relation to the MP average and made Malwa a relatively prosperous region. While raising the overall land productivity of Malwa region (and, of course, moving many small and marginal farmers out of poverty), this cycle not only eliminated all other crops but put an enormous strain on the limited water resources of the region.

The social context of the region also supported adoption of new crops and new irrigation technologies. The average size of holdings in Malwa is bigger compared to other parts in Madhya Pradesh. The prominent landowning communities, mainly Rajputs, Saindhavs, Gujjars and Patidars, who owned relatively large landholdings enjoyed political patronage and took to farming innovations in a major way. Among the regions of MP, except North MP, Malwa has the least concentration of tribal population. Politically articulate farming communities of the region were able to form strong electoral coalitions and strongly lobby for their demands, including increased market access, higher output prices and huge subsidies in input costs like water and electricity. The power pricing regime in the state, till recent years, has been a flat rate system based on rating of the pumpsets. The state also was among the first to undertake APMC reforms and introduce direct farmer access to agricultural markets. Such favourable circumstances have been fully taken advantage of by the strong agrarian castes of the region.

In recent years, the state in Madhya Pradesh has been implementing a huge farmer support programme, which includes assured supply of inputs (including electricity) and massive public procurement of wheat. Madhya Pradesh has become the second largest contributor of wheat to the public procurement system, surpassing Haryana (Krishamurthy, 2014). With the strong nexus observed between electricity pricing, supply and groundwater as well as an assured market for groundwater-irrigated crops, it is likely that groundwater availability in the predominantly agricultural Malwa will further reduce.

Some estimates of state support to agriculture

One common theme in all the four cases discussed above is the strong state support to agriculture. To what extent is this reflected in the macro-indicators like public investment in agriculture and planned public spending on agriculture and allied activities? Table 6.13 summarises the data. It shows that these states have been making considerable fiscal commitments (ranging, on an average, between 15–20 per cent of total development expenditure and 10–15 per cent of revenue expenditure) in their annual budgets to agriculture and allied sectors during the period 1990–2010. Even though this support is potentially available for all agrarian regions within each state, only a few regions seem to have gained by it. This brings us back to the observation that it is not the benevolence of the developmental state but the strong and active coalition of farming castes (mainly the middle peasantry) exerting influence in state policy which has engendered rapid growth in a few agrarian regions within these states.

Table 6.13 Statewise Share (%) of Public Expenditure on Agriculture, Rural Development and Irrigation in Total Public Expenditure, 1990–2010

State	*Share in Development Expenditure*				*Share in Total Revenue Expenditure*			
	1990–1995	*1995–2000*	*2000–2005*	*2005–2010*	*1990–1995*	*1995–2000*	*2000–2005*	*2005–2010*
Andhra Pradesh	31	27	25	26	21	18	15	17
Gujarat	26	25	19	16	18	17	12	9
Madhya Pradesh	31	27	23	28	21	17	13	16
Rajasthan	28	21	19	21	18	12	11	13
All States	30	26	21	21	19	15	12	12

Source: RBI Database on State Finances, Reserve Bank of India.

The estimates of state level gross fixed capital formation (GFCF) are highly unreliable. Different states follow different conventions in reporting, which makes overtime comparison of these estimates difficult. However, using the estimates collated by EPW Research Foundation (EPWRF, 2009), we have tried to see how the share of agriculture in public sector GFCF has moved over the years in different states. Available estimates for three states are given in the following table. Estimates are not available for Rajasthan.

Table 6.14 Statewise Share of Agriculture in Gross Fixed Capital Formation at Current Prices, 1993–2005 (GFCF-A/GFCF-T %)

Year	*Andhra Pradesh*		*Gujarat*		*Madhya Pradesh*	
	Public Sector	*Total*	*Public Sector*	*Total*	*Public Sector*	*Total*
			1993–94 Series			
1990–91	–	–	40	–	–	–
1991–92	–	–	36	–	–	–
1992–93	–	–	33	–	–	–
1993–94	13	9	36	–	12	15
1994–95	11	9	33	–	11	13
1995–96	11	8	40	–	10	13
1996–97	11	7	35	–	12	15
1997–98	14	9	33	–	13	15
1998–99	13	9	34	–	12	15
1999–2000	15	10	27	–	13	16
2000–01	13	9	30	–	12	15
2001–02	12	10	27	–	12	16
2002–03	14	11	21	–	12	16
			1993–2000 Series			
2003–04	16	13	27	–	–	–
2004–05	25	15	39	–	–	–

Source: EPWRF, 2009.

From the table, it would appear that agriculture has retained a steady share in total GFCF as well as GFCF in the public sector in these states. Though it may be incorrect to read too much into these estimates, they also seem to corroborate the story of sizeable public support to agriculture in these states.

And those lagging behind…

We have discussed above a few agrarian regions which have been able to break out of their "low level equilibrium trap" and raise their agricultural productivity and record high rates of growth. A set of favourable circumstances have enabled this movement, which also have resulted the economy stretching the natural ecological limits at least in a few cases. The question would then arise as to why some other regions, equally poor and almost in a similar situation to those described above till a few years ago, have remained at that level. Detailed explanation would again require getting into the specific situation of each of these regions, which is beyond the scope of the present paper.

However, one general observation that can be made is that at least half of the currently "backward" regions have high incidence of tribal population. Recent studies have shown the high correlation between backwardness and preponderance of tribal concentration (Bakshi et.al., 2015)[7]. Examples of backward agrarian regions with high concentration of tribal population are: Jharkhand (Bihar South), Odisha South, Madhya Pradesh regions, Chhattisgarh and the North East region (even though they are not covered in this paper). Hence, "being tribal", seems to the common feature of at least 50 per cent of the low productivity agrarian regions in India. How could this translate into pervasive backwardness? The unique feature of tribal demography in India is that outside the North East, most tribal communities live in district and sub-district units where they are a minority. This very distinctive 'enclavement' of the tribes is a result of long drawn out historical encounters involving the subjugation of the tribes by more dominant communities. This enclavement provides objective basis for the marginalisation and exploitation of tribal communities through interlocked modes of exchange where commodity, credit and input markets are closely interlinked (Bardhan, 1989; Bardhan and Rudra, 1978; Olsen, 1996). These markets often function in a highly exploitative manner and become a vehicle for the exercise of power relations for surplus extraction (Bhaduri, 1983). We suggest that this model, initially proposed for backward agriculture in general, is still valid in the case of the tribal contexts that we encounter in backward regions of India.

Moreover, tribes have been driven over centuries, further and further away from the alluvial planes and fertile river basins to the 'refuge zones'- the hills, forest, arid and semi arid tracts. The undeniable fact is that they do inhabit some of the harshest ecological regions of the country today and constitute a marginalised and highly splintered vulnerable group without voice in India today. Even here, the search for valuable natural resources such as forests, minerals etc., lead to a new situation of extractive institutions coming up in tribal areas, supported by the state. This situation of state-supported 'development by dispossession' led by corporate capital inevitably calls upon the resistance by the people, at times even with armed struggle. Many tribal dominated regions are in ferment now.

While this explains probably only half of the phenomenon of backwardness, the other half, in regions such as Bihar North, Uttar Pradesh South (Bundelkhand) or Uttarakhand calls out for a different explanation. More detailed research is needed on the nature of social and ecological constraints contributing to backwardness in these regions.

What does One Make of This?

While discussing regional disparities in agricultural growth within China and the measures adopted the state for balanced regional development, KN Raj wrote:

> By the early 1970s the lack of material incentives on this account was evidently becoming a serious problem in mobilising labour for collective activity.... But it has to be then also recognised that the large-scale investment activity in agriculture which the organisational innovations made possible was an important and even indispensable phase in development. Prices and other material incentives can evoke substantial increases in output only after the other constraints have been effectively relaxed (Raj, 1983).

Focusing on the agrarian regions below the state level, this paper has attempted to understand the factors contributing to regional differentiation and growing inter-regional inequalities in India. While the coexistence of these variables in spatial clusters is only indicative of the dynamic processes at work, greater empirical explorations are needed to unravel aspects of these transformations in specific contexts. We have asked the question how a backward, low productivity agrarian region has been able to break out of its poverty trap and achieve rapid agricultural development. Broadly, three sets of factors seem to be at work across all regions considered. First, irrigation development, especially from groundwater, seems to have been a major agent of change. But this is not an unqualified achievement of private investment and the free play of market forces. As pointed out above, tapping groundwater for irrigation is contingent on the availability of electricity as well as on well developed markets assuring remunerative prices to farmers. These are critical areas of public investment. This leads to the second set of factors clustered around the state's support to agriculture. In all regions considered, the state has implemented strong farmer support policies, not only in terms direct or indirect subsidies to agriculture but also through policies leading to market development and market reform. Madhya Pradesh is a classic case in point. Drawing upon the experience of regions like Malwa and North-East Rajasthan, we have also highlighted the ecological constraints on irrigation-intensive growth in water-scarce environments as also the possibility of growing *intra-regional* disparities between social groups. Finally, this state support to agriculture seems to have been a consequence of the consolidation and mobilisation of the middle peasantry, who have emerged as a powerful and influential group in policy and has also managed to gain support in the implementing arm of the state, namely, the bureaucracy. The network of relationships forged by these groups with the state on the one hand and the market mechanism (including banks and financial institutions) on the other seems to have contributed substantially to change. By the same token, the tribal-dominated regions which have remained backward seem to have failed to do all these due to a variety of reasons. Hence, a region's agricultural advancement and/or backwardness owes as much to their initial conditions as to the mechanisms utilised for mobilisation of support for agriculture.

Endnotes

1. In addition to being too detailed, the NSS regional classification also creates problems as the definitions keep changing between successive rounds of NSS. Hence, we have used the grouping into regions as per the latest NSS survey and clubbed districts accordingly.
2. Agricultural land productivity refers to the value of production per hectare, which is derived by dividing the value of production of 35 crops with the cropped area under 35 crops in each region.
3. The latter, indeed, is the familiar story of cumulative causation in development economics (Myrdal, 1957; Nurkse, 1961). One variant of this is the story of a backward economy being caught in a 'low level equilibrium trap', which needs to be broken through with a 'big push' public investment (Rodan, 1944). The experience of backward regions in India bears witness to the distilled wisdom of this insight.
4. I gratefully acknowledge our debt to Kantha Murali's paper in this volume, from where I have borrowed this concept.
5. There seems to be some good advice available for the state in terms of sustainable management of its groundwater resources (IWMI, 2011; Shah, 2012). However, very little of this is visible in the public policy on water resources currently being followed in the state.
6. It is a mistake often made to put the entire burden of expansion of tubewell irrigation on private investment. While farmers may have invested in their own money in irrigation equipment, what indeed facilitated the expansion of such irrigation has been the public investment in rural electrification in the region. Electrification of villages in Malwa goes back to 1980s and seems to have facilitated introduction of tubewells in the region.

7. This paper is drawn from the study done for the Planning Commission for identifying criteria for ranking blocks in terms of their backwardness. This would enable them receiving additional support under the Backward Regions Grant Fund (BRGF). A complete list of the districts and blocks ranked on these criteria is available at www.planningcommission.org.

References

Bakshi, Sanchita, Arunish Chawla and Mihir Shah. 2015. 'Regional Disparities in India: A Moving Frontier.' *Economic and Political Weekly* 50 (1): 44–52, January 3.

Bardhan, Pranab. 1989. 'The New Institutional Economics and Development Theory: A Brief Critical Assessment.' *World Development* 17 (9): 1389–1395.

Bardhan, P. and Ashok Rudra. 1978. 'Interlinkage of Land, Labour and Credit Relations: An Analysis of Village Survey Data in East India.' *Economic and Political Weekly* 367–384.

Bhaduri, Amit. 1983. *The Economic Structure of Backward Agriculture*. London: Academy Press.

Bhalla, G. S. and Gurmail Singh. 2012. *Economic Liberalisation and Indian Agriculture: A District Level Study*. New Delhi: Sage Publications.

Bharadwaj, Krishna. 1982. 'Regional Differentiation in India: A Note.' *Economic and Political Weekly* 17 (14/16, Annual Number): 605–614.

Census of India. 2011. *Final Population Totals*. New Delhi: Registrar of Census Operations, Government of India.

Central Ground Water Board. 2011. *Dynamic Ground Water Resources of India (as on March, 2009*. New Delhi: CGWB, Ministry of Water Resources Publ., Government of India.

———. 2014. *Dynamic Ground Water Resources of India (as on March, 2011*. New Delhi: CGWB, Ministry of Water Resources Publ., Government of India.

Dubey, Amaresh. 2008. 'Consumption, Income and Inequality in India.' Background paper prepared for *India Poverty Assessment Report*.

Dubey, Amaresh and N. Srivastav. 2007. *Regional Disparities in Poverty Incidence and Levels of Living in India*.

EPW Research Foundation. 2009. *Domestic Product of States of India, 1960–61 to 2006–07, Second Updated Edition*. Mumbai: EPWRF.

Government of India. 2010. *Report of the Committee for Consultations on the Situation in Andhra Pradesh (Srikrishna Committee) Volume 1*. New Delhi: Government of India

Jha, Raghabendra, R. Gaiha and A. Sharma. 2006. 'Mean Consumption, Poverty and Inequality in Rural India in the Sixtieth Round of the National Sample Survey.' *ASARC Working Papers 2006–11*. Australia: Australia South Asia Research Centre, The Australian National University.

Jodhka, Surinder S. 2014. 'Emergent Ruralities: Revisiting Village Life and Agrarian Change in Haryana.' *Review of Rural Affairs, Economic and Political Weekly* 49 (26 and 27): 5–17, June.

Krishnamurthy, Mekhala. 2014. 'Agricultural Markets: A Regional Perspective.' In the *India Rural Development Report, 2014*. New Delhi: IDFC Foundation.

Kumar, Dharma. 1965. *Land and Caste in South India: Agricultural Labour in the Madras Presidency during the 19th Century*. New Delhi: Cambridge University Press.

Lersche, Jens. 2014. 'Regional Patterns of Agrarian Accumulation in India.' In *Indian Capitalism in Development*, edited by Barbara Harriss-White and Judith Heyer. New Delhi: Routledge.

Ludden, David. 2002. 'Spectres of Agrarian Territory.' *The Indian Economic and Social History Review* 39 (2–3): 233–257.

Mishra, Srijit. 2014. *Incidence of Poor and Poverty Risk in India across NSS Regions for Rural and Urban Areas, 2004–05 and 2009–10, IGIDR Working Paper 2014–21*. Available at, http://www.igidr.ac.in/pdf/publication/WP-2014–021.pdf.

Myrdal, Gunnar. 1957. *Economic Theory and Underdeveloped Regions*. University Paperbacks. London: Methuen.

Nurkse, Ragnar. 1953. *Problems of Capital Formation in Underdeveloped Countries*. New York: Oxford University Press

Olsen, W. 1996. *Rural Indian Social Relations: A Study of Southern Andhra Pradesh*. New Delhi: Oxford University Press.

Palshikar, Suhas. 2006. 'Caste Politics through the Prism of Region.' In *Region, Culture and Politics in India*, edited by Rajendra Vora and Anne Feldhaus, 278-91. New Delhi: Manohar.

Patel, Surendra J. 1991. 'Growing Regional Inequalities in Gujarat.' *Economic and Political Weekly* 26 (26): 1618–28, 1618–1623.

Planning Commission. 2012. *12th Five Year Plan, Planning Commission*. New Delhi: Government of India.

Raj, K. N. 1983. 'Agriculture and Growth in China and India: Role of Price and Non-Price Factors.' *Economic and Political Weekly* 18 (3): 69–74, January 15.

Raj, K. N. 1985. 'Introduction.' In *Essays on Commercialization of Agriculture in India*, edited by K. N. Raj, Neeladari Bhattacharya, Sumit Guha and Shakti Padhi. New Delhi: Oxford University Press.

Rosenstein-Rodan, Paul. 1943. Problems of Industrialisation of Eastern and South Eastern Europe.' *The Economic Journal* 53: 202–211, June–September..

Shah, Tushaar. 2009. *Taming the Anarchy: Groundwater Governance in South Asia, Resources for the Future, 310*. Colombo: Washington DC and International Water Management Institute.

———. 2014. 'Generating Agrarian Dynamism: Saurashtra's Lessons for Vidarbha.' *Economic and Political Weekly* 49 (26–27): 86–94.

Shah, Tushaar, Ashok Gulati, Hemant P. G. Sreedhar and R. C. Jain. 2009. 'Secret of Gujarat's Agrarian Miracle after 2000.' *Economic and Political Weekly* 44 (52): 45–55, December 26.

Singh, Nirvikar, J. Kendall, R. K. Jain and J. Chander. 2011. *Regional Inequalities in India in the 1990s: Trends and Policy Implications, DRG Studies*. Mumbai: Reserve Bank of India.

Thorner, Daniel, ed. 1996. *Ecological and Agrarian Regions of South Asia circa 1930*. Karachi: Oxford University Press.

Tillin, Louis. 2014. *Remapping India: New States and their Political Origins.* London: C. Hurst & Company.

Vakulabharanam, Vamsi. 2004. 'Agricultural Growth and Irrigation in Telangana: A Review of Evidence.' *Economic and Political Weekly* 39 (13): 1421–1426, March 27.

Vakulabharanam, Vamsi and Sripad Motiram. 2014. 'The Dissolution of "United" Andhra Pradesh Insights from Growth and Distribution Patterns, 1956–2010.' *Economic and Political Weekly* 49 (21): 59–70.

Urban Labour Markets

Picture 7.1 "Why has no one turned up at the office today? Is a cricket match on somewhere in the world?"

Source: Laxman, 2005, 46.

Picture 7.2 "Don't you fellows read newspapers or listen to ministers speak? India is shining and feel-good factor is spreading all over, and you chaps have come with good old demands?"

Source: Laxman, 2005, 35.

7

Public Sector Employment

What has Changed?

R. Nagaraj[1]

Introduction

No careful account of India's political economy is complete without reckoning with the size and composition of public sector employment, invariably described as a leviathan, bloated, dysfunctional and inefficient – and, as caricatured in R. K. Laxman's countless cartoons in *The Time of India* for decades (Picture 7.1 and 7.2 for illustrations). These workers form a vital constituency in electoral politics, as they are well represented in the trade union wings of most political parties. Moreover, unity of this section of the organized working class – cutting across party lines – is also evident in how it manages to protect its interest in securing periodic pay rise under the Central Pay Commission.[2]

That the white-collar workers form a significant constituency in varied accounts of India's political economy is widely acknowledged. If they were part of the 'intermediate regimes' in K. N. Raj's (1973) account, they were also a constituent of Bardhan's (1984) 'professional in the public sector' as a propertied class; they were the *salariat* in Patnaik and Rao's (1977) formulation of a mixed underdeveloped economy (emphasis as in original); and, they were among the rent-seekers in T. N. Srinivasan's (1985) neo-classical political economy story.

Most scholars, in line with their preferred view, have too readily accepted the above characterizations as self-evident, without being obliged to examine the evidence. It was perhaps Ashok Desai and Ena Desai, from a libertarian political perspective, made the only careful and critical analysis of public sector employment – in a multi-country volume edited by Gus Edgren (1986) for the ILO-ARTEP, titled *The Growing Sector*. Piecing together evidence from diverse sources, Desai and Desai explained the growth in public sector employment by India's ability to tax and spend.

If there was one aspect of the market-oriented reforms that had wide appeal, cutting across theoretical perspectives and political persuasions, it was to curb the size of the bureaucracy to reign in the fiscal deficit. While the political right advocated shrinking the state as an end in itself, many others made a case for modernization and decentralizing the bureaucracy for better services delivery – a political imperative in a deepening democracy. This was argued to be feasible by replacing the "unproductive" army of unskilled and semi-skilled office workers, by qualified professionals and by investment in office automation.

Nearly three decades after Desai and Desai's factual account of the 'growing sector', and a quarter century of the market-oriented reforms, how has public sector employment fared? Has the leviathan been tamed? Has it been restructured in line with the democratic aspirations for better and responsive public services delivery? Has the bureaucracy become more productive with office automation (popularly called e-governance)? How does the reform of public employment in India compare with similar efforts elsewhere?

This chapter addresses some of the above questions. Drawing upon many studies and official sources, Section I presents the long-term trends in public sector employment and wages. Section II shows a contrasting employment trend for the last decade using the NSS sample survey data. Seeking to reconcile the divergent trends, Section III offers a tentative, political economic, explanation for the observed variations. Summarizing the main findings, Section IV concludes the study.

Employment and Wages: Official Series

Employment size

In 2009–10, as per the *Economic Survey*, public sector employed 18 million persons, aggregated over all levels and forms of government constituting 4 per cent the national work force. Their wages amounted to 8 per cent of GDP. Contrary to popular belief and scholarly opinions, the size of the public employment in India is not large, relative to its population and in comparison with other countries. Though comparable cross-country data are hard to come by, the few available figures seem to attest this fact.

For instance, the US in 2012 (combined for all levels of the government) employed 22 million persons constituting 15 per cent of the workforce (Rampell, 2012). As per a news report, in 2011, for every 100,000 residents, India had 162.3 government servants; the corresponding figure for the US was over four times larger at 768.1 (*The Hindu*, January 30, 2012). Considering that the size of public sector in the US is small, relatively to other developed countries, one can reasonably infer that public sector employment (relative to population) in the advanced countries is much higher than in India.

How would India compare with developing economies? Available data are dated and scanty, but the information put together in an IMF study does not suggest India to be an outlier (Kraay and Rijckeghem, 1996). Therefore, India's public sector employment – to get the facts right – is not bloated, adjusted for population size, and in a comparative perspective.

Figure 7.1 shows the distribution of public sector employment in 2012 by the levels of government. State (provincial) and local governments accounted for about one-half of the employment: expectedly so, since the local administration is responsible for service delivery – as in most countries. The central government employees consist of 14 per cent of the total; the rest is accounted for by "quasi-government" that includes public sector enterprises (PSEs), electricity boards, road transport corporations and so on.

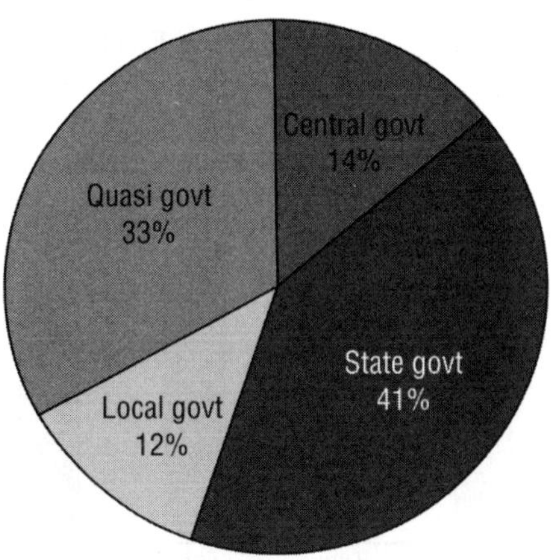

Figure 7.1 Public Sector Employment in 2012

Source: *Economic Survey*, various issues.

As per the official estimates, public sector employment rose from 7 million in 1960–61 to peak at 20 million in 1997, declined thereafter to 17.6 million (by about 12 per cent) by 2012 (Figure 7.2). The decline is, however, sharper relative to population: from 2271.4 workers per thousand in 1991 to 1465 workers in 2012 (declined by 36 per cent) (Figure 7.3). Evidently, the liberal economic reforms are responsible for the decline, as successive governments, regardless of their political leanings, have persisted with the policy of trimming government payroll – similar to what happened in the advanced economies after the right wing political regimes took roots since the late 1970s.

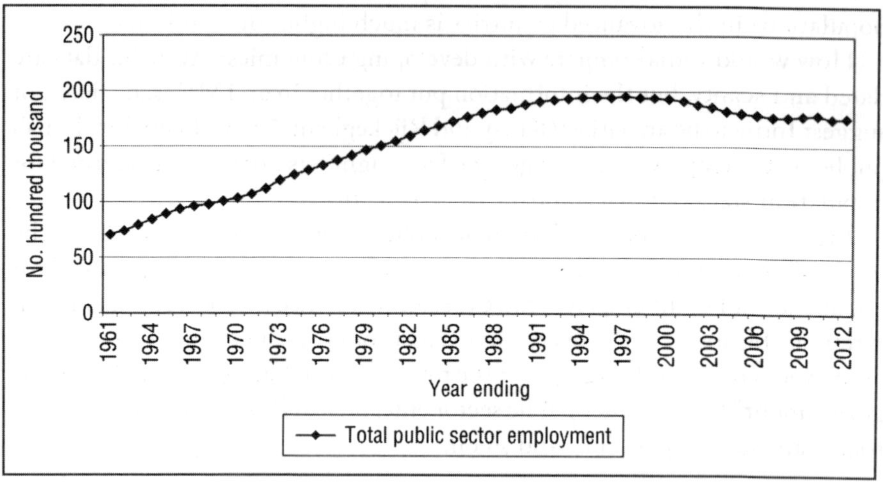

Figure 7.2 Total Public Sector Employment

Source: *Economic Survey*, various issues.

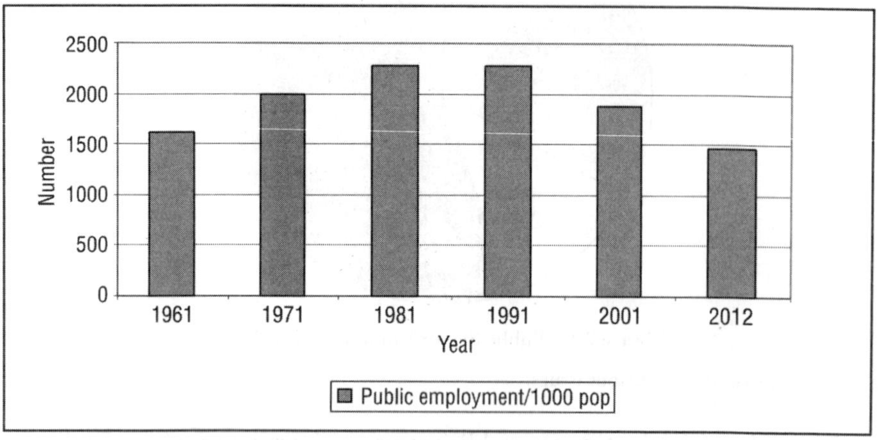

Figure 7.3 Public Sector Employment per 1000 Population

Source: *Economic Survey*, various issues.

The employment structure

Table 7.1 shows the absolute numbers of employees, and percentage change in employment over the years by types of government, from 1961 to 2012. During the employment boom (1961–81), most of the increase occurred in (i) quasi government (broadly representing the widening role of the state in the production of goods and services), (ii) followed by state governments. However, much of the contraction (during 1991–2012) has happened in central government – both in absolute and in percentage terms – followed by quasi government.

Table 7.1 Composition of Public Employment by Levels of Government

(in 00,000)

Year	*Central Govt*	*State Govt*	*Local Govt*	*Quasi Govt*	*Total*
1961	20.9	30.1	11.7	7.7	70.5
1971	27.7 (32.6)	41.5 (37.9)	18.8 (60.7)	19.3 (150.7)	107.3 (52.2)
1981	32.0 (15.5)	56.8 (36.9)	20.4 (8.5)	45.8 (137.3)	154.8 (44.3)
1991	34.1 (6.6)	71.1 (25.2)	23.1 (13.2)	62.7 (36.9)	190.6 (23.1)
2001	32.6 (-4.4)	74.3 (4.5)	22.6 (-2.2)	61.9 (-1.3)	191.4 (0.4)
2012	25.2 (-22.7)	71.8 (-3.4)	21.1 (-6.6)	58.0 (-6.3)	176.1 (-8.0)

Note: Figures in the brackets refer to percentage change, over the previous year.

Source: *Economic Survey*, various issues.

Figure 7.4 depicting just the annual growth – netting out the effect of the levels by indexation – shows employment grew most rapidly in the earlier decades, in quasi government. A similar picture also emerges from the data for the central public sector enterprises (PSEs) – clearly related to growth in public investment in industrial sector, reflecting the national development strategy (Figure 7.5). Expectedly, this is also the branch of government employment that declined rapidly after the reforms. In other words, the long-term expansion and followed by the contraction in public sector employment is clearly related to the changing role of the state in economy.

Sectoral composition of public employment shows that a little over one-half of the workers are employed in community, social and personal services (including public administration and defense) (Table 7.2). Sectors in which employment contracted since the early 1990s are (i) manufacturing, (ii) construction (state's withdrawal from producing goods) and (iii) transport and communication (technological change). To illustrate, the change-over from coal to electric locomotives in railways, and from electromechanical telephone exchanges to electronic exchange significantly displaced workers in transport and manufacturing sectors respectively.

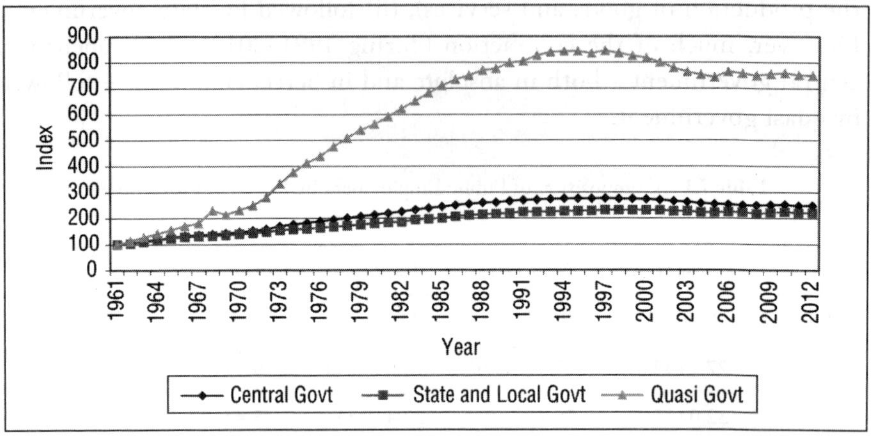

Figure 7.4 Employment Growth in Various Levels of Government

Source: *Economic Survey*, various issues.

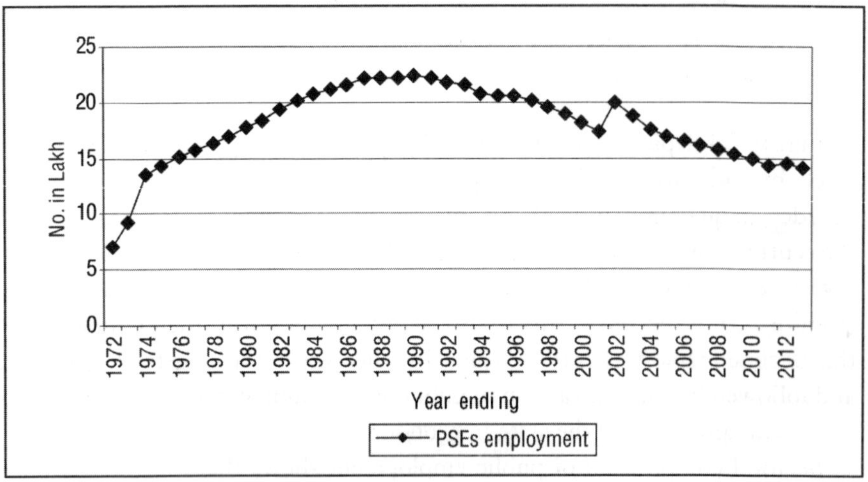

Figure 7.5 PSEs Employment

Source: *Economic Survey*, various issues.

Table 7.2 Sectoral Distribution of Public Employment

(per cent)

Sector	*1961*	*1971*	*1976*	*1986*	*1991*	*2000*	*2011*
Agriculture & allied	2.6	2.6	2.7	3.0	2.9	2.7	2.8
Mining	1.8	1.7	5.4	5.5	5.2	4.8	6.3
Manufacturing	5.2	7.5	8.4	10.3	9.7	7.9	5.9
Elec. Gas and water	3.2	4.0	4.0	4.4	4.8	4.9	4.8
Construction	8.6	8.2	7.5	6.7	6.0	5.7	4.9
Trade	1.3	3.1	0.4	0.7	0.8	0.8	1.0
Transport, storage & communication	24.0	20.6	18.2	16.6	15.9	15.9	13.8
Finance, insurance & real estate			3.7	5.8	6.3	6.7	7.9
Community, social and personal services	52.9	52.2	49.8	47.1	48.4	50.6	52.7
Total (in absolute no. in 100,000)					190.6	191.4	172.7

Source: *Economic Survey*, various issues.

As is widely known, the pyramidical structure of government employment has a large base of unskilled and semi-skilled employees – consisting mainly of clerks, peons, drivers and attendants – supporting a tiny fraction of career bureaucrats and political executives at the top – largely a colonial legacy. Liberal reforms of the last two decades have made modest efforts to rationalize the bureaucratic structure. One suspect, much of the reduction in employment in administrative services is on account of contracting out (outsourcing) of the auxiliary services such as, transport, maintenance, running of canteens, security services etc to private agencies – besides natural attrition.[3]

Distribution of public employment by type of cadres and by occupation is unfortunately not available to discern the changing composition of public employment. Limited information available from the 6th pay-commission report for the central government employees shows the following distribution: senior civil servants – that is, 'gazetted' officers – form a tiny fraction (5 per cent) of the total (Table 7.3). The decline in employment is mostly on account of Group D (or class IV) employees. In fact, after the last pay revision in 2009–10, the central government has, in principle, abolished this category of employment, signaling the official intent to restructure the lower end of the bureaucracy.

Table 7.3 Composition of Central Government Employment by Category of Employees

(Per cent)

	Employment in (000)	*Gazetted officers*			*Non-gazetted officers*		
		Total	*Class 1/ Group A*	*Class 2/ Group B*	*Class 2/ Group B*	*Class 3/ Group C*	*Class 4/ Group D*
(1)	*(2)*	*(3)*	*(4)*	*(5)*	*(6)*	*(7)*	*(8)*
1994	4023	5.1	1.8	3.2			
2005–06	3109	5.1	2.5	2.6	1.9	66.6	26.3
2006–07	3109	5.1	2.5	2.4	2.0	66.8	26.3
2007–08	3119	5.0	2.5	2.4	2.0	67.1	26.0
2008–09	3107	4.9	2.6	2.6	2.5	67.4	24.9
2009–10	3068	5.2	2.7	2.6	3.1	91.6	
2010–11	3082	5.2	2.7	2.5	3.8	91.0	
2011–12	3085	5.3	2.9	2.5	3.7	91.0	

Source: 6th Central Pay Commission Report.

The other reason for the decline in public employment is natural attrition, on retirement of those who joined the service during the boom decades of the 1960s and the 1970s. Moreover, central government has frozen fresh recruitment, leaving large number of posts vacant, amounting to 18 per cent of the 'sanctioned positions' in 2012.

Public sector wages

The wage-setting mechanism of the 'Pay Commission' award for the central government employees – keeping in view the government's mandate to be an ideal employer – is believed have led to a steady rise in real wages regardless of their productivity, setting the floor for the rest of the organized sector. As Mrinal Datta Chaudhuri said:

> There is an established procedure for determination of salaries and other benefits for the employees of the central government … Periodically government of India appoints a pay-commission. Members of the commission usually retired judges, members of the parliament, senior civil servants and academics.
>
> The award of the pay commission for the central government employees becomes reference point for the rest of the public sector … (Datta Chaudhuri, 1996, 17–18).

Have public sector wages – as hinted by the above view – grown at a faster rate than in the rest of the economy? Considering that these workers are unionized, and constitute a vital constituency in the electoral politics, there are reasons to believe it to be the case. Moreover, as public employment is meritocratic – that is, the selection is often based on fiercely competitive public examinations – it is reasonable to expect such employees to receive higher (efficiency) wages to compensate for their qualification, skill, and experience.

What does the evidence tell? As public sector wages data are not readily available, a definitive answer is hard to come by. Compiling the information from central wage commission reports, Eapen (1980) showed that the real earnings of officers had declined by about 40 per cent between 1960 and 1972, though the wages of peons (the lowest category of government employees) has remained roughly constant. In a similar but wider exercise for a longer period, from 1960 to 1983–84, Desai and Desai (1986) found that the wages of all categories of public servants had declined in absolute terms rather steeply: the indexed value of real earnings fell from 100 in 1960–61 to 34 in 1983–84 for the Class I officers. Yet, during the same period, the lowest category employees' real earnings rose to 135. Thus, during the early post-independence decades (1960s to 1980s), public sector real wages declined in absolute terms, and the wage differential between the lowest and the highest category of workers narrowed – indicating progressivity in the public sector wage setting mechanism.

For more recent years, we have examined the data for six years from 2005–06 to 2011–12 for central government employees – a period in which the 6th pay commission award was granted. During this period for all categories of central government employees, on average, real wages rose by 7.9 per cent per year – compared to per capita income growth of 6.8 per cent per year.

There is another data set which could also throw some light on the wage question. Wages paid in PSEs, as reported in the annual *Economic Survey*, is available since 1972. This series may not exactly track the government wages, but is likely to be close to it, for the reasons mentioned above. The data show, over the four decades on a trend basis, the average real earnings in central PSEs rose 5 per cent per year, compared to per capita income growth at 3.6 per cent per year – clearly demonstrating faster growth in public sector wages. However, the apparent gain for PSEs' workers may disappear considering that PSEs' employees represent better educated, technically qualified and experience workforce.

From the foregoing evidence, it is hard to infer that earnings in public sector have grown disproportionately faster than per capita income growth, or that public employees were able to corner a growing share of the national output for themselves (as popularly believed). However, such a conclusion needs to be qualified bearing in mind the data limitations. The wage data analyzed above do not include imputed value of the non-wage benefits of government employment – such as subsidized housing (albeit for a small fraction of employees), access to subsidized schooling, and health services; and above all, job-security and defined-benefit pension for the employees and their families (until 2004).[4] In an economy with practically no universal social security and deteriorating public services, the monetary value of such non-wage benefits could therefore be substantial. Hence the real earnings reported above could underestimate the true compensation received by public employees.

To recapitulate the findings on wages, it seems hard to sustain the view that over the long run, real wages in public sector have risen disproportionately faster than per capita income, albeit such an inference needs to take into account the non-wage advantages such as pension, and the job security enjoyed by public sector workers, which could amount to significant welfare gains in an economy with practically no social security benefits outside the formal sector.

Alternative Estimates Based on the NSS Data

We now report alternative estimates of public sector employment, as seen in the NSS sample surveys of employment and unemployment (the thick rounds) for the years 1999–2000, 2004–05 and 2009–10 (Table 7.4).[5] In 1999–2000, the NSS estimates of public sector employment were lower (at 16.2 million) by 20 per cent than the official estimates (reported in *Economic Survey*) at 19.4 million.

Table 7.4 Alternative Estimates of Public Employment

(in ,000)

Year	*NSS*	*Official*	*Difference (%)*
1999–00	16,148	19,415	(-) 20.2
2004–05	19,784	18,197	8.0
2009–10	22,563	17,795	21.3

Source: NSS Employment and Unemployment Surveys, primary data.

However, during the 2000s, while the official government employment contracted by 8 per cent, the NSS data reports an incredible 40 per cent rise (to 22.6 million). In other words, the NSS reports an annual employment growth rate of 3.4 per cent – more than double the growth rate of employment in the economy at 1.5 per cent per year. This holds true for majority of the states (accounting for over 90 per cent of the total), except for Karnataka. In fact, backward states of Bihar, Jharkhand, Himachal Pradesh and Jammu and Kashmir have more than doubled their employment size during the decade (Table 7.5).[6]

Table 7.5 State-wise Distribution of Public Employment for 1999–2000 and 2009–10

(per 000)

Principal States	*1999–00*	*2009–10*	*% change*
AP	1,404	1,635	16.5
Assam	411	567	37.9
Bihar+Jharkhand	523	1,094	109.3
Gujarat	937	1,004	7.2
Haryana	378	591	56.2
HP	161	446	176.4
J&K	174	478	174.8
Karnataka	918	857	-6.6
Kerala	579	874	51.1
MP+Chathisgarh	1,251	1,942	55.2
Maharashtra	2,276	2,711	19.1
Orissa	625	892	42.8
Punjab	476	682	43.3
Rajasthan	820	1,546	88.4
TN	1,296	1,791	38.1
UP+Uttarkhand	1,640	2,655	61.9
WB	998	1,451	45.3
Sub-total	14,867	21,215	42.7
% of total	92.1	94.0	

Source: NSS Employment and Unemployment Surveys, primary data.

To get a perspective, Table 7.6 shows decadal compound growth rate of public employment since 1961 using the official estimates. Interestingly, the employment growth rate during the 2000s (as noted in the NSS estimates) is close to those recorded during the boom of the 1960s and 1970s.

Table 7.6 Annual Growth in Public Employment

(Per cent)

Years	*Growth rate (per cent per year)*
1961–70	3.9
1971–80	3.5
1981–90	1.9
1991–00	0.1
2001–10	(-) 0.7
2000–10	3.4

Note: Compound growth rates from 1961 to 2012 computed using official data, for 2000–10, the NSS estimates are used.
Source: *Economic Survey*, various issues; NSS Employment and Unemployment Surveys, primary data.

If the NSS estimates are correct (as most economists and policy makers trust these numbers), what could possibly account for the boom, especially in times of fiscal stringency, and of an official ban on fresh recruitment? *Prima facie*, it could be argued that rapid economic growth in 2000s increased public resources, which were used for providing better public services (as promised in various rights based legislations) resulting in employment expansion. To verify the proposition, a simple correlation coefficient is estimated between the following pairs of variables for a cross-section of the 17 major states, separately for 1999–2000 and 2009–10:

(i) (a) Public employment per 1000 population and (b) per capita income,
(ii) (a) Public employment per 1000 population and (b) human development index (HDI).

The findings are as follows: For 1999–2000, the correlation coefficient for (i) above is statistically significant with a positive sign, for 2009–10 the correlation coefficient is not significant. For (ii) above, in 1990–2000, the correlation coefficient is zero; in 2009–10, the correlation coefficient is positive but weak (significant at 90% level of confidence). What can one make of these statistical associations? Very little. They do not offer an unambiguous evidence for the foregoing proposition. So, what could possibly explain the boom in employment as revealed in the NSS data?

A suggested hypothesis

The NSS data for 2004–05 and 2009–10 provide information on the length of the job contract (Table 7.7). It shows that a growing proportion of public employees have short-term contracts, implying these are temporary workers. This is a significant observation since most government employment tends to be regular and permanent.

Table 7.7 Length of Job Contract

(Per cent)

Type of job contract	*2004–05*	*2009–10*
Less than a year	26.2	70.0
More than 3 years	37.7	59.9

Source: NSS Employment and Unemployment Surveys, primary data.

The divergence between the official data and the NSS estimates seems to suggest a deeper story. While the official government pay roll (consisting of regular and permanent employees) has declined, NSS employment surveys show a boom, especially of those with short term contracts. The contradictory trends seem to capture those employed in sub-contracted (or out-sourced) services. Since, as a matter of policy, low-end services are being increasingly outsourced, such workers usually have short-term contracts, as seen in the NSS surveys.[7]

If the forgoing interpretation is valid, then the decline in public employment in official statistics is factually correct, but materially not. In effect, it is yet another instance of informalisation of formal employment as widely reported in the organized sector in India.

This section, in sum, showed that the employment with regular and permanent jobs in public sector has contracted, but those working for outsourced agencies providing services to government have witnessed a sharp rise during the last decade. These trends imply that there has perhaps been very little restructuring and re-orientation of public employment towards skill intensive public services.

Understanding the Size and Trends

What are the implications of the foregoing empirical findings for India's political economy? With 4 per cent of the total work force, the size of public sector employment is not large – in fact, it is small by the standards of the advanced economies. But, its composition seems archaic, quite in contrast to that in developed economies, where the bureaucracy is decentralized and oriented towards providing public services (as expected in welfare states).

Official figures show a 12 per cent contraction in public sector employment since 1997, most of which is in central government and in PSEs – very little in state and local administration. So the decline in employment could simply represent retirement, and voluntary retirement schemes (VRS) initiated in the central government after the reforms decided to shrink public employment.[8] Such a trend may gladden the libertarians, who would commend the reformists for shrinking public employment even as economic growth has accelerated.

Such an inference could however be premature since overall public employment – employed directly as well as indirectly - has in fact been rising, as evident from the NSS estimates shown above. It also implies that there has been practically no administrative modernization or restructuring to meet the growing demands placed on the state. In the sixth pay commission award, the central government has abolished Class IV employees by *en mass* promoting them to the next level, without restructuring their job-content or service conditions. It is not known if a similar change has occurred in states and local administration. One suspects, probably not: because there has practically been no contraction in employment at the state and local levels.

For improving the delivery of social services and meeting their growing demand, what is needed is perhaps not contraction, but restructuring and modernization of public services – towards a contemporary welfare needs, and being responsive to the growing democratic aspirations. Now with many rights-based entitlements enshrined in the constitution, the need to re-orient public employment is all the greater.

There have been many official committees and commissions to reorganize public administration – most recent one being the Veerappan Moily commission on administrative reforms (http://arc.gov.in/) – but no government has shown the inclination to implement them. Herein lies, we would hypothesize, a political economic explanation of the foregoing trends in public employment, tied to the electoral politics.

In the intermediate regime thesis referred to in the introduction, the numerically significant public servants and petty producers were valuable in electoral terms and were perceived as a bulwark against the big business and foreign capital. But, the erstwhile beneficiaries of the state capitalism seem to have outgrown the need for the state support they received, and they seem to have now tightly embraced foreign capital and big business (NRIs are a big proxy of this group).

If so, with a right ward drift in politics, what prevents political parties from dumping public employees from their electoral calculus? Our tentative explanation is as follows: Public servants – be it a senior civil servant, or a humble peon – continue to remain the backbone of the political set up as they are needed to grease and turn the wheels of the patronage system on which electoral politics runs. The following examples are illustrations of the argument:

1. As lower level government employees form the foot soldiers for conducting elections, they probably play a vital role in subtly influencing electoral outcomes. Therefore, any political party would confront the non-gazetted officers (NGOs) at its peril. For example, in the 1989 assembly elections in Andhra Pradesh, NT Rama Rao, the charismatic Telugu film idol and the founder leader of the Telugu Desam Party (TDP) antagonized the lower bureaucracy by refusing to concede their wage demands almost until the assembly elections. He sought to pit the NGOs against the masses of poor in public spending (with a clear eye on the electoral gains), but lost the elections badly, as the lower bureaucracy apparently worked insidiously to defeat TDP to teach the nascent regional party a political lesson.[9]
2. If corruption is the grease, cadres of bureaucracy are the wheels of the patronage system. Winning elections in India require huge sums of money, mostly obtained by corrupt means, and the bureaucracy is the conduit through which corrupt money flows to politicians and political parties. Moreover, as politics in the vast rural country is as yet a labour intensive activity; politicians need to provide a regular source of income to their supporters (as a reward for loyalty). Doling out public jobs at the local level is a sure means of maintaining the support base, which remain the pivots of the patronage network. So, we would hypothesize that it is the political patronage system that keeps public employment growing (or, at a minimum, keeps it from declining despite the known means of doing so) impervious to the opportunity cost of such employment on economic growth or for equity.[10]

Fiscal deficit targets may have restrained central government employment growth, but probably not so at the state or local levels. Interestingly, despite the hardening of the budget constraint after the passage of the Financial Responsibility and Budget Management (FRBM) act, state governments have managed to keep employment growing in all but one state (Karnaraka). Thus, regardless of the political party in power, the states have preferred to reduce public investment (thus foregoing potential output and industrial growth), rather than shrink government employment. This seems suggestive of the pivotal role government servants play in the patronage network.[11]

Ordinary citizens are often outraged when faced with petty corrupt practices in their daily lives – such as a traffic cop collecting *mamool*, or a sub-registrar collecting bribes for approving a house plan or, property registration. But what mostly remains hidden from the public eye is that often the cop or the sub-registrar who collects bribes could just be the front end (or the last mile) of the chain of corruption for a local politician or a minister or political party, to whom the bribes get routinely passed-on without batting an eyelid. The person who collects the bribe probably gets a cut to recoup his or her costs incurred in getting the job. Such practices seem by now quite institutionalized, and not a one-off occurrence. So, the entire network of lower-level bureaucracy is perhaps a necessity for the patronage system to support the political order (see Box, as an illustration of the argument). Hence, given the cost of running the risky business of electoral politics, it is perhaps hard to expect the political executives to rationalize the system of employment that could cut the umbilical cord of electoral finance.

Box: Officer says he was 'harassed' for asking his share of bribe

The Hindu, Bengaluru, November 20, 2015, by, K. V. Aditya Bharadwaj

This officer from the Excise Department has redefined entirely the idea of "honesty" and chosen to make the business of taking bribes an "on-record" negotiation.

While replying to a show-cause notice, he has candidly said that he was being "harassed" for asking for his "rightful share" in the bribe money collected in Tumakuru district. He has gone on to reel out details of the money collected from bars in the district in 2014. The official's reply to the show-cause notice was on Thursday brought to the attention of Upalokayukta Subhash B. Adi by an RTI activist after reportedly exhausting all redressal mechanisms within the Excise Department. Mr. Adi has now served notice to the Excise Commissioner seeking an explanation as to why no inquiry was held or action taken, though the details of corruption was put "on record".

H.S. Shivappa, a Deputy Superintendent of Excise, Tumakuru, was served a show-cause notice by the Superintendent of Excise on an administration issue. Mr. Shivappa filed his reply on January 16, 2014, in which *he has recorded in detail the "economics of bribe" in the district and how it was divided among the officials. Mr. Shivappa is presently serving in Pandavapura sub-division, Mandya. The officer has stated that from each of the 300 bars in the district, Rs. 3,500 to Rs. 4,000 was collected every month, amounting to Rs. 12 lakh as "monthly mamool" and around Rs. 75 lakh was collected during the licence-renewal period in June-July 2013 in the name of Excise Minister and Deputy Commissioner.*(emphasis added).

"Even six months after the money was collected, you hadn't given me my rightful share like you have distributed among other officers. Instead, you served me a notice the next day I sought my share," he has said.

The officer has on record revealed the inner workings of bribery in the Excise Department. No efforts have been made to check corruption and the officer who sought a share in the bribe is still serving in Mandya.

For details, see: http://www.thehindu.com/news/cities/bangalore/officer-says-he-was-harassed-for-asking-his-share-of-bribe/article7898067.ece?homepage=true?w=alstates (accessed on November 20, 2015).

Surely, the form of corruption has evolved lately; it may not be as naïve or simplistic as portrayed above. It is no longer an entirely cash business requiring to change hands physically. In the light of the recent spate of scams, which are of completely different orders of magnitude, it is amply demonstrated how politicians have acquired business acumen in demanding and securing financial favour in terms of equity stakes in corporate entities (in a complex web of shell companies and trusts).[12] Though the evolved form of corruption may have become less 'labour-intensive', one suspect, it still calls for skilled hands to camouflage the operations, and to cover the tracks – lest the information trail (in the internet age) may yet spill the beans. So, despite the more sophisticated forms of corruption, need for services of government employees to support the political system seem to remain as yet.

To recapitulate this section: While public sector employment as per the official estimates has contracted by about 12 per cent between 1997 and 2012, NSS surveys find a boom in it: growing annually at 3.4 per cent between 2000 and 2010 – more than twice as fast as the economy-wide employment growth at 1½ per cent per year. This we have attributed to sub-contracting or outsourcing of many routine services, and increasing use of temporary daily-wage workers at the local level for service delivery; for example, workers in many government programmes like Angawadi or ICDS. In other words, there has been informalisation of public employment without accompanied by modernization of bureaucracy.

What could possibly explain this? Two reasons, in our view, both emanate from electoral politics. One, no political party at the state level would like to offend the local bureaucracy as it could subtly jeopardizing its electoral prospects since the lower administrative staff invariably form the foot soldiers of the election machinery. Two, bureaucracy is the junior partner in turning the wheels of corruption, which is the life line of financing elections in India.

Conclusion

The main empirical findings of the study are summarized as follows:

1. Four per cent of India's workers are employed in public sector, receiving 8 per cent of GDP as their wages.
2. Relative to population, public sector employment is small – just one-fifth of the size in the US (which is widely known to have small public sector among the developed nations). Hence, contrary to the popular perception, India's public employment is not disproportionately large (adjusted for population size).
3. However, its composition is different: majority of them work in public administration and defense and in industrial sectors. Skilled and professional services (taking class I and II employees as a proxy) form just 5 per cent of the central government employment; most government jobs consist of unskilled and semi-skilled work. In developed countries, public employment is mostly in services and in skilled occupations – providing health, education and social services.
4. Public sector employment grew from about 7 million in 1960 to about 20 million in 1997, but declined thereafter. These changes are broadly reflective of changing role of the state in economic development. Most of the decline is in central government and in public sector enterprises (quasi government). Proximate reasons for the decline are natural attrition (retirement), and voluntary retirement schemes (VRS).
5. From 1960s and to the 1980s, real earnings of government employees declined, and the wage dispersion between the highest and lowest category of workers narrowed. The trend however got reversed in the last decade.
6. The wage trends need to be interpreted with caution for two reasons. One, public employees constitute the nation's meritocracy demanding

fair compensation for education, skill and experience (efficiency wage argument). Moreover, the wage trends noted above are vitiated by many non-wage benefits available to public servants.

7. While the official estimate of public employment has contracted, NSS sample survey estimates show a boom during the last decade, growing more than twice as fast as the economy-wide employment growth rate. Much of it is of short term nature, suggesting that such workers are employed by service providers for the government. The contradictory trends noted above implies that while those employed by government have contracted, but they are replaced by those employed by service providers for the government.
8. This also implies that there has been little occupational restructuring towards skill intensive services, use of office automation and decentralization. As fresh recruitment is practically frozen in the central government, there are apparently shortages of many kinds of technically skilled staff, adversely affecting the quality of public services.

Why has there been practically no reorganization of public employment (or the state's inability to do so) to meet the growing demand for professional services, away from the archaic, colonial structure of bureaucracy? There are, we contend, political economic reasons for the persistence of the status quo. We have hypothesized two plausible explanations for it, both having their roots in the nature of India's democratic polity and its electoral financing.

One, no political party (or formation) would like to antagonize the non-gazetted officers (that is, lower level bureaucracy), who are usually in-charge of conducting elections and hence could subtly influence the electoral outcomes. Second, perhaps more important, reason is that the bureaucracy is the machinery (or the conduit) that delivers bribes to the political class, which in turn, creates or sustains bureaucracy by positioning their chosen persons at the critical cross sections in public decision making.

Surely, modes of political corruption have increasingly become sophisticated – wholesale and corporate – and, hence perhaps less 'labour and cash intensive', as the recent spate of scandals have revealed. Yet bureaucracy seems vital to avoid the electronic paper trail, and to cover the tracks, and hence the perpetuation of the status quo.

To answer the question posed in the chapter's subtitle, "What has Changed", our answer is: Not very much; a slight decline in direct employment, more than compensated by those indirectly employed via services providers, and very little reorganization to meet the growing demand for public services. We have contended that there are powerful political economic reasons for the persistence of the status quo. If our contentions are reasonable and substantial, then the chances of the reorganization and modernization of public employment in the near future to meet the felt needs of the citizens seems remote.

Endnotes

1. Acknowledgements: I would like to thank the publisher's referee for his or her comments which helped me in revising the paper. I would gratefully acknowledge Suhas Palshikar's detailed response to the earlier draft, though I am not sure if I have addressed all his comments and suggestions. I also thank C Rammanohar Reddy and the conference participants for their comments and suggestions. I am indebted to Vikash Vaibhav and Sumit Mishra for analyzing the NSS and Census data respectively.
2. The following news item illustrates the argument. 'Hike not in sync with inflation, say trade unions", the title of a news item in the *Times of India* (November 21, 2015), in the context of the 7th pay commission report just submitted to the central government. The news report said: "*Joining ranks against the 7th Pay Commission recommendations, national trade unions linked to BJP-RSS as well as to the Left parties said on Friday that the proposed hike was the lowest in many decades and were not in sync with inflation.*' (For details: http://epaperbeta.timesofindia.com/Article.aspx?eid=31804&articlexml=Hike-not-in-sync-with-inflation-say-trade-21112015017027, accessed on November 21, 2015). Emphasis added.
3. Organizationally, PSEs were the old post-war style (not just) vertically integrated manufacturing enterprises, but also townships (often located in remote places) providing most civic services. After the reforms PSEs were allowed to contract out most of these services, thus reducing their direct employment.
4. The rule was changed in 2004; new government recruits now get defined contribution pension, under National Pension Scheme.
5. We have restricted the analysis to a few broad aggregates, as the quality of the estimates for finer classification may not be accurate, given the sample size and its design.
6. Interestingly, the Left front ruled West Bengal reported a growth rate of just about the average of the states, despite its avowed political sympathy for the organized labour.
7. Strictly speaking, this points to an error in the NSS surveys as these workers are employed by service providers, not by government *per se*. Our judgment – based on an earlier experience of studying sub-contracting in manufacturing industries – is that the NSS surveys are not so finely designed as to distinguish between those directly employed *by government*, and those by the service provider *for government*. Further, the fact that central government, in principle, does not have any class IV employee on its rolls since 2009–10 it clearly indicates that the services rendered by these employees are now outsourced with workers having short term labour contracts.

8. Apparently, the ban on recruitment in the central government since 1991 seems to have created shortage of qualified professionals like statisticians, city planners, doctors and so on, without really changing the employment structure.
9. Analysing N. T. Rama Rao's defeat in the 1989 assembly elections, Shatrugna said, 'There were other reasons for the downfall of NTR. For instance, the NGO's wage issue which remained unresolved for a long time was thrashed out in favour of the employees just a few days before the elections... In the same manner, the reduction of age of retirement from 58 to 55 (which was not approved by the Supreme Court) had also tarnished the image of the party and NTR in particular. ... It appears that, peeved at the humiliating attitude of NTR, the NGOs by and large voted against the TDP.' (Shatrugna, 1989, 2697).

   In another analysis of the same electoral result, Narayan Rao and Sunder Ram said, '... NTR's anti-people's policies have alienated his party from various sections of the people, the prominent one being the anti-NGO policy affecting over eight lakh government employees. Although NTR conceded all their demands after the polls were announced, the NGOs were convinced that the move was merely an electoral ploy. ... The NGOs and the unemployed youth, particularly the new voters in the age-group of 18–21 seem to have stood by Congress (I) in 1989 elections and tilted the scale against the TDP.' (Rao and Ram, 1990, 558).
10. The recent espionage scandal in the petroleum and coal ministries leading to leaking of official secrets by low level employees to consultants and so-called journalists seems to illustrate my argument. It is an open secret that peons and clerks are often the conduits of corruption that often has the tacit blessings of the political masters.
11. Further, outsourcing of services in government probably opens up another avenue of patronage via doling out small contracts to the chosen few. Whether such contracting out really reduces the cost of providing the services depends on contract design and its execution (Vickers and Yarrow, 1991). If not, all the inefficiencies of the earlier system (of regular and permanent employment) may remain intact, but may now go undetected, as the contracts are rarely made public. It may only imply that contractors may now appropriate the 'rents' that earlier accrued to public employees (instead of reducing costs to government).
12. As Sucheta Dalal, the financial journalist, noted:
   There was a time when politicians did politics and used businessmen to raise money as they approached the elections. Then politicians started being sleeping partners in business ventures and then, they themselves became businessmen in their own right – owning real estate, education and other service businesses. But the most sophisticated of their moves has been to create shell companies whose shares are sold to businessmen at a stupendous premium (per share), ensuring neatly laundered, possibly tax paid wealth for our *netas*. There is no need for *benami* holding. It is all white and perfectly legal. Those, who bought shares on these shell companies usually, got concessions, mines, and large tracts of land in return (Dalal, 2012)

References

Bardhan, Pranab. 1984. *The Political Economy of Development in India*. New Delhi: Oxford University Press.

Dalal, Sucheta. 2012. 'The Premium Game: How Politicians Generate White Money through Shell Companies.' *Moneylife*. Available at, http://www.moneylife.in/article/the-premium-game-how-politicians-generate-white-money-through-shell-companies/27191.html.

Datta Chaudhuri, Mrinal. 1996. *Labour Markets as Social Institutions in India, IRIS-India Working Paper No. 10*. Delhi: Delhi School of Economics.

Desai, Ashok and Ena Desai. 1986. 'India.' In *The Growing Sector: Studies in Public Sector Employment in Asia*, edited by Gus Edgren. New Delhi: ILO-ARTEP.

Eapen, Mridul. 1980. 'Trend in Public Sector Employment and Earnings, Part I and II.' *Social Scientist* 8 (8 and 9): 3–21, 38–51.

Kaary, Aart and Caroline van Rijckeghem. 1995. *Employment and Wages in Public Sector: A Cross-Country Study: IMF Working Paper No. 95/70*. Washington D. C.

Laxman, R. K. 2005. *Best of Laxman: The Common Man Casts his Vote*. New Delhi: Penguin Books.

Patnaik, Prabhat and S. K. Rao. 1977. 'Explanation of Crisis in Mixed Underdeveloped Economy.' *Economic and Political Weekly* 12 (6–8): 205–218.

Raj, K. N. 1973. 'The Politics and Economics of "Intermediate Regimes".' *Economic and Political Weekly* 8 (27): 1189–1198, July 7.

Rao, K. V. Nayaran and D. Sundar Ram. 1990. 'Political Developments in Andhra Pradesh, 1978–1989: A Study.' *The Indian Journal of Political Science* 51 (4): 540–564, October-December.

Rampell, Catherine. 2012. "Big Government.' Isn't So Big by Historical Standards. It's Also Shrinking.' *The New York Times*, July 27.

Shatrugna, M. 1989. 'NTR Ratham Grinds to a Halt.' *Economic and Political Weekly* 24 (49): 2696–97.

Srinivasan, T. N. 1985. 'Neo-Classical Political Economy, State and Economic Development.' *Asian Development Review* 3 (2): 38–58.

Vickers, John and George Yarrow. 1991. 'Economic Perspectives on Privatisation.' *Journal of Economic Perspectives* 5 (2): 111–132.

8

New Paradigms of Labour Relations

How Much do They Explain?

Supriya Roy Chowdhury

Introduction

Labour studies in the current scenario are understandably in difficult times. Our traditional subjects of research are disappearing: strikes and other forms of industrial disputes, collective bargaining, trade unions, left parties and so on. Displaced from the spaces – factories and fields – in which labour scholars have historically imagined them, the so called working class is physically scattered and in what could be described as political wilderness. Informal work or the informal sector has become the most commonly used term for describing workers who work, but who do not have regular or assured work, income, or work-related social security. The domain of informal work is vast and diverse. Perhaps one of the most challenging tasks in labour studies has been to provide a definition which captures both the essence and the wide ranging complexity of informality, as well as a coherent imagination of a possible politics of informal workers qua workers. Neo classical economists have defined informality as absence of state regulations, and in recognition of the sector's diverseness have conceded that there is a range (more or less) in terms of absence of regulations, and also, importantly, that formal and informal, therefore, must be seen in a continuum, rather than as mutually exclusive.[1] This unifying definitional framework, is a useful first cut, but does not provide any clues to understand the complexity, or the historical specificity of informal work in the present times.

On the other side of the intellectual divide, left leaning critiques of capitalism, in general, and dependency inspired theories, in particular, explain informal work, particularly in developing countries, but also increasingly in the west, as generated by the contradictions of capitalism in a technologically driven world of global capital. Other left-leaning theorists have seen petty self employment as the domain of exclusion – the need economy – which provides subsistence to workers excluded by the global-capital driven economy. Informality, as a domain of exclusion, is, on this view, structured by global capitalism[2]. Such theories are intrinsically attractive for a broad understanding of the political economy of development; the push cart seller or the pavement vendor in third world cities may well be a product of the dynamics of global capital. It is nevertheless difficult to imagine the precise points of interface/conflict between the huge domain of self employed workers (who may also double up as casual wage earners) and global capital. This diffusion of the class structure of the workforce is of course reflected in the domain of activism. The steady decline of trade union power, and the emergence of a large number of other actors into the domain of labour activism (NGOs, CSOs, Social Compliance agencies, global monitors, and so on), have greatly diffused the context in which labour related issues are addressed. Thus, if informal work is hard to define, the domain of political agency or collective action relating to informal workers is even harder to conceptualize.

There has now emerged an overall consensus around an umbrella-like formula that informal workers must look to the state rather than to private employers, and must ask for social benefits, rather than for wages. This perspective of a redefined relationship between workers and the state is anchored in a broader, emerging world view of the possibility of bringing back a more proactive state, particularly in the context of globalization and economic liberalization. Scholars of different hues appear to agree that even as expanded markets create greater wealth and inequalities, democracy provides a context where the relatively disadvantaged can push the state to create welfarist provisions[3].

However, a central question, that of political agency, remains unaddressed in this perspective. Historically, welfare or redistribution have rarely been gifts of states, and are in fact closely linked to political struggles of the poor, led by trade unions, social democratic or left leaning political parties. In the current context, the economic structure, broadly speaking, and the world of informal livelihoods, in particular, shape and constrict the political agency of the poor. In what ways, for example, does the shrinking of the organized labour force determine the dynamics of welfare politics? Given the centrality of informal work in the economies of developing countries, can we indeed make a substantive set of connections between the political economy of the informal sector, a possible politics of welfare, and the state?

Two new scholarly works on labour in South Asia which have appeared in recent years are important interventions into the debate on labour and political representation in South Asia broadly, and in particular in India. Providing a broad endorsement of labour practices in the informal sector, both scholars appear to hold the view that informal workers hold the state accountable, via the democratic system, the state needs industrial workers as workers, and as voters. This underpins a fundamental mutuality, labour works for unregulated wages, while empowered to bargain for social benefits from the state. Rina Aggarwal (2012) in a comparative study of bidi and construction workers across three Indian states found that early workers movements in these sectors strove to transform the informal workforce in the mirror of formal workers. More contemporary movements reflect a gradual shift of attention from employer to the state, from work and wage related issues to more general social welfare related rights. According to her, this represents class politics (workers use their worker identity cards to get state sponsored social insurance) and an alternative labour movement model. 'Significantly, their emerging identity simultaneously asserts their informality and their position within the working class. Their identity is not expressed as an antithesis to capital.' This then leads Aggarwal to the conclusion that this alternative model 'incorporates the informal sector as an active participant in capitalist growth.' Informal sector workers are pressing for these rights to housing, health and education, and in doing so participating in some kind of a redefined version of 'class' politics. No longer are workers interested in wage or other work related issues. Nevertheless, class still acts as an agency for putting forward the claims of the dispossessed. Teitelbaum (2011) in a study of industrial disputes in three Indian states came to similar conclusions. Democracy, according to him, facilitates the peaceful resolution of disputes, and therefore, enhances the prospects of industrial and economic growth. Political parties need industrial workers' political support during elections. Therefore, it is to the interest of political parties to facilitate the resolution or prevention of industrial disputes (through trade union activities).

Can one indeed talk about industrial worker welfare through state-sponsored social security, in a context where the issue of wages remains unaddressed? What are the political spaces available to informal workers to press their social welfare claims on the state? Finally, within a democratic framework, what are the ideologies and institutions which are constitutive of informal workers as a political force, if at all?

I draw below from a recent study of construction workers in Bangalore. This study highlights that close to half of the workers surveyed earned less than the minimum wage, and work availability in the city was insufficient and irregular. State sponsored social security, through Welfare Boards, is provided in terms of accident insurance, pension, scholarships, and so on. The claims recognized by the state, and sought to be implemented through the Boards, do not speak of wages, income, and housing, the three most important points of deprivation in the lives of construction workers. The number of workers registered in the Boards is low, and awareness and implementation of the welfare measures remains partial and inadequate. My findings are confirmed by other studies of construction workers, conducted across the private and public sectors. Overall the situation speaks of deprivation on both fronts, wages and social security. These findings raise serious questions about the emerging paradigms in labour studies, discussed above, that state sponsored social security can address the plight of industrial workers whose wages are low and unregulated. More broadly, these findings throw open central questions of collective action and political representation of informal workers.

Construction Workers in Bangalore

Industrial labour must be seen within the broader framework of the urban political economy. I highlight features of urban development in Karnataka in brief, which have a particular bearing on the issue of poverty of occupational groups like construction workers. An important feature of Karnataka's development is the preponderance of agricultural employment, in a context where agriculture's share in GSDP is continuously shrinking[4]. While this is a feature of the national economy as well, this persisting trend has led scholars to raise questions about the nature of urban economic growth. Overall, if a large number of people remain tied to agriculture; this is because of the lack of appropriate employment opportunities in urban areas[5]. In Karnataka, the sectoral pattern of growth highlights the narrowness of economic growth. Karnataka is one of the top industrialized states. However, a closer look reveals that in terms of the share of the secondary sector in GSDP, Karnataka ranks fifth amongst industrialized states, and the share of industry in GSDP has actually declined in recent years, from 29% in 2004–5 to 26% in 2011–12; employment in the secondary sector remains low, particularly in comparison to other states, at 18%, while employment in the tertiary sector is 26% and in the primary sector, a much larger 56%[6]. Industry's lowest share in GSDP as well as in employment creation, and the decline of this over time, has been a matter of concern for successive governments. Karnataka's recent economic development is acknowledged to have been led by the growth of the services sector, which increased its share of GSDP from 51% in 2004–5 to 56.3% in 2011–12. The service sector's growth remains central to national and regional growth. This trajectory, however, must be seen in the context of an emerging debate amongst scholars and policy makers as to whether the growth of services can lead development in countries like India, where a large proportion of the workforce remains unskilled and unable to access the kind of jobs generated in the services sector[7]. This brief outline provides the backdrop for the discussion of work and welfare of construction workers, who constitute the largest number of the unskilled urban workforce.

In 2009–10, Construction workers constituted 10% of the total unorganized workforce, and the industry accounted for 12% of GDP. The Construction industry is the second largest employer after agriculture. Infrastructure development has been a central agenda of successive governments in Karnataka.[8] In Bangalore, the Construction industry has expanded greatly, following the city's recent IT-driven growth. In Karnataka state, there are some 1.5 million workers involved in the construction industry. In Bangalore city, the strength of the construction workforce is 0.35million[9], although the enumeration of this workforce can only be approximate, given the cyclical character of a large proportion of the migrant workforce.

A number of legislative measures have been taken, both at central and state levels, to address wages, working conditions and other welfare related measures relating to workers in this sector. Most significant among these are the Building and Construction Workers (Regulation of Employment and Conditions of Service) Act and the Building and Construction Workers Cess Act, 1996[10]. By these Acts, state governments are empowered to create Welfare Boards in which Construction workers would be registered, and through which they can claim a number of benefits relating to pension, accidents, medical and children's education related expenses, and so on[11]. The Karnataka Building and Other Construction Workers Welfare Board was set up in 2006[12]. The Board's mandate is in the domain of welfare provisions –accident insurance, medical benefits for major ailments and diseases, educational assistance for children, loan facilities for housing, and a pension scheme – rather than fair wages. The state government periodically revises the minimum wage for workers in this sector.

The study was conducted in three different sites in the city of Bangalore[13]. This selection was made in order to represent different kinds of habitations of migrant construction workers: the first two are independent rental housing; the third is employer–provided[14]. Each of the three sites is located in South Bangalore[15]. A total of 300 migrant construction worker households were covered by the study, which used both a questionnaire and qualitative discussions[16]. Construction workers in these three sites are predominantly recent migrants, who came to the city anywhere between a few months to 15 years back. The largest number (61%) appeared to hail from Northern Karnataka (Tables 8.1 through 8.6 show the socio-economic background of migrant construction workers in their place of origin). This confirms conventional understanding of the migration pattern in Karnataka, where dry and un-irrigated land in the Northern regions have historically generated extremely low agricultural incomes, leading to distress migration of poor agricultural families. Thus most of the migrant construction workers (73%) had been employed as daily wage earners in farming and construction activities. In terms of social profile, the majority of construction workers in this study belonged to the scheduled castes. Illiteracy was high (at 58%).

Table 8.1 Region of Migration

Region	*Share of Migrants (%)*
North Karnataka	61.89
Andhra Pradesh	11.89
Eastern India	18.85
Others	7.38
Total	100.00

Source: Based on author's field work in three slums in South Bengaluru.

Table 8.2 Occupation before Migration

Occupation	*Share (%)*
Agriculturist	40.16
Daily labourer	24.58
Construction worker	8.20
Others	1.23
Not answered/no work	25.83
Total	100.00

Source: Author's field work data.

Table 8.3 Caste Structure of Construction Workers

Caste	*Share (%)*
SC/ST	62.14
OBC	15.23
General	7.00
Others	15.64
Total	100.00

Source: Author's field work data.

Table 8.4 Education Profile

Education	*Share (%)*
Illiterate	57
Up to V class	27
Up to X class	8
SSLC	6
PUC	2
Total	100

Source: Author's field work data.

Table 8.5 Households who Possessed Land in Village

Site	*Share (%)*
Labour Colony	62.65
Nagavarpallya	53.52
Pai Layout	42.86

Source: Author's field work data.

Table 8.6 Average Land Owned by Households in Village

Site	*Per Household (%)*
Labour Colony	4.50
Nagavarpallya	4.00
Pai Layout	1.94
Average	3.75

Source: Author's field work data.

Work and income

The largest number in this study, close to 72%, described themselves as '*kuli*' or "worker". This refers to work such as digging earth, breaking or carrying bricks, carrying cement or other items such as water, in short, any work relating to construction which does not require any kind of skills or training, and can be performed by any person. Comparatively, the percentage of skilled workers was very low, at 21%, including maistry, electrician, carpenter, grinder/welder (Table 8.7). The industry itself offers little scope to migrant workers to acquire skills that would enable them to improve their occupational status.

Table 8.7 Different Categories of Workers (in percentage)

Maistry	18.11
Worker	71.19
Carpenter	1.23
Electrician	1.15
Grinder/Welder	0.82
Driver	3.20
Others	2.8

Source: Author's field work data.

As this study was conducted during 2011–12, one could look at the wage structure (Table 8.8), in terms of the minimum wage which was stipulated in 2010, as Rs. 135.60 per day, (which amounts to Rs. 3254 for twenty four days of work per month)[17]. First, about 25% were getting less than Rs. 110 per day, and 46% were getting in the range of Rs. 110–150. Assuming that in the latter group, perhaps half were receiving below Rs. 135, then around 48% in the sample were receiving below the minimum wage. The survey revealed that only about 10% were getting more than Rs. 200, (Table 8.8) and in this category, the largest number were skilled workers (Table 8.9). The other significant feature of course is that women workers in the construction industry continue to constitute the extreme bottom of the heap. Women constituted around 25% of the workforce across the three groups studied. As Table 8.10 shows, in the category of those earning less than Rs. 100, only 4.3% were men, while more than 80% were women. Women's share in the workforce declined in the next two higher wage categories, and significantly, in the two highest wage categories, (Rs. 150–200, and above Rs. 200), there were no women workers at all (Table 8.10).

Table 8.8 Wage Structure (in percentage)

Below Rs. 110	*Rs. 110 –150*	*Rs. 150–200*	*Above Rs. 200*
25.82	46.31	18.03	9.84

Source: Author's field work data.

Table 8.9 Category of Work among Those Who are Earning More than Rs. 200 per day

Work categories	*Total*
Maistry	16
Electrician	2
Other plumber/tiles	2
Worker	10
Total	30

Source: Author's field work data.

Table 8.10 Distribution of Male and Female Workers across Wage Structure

	Male	*Female*
Less than Rs. 100	4.3	81.0
Rs. 100–135	22.0	15.5
Rs. 135–150	37.1	3.4
Rs. 150–200	26.8	0.0
Rs. 200 and above	9.8	0.0

Source: Author's field work data.

In any analysis of informal workers, one has to factor in some amount of under reporting of incomes. From general observation, it would seem that in Bangalore, skilled construction workers may get between Rs. 250–350 per day, sometimes even more. Yet in our survey, very few, even of those who reported skilled work, acknowledged receiving Rs. 250–350. It is worth noting, however, that the relationship between wages and earnings is fairly complex. Work availability is highly variable. Across the three settlements, the average work availability was only 15 days per month. Although daily earnings may be higher than what was reported, the actual monthly income was not a reflection of daily wages, translated into twenty -four days of work.

Wages and other entitlements are highly variable across the city depending particularly on the nature of the project, the employer (whether government or private builder). A survey of 169 workers, working for private builders in Bangalore, conducted in 2011 (Prasad et al, 2011), reported that 25 per cent of workers were receiving wages less than the minimum wages stipulated by the Government of Karnataka. About 25 per cent workers in this survey were in the above Rs. 200 category. This study also mentions a specific category of Rs. 300 and above, in which 5 per cent workers are placed. The findings of this study, thus, were approximately similar to the findings in my study.

In contrast, it is found that workers in large government infrastructure projects earn a higher wage than what is available to those working for private builders of commercial and residential complexes. The wage structure of workers employed in the construction of the Bangalore Metro Railway was considerably higher.[18] Around 62 per cent workers were paid in the range of Rs. 6000–9000 per month, which meant that the daily wage for a large percentage of workers was more than Rs. 300, and work was available for all six days of the week. More remarkably, about 24 per cent of the workers were paid a monthly salary that ranged from Rs. 9000 to Rs. 15,000 per month, while only 14 per cent were in the lowest salary bracket, Rs. 4,000 to Rs. 6000 (Madhu Sudan, 2013).

Beyond wages, household income levels explain extreme poverty in the three settlements which I studied (Table 8.11). Across the three settlements, nearly 40 per cent are dependents, and of those who work, average work availability is 15 days in a month The per capita income distribution (Table 8.12) shows that an alarming 29 per cent of the members of the households studied were in the below Rs. 500 category. While the largest percentage of members (41 per cent) were in the Rs. 500–1000 category, there is a declining percentage of members in the higher income categories, and only 30 per cent of the members have a monthly per capita income of more than Rs. 1000. The poverty line for urban Karnataka in 2010–11 was Rs. 892.

Despite the hardships associated with working in this industry, there is of course an obvious economic rationality of the workers' move to Bangalore. The survey showed us that the majority had moved from situations of complete absence of work, income, and assets. Bangalore promises higher wages in this sector, and sometimes free housing. The reality of course, as indicated above, is that of low incomes, with uncertain work availability, absence of medical leave, and often, large numbers of dependents. The extreme instability in their earnings was their daily struggle. *'In one month, barely three weeks of work may be available.' 'One week there will be work, next week there is no work'*, said two men from the same family who had moved from a village in Raichud District. In the absence of the daily wage, they try to make do with their meagre savings, or take a small loan from a neighbour, a small credit from the local grocer. The perception that potentially it is possible to make more money is an enticement that keeps them in their miserable shacks, and beckons others. *'Compared to native, things are better here. We earn to live'* said Rukmini from Gulbarga in North Karnataka.

Table 8.11 Poverty in the Three Settlements

Site Name	*Poverty Ratio*
Labour Colony	69
Nagavara Palya	47.9
Pai Layout	75.3
Total	64.8

Source: Author's field work data.

Table 8.12 Per Capita Income Distribution (in percentage)[23]

	Upto Rs500	*Rs. 500–1000*	*Rs. 1000–1500*	*Rs. 1500–2000*	*Above Rs. 2000*	*Total*
Labour Colony	33	40	20	6.0	1.0	100
Nagavar Pallya	19.6	38.5	23.7	11.2	7.0	100
Pai Layout	32.9	46.6	11.0	2.7	6.8	100
Total	29.1	41.4	18.4	6.6	4.5	100

Source: Author's field work data.

Multiple vulnerabilities

Of the three groups studied, almost all workers in the Labour Colony, who were employees of a private construction company, were registered in the Welfare Board. In the other two groups, (workers moved frequently between employers) registration was low, at about 20 per cent in each group. But whether registered or not, in all three settlements workers had very little actual information about their entitlements associated with the Welfare Board. Across different domains, construction workers are systematically denied access to the benefits (water and toilets at the workplace, sick leave, accident or other insurance) which have been mandated by the Building and Other Construction Workers Act of 2006 in Karnataka. While Contractors (individuals or agencies) were seen to have played a central role in the recruitment of workers across the three settlements, they were not proactive in getting workers registered, or in raising awareness amongst workers of their claims through the Boards. Prasad (2011), in the study mentioned above found that about 76 per cent workers were not even aware of the Karnataka Welfare Board. Of the 20 contractors who were interviewed in that study, only six were aware of the construction workers Welfare Board.

More tellingly, the study on BMCRL workers, mentioned above, narrates the denial of basic rights at the work place. BMRCL workers were registered in the Welfare Board. However, basic facilities such as drinking water, toilets etc, which should mandatorily be provided by the employer in any construction site, were not available to BMRCL workers Even more remarkably, the study highlighted the large number of injuries and deaths of workers (fourteen major accidents were reported during 2007–2012) that had occurred in different BMRCL sites due to absence of necessary precautions being put in place by contractors, and that most of these victims and their families had failed to get any kind of compensation. The Contracting Company, (as well as the BMRCL, although it was the principal employer), failed to ensure that accidents were reported to the local Compensation Commissioner, through the Welfare Board in which the accident victim may have been registered Thus, the basic institutional structure which the 2006 Act sought to create for the welfare of construction workers, was in a sense by passed by the BMCRL, and more poignantly, state responsibility for accident victims or their families could not be enforced, even in a situation where the workers were working for a large public project.

Housing, shelter and schools

Every day vulnerabilities faced by this migrant workforce relate to housing and shelter, water, toilets and sanitation, schools and hospitals. Housing and children's education, particularly highlight state indifference to this workforce. Across the three settlements, two types of housing arrangements were found. First, in Pai Layout and Nagavar Pallya, workers lived on land which they rented from private land owners, in self constructed one-room shanties, which were basically blue plastic sheets held up by bamboo poles. In the absence of toilets, men, women and children used adjacent fields. Each settlement lacked electricity, water connection, and basic sanitation services, was located close to drains, depicting a story of complete absence of hygiene. In the Labour Colony, the Construction Company had provided one small room, with a tin roof and mud walls, for each household, without any separate kitchen, bathing area, or electricity. The Company had provided a borewell and a cluster of toilets at the end of the compound. However, at the time of the study, these toilets had not been used for over a year as they are not maintained because of lack of water supply. The entire community uses the adjacent fields.

The everyday battle of this workforce is with water and toilets. Many are resigned to buying water. However, the most urgent problem, a repeatedly expressed point of extreme agony, is lack of toilets. All the three groups use nearby fields for open defecation. In the night often snakes are seen there. In Nagavar Pallya, which is split into two by a rickety bridge, the older women find it hard to negotiate this bridge in the darkness of the night, on their way to the field. The younger women and girls can relieve themselves only at fixed times of early morning and evening, under cover of dark, and they can only move in groups because of prying eyes and the threat of sexual harassment by men in the neighbourhood. In the rainy season, water flows into the houses. There is no streetlight.

There was collective agreement amongst construction workers that their central need is a roof over their heads, and access to water. Many felt that what they earn would go a longer way if they did not have to pay rent and daily expenditure on water. News about evictions, when the bulldozer arrives and in a few hours huts are razed to the ground and entire communities are left homeless, with their meagre belongings strewn around, feature in regular media reports. Amongst slum communities across the city, NGOs and other social activists, stories of evictions travel back and forth through regular informal channels of communication. For most slum dwellers in Bangalore the fear of eviction is an internalized hysteria, a part of their every day consciousness. A group of residents of Pai Layout live on a piece of land which is part of the railway tract, and pay no rent. They do not know when the government would decide to reclaim and sell this land for commercial purposes. The construction worker community in Nagavara Pallya live on land which is under litigation. Their continuing residence there depends on their good relations with the litigant who collects rent from them, '*we pay him regularly, but how can he protect us if he loses the case*?' said one respondent. In a possible scenario where the other litigant could claim the land, they could be evicted. Although those in the Labour Colony had the advantage of not having to pay rent, this did not seem to lessen the sense of insecurity relating to land and housing. All the participants in the discussion group said that they need help in finding land and for construction of houses. '*Here it is only working and eating. There is no guarantee.*' '*Even though they are giving us houses, any time any one of us can be thrown out*'.

Second, this research revealed that a large number of children of migrants were out of school and working. Figure 4 tells us that of children in the age group of 6–16, amongst males only 35 per cent, and amongst females 44 per cent were going to school. The lower percentage of male children going to school was possibly a reflection of their joining the workforce fairly early in life. In the same age group, 13.95 per cent male children, and 13.36 per cent of female children were working. Of this, 86 per cent of male children, and 72 per cent of female children were working in construction sites (Table 8.13). Taken together, then, this indicates that for the majority of workers migration and employment in the construction industry has not translated to an expanded set of opportunities for their children. Thus a large number of the children of construction workers do not go to school and many of them join their parents to become part of this low paid, unskilled urban workforce[19].

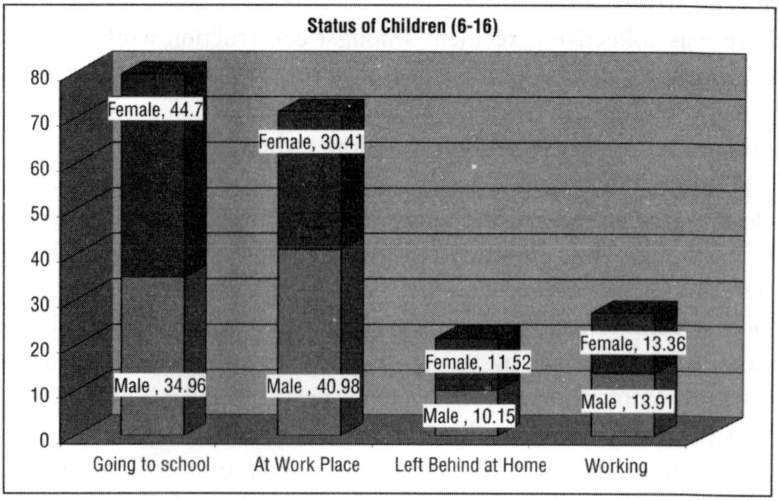

Figure 8.1 Status of Children

Table 8.13 Percentage of Children in Construction Activity amongst Working Children across the Three Sites

	Male	*Female*
Labour Colony	100	100
Nagavar Palya	81.8	100
Pai Layout	90.0	52.9

Source: Author's field work data

Under the Sarva Shikshya Abhiyan, Tent Schools have been set up by the Government of Karnataka for children of construction workers. Tent Schools are meant to provide one or two years of education for younger children, until they can move to a mainstream government school. It was found that most frequently women construction workers use the Tent school near their settlement as a crèche while they work, the facilities available is minimal and very little teaching actually happiness by the single teacher appointed in a Tent School. Children do receive the mid day meal, but no educational or recreational resources have been provided, and rarely do children move on to the mainstream school. One of our discussants, Girish, summarised the issue: '*we are poor, the school is free, and the teacher is not answerable to anyone. No one will take responsibility for poor children. BPL also only for poor people. So no one is responsible for what is given, how it is given, whether it is given*'.

In this environment, then, they have lived for several years, now. Surrounded by uncollected piled up garbage, stinking drains, stagnant pools of water, with low incomes and deprived of basic human rights to water and a protected area of privacy. The future of the next generation does not look different.

Policy, Politics and Civil Society

The setting up of the Welfare Boards in 2006 provided the broad framework of legislated welfare for construction workers. The findings of this research highlight that state-sponsored welfare rarely touches the lives of construction workers. Not only is registration in the Boards extremely low, but there are several important lacunae in what this Act envisions as welfare. The Welfare Boards are in principle required to provide scholarships for children of construction workers, but this applies only to those pursuing studies at the 10th grade and above, and only if the student is staying in a hostel. In principle, the Right to Education Act (2009) provides basic and free education to all, and there are additional supports for children of SC/STs. The reality of course is that few have the opportunity to attend school, there are a large number of drop-outs amongst those who do, and, as the discussion in the previous section have pointed out, and many children of construction workers start working in the construction industry from a young age. Thus, in the absence of educational interventions in the early school years of these children, the provisions for scholarship for high school and college students appear to be unrealistic.

As far as housing is concerned, there is no provision in the Act which speaks to this issue. However, a range of housing schemes for the urban poor have been enacted from time to time (the Valmiki Malin Basti Awas Yojana, and more recently the Rajiv Awas Yojana, to name two). The reach of these schemes remain limited to slums which are notified by the government, and in which the slum dwellers have been given property rights on the piece of land which they occupy. Construction workers, who live in non notified slums, cannot claim property rights on the land on which they live, or avail housing loans. Yet there are no government schemes which actually speak to the housing needs of these large and expanding numbers of workers who seek a living in the city by working in the construction industry.

What are the political and institutional obstacles to a broader conceptualization of welfare for this workforce, and a more rigorous implementation of the Boards? And what are the channels through which the claims of this workforce can be articulated, within a democratic framework? First, in terms of the channels through which construction workers can articulate their needs and claims, one could look at their relations with political parties, trade unions, and civil society associations. The group of workers in the Labour Colony return to their respective villages during elections, those from distant states may not vote at all. In Pai Layput (KR Pura constituency), the 2008 assembly elections led to the victory of Nandeesh Reddy of the BJP[20]. (In 2013, a Congress candidate won from this constituency). Nagavara Palya (C. V. Raman Nagar reserved constituency) is a BJP stronghold. In the 2008 assembly elections, S Raghu of the BJP was elected back to the assembly he was re-elected again in 2013). Thus, in the 2008 elections, while CV Raman Nagar constituency re-elected its BJP MLA, the KR Pura constituency shifted from the Congress to the BJP[21]. In both Wards 83 (Nagavara Palya) and Ward 193 (Pai Layout), local corporators belong to the BJP. Construction workers constitute a small percentage of the voting population in both areas, which are predominantly middle and upper middle class neighbourhoods. During discussions each of the communities said that they had voted for the BJP '*to give them a chance, earlier they had given chance to Congress*'.

The recent history of both these constituencies reveals that there has been little or no interest on the part of local politicians to address the interests of these marginalized communities. This was particularly highlighted in discussions with workers and slum leaders in Nagarvarpalya: the BJP MLA from this constituency, which is reserved, belongs to one of the scheduled castes. However, there is hardly any contact between the MLA and construction workers living on this site, even though the majority in this community belong to the Scheduled castes. Similarly, in Pai Layout, the BJP MLA had made a couple of visits to the construction worker settlement before the elections, but since then there had been no contact with him. In Pai Layout, the locally powerful person is one Cement Nagraj. He is a big supplier of cement to the builders who are constructing large apartment buildings in the neighbourhood, and where most migrant workers in these localities find work. He is also the President of the Pai Layout Residents Association. An extremely wealthy man, he is an active BJP supporter. He has been instrumental in getting the BPL card for some members of the community. It was obvious that this person had played a role in the shift of votes away from Congress to the BJP in 2008 as far as these communities were concerned. However, other than helping several households with the paper work related to applying for the BPL card, no other issues had been addressed during the community's interactions with this locally resourceful person. Thus, even though the construction worker communities regularly participate in elections, they appear to be in a political wilderness.

The lack of attention to these marginalized communities became even more apparent at the level of the local corporation. In Nagavara Palya (Ward 83) projects such as Improvements to Road Side Drain, Mini Water Supply Schemes, and Construction of Individual Houses are listed by the BBMP (as well as mentioned by local corporator) as schemes which will be undertaken, which in turn would directly benefit this community. However, each of these projects remain only on paper, and no headway has been made even in the evaluation of cost of these projects. The workers' sense of political isolation was expressed in the following statements '*No one ever comes, no meetings are held except at election times*'. '*They promise some things, we go after them, then they win and go off, and we come back, like dogs*'.

With regard to unions, in Bangalore, The Karnataka State Construction Workers' Central Union (KSCWCU) has played a leading role in worker registration, and organization around rights based issues. The KSCWCU is an independent union, affiliated to the National Centre for Labour, and with close links to the Janata Dal (S). The KSCWCU has about 62,000 members across Karnataka. In Bangalore, as mentioned in section 1, the total number of construction workers is difficult to determine with accuracy; not more than 10 per cent of this workforce is unionized through the KSCWCU. The major areas of concern of the KSCWCU has been on welfare issues like helpline, housing, increases in the quantum of benefits available through the Welfare Boards and so on. There has been less focus on the issue of fair wages, nor any politically visible activities for greater regulation of work and employment relations in the Construction sector. A second large union in this sector is the Karnataka State Building and Other Construction Workers Federation, affiliated to the AITUC. The Federation's activities have been mostly confined to efforts to lobby with successive governments in the state to arrive at a redefinition of construction workers, with special focus on the needs of those who are engaged in hazardous work within the industry. Within this framework, the Federation has lobbied for workplace security, specifically, and social security more broadly. The Federation, similar to the KSCWCU, has not pressed on issues relating to wages.

A large number of NGOs are engaged with construction workers. It should be noted, however, that typically NGO interest in this sector is an indirect fall out of their involvement with slum communities and the urban poor, broadly speaking. Construction workers constitute a large percentage of the urban poor. However, NGOs are even less interested in wage related issues than are trade unions in this sector. Education, housing and health related issues have been dominant in the NGO discourse on construction workers. In both, Pai Lay Out and Nagavar Pallya, APSA had been engaged for some years. The NGO's activities related mainly to enabling the workers to register themselves with the Welfare Board and managing the Tent School adjacent to the Pai Layout Settlement. In addition, APSA runs a school for poor children, with a large number of children of construction workers. In the Labour Colony, we found no significant NGO intervention except that that management of the crèche, provided by the building Company, had been entrusted to an NGO. The activities of both NGOs appeared to be limited to the groups of workers that they were working with, and to specific issues, particularly with regard to education of children. NGO activities did not appear to be related to broader or even city-wide engagement with issues of deprivation affecting construction workers[22].

Conclusion

Returning to the now widely shared view that informal labour must turn from wage related issues, focussed on private employers, to social security related issues, focussed on the state. The implicit messages here is that even while the market is acknowledged to generate the relative marginalisation of informal workers, nevertheless there is the possibility that informal workers might achieve a decent standard of living through state-provided welfare. In the light of the findings presented above, one could point to some obvious flaws in this argument. First, where more than half of the workforce are not even getting the minimum wage, neither is work availability regular nor assured, the argument that wage is less important than welfare appears to fall on its face. Second, this entire argument would appear to rest on the assumption that democracy allows informal workers the space for collective organization and political representation through which their social welfare related interests could, at least partially, be addressed. The material presented above indicated that legislation addressing construction workers welfare issues is limited in scope, and unrelated to workers' real needs (such as housing, and primary education facilities for children of construction workers), and secondly, that the reach of these policies remains constricted by low registration of workers in the Boards and the fact that workers themselves remain unaware of their rights, lacking access to social and political organizations for collective representation. It appeared that the absence of collective action in the form of unionization was a major factor that prevented the implementation of minimum wages stipulated by government, as well as the basic conditions of service and welfare stipulated by the Building and Other Construction Workers Act of 1996/2006. The 1996 and 2006 Acts relating to Welfare Boards for construction workers came as a response to many years of NGO and trade union pressures. While the Acts introduced a system of regulations, little was done to address the central question of how regulations can be implemented in an industry where the workforce is scattered and migratory. The dynamics of work in Bangalore's construction industry thus raises fundamental questions with regard to the problem of organizing the unorganized.

Beyond this, there is the question of where industrial workers stand vis-a-vis political parties, and the state. The argument that 'competitive democracy requires parties to mobilize workers as a base of support ....' (Tietelbaum, 2012) assumes that workers, qua workers, are a constituency. This assumption is problematic in the present context. Organized workers, who arguably, might have a distinct political identity as workers, are a small fraction of the workforce. Informal sector wage earners lack security of tenure, rights to collective bargaining and freedom of association. Self employed informal workers rarely share an occupational identity and most often lack any kind of collective front. Expectedly, mobilization of political support of workers, qua workers, rarely happens. Dominant political discourses in India construct the voter in terms of identities that are social and religious, not economic, and the distributional discourse has shifted from work related rights to basic rights. However, the basic rights discourse is pinned to universalized categories, such as citizen, rather than occupational categories such as worker. It could be said that at the present time, there is really no political vocabulary for mobilizing the industrial workforce, qua workforce. Finally, arguments in defence of informality– for example, for unregulated wages– are perhaps well anchored in economic efficiency arguments, and in the broadly dominant neo liberal policy paradigm. Within this paradigm it is somewhat naïve to be speaking of state support for informal workers and informal workers' hold upon the state. The material discussed above points out that state laws are hugely inadequate to support informal workers welfare needs, and their political resources to shape state policies and implementation are very limited.

Endnotes

1. See, for example Guha Khasnobis: 2006 Kanbur: 2009;
2. On this, see particularly, Sanyal (2007, 2009).
3. This literature is vast and varied. For a sampling, see Castells, 1987; Sen, 1994, 2000; Stiglitz, 2000; Chatterjee, 2008
4. The contribution of primary, secondary and tertiary sectors to Karnataka's GSDP (at 2004–05 constant prices) in 2010–11 has been 16.06 per cent, 28.48 per cent and 55.35 per cent respectively. Agriculture's share in the GSDP halved from 36 per cent in 1993 to 18 per cent in 2005, further to 16 per cent in 2011/12 and to 15.3 per cent in 2012–13. However, employment in agriculture decreased from 65 per cent in1993 to just 61 per cent in 2005. In 2009–10, agriculture's share in employment stood at 56 per cent, (the corresponding figure for all India being 53 per cent). Therefore, the share of agricultural employment in Karnataka declined by only 5 % between 2005 and 2010. While the contribution of industry to GSDP declined from 27 per cent in 2011–12 to 25.9 per cent in 2012–13, that of the service sector has increased significantly, from 56.9 per cent to 58.8 per cent during the same period. (GoK, 2013).
5. See chapter 2 for more discussion.
6. Economic Survey of Karnataka: 2013
7. See Absan and Narain (2007).
8. Several projects such as the Karnataka State Highways Improvement Project, the NABARD-Assisted Rural Infrastructure Development Fund scheme, the Pradhan Mantri Gram Sadak Yojana etc have been in place since the early 2000s. Central to these programmes has been the task of building state highways and rural connectivity roads. During 2012–13, 3710 Km of SHs had been taken up at an estimated cost of Rs. 1423 crores, and a total budget allocation of Rs. 500 crores had been made. The Rural Infrastructure Development Fund has been implemented in five phases. Such projects are supported through government and other agencies (such as World Bank, and the Asian Development Bank) funding.
9. Ministry of Labour, GoK, 2010.
10. Inter-State Migration Workers' Act, 1979
11. The salient features of the Building and Construction Workers Act are the setting up of an Advisory Committee at the central and state levels to advise the governments on issues related to construction workers, provision of registration of each establishment within a period of 60 days from the commencement of work, in order to ensure that builders maintain compliance with the laws; provision for registration of building

workers as beneficiaries under this Act; and importantly, provision for constitution of Building and Other Construction Workers Welfare Board by every State government. By the Cess Act, builders are required to pay a given percentage of the project cost (as Cess) to the Board, through which workers welfare expenditures would be met.

12. Builders are required to pay a certain percentage of the project cost towards the Welfare Board.
13. The first site, Pai Layout, is a newly developed, fairly prosperous neighborhood about half a kilometer off the National Highway-7. The area has developed around the need to provide middle/upper middle class housing, possibly in response to the growth of the IT sector in the adjacent area of Sarjapur Road. The neighborhood is crowded with closely built, medium to high rise apartment buildings. The housing site of construction workers nestles in a plot which is a triangle surrounded by three high rise buildings. This site came up in 2003. There are approximately 350 huts here, on two sides of an open drain. While one side belongs to railway tracks, and therefore the workers occupying this site do not pay any rent, the other side belongs to a private land owner, who charges a rent of Rs. 200–250 per hut.

    The second settlement, in Nagavarpallya, is also in two parts, one on each side of a huge drain, the two parts of the slum are connected by a fragile bamboo bridge. This settlement, composed of around 250 huts, has been in place for about 10–12 years. The land originally belonged to a devasthan and was granted to the priest by the government. It was subsequently sold, but the sale was contested by other claimants, and is currently under litigation. The migrants who occupy the huts continue to pay rent (Rs. 100–150) which is collected by an advocate on behalf of one of the claimants. This exchange is of course an entirely informal one, with no written receipts given to the rent-payer.

    The third site is a settlement provided by a construction company. The Company calls this Labour Colony. Here housing is provided for construction workers who are employed by the company to work on its different projects. This particular colony is situated close to the Ring Road which goes towards Sarjapur Road from the old Airport Road. A deviation from the main road, through almost 5 Kms of completely undeveloped land, leads to an extremely broken mud road with unkept overgrowth on both sides. Private real estate developers have bought up all of this land. However, following the slowdown in the wake of the 2008 economic recession, there has been no construction on this land. In this particular labour colony there were close to 500 huts. At the time of the study, around 300 households were in residence.
14. Typically, construction workers move, through contractors, from project to project. Therefore, they are not identified with any one company or employer. As such it was decided to conduct the study focusing on housing sites where they live, rather than companies/projects on which they work. However, the third site, Labour Colony, houses workers who are employees of a single company. It should be noted that there are essentially two kinds of Labour Colonies colonies. One, provided by the builder on land which the Company owns, where it houses workers who are employed, by the Company, in different construction sites. Secondly, the building company may

provide housing in a site adjacent to a particular construction site, and then move the workers from there to the next site. The second category of housing is obviously much more temporary than the first.

15. IT and ITES developed predominantly in the southern part of the city, thus leading to an enormous spurt in building activities around IT colonies (Whitefield, Electronic City), offices, residences of the new IT workforce, commercial complexes and other supporting infrastructure such as banks, hospitals, schools and so on. In more recent times, there has been an effort to disperse the IT and related industries to other parts of the city, but the south remain the IT hub.
16. The results of the survey are provided in tables 8.1 through 8.13. The findings are presented as percentages, but are indicative of patterns. The same patterns were in fact found in studies of different sets of slums across the city where a large number of construction workers were present (see our Report, Roy Chowdhury, Supriya, K. S. James, B. P. Vani and N. Sivanna (2013) "Migration, Informal Work and Welfare: a Policy Perspective on Karnataka's Cities". ISEC, henceforth *Report*). However, the limitations of generalization on the basis of a small survey are of course recognized.
17. In 2012–13 the minimum wage was revised to Rs. 176.60 for skilled workers and Rs. 172.58 for unskilled workers. Therefore the minimum wage per month for a skilled worker currently is Rs. 4236 for skilled and Rs. 4140 for unskilled workers
18. While the Bangalore Metro Railway Construction Ltd (BMRCL) is a government enterprise, the work of building the metro railway, in different parts of the city, was given out to contractors. In all, about fifteen contracting companies were involved in this massive enterprise which entailed an expenditure of Rs. 10,000 crores in the first phase.
19. For a discussion of Tent Schools for children of migrant construction labour, set up by the Sarva Shikshya Abhigyan, Government of Karnataka, along with case studies of these schools and of students, see *Report.*
20. Although Reddy's election was later challenged and then set aside by the High Court of Karnataka, he was later reinstated by a Supreme Court Ruling.
21. All seven Wards in this constituency have BJP corporators.
22. For a more detailed critical discussion of civil society involvement in urban poverty issues, see Roy Chowdhury (2009 and 2012).
23. This table was arrived based on the monthly per capita income. To compute household income, daily wages was multiplied with the actual number of days worked. This includes all the working members of the household. Then the total monthly household income was divided by total number of members in the household to arrive at per capita income. This per capita income was further classified as percentage of members having income in different categories.

References

Absan, Ahmed and Ashsish Narain. 2007. 'Labour Markes in India: Developmens and Challenges.' In *Job Creation and Poverty Reduction in India*, edited by Saddiq Ahmed. New Delhi: World Bank and Sage.

Aggarwal, Rina. 2012. *Informal Labour, Formal Politics and Dignified Discontent in India.* New York: Cambridge University Press.

Bhattacharya, Rajesh. 'Beyond the Factory: Globalization, Informalization of Production and the New Location of Labour.' *Economic and Political Weekly* 44 (22): 35–44, May.

Castells, Manuel. 1987. 'World Underneath: The Origins, Dynamics and Effects of the Informal Economy.' In *Informal Economy: Studies in Advanced and Less Developed Countries*, edited by Alejandro Portes, M. Castells and L. A. Benton. London: John Hopkins University Press.

Chatterjee, Partha. 2008. 'Democracy and Economic Transformation in India.' *Economic and Political Weekly* 46 (16): 53–62.

Kanbur, Ravi. 2009. 'Conceptualizing Informality: Regulation and Enforcement.' Available at, www.peple.cornell.edu/pages/sk145.

Khasnabis, Basudev Guha, Ravi Kanbur and Elinor Ostrom. eds. 2006. *Linking the Formal and Informal Econom: Concepts and Policies.* Oxford: Oxford University Press.

Madhusudan. 2013. 'A Report on BMRCL Workers.' *KKNSS*. Bangalore.

Prasad K. S. N., K. V. Rao and H. S. Nagesh. 2011. 'A Study on Building and Other Consruction Workers Welfare Schemes and Amenities in Karnataka.' *SASECH Journal* 10 (1), May.

Roy Chowdhury, Supriya. 2012. 'Civil Society and the Urban Poor.' In *Reframing Democracy and Agency in India: Interrogating Political Society*, edited by Ajay Gudavarthy. London: Anthem Press.

Roy Chowdhury Supriya, K. S. James and B. P. Vani. 2013. 'Migration, Informal Work and Welfare: A Policy Perspective on Karnataka's Cities.' *Planning Department, Government of Karnataka*. Bangalore: Institute for Social and Economic Change (mimeo).

Sanyal, Kalyan. 2007. *Rethinking Capitalist Development: Primitive Accumulation, Governmentality and Post Colonial Capitalism.* New Delhi: Routledge.

Sen, Amartya. 1994. *Beyond Liberalization: Social Opportunity and Human Capability.* New Delhi: ISS.

———. 2002. 'Development as Freedom.' New Delhi: Oxford University Press.

Stiglitz, Joseph. 2002. 'Globalization and its Discontents.' London: Penguin Press.

Tietelbaum, Emaanuel. 2011. *Mobilizing Restraint: Democracy and Industrial Conflict in Post Reform South Asia.* Ithaca: Cornell University Press.

Land and Rural Labour

9

Peripheral Agriculture?

Macro and Micro Dynamics of Land Sales and Land Use Changes in the 'Rural' Economy of Kancheepuram

M. Vijayabaskar and Ajit Menon

Introduction

On the outskirts of Chennai, land is increasingly being converted from the agricultural to the non-agricultural, a process that is often mediated by land sales. This phenomenon confirms recent findings that agricultural land markets are active and that institutional constraints on the sale of agricultural lands are less of an impediment than they were twenty years ago. So how do these land markets function and what are the implications of such markets for agriculture? There are two broadly divergent views about agricultural land markets. The first sees agricultural markets as a way to improve efficiency of agriculture. The second situates such markets in wider processes of development and capital accumulation and often associates it with land grabbing both within and outside of agriculture. We argue that while the activation of agricultural land markets is the result of particular priorities of development, there is a need for a more regionally grounded conceptual and empirical analysis that discloses how state policies impact land markets, what the micro-politics of land sales entail and how such land transactions affect different categories of farmers. By doing so, we also hope to interrogate the over-simplistic use of the tag land grab that often conceals more than it reveals.

Our discussion takes place in the context of Tamil Nadu's socio-economic development over the last two decades which has been characterized by two important features. First, the economy has witnessed a higher overall growth rate than that of the country as a whole. Coupled with declining rates in fertility and advances in public access to education and healthcare, this growth has been accompanied by higher per capita incomes and improvements in human development (Dreze and Sen, 2013; Kalaiyarasan, 2014). Second, despite having witnessed high levels of both economic growth and social development, the agricultural sector has been stagnant with one of the lowest rates of growth of output in the country and a decline in the gross cropped area (Bhalla and Singh, 2009). While declining returns to agriculture and the accompanying crisis has been an all-India phenomenon, it has been more acute in Tamil Nadu (Vijayabaskar, 2010). Moreover, despite relatively high growth rates in certain sub-sectors of agriculture in the recent past agricultural income, as well as returns from farming, have declined. Levels of indebtedness are also high among farming households and multiple livelihood strategies common. Given the fact that over 50 per cent of households still remain in rural areas, this suggests that the benefits of overall growth have excluded many (Census of India, 2011).

The declining returns from agriculture have pushed farmers out of farming either by forcing them to leave agricultural land fallow (land use change) or through sales of land. In Tamil Nadu, the gross cropped area has declined from 73.8 lakh hectares in 1970–71 to 58.9 lakh hectares in 2011–12. The amount of land classified under cultivable waste, current fallows and other fallows cumulatively has increased from 21.36 lakhs hectares in 1969–70 to 28.9 lakhs hectares in 2011–12.[1] The share of land devoted to non-agricultural uses has increased from 11.4 per cent in 1970–71 to 16.7 per cent in 2011–12 (GoTN, Season and Crop Reports). This paper attempts to understand the process of change in land use and the implications of land sales. The case study of a cluster of panchayats near the town of Thiruporur in Kancheepuram district, Tamil Nadu, suggests that both land use change and land sales are significant, hence taking issue with many earlier studies that have suggested that significant institutional constraints prevent land use change and that complex interlocked markets act as a barrier to the establishment of a commercialized land market. We build on an emerging literature that has highlighted an increasingly vibrant land market and suggest that such markets are as important to processes of land use change as state-driven land acquisition. We argue that land use change and land sales have increased because sellers and buyers are able to effectively negotiate the rules and regulations pertaining to land use and land sales. This is possible through a network of actors at the local level including panchayat officials, village administrative officers and a range of land market intermediaries broadly categorized as brokers.

Our other main interest is to map out how different types of rural households are involved in land sales and land use changes. By documenting the micro-processes of land sales, the paper builds on existing literature on land transactions but also supplements it through a more detailed disaggregated analysis across operational size holdings and caste. Specifically, we analyse which farmers sell land, for what purposes and at what prices. We argue that land markets, seen in the context of a declining agriculture, dispossess farmers rather than transfer it to its most efficient users. We selected a region near Chennai as significant land use change and land sales have taken place over the last couple of decades as the city expands outwards. The cluster of villages range from a village where agriculture continues to be significant to one in which almost all land has been sold with a bulk of the sold lands remaining fallow or converted for non-agricultural purposes. It also contains a diversity of castes and some variation in terms of land-size holdings and other endowments.

The paper is structured as follows. In the following section (Section 2), we briefly review the literature on agricultural land markets and highlight the recent changes in characteristics of land markets in India and Tamil Nadu. We make a case for a regional approach to agricultural land markets. Section 3 describes the regional context of Tamil Nadu and the political economy of development in the state. We attempt to relate/embed changes in land markets in the emerging growth and welfare regimes of the state: welfarism's need for revenue, growth in informality leading to problems with resource mobilization, declining returns to agriculture and labour transitions. Section 4 profiles the institutional rules that govern the functioning of land markets and pays attention to changes to these rules and how this has enabled brokers to assume an increasingly important role in the working of land markets. In Section 5, we introduce our study location and identify a few important questions that need further exploration. We also describe our methodology. In Section 6, we put forth our major findings with regard to the declining status of agriculture, the actors shaping the nature of land markets, the processes by which land transactions occur and some key features of an emerging post land transfer local economy. This is done with a view to the wider macro political economy.

Rural Land Markets: Drivers and Outcomes

It is generally believed that an active land market, i.e. a market where exchange of rights over use of land is significant, is essential to ensure that lands are put to their most efficient use. The market mechanism, it is argued, will ensure that over time lands will be transferred from those who use this resource inefficiently to those who can utilize it more efficiently. Deininger, Jin and Nagarajan (2009), for example, argue that when imperfections in credit markets, government policies and household characteristics are controlled for, lands are transferred to more efficient cultivators. In a context where there is considerable evidence that small farms are more efficient than large farms (Gaurav and Mishra, 2011), properly functioning land markets are likely to enable a transfer of lands from large inefficient producers to smaller farmers. Baland et al. (2007) broadly corroborate this finding by arguing that land market transactions in Uganda mitigate inequalities in land endowments.

The counter-argument to this is that land markets are rarely free from imperfections for a number of reasons. Significant credit, insurance and land market constraints persist. New forms of inter-locking of credit and output markets have emerged (Gill, 2004). Production and price risks common within the agricultural sector have been accentuated. Morriss and Pandey (2009), moreover, point to a range of imperfections and information asymmetries in land markets as a result of inadequacies in governance institutions. Added to this is the expected appreciation of land values which makes it more difficult for small farmers to buy land given inflated costs. In fact, the reverse might be true, namely that farmers choose to sell land. This could be the case because while land is seen as an important hedge against risk, holding on to land is not always possible for marginal and small farmers as they tend to have relatively less access to formal risk mitigation institutions. Another important reason that marginal and small farmers might not hold on to their land is their lack of capital to invest in land in a context where returns to agriculture are stagnating or declining.

What we know for a fact is that land markets are more active today than they were a decade or more ago. As Chakravorty (2013) demonstrates, there has been an increase in the levels of activity in rural land markets since the late 1990s which has been accompanied by a tremendous increase in rural land prices in the last ten years or so. Rajshekar (2013) too maps this phenomenon not only in villages located on the outskirts of large cities but even in villages located far away from metropoles across the country.[2]

What we also know is that conspicuous consumption increasingly seems to drive these land markets. Chakravorty (2013) argues that India's high income inequality has led to concentration of income in fewer hands and consequently in the buying of property. Such conspicuous consumption by the wealthy at first led to spikes in urban land prices. Chakravorty (*ibid*) calculates that the urban prices in India are one of the highest in the world in relation to the household income, with prices of residential properties in many localities in cities like Chennai having increased five times during the period 1999–2011 (Chakravorty, 2013). Spillover effects of such price rises may partly explain increases in rural land prices.

The rising prices also offer an exit option for farmers to move out of poorly remunerative agriculture. The political class plays an important role in boosting demand and supply. They constitute a growing source of demand given their ability to invest large sums of black money in land. They also seek rents by facilitating conversion of agricultural lands into non-agricultural land paving way for more of the former to enter the market. The expansion of money supply is also a key factor. According to Chakravorty (2013), scarcity of land has co-existed with poverty and hence kept prices low. This led to the land market reaching a 'tipping point' somewhere around 2000 with the growth in income and credit. Until then, buyers could only buy land through down payment of cash which meant that a large number of buyers who had relatively low incomes were excluded. The expansion in credit for housing increased effective demand for land. Given the inelastic supply of land, this resulted in price increases. Expansion of individual incomes including black money and incomes earned by non-resident Indians compounded this demand.

While Chakravorty's (2013) findings appear relevant to our case study area given its situatedness at the periphery of Chennai and the expanding upper middle class in Chennai, it is important to remember that macro-phenomena are shaped by specific regional contexts. There is evidence, for example, to show that land markets in regions with better safety nets tend to promote better investments in agriculture and land compared to regions with poor safety nets that push marginal farmers to sell lands to meet their basic consumption/reproductive requirements. Deininger, Jin and Nagarajan (2009), based on a study by Vijay (2002), also attribute outcomes to levels of non-agricultural development in the region. Higher levels of non-agricultural development imply better functioning credit and factor markets which in turn may reduce the need for distress sales and therefore allow for land markets to ensure better resource allocation.

Another important issue that might shape land transactions is the actual 'meaning' ascribed to land by those who cultivate it. As Li (2009) points out, land as a resource is quite different from other commodities and hence requires active efforts to ensure that it can be mobilized as a resource/commodity. If the meanings/values attached to land are subjective and vary, it is important to understand such specificities and importantly the factors that shape changes in such subjective valuations over time. For example, do rising land values alter such valuations? And if they do, is it true of all actors within a spatial milieu? In India, peasant and tribal resistance to land alienation or acquisition has occurred in some parts of the country while not in others. Even among farming communities that are seemingly open to land sales, there is evidence of resentment among certain segments (Vijayabaskar, 2013). Oya (2013) highlights the importance of context specificity in understanding drivers, i.e. the need to move away from a mono-causal analysis.

There are, therefore, a number of different scenarios possible in terms of how land markets might work in rural areas. First, purchase of lands by non-residents of the village may lead to the rise of absentee-landlordism with implications for agricultural productivity. Second, as Rajshekhar (2013) suggests, land markets may lead to the emergence of a new class of educated cultivators who can move into modern high value cultivation. The third possibility is conversion of lands away from agriculture which no doubt would have implications for long term food security. State intervention has to therefore be aimed at intervening simultaneously on both fronts, i.e. to ensure commodification and to regulate or slow down the process of commodification. Statecraft requires that the exclusions generated by the process of commodification of land do not lead to adverse outcomes for its users even as it seeks to commodify land through a range of policy and juridical instruments.

Finally, it is necessary to look at these processes at a disaggregated scale. As Sarap (1995) points out, different size classes of farming households might sell land for different reasons. Small and marginal farmers tend to sell more to meet basic consumption requirements or to repay debt. Medium and large farmers, on the contrary, sell lands more as part of rural-urban migration strategies, conspicuous consumption, towards consolidating land holdings, for payment of dowry or to invest in agriculture. These processes are likely to lead to a growing concentration of land with consolidation at the top and pauperization at the bottom which is contradictory to the expectations from a well functioning land market (Deninger, 2009). Krishnaji's (1991) study corroborates these claims. However, authors of another study undertaken in Meerut district of western Uttar Pradesh argue that inequality has increased only marginally despite a large number of transactions (Mani and Gandhi, 1994). Importantly, they argue that the role of speculation in land deals is insignificant. However, Firman (2000), based on his study on large scale rural land conversion in the urban periphery in Indonesia, shows how this process aided by policy measures has led to creation of 'idle lands' with implications for agricultural output, income and employment.

The Regional Context: Incentives and Disincentives to Stay in Agriculture

Development in Tamil Nadu is seemingly being pulled in two directions that make it difficult to *a priori* judge the fate of agriculture and the conversion of land away from agriculture. On the one hand, Tamil Nadu has had a strong emphasis on urbanization. It is one of the most urbanized states in the country and its spread of urbanization is wide. Tamil Nadu also has a larger number of towns per unit area compared to other highly urbanized states such as Maharashtra or Gujarat (MIDS, 1988; Rukmani, 1996). This expansive and diffused process of urbanization has paved the way for better rural-urban linkages than in other states. This has also led to an intensification of short-term rural-urban migration, for example daily commutation or seasonal migration to an urban area. Some village resurveys provide micro-level evidence for this phenomenon (Harriss–White and Janakarajan, 1997, Nagaraj, 2006). This process further manifests itself in a 'shortage of labour' observed in the agricultural sector and a consequent shift to less labour intensive crops like coconut. In addition to such labour mobilities, proximity to urban areas is also likely to have land market implications. Dynamism in small towns or large urban agglomerations like Chennai or Coimbatore may induce surges in land prices fostering another set of incentives to convert agricultural land to land for non-agricultural purposes.

Land is also critical today to the growth strategy of the state embedded as it is within a macro-regime of neo-liberal growth. Neo-liberalism requires several measures to be taken to integrate product and factor markets with the global market. Importantly, this phase of development has also involved a degree of state rescaling of responsibilities with the regional/state governments invested with the task of mobilizing resources for investment and growth. This move has led to the rise of what has been referred to as 'competition states', with state governments competing with one another to attract investments by offering a range of concessions. Offer of cheap land has become an important dimension of state policy in this regard. This incentivizes state governments to assemble large parcels of land free of encumbrances in what are seen as 'attractive' locations. Tamil Nadu has been a pro-active state in this regard and has been able to attract several domestic and foreign investments in sectors such as automobiles, electronics and software. To ensure land for such investors, it has embarked on a policy of creating land banks that involve a steady process of land acquisition not tied to any specific project but which add up to substantial lands held under possession by industrial promotion institutions.

Importantly, land has become critical to the state's resource mobilization efforts in other ways as well. In addition to promoting growth, the state requires financial resources to sustain its expanding domain of welfare provisioning. In a context, where the informal sector continues to contribute more to the growth process, resource mobilization by taxing incomes from these growth segments become exceedingly difficult. Taxing land transactions therefore becomes an important source of resource mobilization. Stamp duties have also come to constitute a critical source and as Mukerjee (2013) has shown, the share of stamp duty in the state's own tax revenue had caught up to the national average by 2007–8, being well below the national average from the mid-1990s (2012). Since 2007–08, the state has also revised the guideline value upwards to ensure that it does not lose out on taxes because of transactions registered at a value much lower than the market value. Despite a fall in the total number of land transactions, the government has been able to increase revenue generation on account of the revised guideline values to Rs. 8055.74 crores in 2013–14.[3] A rise in land prices may therefore have contradictory implications for the state. While an increase in land prices may imply that the state has to give out more to the owners when it comes to acquiring land for promoting investments, it may benefit the state in improving its resource base to sustain its welfarist interventions.

A strong welfarist state has meant that rural people are well-protected and hence might not opt to sell their land. Tamil Nadu is often cited in development literature as a model in terms of its ability to combine economic growth with high levels of social welfare provision (Bardhan, 2014; Dreze and Sen, 2013).[4] The high investments in social welfare have been attributed to the fact that political power in the state has been predominantly drawn from lower castes and classes on the back of a long history of political mobilization among these classes (Harriss, 1999; Wyatt, 2013). Electoral competition among the two dominant regional parties has led to the emergence of a strong welfare regime with its universal PDS definitely being the most important. In addition, there are a range of schemes that are targeted at specific population groups like the old aged, widowed, agricultural workers, construction workers, other casual workers, traditional artisanal workers, etc. Land has come to play an important role in this expanding regime. Following the promises made in its election manifesto, the DMK led front that came to power in 2006 initiated a scheme of distributing two acres of waste lands to the families of the landless poor to a limited extent. In addition, governments periodically provide pattas to the poor from lower castes for housing.[5]

Moreover, the quality of urban employment has been far from satisfactory. Tamil Nadu has fared relatively poorly in terms of employment generation in manufacturing (Vijayabaskar, 2014). In addition to declines in employment absorption, there has been a steady erosion of the quality of employment in the sense that much employment generated has been contract-based and casual in nature (Shyam Sundar, 2009). In fact, compared to other industrialized and relatively better off states, the state has witnessed a faster increase in the share of the casual workforce over the last decade (Vijayabaskar, 2014).

It also needs to be remembered that there has been a marginal turnaround in the growth of the agricultural sector in the country and in the state over the last five years particularly in allied sectors like horticulture and livestock rearing. There has also been a marginal increase in the productivity of some of the major crops like paddy and coarse cereals. Both the central and state governments have prioritized the need to revitalize agriculture through a range of measures and schemes to improve the viability of the sector. Finally, in a context of increasing urbanization and improved incomes, it can be expected that the increased demand for high value foods like fruits and vegetables may incentivize farmers to positively respond to this growing demand. The increase in prices of these products over the last three to four years too is likely to provide additional incentives.

In what follows, we will examine which of these 'development pulls' have impacted farmers' behavior more in our selected cluster of villages. Before doing that, we look at the institutional set up that mediates land sales and land use conversion and how that may open up avenues for rent-seeking.

Process and Institutions for Land Sales and Land Conversion

Sale of agricultural lands and land use change are mediated through the institutional structures that govern these processes. Agricultural lands cannot be converted for non-agricultural use without approvals from different departments. When the government acquires lands, such clearances are more easily available to the new buyers. This introduces further distortions and unequal benefits: whereas land exchanged between farmers are valued as agricultural land and hence priced lower, buyers with a clearance for non-agricultural use can resell land at much higher prices. Such a situation opens opportunities for developers who are interested only in seeking rents through land use conversion and sale.

Land sales

Both land sales and land conversion vis-à-vis agricultural land in Tamil Nadu involve a set of processes and government departments. There are no restrictions on land sales, but rather a number of concerns that buyers must address to ensure that the land belongs to the seller and that all legal paper work is in order. The first thing that the buyer needs to make sure of is that the seller has the parent document of the land. This, however, is not enough because the parent document says nothing about the current owner of the land. Hence, after verifying the parent document, the buyer must ensure that the seller is the complete owner of the land. The buyer can get an encumbrance certificate (EC) from the sub-registrar's office. An EC is a certificate that shows that there are no loans or mortgages on the said property and that the property is in the name of the seller. While getting an EC, buyers can also examine the history of transactions pertaining to this land for a period of time.

After getting an EC, the buyer is burdened with a number of other concerns. First, the buyer should see the seller's patta of this land as it is the patta document that indicates ownership. The patta document also tells you whether the property tax has been paid and whether or not there are any dues remaining. It is possible to verify the name of the patta holder in the A-Register which is kept by the Village Administrative Officer (Revenue Department) at the village level. The A-Register gives overall details of all land holdings in the village including the survey numbers, the types of land and the extent of land. The *Chitta* register gives ownership details according to survey number and the *Adangal* register details crops grown according to survey numbers. Finally, the buyer can get a sketch of the concerned land from the Field Measurement Book (FMB).

The buyer, after ensuring that the land is owned by the seller, must then transfer the patta to his name after purchasing the land. After registering the sale deed at the Sub-Registrar's office, the buyer can get a fresh patta from the taluk office. Buyers will have to update the *chitta* and *adangal* registers and also get the latest EC with their name as the rightful new owner.[6]

The sub-registrar's office has a set of guideline values for all land. These guideline values, which give a rough approximation of the value of a given quantity of land, are obtained after an elaborate process of consultation amongst government departments at different levels. The first step is known as *vaakumoolam* or testimony. Vaakumoolam involves discussions with ward members and panchayat members with regard to recent transactions at the village-level. The next step involves discussion between the Block Development Officer, the Agricultural Officer, the Sub-registrar, the Tehsildar and the Assistant Director Guideline, Sub-registrar's office. Collectively, they recommend guideline values for different types of land. This is then taken up at the district level by the Department of Town and Country Planning (DTCP), the District Revenue Officer and the District Collector. Finally, the Deputy Inspector General of Registration 'adjusts' and sets the guideline values.

Guideline values are set according to land use classifications. There are more than fifty different land use classifications but usually within a revenue village at least 10–15 different categories of classification. Lands are generally categorized within the broad categories of irrigated land, rain-fed land and special status land. Within these categories, there are sub-classifications based on soil quality.[7]

Land conversion

The process of converting land from agricultural use to non-agricultural use is a more complicated process as it might require a clearance. While lands classified as 'dry' can be brought under non-agriculture use, conversion of wet lands requires a No Objection Certificate (NOC) from the Collector. The conversion of wet land requires clearance because of the fear that it will impact adversely on agriculture. Consequently, the Department of Town and Country Planning amended the Town and Country Planning Act, 1971, by inserting Section 47(A)[8] which stated that the district collector, not the tehsildar, had to approve the conversion of wet land after inspecting the existing irrigation source, seeing what the present status of cultivation is and ensuring that any conversion would not affect any irrigation or drainage channel. Revenue officials say that there should have been no cultivation on a given piece of land for at least four years. It is also important to note that land conversion can also happen as a result of land acquisition by the government.

The multiple rules and actors involved on paper in land use change and land sales makes it possible for different actors to engage in rent-seeking activities. In other words, given the high transaction costs of land use change and land sales, it is possible for brokers to assume a significant role in these processes and to shape the way land markets work in practice.

Study Area and Methodology

Kancheepuram district, bordering Chennai city, has witnessed significant land use change over the last decade. The most notable change has been in terms of net sown area and current and other fallow. The net sown area has declined from 150,036 ha or 33.85 per cent of total area in 2000–01 to 118,635 ha or 26.8 per cent of total area in 2010–11. Consequently, the area under current and other fallow has increased from 10,054 ha (2.3 per cent) and 62,348 ha (14.1 per cent) to 32,802 ha (7.4) and 66, 906 (15.1) for the same period.[9]

Our case study is located in a cluster of four panchayats in Kancheepuram district, Manamathy, Amoor, Kunnapattu and Paiyanur, near Thiruporur, a town located approximately 50 km from Chennai. Thiruporur is situated on the Old Mahabilipuram Road, a corridor of industrial and service sector growth. While pockets of agriculture remain, there is evidence to suggest that push factors away from agriculture are in play as farmers face significant constraints in terms of water availability and growing input costs that are making agriculture increasingly unviable. State policies aimed at promoting the industrial and service sector, on the other hand, act as potential pull factors away from agriculture for farmers who are no longer able to sustain agricultural livelihoods.

The population of the four panchayats is 12,447. The four panchayats are comprised mostly of marginal and small farmers and include predominantly Vanniyars, Scheduled Castes and Mudaliars. The Scheduled Caste population is 6,271, i.e around 50% of the total population. The cluster of panchayats represents a mosaic of land uses: panchayats where agriculture continues to be significant and those where most land is no longer under cultivation. It provided us, therefore, an opportunity to analyse land use changes, and land transactions and the reasons behind them.

We interviewed a total of 173 households with two main purposes in mind: (1) to understand the changing role of agriculture vis-à-vis household income and (2) to capture the nature of and reasons for land use changes/land sales. We tried to the extent possible to select a representative sample across the four panchayats in terms of caste and operational holdings both amongst those who have sold land and those who have not. The villages we studied, as mentioned above, comprised mostly of marginal and small farmers (less than 2.5 ha) which is also reflective of the larger state-wide patterns. Less than ten per cent of the households surveyed owned more than five acres of land. We also tried to capture the diversity of possible household scenarios, i.e. families who continued to cultivate despite poor monsoons over the last few years, families who did not cultivate land but retained their land, families who had sold land and bought land elsewhere and families who sold land for 'household purposes'. Finally, we also spoke to a number of landless households who were more predominant in Manamathy and Paiyanur.

Our other main aim was to understand the process of land sales. Who were the main agents involved at different scales in facilitating land sales? Who were the main buyers of land and what were their main reasons for buying land? This would supplement our analysis of the political economy of land transactions. However, we were not able to speak to buyers of land as the sellers of land were not aware of who had bought their land and brokers were not willing to reveal that information.

Discussion

Policy induced distress in agriculture

Most of the households we interviewed either had left their land fallow this current year (2014) or had cultivated far less land than they had ten years ago. Only 19.8 acres were reported to be under cultivation by the respondent households at present (2014) compared to 128 acres ten years ago. There are a number of reasons for this. First, sources of irrigation have run dry. On the one hand, this is because the monsoon has been under par for the last three years and hence open wells and borewells are either empty or the water table has dropped significantly. On the other hand, while some of the agricultural land is in the command area of tanks, these tanks have for the most part silted due to neglect by the departments in charge of maintenance. Also there has been extensive sand mining in tank beds. Second, labour shortages are reported by cultivators in the area. Farmers told us that though NREGA wages are not high as compared to agriculture, many labourers chose to engage in it as it required little work. Youngsters, on the other hand, had preferences for non-agricultural work. The household livelihood profile, in other words, has diversified to a considerable extent. Many go to work in pharmaceutical firms, hospitals, educational institutions and factories in peri-urban Chennai as unskilled or semi-skilled workers. Some work as skilled manual workers in the construction sector and also as drivers. Firms have also mobilised female workers from the villages by providing commuting facilities in 'company buses or vans'. In a scheduled caste colony, about twenty women work as cleaning staff in a nearby hospital. Though the wages are not high, it offers a secure source of income. Older residents dependent on agriculture however find it difficult to find employment outside agriculture. While a few work as security staff in nearby institutions, most continue to rely on agricultural coolie work whereas women tend to take up NREGS work when available.

Having said this, 28.4 per cent of all households we spoke to continued to report agricultural labour as the primary source of income. This was highest (38.9 per cent) in Manamathy where agriculture was more prominent. Some of the bigger farmers who are able to invest more to deepen borewells are still able to cultivate and hence require labour. These bigger farmers include farmers who have resided in the area for a long time and others who have more recently bought land in the area. Agriculture, therefore, remains viable for those who have more land and capital available. Most of the bigger landowners in this region are Vanniyars and Mudaliars though there are also a few scheduled caste households, mostly from outside, who have significant operational holdings.

Even as agrarian distress driven by policy failures have incentivized farmers to sell their lands, land sales in turn create new problems for those continuing to work in agriculture. Fencing off bought lands by non-locals prevents access to common property resources like grazing lands. Fencing in a couple of instances has prevented farmers from being able to get the harvester or any machine into the farm for working the land. Even getting bullocks access to cultivated land was an issue in one case. Another important problem is access to labour. When more households were involved in agriculture, there was enough employment within the village and farmer households often practiced labour sharing. With the decline in agriculture, more labour exited agriculture posing additional problems for labour access. Further, sinking of deep borewells by non agricultural buyers has led to further reduction in water availability for those continuing to work in agriculture. Finally, there is a clear decline in collective action for ensuring proper common asset maintenance such as that of the village tanks. This is clearly visible in the silting of tanks, non-maintenance of bunds and channels and encroachments along such channels.

Land sales

As highlighted above, large areas of agricultural land in our study area remain uncultivated. Equally striking is the fact that 42.8 per cent of the sampled households have sold land in the recent past. Most of these sales took place from 2004 onwards. According to key informants, till 2004–05, there were hardly any market transactions with outsiders and in fact few sales as a whole. What did exist to some extent was a lease market. Approximately 10 per cent of the interviewed households had previously leased in land. Leasing in of land was more prominent in Paiyanur and Amoor. And a rare case existed where local small farmers bought land from four marginal farmers who had migrated to work as labourers in Chennai.

For the most part, those who sold land did so before the boom in land prices took place. Most sales occurred between 2004 and 2009. Land was sold at prices ranging from approximately 9,000 rupees a cent to 16,000 rupees a cent. Today land in the same area is being sold at one lakh per cent. The larger sellers of land invariably sold a part of their total landholdings and remained in the village whereas marginal farmers sold all their land barring their homesteads. There are clear differences in the bargaining power that marginal farmers bring to the land market as compared to small and medium farmers. Depletion of incomes from agriculture has led to distress induced diversification into informal employment in the non-farm sectors. Incurring of debts due to ill health, marrying off of daughters and at times payment of fees for children's higher education are some of the reasons small farmers sell lands. Relatively better off farmers are better placed to negotiate because of their ability to wait. We came across instances of farmers who sold lands more than a year after the first offer from a non-local buyer. In fact, some farmers continue to wait to sell some of their lands which they presume are likely to get higher prices in future. A couple of medium farmers who had refused to part with their lands were offered land parcels in another part of the village in addition to money by the buyer. A medium farmer in Kunnapattu had also bought lands from neigbouring marginal farmers and then sold them as a consolidated holding to a non-local buyer.

Buyers of land were mostly from Chennai who saw in land avenue for investment. These buyers often sell the land after a few years during which period the land values would have appreciated given the new demands for land. However, there are differences in the nature of buyers. Some are institutional – property developers, real estate firms that buy and sell lands to others who require lands, educational institutions and wealthy individuals including NRIs. Brokers report demand from several wealthy households from the city and at times from other places too. The internet has allowed brokers to reach out to distant buyers including those residing outside the country. Farmland prices appear to be highly correlated with inflation but do not respond to returns from other investments. Investment in farmland is therefore seen as a hedge against inflation and also a means to reduce portfolio risks (Fairbairn, 2014). In the case of land, though investment for speculative purposes happens, its appreciation in value is based on its returns when put to productive uses. However, even non-financial investors in land are increasingly seeking to tap into its income streams as a financial source rather than as productive source.

Our case study area also encompasses an industrial park known as Japan City. Land for this park was bought directly from farmers and consolidated by brokers who then sold the land to the industrial consortium. In other words, the provision of land for industry took place more through consolidation of small holdings as opposed to through land acquisition.

The above brief narrative of land sales in our study area suggests that land transactions have not been about improving the efficiency of agriculture but rather about speculative investment and in a few instances for claimed activity expansion of firms. Importantly, most buyers have left their land vacant and continue to live in the city. Presumably, over time they might sell the land and invest further south on the Old Mahabilipuram Road. The sharp increases in land prices, therefore, appear to have been primarily due to demand for land from real estate and other urban actors from Chennai city. In other words, value of land is increasingly determined by its location rather than by its productivity.

Farmers, on the other hand, while benefiting to some extent from the spike of prices when agriculture was down, have witnessed the price of land soar through the roof and the benefits accrue more to these urban buyers. Moreover, the currently high prices appear to prevent farmers from being able to consolidate their holdings into economically viable units. In one of the villages, Amoor, out of nearly 2,000 acres of cultivable land, key informants say that less than 100 acres continue to remain with local owners. Traditionally, the uneconomical size of agricultural landholdings was attributed to the lack of adequate development of lease and sales markets. However, in these villages, despite sales markets being active, there is not a single inter-village transaction that has taken place among the households surveyed during the last decade. The villages are dominated by marginal and small farmers with many of them holding not more than 1–2 acres of land, with some of them even owning less than an acre. Clearly the size of land on average is smaller than the threshold size. Small and marginal farmer interviewees revealed that the increases in land prices have made land unaffordable.

Simultaneous to the land sales market booming, the lease market has gradually declined. Key informants reported the presence of leasing markets till about 15 years ago. At present, however, leasing markets have virtually ceased to function. None of the households surveyed leased in lands though a few mentioned they had leased in land ten years ago.

The factors underlying the decline in leasing markets are to be sought in regional politics and partly in the regional agricultural sector. Over the last 15 years or so, there has been active political mobilization of Parayars, the numerically largest scheduled caste community in north eastern Tamil Nadu. Viduthalai Chiruthaikal, the party that has been the backbone of this mobilization, has a substantial presence in some of the field villages. This mobilisation is held to have worked against leasing according to some key informants in the village. Landowners are wary of leasing out as they feel that tenant farmers by virtue of their political strength and what are perceived as allowances in tenancy reform laws may prevent any efforts on their part to take control over their lands. Traditional forms of labour control via caste hegemony that allowed for labour to be tied to certain farming households no longer holds true in these villages and this has increased the uncertainty around returns through leasing. In terms of demand, scheduled caste and Vanniyar households do not find it attractive enough to lease in lands given the declining returns and uncertainty in agriculture. The other factor that contributes to this lack of interest in farming is the growing demand for labour outside agriculture in the region.

Skewed gains and different logics across farm sizes

Gains are also skewed across farm size. Most small and medium farmers do not sell all of their lands. Rather they sell a portion and retain a portion where agriculture continues to be practiced. The average size of lands sold amongst the interviewees in our study villages was 1.8 acres. Some farmers have started growing vegetables instead of paddy. But this requires family labour and those with smaller families or those households where members have already moved out of agriculture substantially cannot invest in this. Else in the case of some small and medium farmers, they sell lands in these villages and buy lands in more interior villages. This sale for purchase of land elsewhere has led to the creation of secondary land markets. Prices in these villages are likely to have increased as a result of such purchases. During the course of our fieldwork we also came across such farmers who were holding on to their lands expecting better prices. Importantly, relatively better off farmers are better placed to wait and sell their lands. In the case of marginal farmers, as mentioned above, they tend to sell all their lands and retain only a homestead plot or move to the cities permanently.

The creation of secondary land markets is partly driven by taxation laws. Income from sale of land will be taxed if it is not reinvested back in land within a period of six months from the period of sale.[10] This has brought along with it a shift from peasant cultivation to absentee landlordism. Medium farmers who were cultivating their lands now lease lands in distant villages. They say they seldom visit these villages or take interest in the returns from agriculture. Importantly, farmers with slightly larger land holdings are able to invest the money obtained from land sales in their children's education.

Engineering and medicine continue to be perceived of as the most prospective of educational avenues, and educational institutions to cater to these subjects have expanded in the state over the last two decades primarily through privatization. Fifty per cent of the admissions are through payment of fees which vary depending upon the reputation of the colleges which in turn depend on past placement records. Hence farmers who get larger amounts by virtue of larger farm size holdings tend to afford better colleges. On the other hand, in many scheduled caste and poorer Vanniyar households, youth tend to choose vocational streams like ITI or Diploma courses. Career prospects for these streams are clearly lower than that of professional education mentioned above. Differential access to land therefore perpetuates inequities in the non-agrarian landscapes.

Information, power symmetries and asymmetric gains: the benefits for brokers

When lands are bought, sellers are never aware of the uses to which the lands are going to be put to. Often they do not even know who the ultimate buyer is. Buyers tend to employ real estate firms to negotiate on their behalf. For example, ECC, a construction firm, bought 2,400 acres of land, which included lands from two of the panchayats that we studied. However, ECC did not directly negotiate for this land. The face of the company as far as the villagers who sold the lands were concerned was a family of three men, one of whom was a lawyer. This group, we realized later when we did fieldwork in another panchayat, has been involved in identifying local intermediaries in different panchayats in the district for purchase of land. They use local intermediaries, such as panchayat presidents, to aggregate large parcels of land. This is a gradual process and often gets completed over a period of two to three years.

One of the panchayat presidents, who comes from a most backward caste and from a poor family, was not aware of the purpose for which ECC required lands in his village. But he feels that he is really privileged to have been identified amidst other well to do presidents by such big players. ECC and a few other institutions have also bought lands in villages adjoining the field area a couple of years ago. According to key informants, since they are politically connected, they get prior information of major projects. They are also aware of agricultural lands that are identified by the government for conversion. With this access to information they acquire lands even before conversion or major projects are announced. When the state seeks to attract productive investments or when large private actors seek land, they step in with offers of large parcels of contiguous land. The government gives them market rates which are easily three to four times more than the prices at which they had bought the land. However, such lands are not offered merely for productive investments. They also feed into large scale real estate/housing projects by leading developers which are a component of megaproject development like SEZs. Clearly, access to information by virtue of proximity to political power is critical to their accumulation through rents. Once again, gains are skewed towards the politically and economically powerful actors. The political class too gains across these multiple layers of transactions. Announcement of major development projects therefore are accompanied by gains across different levels of party hierarchy. When land holders are reluctant to sell their lands, brokers hint at the possibility that the government may take over their lands at prices lower than what they are offering.

At the local level, residents/farmers who are either economically more powerful or politically better connected are most likely to act as brokers. One broker that we spoke to held a low level position in the Pattali Makkal Katchi, a party with a strong base in this region. He also had good connections with the VAO. Another was a medium sized farmer who was again seen to be an influential person. They are paid two per cent commission and are responsible for getting the *chitta*, *adangal* and EC for the buyer. Also when there are disputes, or when farmers are demanding more, they negotiate on behalf of the buyer. The role of local intermediaries is, therefore, two-fold. Given the predominance of small and marginal holdings, there is a need to transact with a large number of sellers. Even otherwise, given the poor titling of records in India, transaction costs of verifying titles are high. Intermediaries along with the local political leaders and lower level bureaucrats are essentially required for land aggregation and ensuring of clear titles.

Also brokers, as mentioned above, indirectly threaten farmers by telling them that if they don't sell, the government may take over the land later. Market-based transactions are mediated by local intermediaries, elites, developers and political actors who work the markets to withhold information and limit compensation. Clearly, market based mechanisms are not neutral instruments but rather favour powerful actors who work them to ensure larger gains.

Elements of the emerging local economy

Even prior to land sales, households have been diversifying their livelihood options in ways that merge them into the urban economy of Chennai or Thiruporur. For most marginal farmer households, the dominant non-agricultural jobs include construction labourers, sculptors, fence-fixers toll booth operators, drivers, company supervisors, painters, plumbers and electricians. Some of them are also involved in illegal sand mining from the tank beds. While such jobs are mostly confined to male members of the household, women from sample households took up housekeeping and unskilled jobs in pharmaceutical firms, educational institutions, hospitals and software parks not too far from their villages. The firms or the labour contractors arrange vehicles for women from the villages to commute to work.

Clearly, all the jobs are informal in nature and temporary or casual without any degree of employment security. Most male respondents in the age group 18–30 do not have employment all through the month. Many who work in the construction sector for instance have on average only two weeks of work a month. Electricians and plumbers again alternate between intense contract work and periods of non-work. However casual wage rates in nominal terms have increased considerably and incomes vary between 10,000–20,000 per month. Women employees are employed through contractors and get paid not more than Rs. 6,000–9,000 per month. Their jobs are invariably dead end jobs with few prospects of vertical mobility or acquisition of skills that allow for inter-firm mobility. With land sales going up in the region, peasant families are increasingly being incorporated as labour in the urban economy. There is another important change. Earlier, availability of land for cultivation meant that any setbacks in the urban economy could be compensated by returns from agriculture, however meager. In turn, incomes from the non-agricultural sector would feed into investment requirements in the agricultural sector. Land sales ensure the severance of such linkages. The construction boom in this part of the state and the widening social security net have meant, however, that the sellers do not necessarily perceive the growing insecurity of their livelihoods.

Another important dimension of the emerging local economy is the spurt in income opportunities through rents. We have already highlighted the rent seeking opportunities that opened up because of the brokering and mediating of land transactions. In addition, farmers who have sold their lands have invested in not only farm lands but also bought lands in Thiruporur where they have built small tenements for rental. In addition, some households reported that they rented out JCBs, harvesters, tractors, transplanters and transport vehicles like cars and vans. A few families with connections in the bureaucracy and political parties have moved into real estate activity. Key informants also mentioned that a few people have moved into informal money lending. Some of the older farmers survive on income from interest though many of them said that their livelihoods have become less sustainable in a post-sales environment. A few others have sunk borewells and earn income by supplying water for firms that have come up near these villages.

Conclusion

Looking at factors that induce land use change, Lambin and Meyfroidt (2010) suggest a conceptual dichotomy between endogenous factors, i.e. changes to attributes/factors within the land-ecology system such as depletion of critical ecological resources such as water or soil quality and exogenous changes to the larger socio-economic milieu external to the particular set of lands under consideration. Some examples of the latter include urbanization and generation of new uses of land and labour as a result. While literature has focused on larger macro-level factors such as the need for global capital to seek new outlets for accumulation, the response of local actors with different endowments to these changes have not been examined adequately (Hall, 2013). We suggest an approach that takes into account these two sets of factors and the nature of interactions between them. Importantly, we highlight that even endogenous factors are shaped by policy shifts that have led to neglect of agricultural growth. Hence, incorporation of institutional variables is critical to understanding or explaining land use changes and working of land markets.

What we have also tried to illustrate is that discussions about land grabs need to take into account the fine line between coercive and voluntary transactions. At one level, when farmers sell their land it is significantly different than when the state acquires lands to promote private capital. At another level, however, we have illustrated that small and marginal farmers often have little option but to sell their lands when their economic situation deteriorates over time. Moreover, the economic situation of farmers seems to have deteriorated as a result of state neglect of agriculture be it in terms of poor maintenance of tanks or in failing to make agriculture more remunerative vis-à-vis other occupations.

We have also tried to highlight how participation in land markets is very much linked to the prevailing nature of policy interventions and specificities of the agrarian situation. Land markets have led to fallowing of land in the short run and to conversion of land into a speculative asset in the medium term.

Our fieldwork indicates that while income inequality may generate demand for rural land as argued by Chakravorty (2013), this demand in turn appears to generate new inequities. Such inequities are tied to size of land holdings, access to information and access to powerful political actors. Credit markets appear to be lacking for meeting the reproductive requirements of marginal and small farmers pushing them into land sales. Relatively well endowed farming households on the other hand are able to negotiate better terms and reinvest in land, other assets and human capital. Local actors often appear to willingly participate in the emerging land economy. However, respondents above the age of 40 expressed concern about the loss of land for agriculture and lack of work for them outside agriculture. Age based differences in response to land markets are therefore evident.

Our fieldwork also reveals the emergence of a livelihood structure that is based on rental incomes and casual insecure work. While macro-economic studies point out how the rise of rentier incomes may undermine incentives for productive investments, the implications of such a local economy for productive linkages are not clear. The growing reliance on casual urban employment may however lead to new livelihood insecurities that cannot be offset by the relatively low returns from agriculture.

Acknowledgement

We would like to thank P. Selvam, B. Nagaraj, R. Ramya and K. V. Preetha for their diligent fieldwork and the many people in our study area who gave us time and shared their thoughts with us. The research was funded by the State Planning Commission, Land Use Board, Government of Tamil Nadu. We alone, however, are responsible for the arguments put forward.

Endnotes

1. For details: http://www.tn.gov.in/dear/4.%20Agriculture.pdf accessed on 7/4/2013 and Season and Crop Report, Tamil Nadu 2011–12.
2. For details: http://articles.economictimes.indiatimes.com/2013–11–12/news/43981081_1_farmland-prices-rs-10-lakh-land-acquisition accessed on September 18, 2014.
3. For details: http://timesofindia.indiatimes.com/city/chennai/Revenue-rises-but-land-deals-in-Tamil-Nadu-hit-a-seven-year-low/articleshow/39318180.cms accessed on September 24, 2014.
4. For details: http://twocircles.net/2013jan07/only_high_growth_does_not_make_gujarat_model_pranab_bardhan.html#.VCJIuWfbaho accessed on September 24, 2014.
5. For details: http://www.tn.gov.in/scheme/data_view/43801 accessed on October 6, 2015.

6. Much of this information related to process with regard to purchasing of land was obtained through multiple discussions with brokers in Thiruporur and Chennai.
7. Interview with clerk at the Sub-Registrar's Office, Government of Tamil Nadu, at Thiruporur on the July 2, 2014.
8. For details: http://www.tn.gov.in/tcp/Amendment_47A.pdf accessed on October 6, 2015.
9. This data was provided to us by an independent researcher who is collecting and tabulating data for all the blocks in Tamil Nadu for the State Planning Commission.
10. This information was provided by a lawyer who wishes to remain anonymous. Interview took place on the March 29, 2014.

References

Baland, J-M., F. Gaspart, J. P. Platteau and F. Place. 2007. 'The Distributive Impact of Land Markets in Uganda.' *Economic Development and Cultural Change* 55 (2): 283–311.

Bardhan, Pranab K. 1980. 'Interlocking Factor Markets and Agrarian Development: A Review of Issues.' *Oxford Economic Papers*, 82–98.

Bhaduri, A. 1986. 'Forced Commerce and Agrarian Growth.' *World Development* 14 (2): 267–272.

Bhalla G. S. and G. Singh. 2009. 'Economic Liberalisation and Indian Agriculture: A State-Wise Analysis.' *Economic and Political Weekly* 44 (52): 34–40.

Chakravorty, S. 2013. *The Price of Land: Acquisition, Conflict, Consequence*. New Delhi: Oxford University Press.

Centre for Agricultural and Rural Development Studies (CARDS). 2009. *National Agriculture Development Programme: State Agriculture Plan-Tamil Nadu, Volumes I and II*. Coimbatore: Tamil Nadu Agricultural University.

Deininger, K., S. Jin and H. K. Nagarajan. 2009. 'Determinants and Consequences of Land Sales Market Participation: Panel Evidence from India.' *World Development* 37 (2): 410–421.

Deininger, K. and G. Feder. 2001. 'Land Institutions and Land Markets.' *Handbook of Agricultural Economics* 1: 288–331.

Fairbairn, M. 2014. '"Like gold with yield": Evolving Intersections between Farmland and Finance.' *The Journal of Peasant Studies* 41 (5): 777–795.

Firman, T. 2000. 'Rural to Urban Land Conversion in Indonesia during Boom and Bust Periods.' *Land Use Policy* 17 (1): 13–20.

Gaurav, S. and S. Mishra. 2011. 'Size-Class and Returns to Cultivation in India: A Cold Case Reopened.' *Working Paper No. 2011–027*. Mumbai: Indira Gandhi Institute of Development Research.

Gill, A. 2004. 'Interlinked Agrarian Credit Markets: Case Study of Punjab.' *Economic and Political Weekly*, 3741–3751.

Government of Tamil Nadu. 1971. *Season and Crop Report 1970–71*. Chennai: Department of Economics and Statistics.

———. 2012. *Season and Crop Report 2011–12*. Chennai: Department of Economics and Statistics.

Hall, D. 2013. 'Primitive Accumulation, Accumulation by Dispossession and the Global Land Grab.' *Third World Quarterly* 34 (9): 1582–1604.

Harriss, J. 1999. 'Comparing Political Regimes across Indian States: A Preliminary Essay.' *Economic and Political Weekly*, 3367–3377.

Institute of Development Alternatives. 2004. *Livelihood Assessment Report* (mimeo). Chennai.

Kalaiyarasan, A. 2014. 'A Comparison of Developmental Outcomes in Gujarat and Tamil Nadu.' *Economic and Political Weekly* 49 (15): 55–63.

Krishnaji, N. 1991. 'Land Market-On Dispossession of Peasantry.' *Indian Journal of Agricultural Economics* 46 (3): 328–334.

Lambin, E. F. and P. Meyfroidt. 2010. 'Land Use Transitions: Socio-Ecological Feedback Versus Socio-Economic Change.' *Land Use Policy* 27: 108–118.

Li, Murray Tania. 2009. 'Exit from Agriculture: A Step Forward or a Step Backward for the Rural Poor?.' *The Journal of Peasant Studies* 36 (3): 629–36.

Mani, G. and V. P. Gandhi. 1994. 'Are Land Markets Worsening the Land Distribution in Progressive Areas? A Study of Meerut District in Western Uttar Pradesh.' *Indian Journal of Agricultural Economics* 49 (3): 330–338.

Madras Institute of Development Studies. 1988. *Tamil Nadu Economy: Performance and Issues*. Company, New Delhi: Oxford and IBH Publication.

Morris, Sebastian and Ajay Pandey. 2009. 'Land Markets in India: Distortions and Issues.' In *India Infrastructure Report 2009: Land – A Critical Resource for Infrastructure*, 13–19. 3i Network, New Delhi: Oxford University Press.

Mukherjee, V. 2012. 'Determinants of Stamp Duty Revenue in Indian States.' Project Report submitted to Centre for Training and Research in Public Finance and Policy. Kolkata: Jadavpur University.

Nagaraj, K. 2006. *Tamil Nadu Economy: Contours of Change – A Secondary Data Exploration* (mimeo). Chennai: Madras Institute of Development Studies.

Oya, C. 2013. 'The Land Rush and Classic Agrarian Questions of Capital and Labour: A Systematic Scoping Review of the Socioeconomic Impact of Land Grabs in Africa.' *Third World Quarterly* 34 (9): 1532–1557.

Patel, Raj. 2009. 'Food Sovereignty: What does Food Sovereignty Look Like?.' *The Journal of Peasant Studies* 36 (3): 663–706.

Rajshekar, M. 2013. 'Great Rural Land Rush: 3 to 100-Fold Rise in Farm Land Prices May Not Bode Well'. *The Economic Times*, November 12.

Ramaswamy, K. V. 2007. 'Regional Dimension of Growth and Employment.' *Economic and Political Weekly* 41 (49): 47–56.

Rukmani R. 1996. 'Factors Underlying High Dispersal of Towns in Tamil Nadu.' *Review of Development and Change* 1 (1): 113–125.

Sarap, K. 1995. 'Land Sale Transactions in an Indian Village: Theories and Evidence.' *Indian Economic Review* 30 (2): 223–240.

Sarap, K. 1998. 'On the Operation of the Land Market in Backward Agriculture: Evidence from a Village in Orissa, Eastern India.' *The Journal of Peasant Studies* 25 (2): 102–130.

Swaminathan, M. 1991. 'Gainers and Losers: A Note on Land and Occupational Mobility in a South Indian Village, 1977–1985.' *Development and Change* 22 (2): 261–277.

Vijay, R. 2002. 'Land Market Activity: A Framework.' *Indian Journal of Agricultural Economics* 57 (4): 714–721.

Vijayabaskar, M. 2010. '"Saving Agricultural Labour from Agriculture": Special Economic Zones and the Politics of Silence in Tamil Nadu.' *Economic and Political Weekly* 45 (6): 36–43.

Vijayabaskar, M. 2013. 'Tamilnadu: The Politics of Silence.' *Power, Policy and Protest: Politics of India's Special Economic Zones*, edited by R. Jenkins, L. Kennedy and P. Mukhopadhyaya. New Delhi: Oxford University Press.

Vijayabaskar, M. 2014. *Income, Poverty and Employment.* Draft background paper prepared for the Tamil Nadu Human Development Report.

Wyatt, A. K. J. 2013. 'Combining Clientelist and Programmatic Politics in Tamil Nadu, South India.' *Commonwealth and Comparative Politics* 51 (1): 27–55.

10

Infrastructures of Growth, Corridors of Power

The Making of the SEZ Act 2005

Preeti Sampat

Introduction

The Special Economic Zones (SEZs) Act 2005 was approved by both houses of the Parliament of India in two days, with little discussion and zero dissent. Introduced as policy by the Hindu-nationalist Bhartiya Janata Party-led National Democratic Alliance (NDA) in 2000, the SEZ Act was enacted by the centre-right Congress Party-led United Progressive Alliance (UPA) which at the time was supported by the Communist Party of India (Marxist).[1] Like Free Trade or Export Processing Zones (EPZs) in the Americas, South-East Asia or China, SEZs in India aimed at creating export-led enclave economies with tax and duty concessions. Ostensibly premised on the Chinese model (that comprises seven large state-owned SEZs with clearly-defined targeted incentives for industries), India's 2005 law went much further. Expanding the existing 11 EPZs model, it envisioned no ceilings on the numbers and sizes of SEZs; eschewed targeted incentives for blanket concessions; and its comprehensive scope included most economic activities—mining, agriculture, manufacturing and services. By April 2011, in six years, the Government of India (GoI) formally approved a whopping 584 SEZs (with 377 notified;[2] GoI, 2011a). This number surprisingly rose from 366 formally approved (142 notified) in August 2007 (GoI, 2007; Table 10.1 and Map 10.1) – the 'global financial meltdown' did evidently little to dampen the enthusiasm for SEZs in India.

In stark contrast, in less than two years of enactment, tenacious resistance against SEZs erupted across the country from peasants' and citizens' groups,[3] forcing the central and state governments to respond variously with violent repression, tactical reversal, negotiation and deference. In Gujarat, Maharashtra, Goa, Karnataka, Tamil Nadu, Andhra Pradesh, Odisha, West Bengal and Haryana, land and resource acquisition for SEZs emerged as a central contention between state forces, corporate developers and peasants' and citizens' groups. In the ensuing furor, in March 2007, 14 people died in police firing protesting land acquisition of 25,000 acres for Indonesian Salim SEZ in Nandigram in West Bengal. As violence escalated in November 2007 with an unclear number of additional people dead (accounts vary from 7 to 100), the state government eventually moved the SEZ out of the area. Similarly, under immense pressure from widespread protests by peasants' and citizens' groups, the Chief Minister of Goa announced a 'new year gift' to the people of Goa on 31st December 2007, and cancelled all 15 SEZs in the state.[4] Three SEZs were notified, two with construction underway; but by 2009, Goa's SEZ policy was officially revoked. By November 2009, one of the most ambitious SEZs on the outskirts of Mumbai city, the Mumbai SEZ, failed to secure even a quarter of the 11,300 hectares of land approved for it, and officially ceased operations. The resistance to (largely medium and large) SEZs as it unfolded across the country from 2007–2010, sent the message loud and clear to the policy establishment – SEZs were bad policy, people would not give up their lands; SEZs had to go.

As they became political hot potatoes, the year 2011 saw a near freeze on the enthusiasm for new SEZs; there were no new proposals and requests for withdrawal of approved SEZs registered a rise.[5] By January 2015, the number of approved SEZs had not just stagnated but reduced from 584 in 2011 to 491 in 2014 (GoI, 2014; Table 10.1) with every Board of Approval meeting for SEZs receiving requests for more withdrawals from developers. SEZs were widely portrayed as failures and victims of the UPA's 'unstable policy environment' by industry representatives and in the media. Partly, this is because of the new Minimum Alternate Tax levied by the Finance Ministry in 2011. Significantly, the Commerce Ministry's decision to disallow forcible acquisition of land for SEZs in 2007, and the decision by several state governments to discontinue any land acquisition for SEZs has been a big blow for developers who sought to institute large SEZs with government support.

Opposition to the institution of SEZs by peasants' and citizens' groups influenced their legal framework. The introduction of a 5000 hectare ceiling on SEZs in 2009 (later revoked); economic processing area requirement revisions from the initial 25 per cent of total land acquired to 33 per cent and to the eventual 50 per cent; as well as a critical order of the Commerce Department forbidding compulsory acquisition of land for SEZs were the result of anti-SEZ protests (GoI, 2009a).

Table 10.1 Approved and Operational SEZs in India

	2007	*2011*	*2014*
Formally Approved	366	584	491
Notified	142	377	370
Operational	Figure unavailable	133	196

Source: http://sezindia.nic.in

This paper analyzes the behind-the-scenes law-making process of SEZs. The formal SEZ law-making process has involved several Ministries, predominantly Commerce and Finance, that have been at loggerheads over them. 'Soft law'[6] settings (by which I refer to industry-bureaucrat conclaves and recommendations by industry in the form of submissions or reports), were powerful influences on the policy framework. Extra-legal influences, like the protests in SEZ areas, influenced political 'course-correction,' but beyond the pale of evidence and shadowing formal and soft law circuits, rumors and gossip point to bureaucratic turf-wars, Ministerial rivalries and high-level corruption as major extra-legal forces shaping the law. These circuits of power have determined the trajectory of SEZ infrastructures in India.

The materiality of infrastructure allows for the possibility of exchange and circulation of goods, ideas, waste, power, people and finance, among other things; and also signifies aesthetic and affective desire and possibility (cf. Larkin, 2013). Infrastructure also signifies paradigms of development. In the post-liberalization period in India there has been a marked shift from the post-independence model of state-led investments in infrastructure, to private investments or Public Private Partnership models (Goldman, 2011; Nilsen, 2010). These 'infrastructures of growth' facilitate the circuits of capital with a deeply embedded (and hackneyed) model of trickle-down development. At the scale envisioned in policy, growth infrastructures fundamentally reconfigure relationships with land and resources[7] – moving people away from agrarian mores and other possibilities of development or infrastructures, and engendering deeper dependence on capital's investment circuits.

Unwittingly for public and private investors, the institution of growth infrastructures by private entities at times also enables successful opposition movements challenging takeovers of land and resources. An ongoing dialectic of institution-opposition is creating contingent revisions in legal frameworks, but the impact of revisions on resistance is minimal, as people resist dispossession. Any analysis of these significant transformations then, behooves examination of policy-making processes – the who, what, why and when of law-making – that despite ostensibly democratic frameworks are invariably obscured in bureaucratic practices, or rendered invisible in 'corridors of power.'

The materials for this paper were obtained from interviews with senior and mid-level bureaucrats in the Ministries of Commerce and Industry and Finance; SEZ Commissioners and administrators; SEZ developers and unit owners; legal experts; journalists; and academics in and around Delhi, Mumbai and Goa. I also attended four industry-bureaucrat conclaves on SEZs organized by industry and state bodies. I tracked archival records of communications, agendas and minutes of meetings, reports and documents available on Ministerial websites as well as industry, media and academic archives on SEZs.

Contentious communications between the Finance and Commerce Ministries form exclusive infrastructures of information, and were especially hard to come by. The bureaucratic paper trail I cite below proved critical to analyzing the SEZ law-making process and was accessed from documents that two journalists had procured and passed on to me. I could not gain access to these documents on the merit of my requests and Right to Information applications despite persistent effort. My unsuccessful attempts to access key policy-related documents indicated that the refusal of disclosure may indeed point to significant issues in the law-making process. They also underlined the extent to which bureaucratic privilege can derail entitlements and rights of 'ordinary citizens' from policy-making arenas (and I was privileged in many ways, including that I knew the bureaucratic procedures relating to information applications and could eventually secure access to the documents through other sources). I was never meant to trespass in the corridors of power between the Ministries in New Delhi.

Corridors of Power

The revenge of finance

'Liberty will not descend upon a people. A people must raise themselves to liberty that must be earned before it can be enjoyed.' It was a muted Delhi winter afternoon in November 2011 as I made my way up the wide red sandstone steps to the

North Block, when I was greeted by these words inscribed along its arched stone entrance. I was there to meet the Joint Secretary Finance, second in the Finance Ministry's bureaucratic hierarchy. He had chanced to answer my call intended for his personal secretary, and I 'luckily' landed an interview with him without circuitous protocol. As I entered the corridors of the Ministry, I wondered if, somewhat ironically, the inscription was an unwitting invitation to all 'people' across time. I later learned that these were Queen Victoria's words, likely inscribed upon direction of the main designer of the palatial premises and much of colonial New Delhi, Edwin Lutyen (after whom many parts of what is now central Delhi are called 'Lutyen's Delhi').[8]

In his budget speech in March 2011, the Finance Minister had announced a Minimum Alternate Tax (MAT) of 18.5 per cent on booked profits, bringing within the tax net all industries that otherwise enjoyed blanket concessions (hence the title, Minimum Alternate). This had especially distressed SEZ developers.[9] I was eager to understand why the central government was seemingly axing its own foot with the MAT and other proposed measures like the Direct Taxes Code (DTC). The DTC was to replace the Income Tax Act 1961 and among other things, link tax incentives to the scale of investments made by industries, rather than give concessions on profits.

What I got from the Joint Secretary Finance, Rohit Khanna (name changed), was a lesson in 'revenue foregone' (or lost) by the central government as a result of existing tax concessions. He explained that the diversion of export-oriented industries from the Domestic Tariff Area (DTA) to SEZs[10] was the reason behind the zero growth of exports from the domestic area in recent years, and the 100 per cent growth of exports from SEZs. I also learned that the SEZ 'model itself was flawed.' Instead of promoting manufacturing, he asserted, the 'model was catering too much to the services sector, [and] services never needed a boost since they were anyway doing well.' He argued that it was sufficient to reduce taxes for units in SEZs, but the country could not afford to give up revenue from SEZs altogether (interview on November 24, 2011).

This interview clinched my interest in the deeply divided motives and arguments of the Ministry of Finance (MoF) and the Ministry of Commerce and Industry (MoCI) over SEZs that several sources were alluding to. As I dug deeper, interviews with bureaucrats and developers, as well as bureaucratic paper trails between the two Ministries revealed that the differences over SEZs were entrenched, pointing to intense rivalry, mistrust and policy divergence.

In March 2012 however, the Finance Ministry released a 'harmonized' definition of infrastructure. The new definition created consistency across various laws and Ministerial departments for smoother implementation of 'infrastructure' projects. A 'master list' deemed as infrastructure *all public and private* undertakings for transport, communication, energy, water and sanitation and social and commercial infrastructure; commercial infrastructure included private investments in health, education, SEZs, industrial parks and tourism facilities (GoI, 2012; Table 10.2).

On the one hand, Finance[11] had deliberately stymied the SEZ model by introducing the MAT and the DTC, and on the other it sought to facilitate the smoother implementation of 'infra' projects. While SEZs were not liable for forcible acquisition under a departmental order from 2007 (GoI, 2007, 2009), their inclusion in the list seemed to open a possibility for doing this under the new framework for land acquisition being proposed at the time.[12]

I learned over the course of research that the differences between the Commerce and Finance Ministries modeled divergent policy imperatives for the central government. Finance oriented towards a model of economic growth with revenue collection for state expenditures, while Commerce took a more hard line approach of 'minimal government,' allowing capital a freer run with subsidies and concessions. But what constituted infrastructure, and its significance for 'economic growth,' was undisputed between the two.

Table 10.2 List of Sub-sectors for Infrastructure Lending

Category	*Infrastructure sub-sectors*
Transport	1. Roads and bridges 2. Ports[1] 3. Inland Waterways 4. Airport 5. Railway Track, tunnels, viaducts, bridges[2] 6. Urban Public Transport (except rolling stock in case of urban road transport)
Energy	1. Electricity Generation 2. Electricity Transmission 3. Electricity Distribution 4. Oil pipelines 5. Oil/Gas/Liquefied Natural Gas (LNG) storage facility[3] 6. Gas pipelines[4]
Water & Sanitation	1. Solid Waste Management 2. Water supply pipelines 3. Water treatment plants 4. Sewage collection, treatment and disposal system 5. Irrigation (dams, channels, embankments etc) 6. Storm Water Drainage System 7. Slurry Pipelines

Contd.

Contd.

Category	*Infrastructure sub-sectors*
Communication	1. Telecommunication (Fixed network)[5] 2. Telecommunication towers 3. Telecommunication & Telecom Services
Social and Commercial Infrastructure	1. Education Institutions (capital stock) 2. Hospitals (capital stock)[6] 3. Three-star or higher category classified hotels located outside cities with population of more than 1 million 4. Common infrastructure for industrial parks, SEZ, tourism facilities and agriculture markets 5. Fertilizer (Capital investment) 6. Post harvest storage infrastructure for agriculture and horticultural produce including cold storage 7. Terminal markets 8. Soil-testing laboratories 9. Cold Chain[7] 10. Hotels with project cost[8] of more than Rs. 200 crores each in any place in India and of any star rating; 11. Convention Centres with project cost[8] of more than Rs. 300 crore each.

Note:
1. Includes Capital Dredging
2. Includes supporting terminal infrastructure such as loading/unloading terminals, stations and buildings
3. Includes strategic storage of crude oil
4. Includes city gas distribution network
5. Includes optic fibre/cable networks which provide broadband / internet
6. Includes Medical Colleges, Para Medical Training Institutes and Diagnostics Centres
7. Includes cold room facility for farm level pre-cooling, for preservation or storage of agriculture and allied produce, marine products and meat.
8. Applicable with prospective effect from the date of this circular and available for eligible projects for a period of three years; Eligible costs exclude cost of land and lease charges but include interest during construction.

Source: http://www.rbi.org.in/.

The institution of the SEZ model in India met two key sources of resistance that transformed its implementation trajectory. One was the intense peasants' and citizens' resistance to land acquisition, especially for large and medium SEZs; and the other, somewhat unlikely, was the Ministry of Finance, which objected to their scale, scope and tax and duty concessions from the word go. While resistance highlighted dispossession, corruption and real estate scams in the institution of SEZs, Finance consistently warned of their potential for 'land-grabs,' speculative investment in real estate, transfer of existing industries to SEZs and the 'revenue foregone' by 'concessions.' These two arenas of resistance effectively dampened the SEZ model, changed the rules of the SEZ law (or game), and influenced the formulation of the new land acquisition law.

Policy imbroglio (Hotel Le Meridien, July 2011)

An industry-bureaucrat conclave on SEZs was organized by the influential Associated Chambers of Commerce (ASSOCHAM) in the post-MAT period of 'uncertainty' in July 2011. The meeting (held in the plush five-star Le Meridien Hotel) anticipated the growing policy imbroglio with SEZ 'withdrawals' and 'surrenders.' I reproduce below excerpts from the presentations of two key actors, then Commerce Secretary (highest ranking bureaucrat of the Ministry) Arjun Vajpayi (name changed), and a prominent Delhi-based SEZ corporate lawyer from Vaish Associates, Hitender Mehta. Their arguments capture the hedging by the Commerce Department over MAT and land acquisition on the one hand and the growing disquiet among investors over SEZ 'policy reversals,' on the other.

The day-long panels at the ASSOCHAM convention were held in a large convention hall of the hotel and featured a range of talks, from the Commerce Secretary, the (next in line) Joint Secretary Commerce, Commissioners from various SEZs, representatives of Free Zones from Turkey and Oman, SEZ developers, industrialists and legal and taxation experts. Unrest in the SEZ industry in the aftermath of the MAT and land acquisition issues shaped the proceedings of the day.

The Bureaucrat

Then Commerce Secretary Arjun Vajpayi was moved up the agenda as the first speaker, as he had "to leave soon after for another meeting" (industry's palpable unrest over MAT was possibly factored into his schedule). His speech revealed the Commerce Ministry's disposition around the MAT and land acquisition at the time, and indicated the agenda items Commerce was open to discuss, and those that it would not. He highlighted two related issues, the concentration of SEZs in a few states around metropolitan centers and the need to reach the "hinterlands."

In an obviously elite accent, he began with a reprimand:

> ...Most of your SEZs are concentrated in about six states. Those six states also account for 92 per cent of total exports from the SEZs. Which means

> it's not merely the number of SEZs but the concentration is complete, almost total in terms of exports emanating from Maharashtra, Gujarat, Tamil Nadu, Andhra, Kerala and Karnataka. Even within those states, by and large, you would be spot on if you just looked at the major cities and looked around them. That's the second problem [that] within the states where they're coming up, the concentration is in highly selected areas.

Adding that the main motivation behind SEZs was a 'hassle-free environment' with 'infrastructure provision' to facilitate production, he said, tax concessions were secondary, the first priority was a 'good environment for producers.' 'Labor, land and infrastructure' he said, are 'pan-India difficulties, with power and water shortages, inadequate roads, connectivity and ports.' SEZs were to take care of 'infrastructural bottlenecks that are worse now than at the time SEZs were envisaged in 2004.' For a businessperson outside zones, he said 'wage rates are going up and I may lose my edge, and I may need to get out of the business.' Land he added 'is a major issue in the country. It is just no longer possible, given the agitations that have taken place over the last 4–5 years, and the very complicated politics that is involved in all of this, to get hold of large parcels of land, and say this is an SEZ.'

Snapping his fingers then:

> You know, there may have been a time when you snap your fingers and you could get a 1000 hectares. It's not gonna happen now. And if its not gonna happen now, what are we gonna do? Are we just gonna sit around and do nothing about it, or do we need to start having a second look? At both the SEZ Act and the rules?
>
> This concentration of SEZs all along metropolitan hubs, has got to end. Simply because the price of land has reached astronomical levels [in these areas]. Now, if you're real-estate developers, it doesn't matter. You buy land at astronomical levels, you sell it on at astronomical levels. But you're *not* real estate developers, you're *manufacturers*. Land, is only an instrument in your [business]. That regional concentration has to end. You have to get out of the Bangalores and the Hyderabads and the Kolkotas, you have to go into the hinterland. Because you're going to get land cheaper there. And you're going to get labor cheaper there, you're not going to get labor cheaper in Bangalore. If you don't [move] it won't happen. I *assure* you, it is far more difficult to get land in a village near Noida [suburb of Delhi], then it would be in a land [sic] in the boonies. I understand the concern of the DTC [tax concessions being linked to investments] and what have you. But, even if you fix the MAT and all those issues, you will have these three big problems to cope with. And the

> quicker you guys, collectively, think about what needs to be done on those matters and tell us, the better it would be to deal with the problems that may arise in the next five years (emphases in original, speech July 27, 2011).

After his speech, a developer posed a question regarding cooling investor interest in SEZs post MAT. Vajpayi assured the participants that the taxation concerns of industry would be given 'fair hearing with the Parliamentary Affairs Committee' constituted for the issue. He urged again that industry focus on the three issues of 'land, labor and infrastructure' for the long term (and forget about MAT). After this, he left the meeting.

His attempts to deflect developer and industry concerns over MAT and the proposed Direct Taxes Code (DTC) however, failed. It became clear over the day's proceedings that the convention had been convened primarily for SEZ developers and units to gauge how 'serious' the central government was about revoking their promised tax benefits with the MAT and DTC. The Secretary's suggestion of focusing on 'investment in the hinterlands' was not enticing, and ignored for the rest of the day.

The Lawyer

Towards the end of the day, Advocate Hitender Mehta, a legal expert on SEZs, spoke on the two 'burning issues,' MAT and land acquisition. I juxtapose below the concerns he raised as a counter to Secretary Vajpayi. His presentation highlighted the agitation within industry circles with the 'policy instability' unleashed by the MAT, the DTC and increasing activism by the higher judiciary in land acquisition cases.

Advocate Mehta began by exhorting developers to petition the Supreme Court against the MAT. He noted that in a recent interview he had heard Commerce Secretary Vajpayi argue for the reduction of the MAT from 20 percent[13] to 10 per cent. This he said, meant that the Commerce Ministry was 'resigned' to the MAT and only willing to 'bargain' over it. He pointed out that the SEZ Act had its own tax regime and its 'rules of business' clearly mandated that any change in fiscal incentives to SEZs was to be initiated by the Commerce Ministry. He added that, 'Personally I am seeing this as a backdoor amendment which Finance Ministry has chosen to do.' Only three petitions had been filed in the courts thus far he said, and he felt that others needed to step up: 'unless they [other developers] take action, they initiate some sort of resistance process, Ministry of Finance may not actually then come down to [renegotiating] the terms.'

On land acquisition, stressing that no compulsory acquisition is allowed for SEZs, he added:

> '…but now issue comes up, previous acquisitions done by the state governments are being questioned. And there are some court rulings, one by Supreme Court in Noida case, [of] 156 acres. They ruled down the acquisition by the state government! They said now this is to be restored!'

Similarly raising alarm over a High Court order of the demolition of the DLF SEZ in Gurgaon[14] he added:

> 'Another thing is coming. In Gurgaon, my friend from DLF is sitting, 22-year old acquisition by the state was reopened. And Punjab and Haryana High Court, they passed an order to demolish a functional SEZ! I don't know whether they've [the judges] visited this SEZ or not, the kind of infrastructure that has come up, whether they've seen this or not, but it is scary, to see what kind of jurisprudence is evolving! Luckily, this decision has been stayed by the Supreme Court, but still, the final outcome is awaited. And in Noida we are now hearing that cases of 1976 onward, they are contemplating to reopen. So where is the stability of law?'

Highlighting the Jagpal Singh vs State of Punjab judgment of January 2011, he explained:

> 'The Supreme Court, what they're thinking I'm just trying to bring out to your notice. They're actually questioning state government acquisitions. This [case] was in particular reference to the *gram sabha* [village assembly] acquisitions. And they come down very heavily and they cited this in their judgment. That in U.P., [the] consolidation of land holdings Act is widely misused and with the connivance of consolidation authorities. And surprisingly U.P. government has not chosen to object to this, so let us say that they have accepted it. And Supreme Court goes on, saying that 'similar [acquisitions] may have been practiced in other states. The time has come to review all these orders by which the common village land has been grabbed by such fraudulent practices.'

Pausing for a dramatic moment he then exclaimed:

> 'It, it actually leaves me in a shivery condition! And before parting with this case what they've said, it's even more scary! They give direction to all the state governments in the country, that they should prepare scheme of eviction of illegal unauthorized occupants of *gram sabha*, *gram panchayat*, *peromboke*

> [village commons], *shamalat* [grazing lands] land and these must be restored to the *gram sabha*! This is quoted from the Supreme Court Judgment! And then they say the political connections, or, huge expenses incurred in construction, these are no excuses.'

He concluded:

> Now I leave it to you to just, think about this, review this and what kind of jurisprudence is evolving. And it would be a message for investors also, if they want to invest in the SEZs, particularly developers, they need to take care of this situation also.' (presentation July 27, 2011).

Needless to add, legal developments and fresh litigation are great foraging grounds for lawyers and tax experts, and Mehta's alarm may well be motivated by enlightened self-interest. Regardless, while Secretary Vajpayi tried to deflect attention from the MAT, Advocate Mehta advocated a frontal confrontation. Both highlighted the tax and land issues to very different ends. These presentations captured the widening gap at the time between Commerce's ability to deliver industry's expectations and the sundering of the 'consensus' between capital and the state over SEZs. After the July convention, several 'stake-holder' discussions were held by the Commerce Department in an effort to soothe industry unrest, and while changes in operational rules were subsequently made (see below), the major issues of MAT and land acquisition remained unresolved and festering.

The backlash was potent. As industry had to bite back, there was growing and frequent industry decrial of 'unstable policy' or 'policy paralysis' engendered by then ruling Congress-led UPA. Though not confined to SEZs, this decrial especially intensified in the last two years leading up to the 2014 election year.[15] The endorsement of the controversial then-Chief Minister of Gujarat, Narendra Modi as an ideal Prime Ministerial candidate by major Indian business houses; their support for his spectacular high-tech 'Presidential-style' election campaign; and the BJP's resounding victory under his leadership with Modi's elevation to Prime Minister, have also to be seen in this context of capital's dissatisfaction with the UPA.[16]

Making the SEZ Law

The Indian economy was relatively insulated from the 'global' financial crisis in 2008–11 by a combination of monetary policy, expanding domestic market and capital, and a mixed-bag of stimulus and welfare entitlements (Subbarao,

2009; UNDP, 2011). As a result, Indian capital invested enthusiastically in the initial SEZ promise of land, resources, infrastructure (water and power were to be supplied 24x7 to SEZs) and potentially, the labor of dispossessed peasantry. As is evident from the jump in the numbers of SEZs from 2008 to 2011 (366 to 584), while the SEZ model was to facilitate India's global economic integration, this was not necessarily at the behest of global capital seeking to come in, although global investors were certainly on the 'invitation list,' for instance the Indonesian Salem SEZ in West Bengal or the South Korean POSCO SEZ in Odisha. Global capital influenced the SEZ policy framework through the involvement of consultancy firms like McKinsey in SEZ policy formulation. The SEZ model as it bore out however was more in keeping with the aspirations of domestic capital with its growing global reach and interest in real estate (this also becomes evident from the low number of operational SEZs, only 196 operational in 2014 out of 370 notified).

I discuss below the SEZ law-making process that has involved frequent inputs from business interests that also partly explain their sense of "betrayal" with the "reversals" of concessions.

'Soft law'

Zerillo (2010) argues that to understand how legality works in social settings we need a more open definition of what law is. He refers to 'soft law' as 'non-binding coercions', those specific procedures and mechanisms aimed at obtaining compliance despite their non-justifiable character. He argues that it is a practical necessity to look at particular sites and locations where soft law originates and takes shape. In the increasing proliferation of law-making procedures and sites and in the privatization of legal regimes, which then draw upon the power of the state for enforcement, soft law becomes 'hard law.' However, coercive settings are arguably more aptly described as 'mixed' or 'private governance' settings. My use of the term 'soft law' here is particular, and refers to non-coercive settings that nonetheless influence law-making.

The milieu of liberalization and export-led growth facilitated the SEZ policy framework through its genesis and evolution. The Commerce Ministry's approach to SEZs saw their legal framework evolve in frequent consultation with developer and industry interests. Reports and recommendations by industry also formed 'soft law' in the making of the SEZ law.

In 2000, then Commerce Minister late Murasoli Maran of the BJP-led NDA announced the new SEZ policy. Deeply impressed by a visit to China's Shenzhen SEZ in early 2000, Maran incorporated SEZs in the Export-Import policy that same year, calling for 'a significant break with the past' through the introduction of a 'simple and transparent policy' without 'inspector-raj' and with '100 per cent FDI' (*The Hindu*, 2000).

In 2001, a report of the global management consultancy firm McKinsey & Company (2001) prepared at the initiative of then Prime Minister Atal Behari Vajpayee recommended: 'Over the next 5 years India could attract FDI of over US $11 billion in the exports sector. Major action required for doing so is the creation of SEZs offering world class infrastructure and other facilities.' A 2003 press release issued by the Commerce Minister cited this report and its call for SEZs (GoI, 2003a), as did the 2003 proposal of the Commerce Ministry to enact a new SEZ law (GoI, 2003b). The proposal also referenced interactions held with Indian financial institutions, leading to the establishment of a committee under the leadership of the Industrial Development Bank of India. The committee recommended provisions for a legislative framework for SEZs that would promote greater confidence in the model among financial institutions.

In 2004, a joint Chamber of Indian Industry (CII) – McKinsey report recommended that the government needed to remove barriers to export-led growth; to encourage SEZs, two key recommendations asked for simpler administrative procedures and flexibility in hiring contract labor. Indeed, a 'single-window clearance mechanism' for approvals, and flexibility for state governments to relax labor and environment laws found their way into the legal framework of SEZs. Reports and submissions by global and domestic corporate consultants and interest groups found voice in the SEZ policy and legal framework as it evolved.

Ongoing engagement is reflected more recently in conclaves addressing industry concerns over SEZs organized by government and industry bodies. These meetings like the ASSOCHAM one mentioned earlier are organized by important industry lobby groups and Commerce Department affiliated bodies. Of the three others I attended between 2011–12, one was organized by the Chambers of Indian Industry (CII) and two by state-led bodies, the Export Promotion Council for EOUs and SEZs (EPCES), and the Santacruz Electronics Export Processing Zone (SEEPZ) in Mumbai. Along with key developers, most of these had senior and mid-level bureaucrats from the Commerce and Finance Ministries in attendance. At least two of them, the one organized by ASSOCHAM and the other by the Export Processing Council, were held in plush hotels and three accompanied lavish meals.[17] Three were day-long meetings and one was a half-day consultation.

The first 'stake-holder consultation' in the post-MAT scenario was organized by the Export Processing Council in September 2011 at The Hans Hotel in central Delhi. Like the ASSOCHAM meeting earlier in the year, here again, officials flagged the issues of the concentration of SEZs near urban areas (Map 10.1), while developers complained about MAT. Revenue department officials in attendance felt obliged to explain that there was clear rationale for taxation and that Revenue was not against SEZs per se. Officials requested suggestions for improvements in the investment environment for SEZs, and developers asked for reductions in duties for sale in domestic areas given the slow global demand, and relaxation of norms for servicing domestic customers in SEZs. Other issues discussed at The Hans, such as the relaxation of minimum land and contiguity of land requirements, the broad-banding of sector-specific SEZs to allow additional sectors into operational SEZs, had also come up in the ASSOCHAM convention.

By November 2011, based on recommendations from The Hans consultation and other submissions by developers and industry bodies, the Commerce Department came up with a draft discussion paper to further facilitate discussions, identify 'problem areas' for industry and resolve them through new rules for the law. The discussion paper identified several issues: the minimum area requirements for SEZs; contiguity of land parcels; 'broad-banding' of sector specific SEZs to attract more investors; allowing domestic customers to be serviced in non-processing areas; the increasing unattractiveness of SEZ fiscal incentives; and leveraging domestic sales for SEZ products and services[18] (GoI, 2011b).

It identified four 'adverse perceptions' of SEZs 'on account of a few black sheep' that were 'causing damage to 'Brand SEZ:" (i) that SEZs are about 'garnering control of land'; (ii) they were 'tax havens leading to loss of government revenue'; (iii) that there were coordination issues between various government departments undermining the Single Window Mechanism of SEZs; and iv) that the fiscal policy environment for SEZs was 'unstable.' It acknowledged that as a result of these 'perceptions,' there was significant reduction in the number of SEZ proposals; withdrawals of approved proposals, requests for denotification and a reduced interest in setting up new units in SEZs (*ibid.*).

The Commerce Department then used the discussion paper to facilitate discussions in 2011–12 in Mumbai (SEEPZ), Bangalore, Kolkata and Kandla. The discussion paper was also posted on the official SEZ website inviting comments from 'stake-holders.'

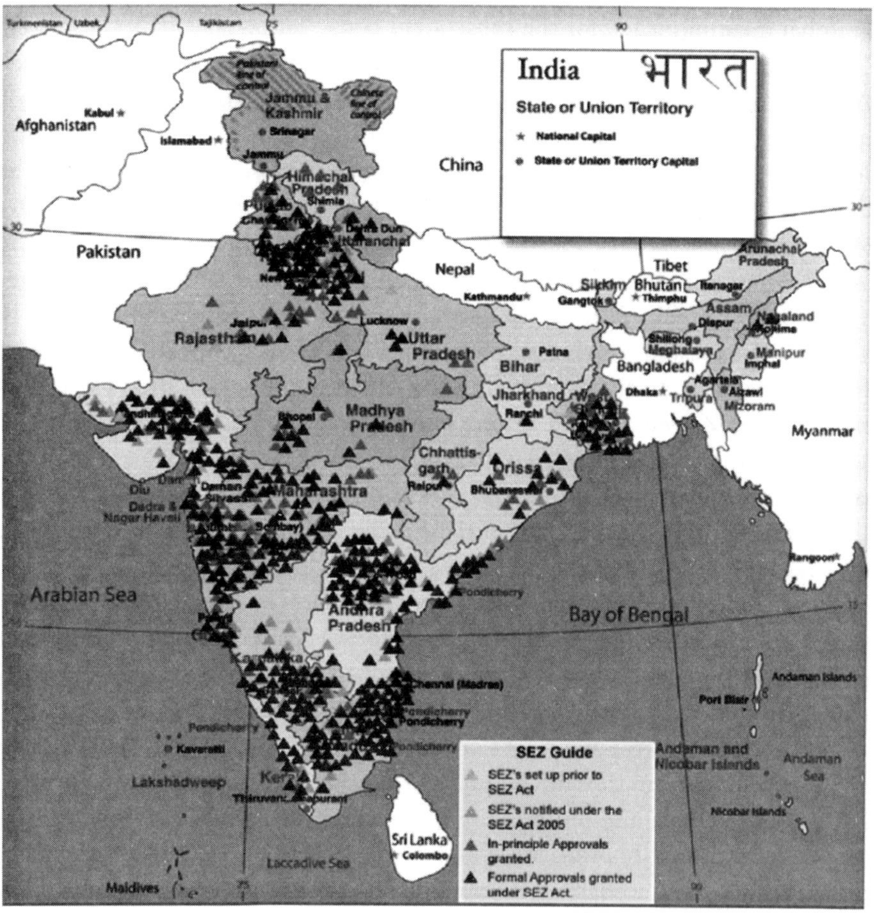

Map 10.1 Distribution of SEZs

Source: GoI, 2011e.

At the SEEPZ meeting in December 2011, a developer proposed the reduction of minimum land requirements to 250 hectares for multi-product SEZs and 40 hectares each for sector-specific and IT SEZs. Representatives of the real estate body CREDAI (Confederation of Real Estate Developers Associations of India) and several other developers raised the issue of 'relaxation of norms' for schools, hospitals and residential areas or non-processing areas in SEZs so that people not working in SEZs are also allowed access to these areas. Easier 'exit options' for developers wanting to quit, or develop and transfer SEZs were also raised. With marked efficiency, the discussion paper on the official SEZ website reflected these fresh proposals within two weeks of the Mumbai meeting, ready for the subsequent consultation.

Many of these recommendations found their way into the changes proposed to the SEZ rules by the Commerce Department. Commerce was clearly attempting to revive the flagging fortunes of the model, although it could not address the core issues of MAT and land acquisition. In August 2013, the Commerce and Industries Ministry finally released new rules, presumably after Ministerial deliberations. The rules were not as wide-ranging as the discussion paper proposals. The reduced minimum area requirement was 500 hectares (from 1000) for multi-purpose SEZs and 100 (from 450) for sector-specific, 10 (from 50) for food processing and none for IT SEZs (as opposed 250, 40 and 40 hectares respectively suggested in the discussion paper). 'Broad-banding' of sectoral SEZs was allowed among industries related to each other and 'exit norms' for investors wishing to withdraw were made more flexible. Domestic sales, access to domestic customers and contiguity norms relaxation were not allowed. It appears that the writ of the Finance Ministry held on attempts at the dilution of the original SEZ concept by the Commerce Ministry.

I met Commerce Secretary Vajpayi one afternoon in February 2012, in his smart office at *Udyog Bhavan* (Commerce House) near the Central Secretariat in Delhi. A popular upbeat bollywood number was playing on the large led screen hooked up to the wall by one side: '*dhoom macha le, dhoom macha le, dhoom*' (let's create an uproar, let's create an uproar, uproar). As I was shown in, he looked up from the files on his table, nodded in terse acknowledgment, lowered the volume and resumed signing the papers in front of him. After a few minutes, he set his files aside and matter of factly proceeded to explain the prevailing SEZ scenario. He explained that there were two to three main issues. The 'politicization' of land acquisition 'was not envisaged' at the time of the law's drafting. There was 'consternation' with MAT among industry circles as SEZ benefits had indeed been rescinded. He added that there were 'things that can be fixed and we're doing it.' Issues that could be fixed included procedural simplification, fixing rules of business and allowing the servicing of domestic customers in the SEZ 'non-processing area,' although not for 'multi-story apartments and hotels' but 'super specialty hospitals and schools' on a 'case to case basis' (interview on February 29, 2012).

'Soft law' practices in the form of industry recommendations consistently informed the legal evolution of the SEZ framework and eventually found their way into 'hard law.' The leverage of these soft law settings suffered greatly from 2011 however, as Finance had its revenge with the MAT. As I show below, the Finance Ministry's compliance in 2005 was coercively obtained through the highest political intervention of the state, the Prime Minister.

Then Prime Minister Manmohan Singh convened a meeting in April 2005 with several Ministers of his Cabinet, to intervene in the matter of Ministerial differences over SEZs, particularly between the Finance and Commerce. A number of issues were 'resolved' and Finance had to back off on its objections to the SEZ framework proposed by Commerce on several counts, most notably on tax concessions that Finance viewed as its legitimate turf. A decision was taken to constitute an Empowered Group of Ministers (EGoM) with special cabinet powers to resolve further differences (F.No.149/61/2003/TPL), and the documents related to EGoM meetings shed important light on how the SEZ policy framework evolved. The EGoM comprised Ministers of Commerce and Industry; Finance; Agriculture; Consumer Affairs, Food and Public Distribution; Home Affairs; Law and Justice; Labour and Employment; Defence; and Communications and Information Technology. The intervention of the Prime Minister underlines the significant political status the SEZ model enjoyed at the time.

The subversion of Finance's opposition by Commerce was critical to the evolution of the SEZ legal framework until 2011. I discuss the standoff over SEZs between the two Ministries in the following section.

Shadowing (Soft) law

How did the Commerce Ministry establish its writ over the SEZ Law in the initial years? The bureaucratic paper trail gives ample evidence of the turf war that played out between the Ministries of Commerce and Finance over SEZs. But there is more to the SEZ law-making process than meets the eye, even more than the 'secret' EGoM and other bureaucratic files reveal. Max Gluckman (1965) in his work on 'law as process,' showed how gossip and scandal revealed the role of shame, social pressure and suasion in legal processes. Here I extend this wider interpretation of legal processes. Analyses of the paper trail and bureaucratic and developer grapevines reveal the role of bureaucratic and Ministerial rivalries and possibly high-profile corruption in determining the legal trajectory of SEZs.

A member of the SEZ Board (of Approval)[19] I interviewed revealed that each Board meeting approved over 25–30 proposals in each sitting of 2–3 hours. The decisions seemed already taken and there was little deliberation discussing the merits of the projects being considered for approval. This rendered the approval process a mere formal exercise.

The Finance Ministry has such complaints on record. In a letter to then Director SEZ on August 7, 2006, a day before the Board meeting was to be held, the Revenue Department raised issue that its representatives had not received copies of the proposals made by applicants that were to be discussed in the meeting. Relevant documents concerning several other agenda items were also not furnished. Revenue asked for the deferral of these agenda items until all relevant documents had been made available, with sufficient time for scrutiny. It cited and enclosed an intriguing December 2005 missive by the Finance Minister to the Revenue Secretary. The missive asked the Secretary to ensure that the Revenue representative in the SEZ Board (and other approvals committees of the Commerce and Industries Ministry), 'be a high-level representative who can speak his [sic] mind and assert his views' and is 'fully prepared with the agenda items.' The letter added, 'If the agenda papers have reached him late, and he has not had time to examine each item, he should insist on postponement of the meeting or at least some items of the agenda on which he has not had adequate notice or time to prepare' (F. No. 178/141/2006-IT.1; RTI document available with author).

The August 7 letter from Revenue also raised issue with the total number of SEZ approvals until then. An initial limit of 150 SEZs had been fixed in a previous EGoM meeting, after which a review of already approved SEZs was to be undertaken. Finance pointed out that the agenda items indicated that the approvals were expected to go well over the limit. The letter recommended waiting for already approved SEZs to become operational before approving any fresh proposals (this is significant given the low numbers of operational SEZs until 2014).

The concerns raised in the letter were subsequently noted by the senior bureaucracy. Additional Secretary Revenue followed up with a letter to Special Secretary Commerce the day after the Board meeting. The letter raised concerns that 'about 100 cases (6th item of the agenda) were considered by the BOA during the 3rd meeting in a matter of about an hour a [sic] quarter and formal as well as "in-principle" approvals were given. Important factors like the financial health of the Developers and their capacity to carry out capital-intensive projects were not discussed. In some cases Developers with lesser area of land were given approvals ignoring those who had bigger areas.' He further raised the issue of the BoA going over the 150 mandated SEZs. (D.O. No. Member(IT)/SEZ/R-683/06; RTI document available with author). In his reply, the Special Secretary Commerce refuted all of the Revenue Secretary's charges adding that the "internal" limit of 150 approvals was reserved for final and not in-principle approvals.

An EGoM was convened within the same month to discuss Commerce's claim of distinction between 'in-principle and 'final' approvals for SEZs and the 'internal guideline' of 150 approvals. A case was made by Commerce that the limit had been an internal one, and referred to final approvals, with no bearing on in-principle approvals. The Finance Minister (FM) again raised concerns of 'revenue loss' from the additional SEZs being allowed to escape the tax net, urging that the limit of 150 SEZs be adhered to. The Commerce Minister (C&IM) countered the Finance Minister with figures of potential revenue generated from additional SEZs. Most EGoM members rejected the distinction between in-principle and formal approvals, but all save the Finance Minister were in favor of removing the limit of 150 SEZs. The FM had to give in. A national daily carried a news item the following day citing sources that claimed that the FM 'waged a lone battle' against more SEZs (Badarinath, 2006).

At the same EGoM, the FM had also raised issue requesting suitable guidelines for SEZ approvals with clearly recorded reasons for approval, rejection or deferral. The approvals procedure could not be discussed in the EGoM, but was taken up by him through subsequent letters to the Chair of the EGoM (then Defence Minister) and the Commerce and Industries Minister. A series of communications over guidelines for approval followed between the Ministries, primarily between Commerce and Finance. The guidelines for approval were eventually drafted and approved two months later, in October 2006 (this series of events constructed from F.No. F.1/3/2006-EPZ; RTI document available with author). The pitched battle between the FM and the Commerce Minister over SEZs interrogates claims of a coherent ideology or interest within 'the state' or indeed any general attributes like 'cunning' (cf. Randeria 2003) for the state; in the SEZ contest, cunning, if any, was maneuvered between the Finance and Commerce Ministers.

Ministerial Rivalries and Corruption

A senior developer I interviewed claimed that the tug-of-war over SEZs between the Finance and Commerce Ministers was a result of the Finance and Commerce Ministers' personal stand-off with each other. He claimed that the 'rush' for SEZ approvals came with many developers lining up to meet then Commerce Minister with bribe money to get their projects approved. This 'income' from SEZ approvals went to ruling party coffers, keeping the party favorably disposed towards the model, and the Minister. This, he argued, did not go down well with then Finance Minister, who felt threatened by the success of the Commerce Minister (interview on December 6, 2011). While the veracity of these allegations of corruption and Ministerial rivalry is difficult (if not impossible) to ascertain with evidence, there was clearly a struggle between the Commerce and Finance bureaucracies and Ministers over SEZs that the paper trails and interviews with bureaucrats, developers and others established.

Bureaucratic Turf Wars

Retired bureaucrat Ravi Menon (name changed) was Special Secretary Commerce during the initial years of the SEZ law's enactment and acknowledged by several developers and bureaucrats as a sincere promoter of the SEZ model.[20] When I met Menon, he spoke passionately of the model and shared brochures and other material with me. He openly accused Finance of being against the SEZ model and creating problems for it with a 'vicious campaign about SEZs being a big scam.' Finance 'insisted' on three representatives in the BoA, he said, and that all decisions in the Board be made by consensus and not majority. Commerce, he added, 'compromised' on these demands (interview on February 20, 2012). Another ex-bureaucrat of the Commerce Ministry subsequently working in the corporate sector accused Revenue bureaucrats of waging a 'turf war' as Commerce was getting all the 'credit' for SEZs (interview on September 20, 2011). A senior academic extremely sympathetic to the SEZ model similarly accused the Finance Ministry of derailing the SEZ model, but put its perceived need for revenue in perspective, adding that such a large part of the Indian economy is 'informal' that any loss of revenue threatens the Finance Ministry. Given the 'drag' on resources by welfare schemes such as the employment guarantee law, the academic explained, Finance feels the need to secure revenue sources (interview on March 1, 2012).

Joint Secretary Finance and the Customs representative from the Revenue Department in the SEZ Board on the other hand, insisted that the loss of revenue with tax concessions for SEZs, their potential for real estate speculation and the diversion of existing industry into SEZs to avail concessions were the prime reasons for raising issue with SEZs (interviews November 24, 2011; February 14, 2012). The paper trail reveals that Finance raised these concerns consistently, from the time the SEZ model was conceived in 2000.

All legal provisions related to taxation and fiscal incentives in India come under the purview of the Finance Ministry. Journalist Suresh points out that Commerce acquired full powers to frame the fiscal and economic policy of SEZs without any responsibility to collect revenue, through an amendment to the Allocation of Business Rules 1961 in November 2002. This was a 'unilateral' decision by Commerce, without consulting the DoR. Revenue discovered this amendment only in September 2003 when a proposal for the SEZ law was sent to it. A previously sent draft Cabinet note on the SEZ Bill in February 2003 also did not mention this amendment. Revenue soon raised issue with this encroachment over its turf (unpublished notes shared September 8, 2011). Documents reveal that the disagreements that developed between the two Ministries were profound. It was only just before the law was to be introduced in the parliament that the meeting of the group of Ministers convened at the initiative of the Prime Minister in April 2005 to prevail upon Finance's misgivings and retain the considerable incentive structure of SEZs (F.No. 149/61/2003-TPL; RTI document available with author). This was the same meeting in which the decision on constituting EGoMs was taken. The meeting approved the draft SEZ Bill, overriding many of Finance's concerns. The Bill was finally introduced in the Indian Parliament in June 2005, and approved in both houses in two days, with little discussion and no dissent.

Finance's reservations over tax incentives likely laid the foundation for what would later develop into a full-fledged war over SEZs between Finance and Commerce, with the 2011 introduction of the MAT and DTC only a latest twist. However, Finance raised cudgels immediately after the enactment of the law, airing concerns now in the EGoMs. Repeatedly through the drafting of the rules for the SEZ law, Finance raised concerns that given the incentives, all existing productive export units would relocate to SEZs doing little for fresh investment. No explicit provision was made in the law for preventing this shift until Finance prevailed upon the Ministerial deliberations. Finance additionally raised concerns regarding distortions in land, labor and capital resulting from uneven development of SEZs with a bias towards urban locations and industrialized states. The Ministry unsuccessfully pushed for the cap of 150 SEZs. It raised concerns of land and resource diversions for real estate speculation in SEZs. And it made repeated threats to Commerce that in the interest of a stable fiscal regime, the latter should desist from meddling in fiscal affairs (F.No. 149/61/2003-TPL; RTI document available with author). The threats of Finance were finally made good in 2011, with the introduction of the MAT.

Ministerial and Bureaucratic Personalities:

How did Commerce initially secure and subsequently lose its leverage over SEZs towards 2011? The academic mentioned earlier alluded to another facet of law-making, that of bureaucratic 'ownership.' Once the initial team of people driving a model or project is gone, through routine transfer, promotion or retirement, a model loses momentum. Thus, the academic explained, in the initial years there was a lot of passion behind the SEZ model. But once the initial team moved out, the subsequent Minister and bureaucrats were either not strong enough to confront Finance, or did not particularly care, allowing SEZs to falter (interview on March 1, 2012). Recalling the Bollywood song playing on television when I had met then Commerce Secretary a few weeks before, I wondered.

Ministerial personalities may have also played a role here. At the time of UPA 1 (2004–09) when the SEZ law was being drafted, the Ministers of Commerce and Finance were equal political heavyweights of the Congress party, P. Chidambaram was Finance Minister from 2004–08 and Kamal Nath was Commerce and Industries Minister from 2004–09. In 2009, there was a change of guard with UPA 2 and while the Finance Minister's portfolio went to another Congress political heavyweight, Pranab Mukherjee (subsequently the President of India), the Commerce and Industries Ministry went to relatively junior, Anand Sharma. In 2011, it was Pranab Mukherjee who introduced the MAT in his budget speech. From 2007 onwards, as outlined earlier, the SEZ environment also became increasingly vitiated with several controversies over land acquisition. Finance had also been pushing for a limit to the number of SEZs, and by 2011 there were already 584 approved with 377 notified SEZs. This combination of factors may have pushed back the leverage Commerce had over the SEZ model and allowed Finance to recover its turf by 2011.

There is, again, no proof to substantiate the allegations of corruption and Ministerial and bureaucratic rivalries, but the paper trail clearly reveals that the Commerce and Finance Ministries have been at loggerheads over SEZs from their inception. I flag these allegations here as that arena of law-making process that lies beyond both 'hard' and 'soft' law but 'shadows' them, present in 'word of mouth,' gossip and rumor, but beyond adequate evidentiary grasp. Analyses of paper trails and interviews indicate their plausible influence over the SEZ law-making process. The bureaucratic paper trail and interviews allude to a larger role for the bureaucracies than the Ministers in shaping the SEZ dynamic. If the vicissitudes of bureaucratic and Ministerial interest indeed determine the fate of critical laws and policies impacting millions of lives and livelihoods, there is an even greater case for more robust and transparent systems of accountability and transparency in infrastructure policy-making.

Legacies of a mixed economy: revenue, welfare and 'inclusive growth'

The issues that the Ministry of Finance raised around SEZs do not only pertain to fiscal incentives that Finance considers its turf, but also to concerns over 'land-grabs,' 'real estate speculation,' the diversion of industry from the domestic area to SEZs and the predominantly service-oriented investment in SEZs when their stated goal was manufacturing. How then did Commerce go so far out on a limb in the context of SEZs?

There is a plausible argument to be made for Ministerial and Departmental bureaucratic dispositions and cultures here. India adopted a 'mixed' economic model upon independence that sought to combine a centrally planned economy with capitalist growth. Finance has traditionally been an extremely powerful Ministry with revenue collection, budget and disbursement functions. The emphasis on public spending and numerous old and new state-led welfare initiatives may have historically engendered the Finance Ministry's dispensation towards revenue collection. This may also explain its deep suspicion of those trying to avoid its jurisdiction, or evade taxes, in this case SEZ developers and investors. This suspicion regarding SEZs may have enabled Finance to apprehend and raise concerns regarding real estate related land grabs and other distortions.

In the post-liberalization period, the Commerce and Industries Ministry is cast in a role of supporting and facilitating capital expansion and accumulation (or 'growth'). As Commerce attempts to champion concessions for capital at public expense, Finance is rooted in a model of revenue collection for the exchequer. The two Ministries are thus cast in contradiction with each other despite an overarching commitment to capitalist growth (Finance has been equally conservative over disbursements under the rural employment guarantee law; Dreze, 2007). The 'policy instability' that industry decried in the 'reversal' of SEZ concessions nonetheless, did not emerge from Finance, but from Commerce's 'break from the past' through tax and other concessions granted to capital in the SEZ model.

A note on 'Consultations'

The infrastructure of "stake-holder consultations" is in stark contrast with the stonewalling and often violent repression of the "stake-losers"[21] opposing the institution of SEZs. Unabashedly skewed in favor of capital, there is no system of hearing or redress for those who stand to lose lives and livelihoods, or even a mechanism to record complaints or objections under the SEZ law-making framework. For formal approval, all that is required is partial acquisition of land by a developer and an undertaking to acquire more land, with the endorsement of the state government in question. Despite a three-year maximum stipulated period of approval, SEZ proposals are regularly renewed on request, keeping people opposing them under constant stress and abeyance. For instance, in the case of the controversial South Korean POSCO SEZ in Odisha, the developer has not managed to fully acquire land for seven years given local opposition, but approval has been repeatedly renewed (GoI, 2013; 2009b). Despite clear ceasing of operations for the Mumbai SEZ as its initial approval lapsed in the face of opposition, the project appears in the formally approved SEZs in 2014. Consultation is skewed entirely in favor of capital, organized in lavish conclaves. If the amendments under the Land Ordinance 2014 come to pass in the land acquisition law, all that stands between the 'stake-holders' and the 'stake-losers' is a Board of Approval circular disallowing forcible land (and resource) acquisition for SEZs.

Infrastructures of Growth

Through the creation of SEZs, capitalists of largely Indian origin attempted to take control of large parts of the most valuable opportunities the large domestic economy offers the global market: land, resources, and arguably some freeing reserves of cheap labor, or dispossessed peasantry (although there is also significant indifference towards the dispossessed; see also Levien 2012). SEZ concessions were not just in the form of tax incentives, but also over administrative and other legal measures for creating 'quasi-corporate city-states.' Disingenuously invoking exceptional legislation, in their scale and scope SEZs in reality sought to establish a normative paradigm of infrastructural development for economic growth. As the ambitious model unfolded, capital and allied forces in Commerce were forced to beat retreat. The state's repressive apparatus unsuccessfully attempted to counter resistance on the ground and bureaucratic and ministerial disagreements between Ministries of Commerce and Finance resulted in policy imbroglios. The grand vision of proliferating urban, gated global enclave economies with state of the art infrastructure and 24/7 services is today in a considerable state of impasse.

In the ruling dispensation of the far-right BJP, a restructuring of Finance may well be on the cards.[22] Going by Ministerial hierarchy, the current Finance Minister Arun Jaitley overshadows the Commerce and Industries Minister Nirmala Sitaraman quite starkly. As the Modi-led regime consolidates and influences shift, the SEZ framework will potentially evolve further. For the moment, interest in SEZs remains low, and the baton has passed on to other infrastructures of growth, such as the Delhi Mumbai Industrial Corridor.

The evolution of the SEZ legal framework has been a multi-layered process. Formal, 'soft law' and other processes in their shadows have shaped the SEZ law-making process, through their inception as policy, implementation as law and evolution in rules. Resistance to SEZs has also effected revisions in their legal framework.

This analysis of the SEZ law-making process reveals that 'the state' is not a coherent or 'cunning' entity (Randeria, 2003), or the 'vertical and encompassing spatiality of power' (Ferguson and Gupta, 2002). More specifically, it is also not only a 'speculative' (Goldman, 2011) or a 'land-broker' (Levien, 2012) state working on behalf of capital. 'The state' instead, is rife with contestation and meanings that diverse actors occupying its offices bring to it. It is an arena of competing ideologies and interests that influence decision-making processes, influenced in turn by historical legacies and political contingencies. This is not to suggest that dominant ideologies of liberalization and capitalist growth do not influence this arena, but their interpretation and effect on policy frameworks are contingent and not given factors. Legality or rule of law then, are unsettled and contested terrain in the wake of the SEZ experience.

What is gained by this view of the state and legality, given the ultimately 'class compromise' character of social democratic states (cf. Sandbrook et al., 2007)? Under conditions of a consolidating Hindu-right regime in India, this raises some important questions. Jaffrelot (2012) argues that the 'saffronization' of Gujarat's administration and judiciary has had grave implications for the victims of the 2002 violence in the state. Would concurrent structural transformation at the central level be effective in infrastructure and development policy, or would historical legacies and political contingencies create internal forces of resistance, as this study demonstrates? As resistance on the streets and villages by those threatened with dispossession remains steadfast and ever emergent, the trajectory for capitalist takeover in India seems checkered. Under what conditions then, could a coherent ideological take-over of 'the state' that successfully counters internal and external resistance emerge?

Endnotes

1. The Left parties withdrew their support to the UPA government in the summer of 2008.
2. Notification is the final stage of approval and indicates readiness to start operations.

3. I use the term peasants' groups here to refer to small and marginal land-owning farmers with less than ten and two acres of land respectively, landless agrarian workers, pastoralists, fisher-folk, forest dwellers and other petty commodity producers. Peasants are also further stratified along ethnicity, religion, caste and gender lines.

   Citizens' groups here refer to coalitions of individuals, often concerned professionals and representatives of Non-Governmental Organizations (NGOs) that coalesce around contentious issues. They are not NGOs in themselves, and often do not take institutional funds or salaries, but comprise voluntary campaigners who raise resources through individual donations.
4. See amkanakasez.blogspot.in; Vekateswaran 2008.
5. See *The Indian Express* (2012); *The Economic Times* (2013); Suneja (2013).
6. Zerillo (2010) refers to 'soft law' as non-binding but coercive processes of closed-door consultations and recommendations that result in non-binding directives, declarations, resolutions, which inevitably come to be enacted as law. This interpretation is disputable, as coercion renders these processes more appropriately in the realm of 'mixed' or 'private governance.' Here I refer to soft law as arguably non-coercive closed-door consultations and recommendations from private bodies that influence law-making (see discussion later in the chapter).
7. This is an underrepresented relation in recent anthropological analyses of infrastructures; see Larkin (2013) for an overview.
8. Herbert Baker, attributed with designing many significant buildings in Cape Town around the time, assisted Lutyen on this assignment, especially for the North and South Blocks. The *Bhavan* itself was built in the early 20th Century by clearing the Rasina and Malcha villages of a few hundred families, with the Land Acquisition Act 1894. This incredibly powerful elite area of Delhi subsequently came to be called Ra*i*sina Hill, alluding to the ruling caste connotations of the name when the syllable 'i' is added to Rasina.
9. Under the SEZ Act 2005 until then, SEZ developers and units enjoyed blanket tax concessions for the first five years of operation, 50 per cent concessions on booked profits for the next five years, and an additional 50 per cent concession on profits 'ploughed back' into investment in the SEZ for the subsequent five. The 18.5 per cent MAT reduced these benefits.
10. SEZs are deemed 'foreign territory' by law for commercial purposes.
11. In the interests of readability I refer to the Finance Ministry as simply Finance and to the Commerce and Industries Ministry as Commerce or Ministry of Commerce through the text.
12. This has borne out in the Land Ordinance 2014 that has removed consent and social impact provisions from acquisition for all manner of investments by 'private entities', including industrial corridors and 'social infrastructure' like private hospitals and entertainment complexes (see GoI, 2014).
13. Developers consistently referred to the 18.5 per cent levy of MAT as 20 per cent.
14. The Punjab and Haryana High Court ordered the demolition of the DLF SEZ in Silokhera village in Haryana in February 2011 because of an illegal transaction between the company and the state government. Petitioners from the village had challenged the

acquisition of over 200 acres of land from their village by the state government and its sale to private companies. The SEZ land had first been sold to another developer for a hospital who in turn sold it to DLF. DLF challenged the order in the Supreme Court and managed to get a stay on the demolition by July 2011 (Ohri, 2011; Sura, 2011).

15. Other factors fueling industry ire have included the number of crony capitalist deals busted by the Central Bureau of Intelligence and subsequently the Supreme Court in recent years.
16. See also Varadarajan (2014) for a trenchant analysis of how the judicial fallout of 'crony capitalism' scandals during the UPA regime have added fuel to industry's (f) ire in supporting Narendra Modi as an ideal administrator.
17. I note the settings of these consultations here as they contrast sharply with the areas where SEZs come up, the 'underdeveloped' countryside. The 'stake-holder' consultations also contrast with the stonewalling and repression of people opposed to SEZs (and similar projects), or the 'stake-losers' (Iyer, 2007), before state forces even acknowledge their reservations and grievances.
18. This demand would defeat the purpose of SEZs as export-oriented enclaves, but industry representatives justified it pointing to the "slow" global economy.
19. When citing sensitive information I have not disclosed interview details that may compromise the informant. This informant was not from the Ministry of Finance however, though Finance representatives on the Board additionally noted similar objections.
20. R. Ghatak (name changed), who was then Secretary Commerce and later moved to Finance, was considered the visionary force behind SEZs, but I could not secure an appointment with him despite several attempts.
21. Iyer (2007) argues that in the case of people threatened with dispossession due to 'development' projects, it is a cruel irony to call them 'stake-holders'; they are instead 'stake-losers.'
22. In his election campaign, Prime Minister Modi often rhetorically announced that he would abolish the income tax when he came to power.

References

2013. 'Eight Developers to Surrender SEZs; 13 Asks [sic] for More Time.' *The Economic Times*, August 25.

CII-McKinsey. 2004. *Made in India: The Next Big Export Manufacturing Story*. Accessed May 19, 2014. Available at, http://www.mckinsey.com/global_locations/asia/india/en/our_people/~/media/AC04DC59EC6943EE876BED2A172EF3C3.ashx.

Dreze, J. 2007. 'Empty Stomachs and the Union Budget.' *The Hindu*, March 9.

Ferguson, J. and A. Gupta. 2002. 'Spatializing States: Toward and Ethnography of Neoliberal Governmentality.' *American Anthropologist* 29 (4): 981–1002.

Gluckman, M. 1965. *Politics, Law and Ritual in Tribal Society*. Oxford: Blackwell.

Government of India. 2003a. 'Jaitley Wants Speedier Implementation of SEZs Parliamentary Consultative Committee of Commerce and Industry Meets.' Accessed

April 24, 2014. Available at, http://commerce.nic.in/pressrelease/pressrelease_detail.asp?id=562.
———. 2003b. 'Proposal for Enact [sic] a Central Act for Special Economic Zones (SEZs) in India.' (RTI Document available with author).
———. 2007. 'Letter to State Governments Regarding Compulsory Acquisition.' April 5. (RTI document available with author).
———. 2009a. *Instruction no. 29.* Available at, http://sezindia.nic.in/.
———. 2009b. 'Minutes of the 37th meeting of the SEZ Board of Approval held on December 15, 2009 to consider proposals for setting up of Special Economic Zones.' Accessed April 10, 2013. Available at, http://sezindia.nic.in/.
———. 2011a. 'Fact Sheet on Special Economic Zones.' Accessed October 14, 2011. Available at, www.sezindia. nic.in.
———. 2011b. Discussion Paper to Facilitate Stakeholder Consultation on Potential Reform of the SEZ Policy and Operating Framework. New Delhi: Government of India.
———. 2012. 'Harmonized List of Infrastructure Sub-Sectors.' Accessed May 5, 2014. Available at, http://pib.nic.in/newsite/erelease.aspx?relid=80634.
———. 2013. 'Minutes of the 56th meeting of the SEZ Board of Approval held on January 18, 2013 to consider proposals for setting up Special Economic Zones and other miscellaneous proposals.' Accessed April 10, 2013. Available at, http://sezindia.nic.in/.
———. 2014. The Right to Fair Compensation and Transparency in Land Acquisition, Rehabilitation and Resettlement (Amendment) Ordinance, 2014. New Delhi: Government of India.
Goldman, M. 2011. 'Speculative Urbanism and the Making of the Next World City.' *International Journal of Urban and Regional Research* 35 (3): 555–81.
Gutiérrez, R. 2012a. 'The Rhythms of the Pachakuti: Brief Reflections Regarding How We have Come to Know Emancipatory Struggles and the Significance of the Term Social Emancipation.' *The South Atlantic Quarterly* 111 (1): 52–64.
———. 2012b. 'Maharashtra Govt Cancels 4 SEZs over Land Acquisition.' *The Indian Express*, July 31.
Iyer, R. 2007. 'Towards a Just Displacement and Rehabilitation Policy.' *Economic and Political Weekly* 42 (30): 3103–3107.
———. 2009. *Water and the Laws in India.* New Delhi: Sage Publication.
Jaffrelot, C. 2012. 'Gujarat 2002: What Justice for the Victims? The Supreme Court, the SIT, the Police and the State Judiciary.' *Economic and Political Weekly* 47 (8): 75–87.
Larkin, B. 2013. 'The Politics and Poetics of Infrastructure.' *Annual Review of Anthropology* 42: 327–343.
Levien, M. 2012. 'The Land Question: Special Economic Zones and the Political Economy of Dispossession in India.' *The Journal of Peasant Studies* 39 (3–4): 933–969.
McKinsey & Company. 2001. *Achieving a Quantum Leap in India's FDI.* New York: McKinsey Global Institute.
Nilsen, Alf. 2010. *Dispossession and Resistance in India: The River and the Rage.* New York: Routledge.

Ohri, R. 2011. 'SC Stays Demolition of SEZ in Gurgaon.' *The Indian Express*, July 6.

Randeria, Shalini. 2003. 'Cunning States and Unaccountable International Institutions: Legal Plurality, Social Movements and Rights of Local Communities to Common Property Resources.' *European Journal of Sociology* 44 (1): 27–60.

Sandbrook, R., M. Edelman, P. Heller and J. Teichman. 2007. *Social Democracy in the Global Periphery*. New Work: Cambridge University Press.

Subbarao, D. 2009. 'Impact of the Global Financial Crisis in India: Collateral Damage and Response.' Speech by Duvvuri Subbarao, Governor of the Reserve Bank of India, delivered at the Symposium on The Global Economic Crisis and Challenges for the Asian Economy in a Changing World. Organized by the Institute for International Monetary Affairs, Tokyo, February 18.

Suneja, K. 2013. 'Sitting on Denotified SEZ Land, Reliance Industries, Parsvnath Eye Greener Pastures.' *The Financial Express*, September 26.

Sura, A. 'Govt's Land Acquisition Quashed by High Court.' *The Times of India*, February 3.

UNDP. 2011. 'India's Job Guarantee Act Emerging as a Ray of Hope in Global Meltdown.' Accessed June 5, 2014. Available at, http://www.undp.org/content/support/en/home/test_area/ourwork/democraticgovernance/su ccessstories/india_s_job_guaranteeact emergingasrayofhopeinglobalmeltdown/.

Varadarajan, S. 2014. 'The Cult of Cronyism.' *Seminar*: 60–63, April.

Vekatasweran, S. 2008. 'Goa Govt Cancels all SEZs.' *The Economic Times*, January 1.

Zerillo, F. 2010. 'The Rule of Soft Law: An Introduction.' *Focaal - Journal of Global and Historical Anthropology* 56: 3–18.

11

Land-based Financing for Infrastructure

What is New about India's Land Conflicts?

Sai Balakrishnan

Introduction

The past ten years has been a decade of land wars in India. Some of the most violent and contentious land conflicts were over the use of land-based financing: the state acquired surplus land, more than was needed for the actual infrastructural project, with the justification that property development on the surplus land can generate revenues and cross-subsidize the building of the new infrastructure. The conflicts over the building of new infrastructural projects, including tolled highways such as the Bangalore-Mysore Infrastructure Corridor and the Yamuna Expressway and new greenfield airports such as the Bangalore International Airport, are clear examples of this new type of land conflict.

Proponents of land-based financing see the mode of financing infrastructure as heralding a new paradigm of infrastructure provision: that of public-private partnerships (PPPs). The frenetic pace of 21st century urbanization in India generates new infrastructural demands that the fiscally strapped Indian state cannot meet by itself. \$1.2 trillion dollars in capital investment for urban infrastructure, 2.5 billion square meters of roads to be paved (which is twenty times the road capacity added in the past decade), commercial and residential space equivalent to the built-up area of Chicago has to be added every year: these are some of the statistics that convey the giddying pace at which infrastructure has to be developed in India (Dobbs, Gulati, Mohan, Sankhe and Vittal, 2010). Advocates of PPPs argue that the public sector lack, by itself, lacks the capacity to mobilize such large-scale financial resources and it has to combine in new ways with private sector financing to meet these infrastructural demands. But infrastructure projects, as long gestation projects, hold little attraction for the private sector. The state, then, has to experiment with new incentives to rope the private sector into the infrastructural sector, and one such incentive is surplus land: the lure of high returns from property development on the surplus land can bring a reluctant private sector into the infrastructural sector. Surplus land, then, is the bait for the private sector to enter infrastructure, in the absence of which India cannot build the new types of infrastructure needed to propel a country with what Raj Krishna disparagingly called the 'Hindu rate of growth' into double-digit growth figures.

Land-based financing is met with vociferous opposition from the critical left. The critical left is unequivocal that the new infrastructural projects are a variation on the old theme of accumulation by dispossession. Post-Independent India has had ambitious infrastructure development programs, starting from the dams (the temples of modern India) to the new tolled highways and international airports. And the cost of development, according to the left view, is disproportionately borne by the country's most vulnerable: low-caste groups, landless groups, and small farmers. The violent and publicized land conflicts of the past decade – Bangalore-Mysore Infrastructure Corridor, Yamuna Expressway – are framed as episodes of land grabbing, with the state (often acting on behalf of the private sector) expropriating land through legal manipulations, and dispossessing peasants and low-caste groups to further corporate and real estate profits (Shiva, 2011; Borras, Hall, Scoones, White and Wolford, 2012). These 'enclosure movements' date back to the Irish and English enclosures of the seventeenth to nineteenth centuries, the dispossession of Native Americans from their land by the new settlers of seventeenth century US, and the land rushes that characterized the African colonial experience of the nineteenth century (Borras, Hall, Scoones, White and Wolford, 2012), and the ongoing infrastructure-induced displacements in India are the new iterations of an old pattern of dispossession.

The optimistic view of land-based financing (henceforth, referred as the abbreviated LBF) sees it as a new phenomenon, and pays little attention to the use of this financing instrument in the past. The critical view, on the other hand, views LBF as an old historical process that plays itself out ad nauseum and pays little attention to what is new about the latest iteration of LBF projects. Here, I argue that LBF has a long, albeit relatively unacknowledged history, in India, but the new generation of post-liberalization and post-decentralization LBF projects marks some critical junctures and departures in India's development history. I use LBF as a window into the new political economy of land in India, including the new role of land in India's development, the new cast of actors involved in these LBF/infrastructure projects, and the distributional implications of these changes on the provision of basic infrastructure. The chapter is in four parts. Part I starts with a very brief overview of LBF in the Indian context. Part II delves into the case of the Bangalore International Airport as a paradigmatic example of the new generation of LBF projects. Part III highlights three key changes between the old and new LBF projects: the new price regime of land, the privatization of surpluses, and the decentralization of surpluses. Part IV shows how these changes come together to produce new land conflicts and new balances of power, and how the recent amendments to the 1894 Land Acquisition Act reflect the challenges faced by the Indian state in balancing the new configurations of class power that emerge in a decentralizing, liberalizing society.

An Overview of Land-based Financing in India

LBF is a form of land monetization, i.e. the process of an asset into money or legal tender. At its simplest, land can be monetized through land disposition, i.e. through the leasing or selling of it. Land can also be used to generate further capital through using it as collateral for raising debt. In its most complex forms, land can be used as the underlying asset for the creation of new fungible and easily transferable financial instruments through processes known as securitization (less common in India, but widely practiced in the West and one of the main reasons for the 2007 global financial crisis).

Land monetization in the form of land disposition is not new to India and dates back to the 1880s when the colonial state set up City Improvement Trust Boards (CITBs). The CITBs acquired agricultural lands outside the city boundaries and built India's first planned suburbs (Nair, 2005). The CITB activities were partly a move to relocate the native poor from slums to these 'model hygienic suburbs' in response to the plague epidemics sweeping through colonial cities, and partly a legitimization of colonial rule through demonstrating the civilizing effects of these rationally planned suburbs over the unsanitary and chaotic native settlements (Kidambi, 2007; Legg, 2007; Nair, 2005). The colonial government framed the Land Acquisition Act – the subject of much recent controversy and debate in India - in 1898 to enable the conversion of agricultural lands in the peripheries into CITB planned suburbs. In post-colonial India, the CITBs took the organizational form of parastatals. Parastatals are hybrid organizations that perform the functions of public agencies, but with the nimbleness afforded to private corporations. They are generally set up to perform specialized functions and as such, are referred to as special purpose governments, in contradistinction to general-purpose governments such as municipalities (Burns, 1994; Foster, 1997). The parastatals that proliferated in the 1960s and 70s are institutional choices to circumvent some of the restrictions imposed on municipalities. For one, the members of parastatals are not elected, but are nominated by the state government. Parastatals then are more insulated from democratic politics and their centralized authority can lead to more efficient and expedited decision-making. Second, they have higher degrees of fiscal autonomy compared to municipalities. For instance, in order to safeguard the public interest, local governments in India can use their landed assets only for public uses (not even public purposes) such as parks, public schools and public hospitals. In contrast, parastatals can develop their land to its 'highest and best use' and dispose of it to the highest bidder. Because parastatals can extract the maximum commercial value from their landed assets, land development parastatals such as the Bangalore Development Authority (BDA), set up in the 1970s, soon became one of the richest public agencies in the city. The BDA acquires privately owned land through eminent domain, subdivides and services the land into developable plots, sells most of the plots to the public at affordable rates, but makes huge profits through selling advantageously located plots such as corner plots through public auctions. Though the BDA has the legal powers to borrow from banks and capital markets (again, something that municipalities were prohibited from doing), their lucrative business in land development and disposition precluded them from looking for any other sources of revenue. Bangalore's water and sanitation provider is also a parastatal, the Bangalore Water Supply and Sewerage Board (BWSSB). The BWSSB also owns large land banks in the city and revenues from land development and disposal enable it to cross-subsidize the provision of basic services to city residents.[1]

In the past two decades, PPPs have replaced parastatals as the key organizational form for structuring LBF for infrastructure. I outline below the use of LBF to finance an ambitious greenfield international airport for Bangalore.

The Bangalore International Airport

In 2006, the National Commission on Infrastructure set up a Task Force to develop a financing plan for modernizing and expanding India's airport infrastructure. Envisioning a capital outlay of around Rs. 40,000 crores, the Task Force strongly recommended public-private partnerships as the only viable strategy for building new greenfield airports and for overcoming the logistical bottlenecks imposed by India's existing publicly owned airports. The new airport policy took its cue from international airports such as Heathrow, where the airport promoters profit not from the revenues generated through aeronautical activities, but from the income generated from non-aeronautical, real estate activities (Peterson, 2009). For instance, most international airports earn the bulk of their revenues from non-aviation activities. The British Aviation Authority, which operates Heathrow and other airports, derives 72 per cent of its revenues from real estate uses (hotels, restaurants, upscale housing and office enclaves, and convention centers) in the land surrounding the airport (KPMG, 2006; Ohri, 2009). The policy of separating aviation income from property development income, and in using the latter to cross-subsidize the former, became particularly important in the Indian context because airports and their connected aviation activities, which are categorized as 'infrastructure,' are subject to pricing controls by the Aviation Authority, and it is only non-aviation/real estate activities that are open to market pricing (Peterson, 2008).

The use of surplus land as a source of financing airport infrastructure was a key element in the financing of the Bangalore International Airport. The industrial parastatal, the Karnataka Industrial Areas Development Board (KIADB), acquired through eminent domain/compulsory purchase 4,017 acres of land in the Devanahalli area in north Bangalore. Of this, 2000 acres is for aviation activities and the remaining land is for property development. The land was transferred to a parastatal agency of the Government of Karnataka (GoK), the Karnataka State Industrial and Investment Development Corporation (KSIIDC). KIADB paid landowners a compensation rate equivalent to the market price of agricultural land at the time of notification, which was around Rs. 600,000 per acre. Since the GoK proposed to develop the airport as a PPP, KSIIDC would enter into a land lease arrangement with the airport concessionaire and lease the land for a specified term. Besides its contribution of land equity, the GoK also committed Rs. 350 crores towards the project in the form of an interest-free loan.

In 2002, following a global bid under the build-own-operate-transfer (BOOT) model, the GoK selected the Bangalore International Airport Limited (BIAL) consortium as the concessionaire for the new airport. The public partners in this PPP are the Airport Authority of India (AAI) and the GoK through its parastatal agency, the KSIIDC. The private sector partners include Seimens Project Ventures, Unique Zurich (the operator of Zurich airport and other airports) and Larsen and Toubro (L&T). The KSIIDC, as the owner of the airport land, entered into a land lease agreement with BIAL for leasing the land to the concessionaire for a term of 30 years and for a lease rate as follows: Re. 1 till the airport opening date, and thereafter as a percentage of the land acquisition cost of Rs. 175 crores - 3 per cent for the first seven years, 6 per cent after the eighth year, and thereafter a sum equaling the rent of the preceding year plus three per cent.

The shareholding pattern of BIAL in 2002, the time of signing the shareholders agreement, was as follows:

Table 11.1 Organizational Pattern of BIAL Shareholders in 2005 and 2011

Shareholders	*Shareholding pattern (%) in 2005*	*Share-holding pattern (%) in 2011*
Private Promoters		
Siemens Project Ventures GmbH	40%	26%
Flughafen Zurich AG Ltd.	17%	5%
L&T IDPL	17%	Nil
GVK Group	Nil	43%
Sub-Total	74%	74%
State Promoters		
Airport Authority of India – (GoI)	13%	13%
Karnataka State Industrial Investment & Development Corporation Limited (GoK)	13%	13%
Sub-Total	26%	26%
TOTAL	100%	100%

Source: Bangalore International Airport Limited (BIAL) website, accessed at http://www.apaoindia.com/?page_id=152.

The acquisition of surplus land for the purpose of property development has generated much controversy. Some have pointed out that it was not necessary for the GoK to lease the land to the consortium whose majority stakeholders are private sector firms. Instead, there are other institutional arrangements that would have enabled the Karnataka government to mobilize financial resources through land, while also retaining control over the revenues generated through property development (John, 2005). Bangalore itself has the earlier precedent of Electronic City, the information technology (IT) hub that rings the southwestern periphery of the city. Lacking the financial resources and the expertise to develop the IT enclave, the GoK took responsibility for land acquisition and property development, and used the revenues from property development to hire developers for the new urban development. Another option is for the public sector to divide the project into its real estate and infrastructure components, to ring fence these finances, and to use the revenues from property development directly to cross-subsidize infrastructure. This model is similar to the land monetization practices of parastatals like the BDA. In the BIAL case, the main intention of the public sector is to attract private sector firms to the infrastructure sector, and this leads to contentious arrangements where the surplus land is directly transferred to private sector control either through a long-term, renewable lease.

In 2009, hardly eighteen months after the opening of the new airport, the GVK Group - supplier of equipment to infrastructure companies such as power plants and airports - acquired 12% stake in BIAL from Unique and 17% from L&T (Table 11.1). In 2001, GVK further acquired 14% stake from Seimens GmBH, thus giving the former management control of the project as majority shareholder. In order to lock-in the private sector capital and to ensure a longer-term commitment to the project, the private sector promoters were subjected to the following lock-in restrictions: Seimens GmBH shall subscribe and hold at least forty per cent of the paid up capital of BIAL for a period of three years after airport opening and no less than twenty six per cent for a period of seven 7 years after airport opening; and Unique Zurich shall subscribe and hold at least five per cent of the paid up capital of BIAL for a period of three years after airport opening. As a construction partner, L&T was not subject to any lock-in restrictions. It is telling that at the end of the stipulated lock-in periods, all three private sector promoters divested their stakes down to the permissible minimum. All three private promoters made windfall profits from their divestitures, as the appreciated cost of land and the non-aeronautical revenues were capitalized into the new share values. In 2005, Siemens invested Rs. 130 crores, Unique Zurich Rs. 55.5 crores, and L&T Rs.

55.5 crores. In 2009, GVK acquired Unique Zurich and L&T's shares at Rs. 485 crores and Rs. 686 crores respectively, and it acquired 14% of Siemens' shares at Rs. 613 crores. In a matter of just four years, the new transferred value of L&T's shares, for instance, are almost ten times its original equity contribution in 2005.

The increased transferred value reflects in the BIAL's balance sheets as increased project cost, and these escalated project costs are ultimately passed on to the public in the form of increased user development fees. Though the Airports Economic Regulatory Authority regulates user development fees, poorly negotiated contracts like the BIAL one saddle the company balance sheets with high costs, leaving both the GoK and the regulatory authority with little recourse but to succumb to pressure and escalate the user development fees. Contracts like the BIAL one defeat the purpose of competitive bidding: the concessionaire was awarded the contract because it quoted the lowest price in a competitive bid which would result in affordable fares for the public for air travel. And yet, the opportunistic exit of these promoters has resulted in escalating project costs and high user development fees.

Land-based Financing – What is New?

Using the case of the Bangalore International Airport as an empirical lens, I outline below three key changes in the political economy of land-based financing for infrastructure. The long history of LBF enables us to track these differences over time, and the change in the organizational form of LBF projects – from parastatals to PPPs – is particularly helpful as a starting point.

New price regime of land surplus

In the earlier era of parastatal-led land monetization, the parastatals acquired un-serviced land from private landowners, they reassembled the fragmented plots into developable ones, installed basic infrastructure, and sold the gridded, serviced plots to the public. It was primarily the change from unserviced to serviced plots that contributed to the increase in land value. In other words, the benefits of urban infrastructure were capitalized into the land values, and it was this land value increment that the parastatals captured. Econometric studies show the rates of infrastructure capitalization in land value: investment in wastewater leads to gains in land value of 3.03 times the cost of investment, piped water supply to gains of 1.02 times the investment cost, and paving roads to gains of 2.58 times (Peterson, 2008).

In the past decade, however, the value of appropriately located agricultural land has increased even in the absence of infrastructural provision. Though it is difficult to get systematic data on agricultural land prices in India, microstudies and spot analyses of compensation rates for recent land acquisitions show the stirrings of a "great rural land rush" with farmland prices rising upto 100-fold in some places (Rajashekhar, 2013). In the Devanahalli area, land value at the time of acquisition in 2002 was Rs. 6 lakhs per acre. In 2004, even before the PPP was finalized and airport construction broke ground, the villages at the fringes of the airport registered land prices of around Rs. 80 lakhs. In 2007–8, the Department of Registration and Stamps notified an upward revision of property guidance values[2] in the Devanahalli districts. The airport was opened in May 2008, and, in the preceding year, in 2007, land in the village of Hire Amanikere was selling at the rate of Rs. 7 crore per acre. These meteoric increases represent a new price regime for appropriately located agricultural land.

It is important to note that not all agricultural land is equally increasing in value, but only appropriately located land, specifically those lands that are at the peripheries of large cities and along infrastructure corridors (Sathe, 2011). The dramatic new price regime for urban and appropriately located rural land has attracted much attention from scholars. Some argue that the price hike is because of a demand-supply mismatch. New demand-side factors – including the demographic shift, the burgeoning middle class and the growth of dynamic new sectors such as information technology (IT) and pharmaceuticals – combine with outdated land regulations that restrict the supply of serviced land, thereby leading to the scarcity and high price of urban land (Annez, Bertaud, Patel, and Phatak, 2010). Others point to the dizzying rush of black money into the real estate sector, and the organized interests that stand to gain from the existing system and that oppose any changes to land regulations (Jagannathan, 2014). Yet others point to growing inequality now manifesting itself through skewed land markets, where the ultra rich (the1 percenters) can afford to pay extremely high prices for the best plots of land, thereby creating a ripple effect in the entire land market (Chakraborty, 2013).

Rather than focusing on the economics of demand-supply alone, I agree with the latter two viewpoints that the new price regime is a more complex product of the new political economy, and specifically of how certain sectors of the economy are liberalized and others are not, which ones are regulated and which ones are not, and the constellation of actors that make these decisions and that benefit from them.

Privatization of surpluses

The BDA and other parastatals have recently come under intense flak for bypassing local elected representatives and for their limited public accountability. (Benjamin and Bhuvaneswari, 2006; Chamaraj, 2009; Goldman, 2011). Having upward channels of accountability to state governments, they are criticized for undermining local democratic institutions, and particularly for contravening the recent efforts at democratic decentralization as envisioned by the 73rd and 74th Constitutional Amendment Acts. Though not directly accountable to the politicized electorate, as public agencies, parastatals do come under the recent transparency law, the Right to Information Act. Questions of public accountability become thornier for the new PPPs. Operating for profit under market conditions, private sector promoters want to maintain their competitive edge through some keeping some proprietary information confidential. These confidentiality requirements are at odds with the accountability norms under which the public sector operates. In the BIAL case, a Bangalore resident challenged the BIAL's refusal to furnish information under RTI (Rajendran, 2008). BIAL argued that since private promoters owned majority stakes in the consortium, it was not a public authority and hence was outside the purview of the RTI. In a definitive judgment, the Karnataka Information Committee, and later the Karnataka High Court, rejected BIAL's argument with the verdict that the airport project is 'substantially financed' by the government and as such it is subject to audits by the Comptroller and Auditor General (CAG). Though the BIAL case tilted in favor of public disclosure, the question is unresolved in other airport cases (including Hyderabad and Chennai) where the matter is still pending in the courts.

Besides public accountability, a key difference between parastatals and PPPs is who captures the surpluses from land monetization. In the case of parastatals, revenues from land redevelopment and disposition are captured by a public agency. These surpluses are then either reinvested in new affordable serviced residential layouts (in the case of the BDA) or to cross-subsidize the provision of basic services (in the case of the BWSSB). Parastatals may not be directly accountable to the public, but surpluses from land monetization accrue to the public (Balakrishnan and Pistor, 2014). In the case of the PPPs, on the other hand, it is not the public, but private shareholders of the promoter companies that benefit from land monetization (*ibid*). The opportunistic exit of L&T from the BIAL consortium reflects the incentives of private sector firms in maximizing the returns to their shareholders. As soon as the airport was completed and the market value of the land around the airport was 'discovered,' all three private sector promoters had their shares valued at more than ten times their investment in 2005, captured the appreciated land value in the new share price and either partially or completely exited from the partnership.

The private sector has benefited from state-mediated transfer of land in the past. Since the early decades of Independence, private sector firms have been amassing vast tracts of land to build their offices and industries on. In the past decade, however, firms have turned to monetizing their land banks. The cash-strapped national carrier, Air India, recently announced plans to sell key plots of land as a financial strategy to revive its sagging balance sheet (Sanjai, 2014). Privately owned textile firms like Arvind Mills and Bombay Dyeing are likewise using their vast land banks to start lucrative real estate developments, and the revenues generated from real estate are helping boost the companies' stock values (Gupta, 2012). Firms that heavily borrowed before the 2008 global financial crisis and that are now saddled with heavy debt in a slow economy have also turned to land monetization to pare their debts: the 10 large business houses whose combined debt accounts for nearly 20 per cent of bank loans in the country are planning ambitious real estate projects on their vast land banks as a strategy for deleverage their balance sheets (Nandy and Datta, 2013). In other words, the land banks no longer serve as the key input factors for the generation of industrial wealth; the land banks themselves become a source of wealth as the returns from property development outpace the returns from even industrial development. Private sector firms are increasingly moving into the infrastructure sector not in anticipation of gains from infrastructural development, but in anticipation of the soaring returns from property development on the surplus land.

Decentralization of surpluses

Though the BDA and other parastatals have been actively acquiring land since the 1970s, it is only in the past decade that these coercive takings have escalated into such violent and visible conflicts. A key protagonist in the recent land conflicts is the group that has been variously identified as the provincial propertied class (Balagopal, 1987), the intermediate castes (Jaffrelot, 2003) and the real estate politicians (Pani, 2013). This class includes caste groups such as the Vokkaligas in Southern Karnataka and the Maratha-Kunbis in Maharashtra, who till now have been the key power brokers within the agrarian economy. The acquisition of privately owned surplus land that would purportedly cross-subsidize the building of new highways such as Yamuna Expressway and the Bangalore-Mysore Infrastructure provoked the wrath of this class of agrarian landowners: the Jats in the former case and the Vokkaligas in the latter. In cases like the BIAL, the surplus land was owned/occupied not by powerful agrarian propertied classes, but predominantly by 'unauthorized cultivators,' i.e occupiers who had been cultivating on government land for decades. The remaining land was owned by authorized cultivators who belonged to more dispersed caste groups, many of them low-caste Dalits. These cultivators with titles to their land received paltry compensation of Rs. 5–6 lakhs. The villages surrounding the airport have seen dramatic increases in land prices. Agrarian elites, both from the region and from surrounding regions, are now actively involved in consolidating these lands through purchasing them from marginal landowners, often with the mediation of local brokers.

In other words, the rising price of appropriately located agricultural land has led to new urban real estate aspirations for certain classes of agrarian landowners – the agrarian propertied classes. These landowners see a lucrative opportunity in converting their agricultural land into high-demand urban land. But, existing regulations governing agricultural land conversion often prevent them from doing so. For instance, the Land Reforms Acts impose strict restrictions on the conversion and transfer of agricultural land. Owners of agricultural land cannot sell, lease or mortgage their land to non-agriculturalists, or to educational, religious, charitable society, trust, company, association or cooperative other than the cooperative farming society.[3] To prevent concentrated land ownership, the acts also placed ceiling limits on agricultural landholdings and any person owning land in excess of the ceiling was prohibited from alienating any or all of the surplus holding. As a result of these restrictions, it was only parastatals like the BDA and the KIADB that could successfully go through the various regulatory steps and develop formal residential and industrial sites on previously agricultural land. These land reforms have been steadily modified and even repealed since the 1990s onwards to enable expedited and unmediated agricultural land conversions. In Karnataka, the changes came in the form of the 1996 amendment of the Land Reforms Act,[4] during the Chief Ministership of Deve Gowda. The amended act enabled agricultural landowners to directly lease their land to certain non-agricultural uses including aquaculture, horticulture, floriculture, housing projects and educational institutions. These uses were also granted exemption from the land ceiling limits. The amended act was justified on the grounds that frequent violations of the old Land Reforms Act defeated the very purpose of the act – the protection of small and marginal farmers – and the new act was merely legalizing land practices that are rampant and that will continue irrespective of the letter of the law. The real motivation for the amendment was political. As an astute politician, Deve Gowda recognized the aspirations of his party's leading political constituency – the Vokkaliga agrarian propertied class – to be a part of the 'India Shining' growth story and to partake in the benefits from a booming real estate sector. The new land reform amendments were intended to remove the parastatals as mediating land agencies and to ease the entry of a politically strong agrarian propertied class into real estate.

These changes have led to the emergence of a new political class that has variously been identified as the 'provincial propertied class' (Balagopal, 1987) or the 'real estate politician' (Pani, 2013). But existing regulations prevent the agrarian propertied class from monetizing their agricultural land. Recognizing the aspirations of this class, astute politicians like Deve Gowda are amending land-use regulations to facilitate the easier entry of the agrarian propertied class into real estate. These landowners are emerging as the new power brokers in urban real estate markets, and they are using their real estate surpluses to further entrench their political power. A review of the mandatory declaration of assets of Karnataka's Members of the Legislative Assembly (MLA) in the past decade reveals a striking trend. In the 2008 Karnataka Assembly elections, 23 of the 30 MLAs received their recent wealth as real estate developers (Merinews, 2009; Goldman, 2011). The trend continued in the 2013 Karnataka Assembly elections. 93% of Karnataka's sitting MLAs are crorepathis and 80 per cent of them are involved in real estate and mining activities.[5] The richest MLA is 29-year old Priyakrishna, with a declared asset value of Rs. 750 crores, and whose father, M. Krishnappa, is a realtor-politician with the fitting appellation of Layout Krishnappa (DC Reporter, 2013; Sastry, 2013). Of the 218 MLAs, nearly 100 of them dropped out of high school or PUC.[6]

What we are seeing then is a new class of elites who straddle the urban-rural economies and who are emerging as urban power brokers using their agrarian land-based sources of power.

Private Land and the 'Publicness' of Infrastructure

Using land monetization to finance infrastructure is not new in India. As evident from the long history of parastatals (and their earlier colonial institutional versions of City Improvement Trust Boards), public agencies have frequently turned to land redevelopment as a source of revenue for public infrastructure. What is new in the new millennial experiences of LBF are the three trends of the new price regime of land surplus, the privatization of surpluses, and the decentralization of surpluses. As India experiments with two key policy changes of liberalization and decentralization, two powerful constituencies that were hitherto kept distinct now start competing over the allocation of land surpluses. Industrial firms whose core business till a few decades back did not include property development are now diversifying into real estate and becoming prominent players in this sector. Agrarian propertied classes that earlier exercised material control over the agrarian economy now use their landed assets to finance their election campaigns and propel them into prominent elected positions at the state level. As the state appropriates privately owned surplus land for financing infrastructure, the flashpoint of the new land conflicts is how the land surpluses are allocated between the financially powerful industrial (now property development) firms and the electorally strong agrarian propertied classes. The Indian state has responded to this conflict through amending the 1894 Land Acquisition Act and amending the terms of transferring agricultural land from one private actor to another, i.e. from agrarian landowners to private sector firms. The policy response of the Indian state reflects a pendulum swing from, at first, capitulating to the demands of the private sector firms, and then, swinging to the other extreme and yielding to the demands of an agrarian propertied class.

Bangalore is replete with new infrastructure projects financed via land monetization. Besides the BIAL project, another infrastructure project that has captured the media and public attention is the Bangalore-Mysore Infrastructure Corridor, a tolled highway connecting the cities of Bangalore and Mysore. Bangalore's public agencies acquired 7000 acres of land for the tolled expressway and handed over the land to the private sector concessionaire, the Nandi Infrastructure Corridor Enterprise (NICE). While the tolled expressway will be handed over to the Karnataka government after 30 years, another 21,000 acres of acquired land was sold to NICE for the building of five new townships along the expressway. In interviews of the author with senior bureaucrats in Karnataka, they conceded that the new tolled expressway is redundant – the intended goal of faster connectivity between Bangalore and Mysore could have been achieved through expanding and improving the existing rail link that exists between the two cities. And yet, an ambitious $ 1 billion expressway project was proposed in order to justify the transfer of 21,000 acres of agricultural land to private sector firms for real estate development. The exit of Siemens, Unique and L&T in the BIAL case vividly captures the incentives of private sector promoters who enter the infrastructure sector only for the gains to be made from property development. Since the returns from property development are faster and higher than the long gestation infrastructure projects, private sector promoters find ways to exit the poorly negotiated PPP contracts as soon as they are able to capture the appreciation from land redevelopment.

One could argue that in both these cases, state agencies could indiscriminately transfer agricultural land from one class of private actors to another because of the low compensation regime. A fair market value compensation for acquired land, or 'just compensation,' is generally justified based on the principles of utility and fairness. The utility principle argues that when governments are obliged to pay fair market value compensation, the price system deters governments from acquiring more land than is needed for the public use/ public purpose, and it incentivizes the government to utilize the condemned land most efficiently. In the absence of compensation, the government is not paying for the full cost of its regulations and the costs of government regulation are not fully internalized. The fairness principle argues for compensation so that the costs of a public infrastructure, i.e. infrastructure that is enjoyed by a diffuse public – is not disproportionately borne by a small group of landowners. Had the compensation rate not been determined by government diktat, and had it been more reflective of the market price of urban land, the state would have been more fiscally prudent in its land acquisition, and the agrarian landowners would not have been so unfairly excluded from the surpluses from land redevelopment.

These coercive land acquisition practices however did not go unchallenged. Agrarian propertied classes reacted vociferously to these acquisitions that deprived them of capturing the windfall profits from monetizing their converted agricultural land. Faced with a huge public backlash that was spearheaded by dominant caste landowners across the country, the Indian state teetered to another extreme position and introduced a new compensation regime for land acquisition. The 2013 Land Acquisition, Rehabilitation and Resettlement Act (LARRA) obliges the state to compensate land at the rate of two times the prevalent market value for urban land and four times the market value for rural land. The marked-up compensation regime in one stroke shifts the decision-making process on land acquisition from government diktat to the market. In doing so, it overcompensates the small group of agrarian landowners whose lands are needed for the new infrastructure. In relying on the price system to allocate land, the Indian state will now be forced to prioritize those infrastructure projects that promise high rates of return so that it can recover the high costs of land acquisition. The use of LBF for infrastructure reinforces spatial imbalances: infrastructure will be developed in already prosperous areas where the land values are high enough to enable LBF. In addition, the new compensation regime further skews infrastructural development towards international airports, tolled expressway and other types of infrastructure that can generate higher user charges and achieve higher cost recovery, and away from public infrastructures such as rural roads and rural irrigation systems.

The question of the right compensation price for land is removed from the larger context of the type of public infrastructure needed for India at specific moments of its development trajectory. The state acquired private land for the Bangalore international airport under the old Land Acquisition Act and compensated the existing landowners with a low rate that did not capture the value of the land value increment. Those who bore the cost of the new project through losing their land – the unauthorized cultivators and authorized marginal landowners – had little voice in determining the type of infrastructural project that would come up on their land. In other words, these marginal landowners gave up their land for an infrastructural project – an international airport – that they would in all likelihood never use or benefit from. The question of what type of infrastructure is needed for the Devanahalli region was insulated through vesting decision-making in the PPP company. The new compensation regime mandated in the 2013 LARRA, in a different way, insulates the deliberations of the type of public infrastructure needed for different regions from the public domain. In relying on the price system, the Indian state has effectively ceded decision-making control to the market (Balakrishnan and Pistor, 2013). Instead of crucial decisions on public infrastructure being sited in the public domain, they are being increasingly depoliticized, first through outsourcing them to technocratic organizations like parastatals and now through a turn to the market.

In the BIAL case, the poorly negotiated contract led to escalation in project cost, and the state legislative assembly had little choice but to authorize the hike in the user development fees. Now, with the marked-up compensation regime of the new land acquisition act, democratic forums have little choice but to choose infrastructure projects that are financially viable, given the high costs of land acquisition. In the Indian state's careening from responding to the demands of one constituency – the financially powerful urban firms – to the demands of another constituency – the electorally strong agrarian landowners – the question of the type of infrastructure needed for the inclusive growth of the other diverse publics remains unattended. The choice of infrastructure – whether a country with limited resources should invest them in rural roads or tolled highways, in rural irrigation projects or urban international airports – is a contested one, with different publics having different preferences. Countries like Brazil are innovating with new experiments such as participatory budgeting, so that these contested decisions can be more firmly and closely entrenched in the politicized electorate. India on the other hand is further depoliticizing these difficult choices, leaving even its formal deliberative bodies like the state legislative assemblies with their hands tied in making decisions on public infrastructure.

Endnotes

1. Interviews with bureaucrats and researchers in Bangalore.
2. Guidance value of immovable property is set by the State Government through a committee constituted by the Inspector General of Registrar. Guidance value marks the minimum value below which a property cannot be registered, and is used primarily to determine the stamp duty and registration fees for land transactions.
3. Sections 79A and B of the 1961 Land Reforms Act.
4. See (Nair, 1996) for a critique of the 1996 amendment.
5. Source: Affadavits submitted by candidates contesting the 2013 Karnataka Assembly elections, accessed at the Association for Democratic Reforms (ADR) maintained myneta.org website: http://myneta.info/karnataka2013/index.php?action=show_winners&sort=default
6. Ibid.

References

Annez, P., A. Bertaud, B. Patel and V. Phatak. 2010. *Working with the Market: Approach to Reducing Urban Slums in India.* Washington, D. C.: Sustainable Development Network, The World Bank.

Balagopal, K. 1987. 'An Ideology for the Provincial Propertied Class.' *Economic and Political Weekly,* 1544–1546.

Balakrishnan, S. and K. Pistor. 2014. 'Governing Land and Water Resources: The Demise of Collective Voice.' *Unpublished mimeo.*

Benjamin, S. and R. Bhuvaneswari. 2006. 'Urban Futures of Poor Groups in Chennai and Bangalore: How these are Shaped by the Relationship between Parastatal and Local Bodies.' *Local Governance in India: Decentralization and Beyond,* edited by Jayal, Niraja Gopal, Amit Prakash and Pradeep Sharma. New Delhi: Oxford University Press.

Burns, N. 1994. *The Formation of American Local Governments: Private Values in Public Institutions.* New York: Oxford University Press.

Chakraborty, S. 2013. *The Price of Land.* New Delhi: Oxford University Press.

Chamaraj, K. 2009. 'Parastatals and Task Forces: The New Decision-Makers.' *India Together,* February 22.

DC Reporter. 2013. 'Ayukta Cops Give MLA Clean Chit.' *Deccan Chronicle*, January 25.

Foster, K. 1997. *The Political Economy of Special Purpose Government*. Washington D.C.: Georgetown University Press.

Goldman, M. 2011. 'Speculative Urbanism and the Making of the Next World City.' *International Journal of Urban and Regional Research* 35 (3): 555–581.

Gupta, J. 2012. 'Monetising Land Bank to Prop Up Textile Firms'. *Business Standard*, April 3.

Jaffrelot, C. 2003. *India's Silent Revolution: The Rise of the Lower Castes in North India*. Orient Blackswan.

Jagannathan, R. 2014. 'Unaffordable Property: Land is Scarce, Prices Can Only Rise.' *Firstpost.com*, March 26.

John, J. 2005. 'Real Estate Matters.' *Economic and Political Weekly* 40 (11): 1015–1017.

Kapur, D., T. Somanathan and A. Subramanian. 2014. 'Land-Shackled – I.' *Business Standard*, July 20.

Kapur, D., T. Somanathan and A. Subramanian. 2014. 'Land-Shackled – II.' *Business Standard*, July 21.

Kidambi, P. 2007. *The Making of an Indian Metropolis: Colonial Governance and Public Culture in Bombay, 1890–1920*. Aldershot.

KPMG. 2006. *India's Airports: Now Boarding for Growth*. Mumbai: KPMG.

Legg, S. 2007. *Spaces of Colonialism: Delhi's Urban Governmentalities*. Malden, MA: Blackwell Publishing.

Merinews. 2009. *Money Power to Dominate Polls in the South?*, March 2. Accessed October 6, 2014. Available at, http://www.merinews.com/article/money-power-to-dominatepolls- in-the-south/15714396.shtml.

Nair, J. 1996. 'Predatory Capitalism and Legalized Landgrab: Karnataka's Land Reforms.' *Economic and Political Weekly* 31 (5): 251–252.

Nair, J. 2005. *The Promise of the Metropolis: Bangalore's Twentieth Century*. New Delhi: Oxford University Press.

Nandy, M. and A. Datta. 2013. 'Firms Tapping 'Real' Wealth in their Books.' *Livemint*, February 4.

Ohri, M. 2009. *Airport Privatization in India: A Study of Different Modes of Infrastructure Provision*. Accessed October 14, 2013. Available at, http://www.ipe.ualberta.ca/en/EventsandSeminars/TransportationConferenceBanffA/~/media/ipe/ConferencesAndLectures/TranspBanff/TransportPaper-Ohri.pdf.

Pani, N. 2013. 'Globalization, Group Autonomy, and Political Space: Negotiating Globalized Interests in an Indian City.' *Unpublished mimeo*.

Peterson, G. 2009. *Unlocking Land Values to Finance Urban Infrastructure*. Washington D.C: Public-Private Infrastructure Advisory Facility (PPIAF), World Bank.

Peterson, G. 2008. 'Unlocking Land Values to Finance Urban Infrastructure: Land Based Financing Options for Cities.' *Gridlines, Note No. 40*.

Rajashekhar, M. 2013. 'Great Rural Land Rush: 3 to 100-fold Rise in Farm Land Prices May Not Bode Well.' *The Economic Times*, November 12.

Rajendran, S. 2008. 'RTI Act Applies to BIAL: Panel.' *The Hindu*, August 19.
Sanjai, P. 2014. 'Air India, NBCC Tie Up for Monetization of Assets.' *Livemint*, August 19.
Sankhe, S., I. Vittal, R. Dobbs, A. Mohan and A. Gulati. 2010. *India's Urban Awakening: Building Inclusive Cities Sustaining Economic Growth.* McKinsey Global Institute.
Sastry, A. 2013. 'Bachelor Priya Krishna's Assets are Over Rs. 900 Crore.' *The Hindu*, April 17.
Sathe, D. 2011. 'Political Economy of Land and Development in India.' *Economic and Political Weekly* 46 (29): 151–155.
Shiva, V. 2011. 'The Great Land Grab: India's War on Farmers.' *Aljazeera*, June 7.
White, B., S. Borras, R. Hall, I. Scoones and W. Wolford. 2012. 'The New Enclosures: Critical Perspectives on Corporate Land Deals.' *Journal of Peasant Studies* 39 (3–4): 619–647.

12

Political Economy of Land Acquisition and Resource Development in India

Shashi Ratnaker Singh

Land Acquisition: The Contested Domain

Land is a non-expandable factor of production . This very finiteness tends to cause competition for this scarce resource between various economic activities. In capitalist societies, the industrial and service sectors, dominated by the bourgeoisie and supported by the state's right of eminent domain, adopt land usurpation and acquisition by hyper commercialisation and commodification of land. The land acquisition process in India has come under close scrutiny within the overall context of economic growth and transformation from an agrarian economy to an industrial economy. Land acquisition with regard to resource based project becomes more complex as these resources are geographically located and projects becomes region specific.

The traditional argument as posited by the Lewis Model states that economic growth requires structural change in the economy whereby surplus labour in traditional agricultural sector with low or zero marginal product, migrate to the modern industrial sector with high rising marginal product. This promotes industrialization. The Lewis model necessitates structural change and thus explains the emergence of a dual economy. Land becomes a pre-requisite for industrialization. It implies that land has to change character from its present use to industrial use. The debate about industrialization and land acquisition is thus about how political, social and economic forces are acting in concert to transform the economy. At a more basic level, this problem occurs because the emerging industrial sector usually does not have the level of employment intensity as the existing agricultural activity. Moreover, affected people are not immediately employable as the only marketable commodity they possess in the absence of skills valued by the market, is their labour. This alienates the peasantry from their traditional means of livelihood and more often than not results in social turmoil and unrest.

Many developing countries, including India, have been undergoing this process of transformation over recent decades raising several questions about the true nature of the welfare state and its role in protecting the right to property. In India, the role of the state seems to have got reversed; after independence, through land reform, the government attempted to create a socialistic pattern of society through redistribution of land, which is now being reversed through increased acquisition of land from small and medium owners for industrialisation. Sixty years of 'planned' development in India have also entailed large scale forced evictions of vulnerable populations, without countervailing policies to assist them to rebuild their lives. Most of the negative aspects of displacement, such as undervaluation of compensation and its payment in cash, lack of information, failure to prepare in advance a comprehensive plan for rehabilitation, failure to restore lost assets or livelihoods, traumatic and delayed relocation, problems at relocation sites, multiple displacement and neglect of the special vulnerabilities of the most disadvantaged groups result from the existing law and the policies. This raises a crucial question: Is India moving on a path, which segregate society and enclaves economic spaces in a way that essentially excludes the majority from development?

The vast literature generated over recent decades on land acquisition, mining, resettlement and rehabilitation issues in the country has largely focused on recording the detrimental social, cultural and economic consequences of development projects on the lives of local project affected families. Development analysts, civil society and media have pointed to the inadequacy of the current normative and legal policy framework, in particular of the pivotal notion of eminent domain underpinning the Land Acquisition Act (of 1894). This literature has been useful in identifying systemic problems underpinning resettlement and rehabilitation in India (in addition to eminent domain, analysis from political economists that points to intractable power relations that nullify efforts to sustainably assist project affected families).

Every year dams, mining, highways, ports, urban improvements, pipelines and petrochemical plants and other such industrial development projects globally displace about 10 million people. (Cernea, 2000a). In India alone involuntary resettlement is estimated to have affected about 50 million people in the last five decades (Roy, 1999). Three-fourths of those displaced in India over five decades still face an uncertain future (Cernea, 2000a). The resettlement process has frequently been taken to be complete once compensation was paid to the affected people and they were relocated to a new resettlement site. Traditionally, little thought went into addressing the factors that limit the benefits available to project affected families, making a series of rehabilitation action plans unsustainable in the long run.

People displaced by development projects confront a variety of impoverishment risks that include landlessness, joblessness, homelessness, marginalisation, increased morbidity, food insecurity, loss of access to common property, and social disarticulation. (Cernea, 2000 and 1995) If resettlement is not to leave people worse off than before, it must be addressed as a process of sustainable development (Cernea, 2000; Scudder, 2005, 1997). Still persisting colonial laws govern the regime of displacement and rehabilitation. The decisive discursive category is here that of the 'oustee' who, of course were the rightful owners of property in recent past. And a series of cumulative consequences of displacement are now compensated under the Land Acquisition Act, 1894 through a consolidation of temporalities of many future deprivations (Baxi, 1989). In case of development- induced displacement, rehabilitation becomes a necessary legal and moral responsibility on the developer's part and it depends on the state and developers to transform these events into a developmental opportunity for the affected families. However, the past displacement experiences of the Indian states suggest that the affected families are the worse affected in this process and they do not receive any direct benefits from such projects, for which they sacrifice their land and livelihood.

The meaning given to compensation has been dominated by its equation with the market value, or the notional value of the land in the market. This treats the displaced person as a willing seller. Compensation is seen as the means for reducing the injustice inherent in acquisition. The limited understanding of compensation has eroded its moral base. The notion of total compensation being unknown to the law – it is ill equipped to internalise the immoderation which acquisition may entail (Ramanathan, 1995). The land acquisition process also tends to be individual centric and compensation is not sensitive to the displacement of communities. The trauma involved in displacement, the fragmentation of communities, the breakdown of support structures, the deprivation of displaced populations, the increased susceptibility to exploitation where protected populations are dislocated, are usually neglected by the law of compensation. The only significant reparation for displaced persons guaranteed by law is the payment of monetary compensation for compulsorily acquired individual assets, mainly land or houses. However, the manner in which the law is framed and interpreted ensures that the displaced landowner or house-owner is always the loser.

Existing provisions and practices of determining land price

The provisions of the Land Acquisition Act of 1894 relating to the definition of compensation, the method of fixation of compensation and its disbursement are replete with loopholes that cause many difficulties for displaced land holding households. In this context, neither the existing Land Acquisition Act, 1894 nor the Land Acquisition Resettlement and Rehabilitation Act 2013, (LARR) prescribe any appropriate methodology for the determination of rate at which land should be acquired. The Land Acquisition Act, 1894 uses different terms to denote the sense of 'quid pro quo'. In section 11 (i), it uses the words 'value of land'; in section 11 (iii), phrase 'compensation' used; section 15 of the act changes to phrase 'amount of compensation'; section 23 switches to term 'market value of the land'. And, no where in the Act, have any of these terms been adequately defined. Consequently, they have been used interchangeably at the level of field assessment causing great damage to the rights of the landowners.

In the absence of any clear value for rate of land, different *ad hoc* practices, predominantly two, have gained ground. First, rates used in registered sale deeds in neighbouring areas (project notified region) are averaged over three years. Second, the stamp duty rate, known as the collector rate, is taken as market value of the land. The first is more prevalent than the second. However, most land transactions in India are grossly undervalued to evade registration fees. Therefore, the oustee receives a rate which is typically much below the market rate, and the solatium of 30 per cent (or even 100 per cent or multiplying circle rate with 2 or 4 times as is being proposed in a new LARR Act 2013 by the Government of India) does not bridge the gap between the market and the registered prices. These practices seem to have grown primarily out of convenience rather than adoption of any scientific approach. This lack of predictability in the process of determining land value has added to the intrinsically contentious nature of land acquisitions, and contributed to the social unrest that inevitably accompanies such proceedings.

Significant judicial pronouncements on determination of land price

One natural consequence of this lack of clarity in the Land Act is that it has led affected people to frequently turn to the courts for guidance in interpreting the different provisions. The courts in turn have issued a variety of judgments in an attempt to guide administrators on what factors need to be taken into account in determining the value of the land to be acquired. The most salient guidance with respect to the valuation of land can be summarized as follows:

1. The opinion of experts can be taken into account in determining the market value of land (AIR 1959, SC 429),
2. The Collector should not neglect the non-agricultural potential of the land in question (Bhojraj vs Collector of Durg, 1979 JLJ 24),
3. In A. Gopalakrishan vs Special Deputy Collector, AIR, 1980 SC 1870), The Supreme Court of India has suggested that the following factors be taken into consideration in determining the compensation amount in an acquisition process:
   - Nature and location of land to be acquired
   - Present use of land to be acquired
   - Nature of use of nearby lands and their effect on the land under consideration
   - Capacity of the land being acquired.
4. Market value should be equal to the price at which a willing seller would give it to a willing buyer (1964 JLJ 231: 1964 MP Law Journal 299),
5. Market value of similar land in the past should be taken into consideration (1961 MP law journal 1219),
6. If the agricultural land to be acquired falls within urban body limits, an enhanced compensation amount should be paid (Deep Chand vs State of UP, AIR1980 SC 633),
7. Market value paid for small pieces of land cannot become the basis of land rates (1970 JLJ 466),
8. The assessment of land revenue can be a good indicator of market value of the land (Chatarbhuj vs Collector Raigad, AIR 1964),
9. Under some conditions, the prevailing rent or rate of tenancy can be taken into consideration for determination of land rate (Ramnarain vs State, AIR1963 MP 35)

These judicial pronouncements by different courts and at different periods of time do expound certain principles but do not create a template for determination of market value of the land. It is the responsibility of the legislators to learn from these experiences and with the help of subject experts they develop a sound and practical approach, acceptable to all stakeholders rather than such populist approach of multiplying land rate by 2 or 4 times. The objective should be to address the issue of restoration of livelihoods and for the farming community the only way to restore their livelihood is to restore their agricultural land, so emphasis must be given on replacement value of the lost assets.

Rationale for compensation

The rationality of compensation in context to land acquisition and resource development can be conceptualised under following heads (Figure 12.2): Economic, Spatial, Legal, Social/Ethical and Political. However, it is extremely complex to quantify community resources and livelihood with regard to expropriation and perhaps it will be inappropriate to even attempt to do so. But, unfortunately the legal provisions and the powers of eminent domain only leaves with the option of expropriation which is subject to debate whether it is 'just' or 'unjust'.

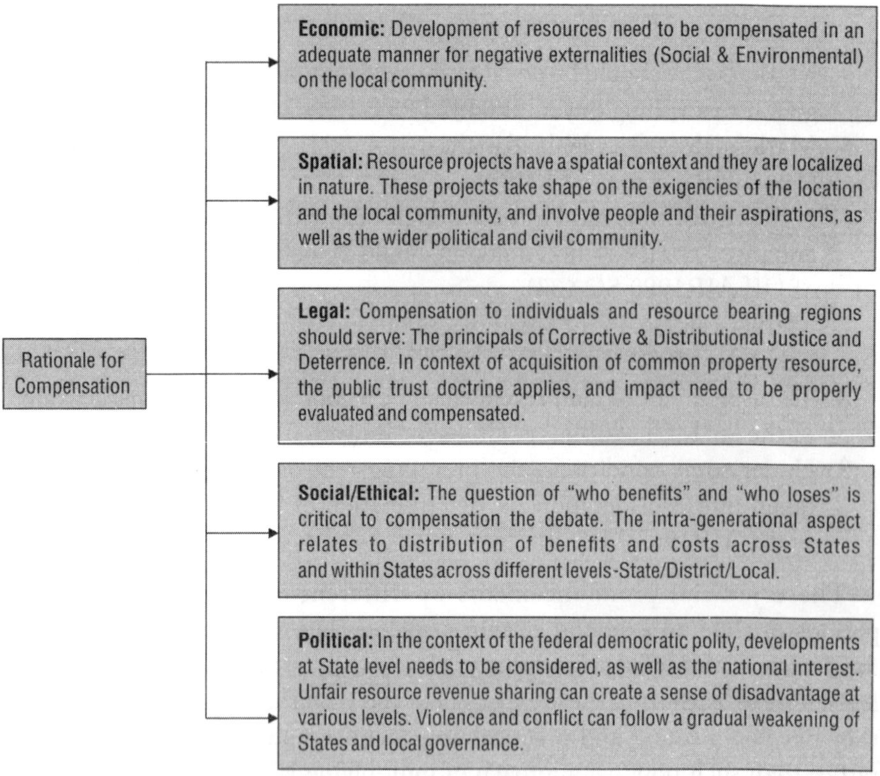

Figure 12.1 Rationale for Compensation: Land Acquisition and Resource Development

Source: Author's own illustrations.

Resource Federalism: 'Who' gets 'What' 'Where' and 'How'?

The role of resource development in regional development is a subject of debate between dependency theorists, who argue that resource development obstruct a balanced development process, and comparative advantage theorists, who argue that resources can expedite development. The literature suggests that the natural resources have the potential to provide a significant comparative advantage relative to other economic sectors by virtue of generating resource rent, which is surplus above normal returns to other factor of production. However, there are considerable risks in resource led growth, including the propensity to dissipate rent, increase community instability and several other externalities (social and environmental). The natural resources are geographically unevenly located (spatially) and the resource development projects have larger national and public interests. But there are layers of 'public' who gets affected in positive and negative manner by resource development projects: gains from their development accrue to large common market though the process also affects local lives/ livelihood and environment.

In context to this study, analysing the way federalism plays out in natural resource sector is very critical at this juncture of the evolution of the Indian political system, given its commitment to a more decentralized system of governance. In no sector such an engagement is more urgent than in the context of natural resource development, given the sharing of administrative and fiscal powers, along with growing responsibilities at the local government level. A federal government has been defined as an association of states, which has been formed for certain common purpose, but in the member states retain a large measure of their original independence.[1] The constitution of India stipulates a union of states but the drafting committee of the constitution made it clear that though India was to be a federation, the federation was not the result of the agreement of states to join in the federation and therefore, no state has a right to secede from it. A central issue, both from the point of the working federalism and in terms of the impacts that the resources development can have on local people, is the monitoring, regulation and enforcement of laws and rules in place. Both centre and state collect revenue through different taxes and levies imposed on minerals development under different legislations. In the given precarious fiscal situation of the mineral bearing States, there is a question with regard to the powers exercised by the Centre vide the Mining and Mineral Development and Regulation (MMDR) Act on fixation of royalty rates for a resource that is in principle owned by the States. There is also a discontent with the manner by which revisions are done by the Centre in terms of their periodicity. The necessity to arrive at a fair royalty is critical for the state and should not be dealt as a commercial activity only, but should also consider the ecological and social aspects of mining. The term 'regional' used in the paper refer to the governments at the state and local level. The central government collects revenue in the form of excise duty, forest conservation charges, and corporate taxes and so on. Apart from these taxes, some states like West Bengal impose a cess (primary education) on minerals. Table 12.1 summarises some of the main payments in case of resource development (minerals) and these payments are charged across different levels of government at different stages of mining cycle.

Table 12.1 Key Payments Land and Mining

Royalty and Dead Rent
Compensatory Aforestation and NPV (forest land)
Fees
Land Acquisition, R&R Payments
Income taxes
Local taxes
Environmental Fees
Water cess
General sales tax
Local taxes
Labour welfare cess
Cess on coal bearing lands

Source: Author's own illustrations.

With the opening of the economy and entry of private capital, there has been growing interest in resource projects by national and multinational corporations in the mineral bearing states. The lack of clarity about the nature, basis and rational of compensation and a recognition that the issues relating to fair compensation to the individuals and resource bearing regions are very important in the context of the federal democratic polity of the country, are the main motivations for this study. The complexities for resource development policy and consequently for compensation issues arises from the roles that resources perform and values attached to them. Understanding the issue of compensation for resource development requires a multifunctional view of resources and a multi-dimensional perspective- spatial, economic, legal, social and political. Such a perspective enables an understanding of the impacts that these projects have on the community and the region, and the need to be attentive to them if resource development is to truly be in the national interest.

Resource curse and compensation debate

There is an extensive literature on the Resource Curse, which suggests that regions or economies rich in natural resources are poor in developmental outcomes. Wheeler (1984) found that within Sub-Saharan Africa, countries that were rich in minerals grew more slowly than those that were not rich in minerals during the 1970's. Sachs and Warner (1995) examined the experiences of a large and diverse set of natural resource economies between 1970 and 1989 and found that natural resource abundance was negatively correlated with economic growth. Other scholars have presented evidence to suggest that the economic problems of resource abundant countries have gone beyond poor levels of economic growth. Leite and Weidmann (1999) found that natural resource abundance tends to worsen corruption. Finally, Ross (2003a) found that oil wealth and non-fuel mineral wealth are associated with bad outcomes for the poor in terms of poverty and human development levels.

It is now well recognised across the world that wealth generated by the mining sector comes at a substantial development cost. This has also been exhaustively documented in India. In fact, the major mining districts of India are among its poorest and most polluted (Bhushan, 2008). Considering the negative externalities of the mining sector, new policies and practices are being explored and implemented across the world to ensure that mineral wealth can be converted into sustainable development benefits for local communities. Many mineral rich countries have enacted legislation in which provisions of benefit sharing with the local communities are explicitly stipulated.

The mining and quarrying sector constituted about 2.26 per cent of GDP in India during 2010–11 (Source: IBM). Coal occupies an important position amongst minerals, as about 60% of India's energy needs are met through coal. In states like Chhatisgarh and Jharkhand, the contribution of minerals in the SDP is higher than 10 per cent and next only to agriculture and manufacturing. Further, income from royalty from minerals is a significant contributor to revenues in states like Chhatisgarh, Jharkhand, Odisha and Madhya Pradesh. Royalty was the single most important contributor to non-tax revenue in some of these states. Examining the contribution of various minerals to the royalty revenue in these states, it is seen that coal accounts for 65–90 per cent of the royalty revenue in Chhatisgarh, Jharkhand, Odisha and Madhya Pradesh. Other important minerals in terms of their contribution to royalty in these states are limestone, iron ore, bauxite and chromite.

The top 50 mining districts, in terms of value of mineral production are in 13 states. Jharkhand has nine of these districts, Odhisa, Madhya Pradesh and

Chhattisgarh six districts each, five are in Andhra Pradesh, and four districts in Maharashtra. The top 50 districts in India based on value of mineral production, together account for more than 85 per cent of the value of mineral production in the country (CSE, 2011). Another significant fact about these districts is that most of these mineral rich areas are affected by 'Naxalism'and declared as extremist affected regions by the Government of India. The appropriation and exploitation of natural resources have frequently been mentioned as a cause of civil wars. Several studies both from economic (Collier and Hoeffler, 1998, 2004; De Soysa, 2000) and political science (Kaldor, 1999; Klare, 2001) perspective suggest that natural resource abundance is an important determinant of the occurrence of internal armed conflict. However, Ross (2004) warns that the empirical linkage between natural resources and civil war is fragile, and proposes that the resource-conflict relationship should be differentiated with respect to both the type of natural resources and the kind of civil conflict.

In the context of resource development, land emerges as an important and highly volatile issue at many points during the life cycle of a project. Corporations need to secure access to land and community consent, and communities need to be assured that land rights are properly recognized, that free and informed consent is obtained, and appropriate compensation policy is in place where land is lost or affected. Past experience demonstrate that people in project areas, contribute to a project through the land that they give up, and that the project would not possible without access to this land. And yet payments made to the project affected people are only for damage created or for loss incurred, they do not necessarily create a benefit. Communities or individuals beneficiaries in project, and the loss of opportunity for the affected people in benefiting from enhanced land values as a result of resource development are not recognized. Even when land rights of local people are clear, these resources tend to be valued more cheaply in a deal, as negotiations depend on the distribution of information, power and influence and these are typically asymmetrical. Women are specially affected when productive assets, such as arable land are lost to mining because of their greater dependence on agriculture, as men migrate to mining or other non-farm jobs. Compensation payments by project authorities for this land are one time payments, which tend to go to the males of the household and which are often used for immediate consumption needs rather than investment purposes.

Land is a particularly contentious issue with regard to resource development in tribal populated areas. The Constitution of India provides specific protection to tribal rights over their customary resources, particularly in Schedule V and Schedule VI. The existing literature and past experience reflect that resource policy has either ignored or not engaged centrally with project affected people especially in tribal area and the creation of institutions for equitable distribution and sharing of project benefits. The negative externalities associated with resource development suggest that compensation demands by resource bearing states (See memorandum to central finance commission from the mineral rich states), cannot be seen as just an Union-states issue, but also involving the sub-state, local level, wherein various groups have interests in resource development or their non development.

Resources: development and externalities

Resource development has associated social, resource, cultural and environmental costs. Mineral development, for example, has the potential to be both beneficial and detrimental to poverty reduction. At a macro level, research suggests that a state's dependence on the export of non fuel minerals tends to hurt the welfare of the poor (Ross, 2003). At a micro level, while new income and mine supported social services can help reduce poverty, land alienation and deterioration, loss of access to common property and services, loss of traditional livelihoods, crowding out of agriculture, increased morbidity and mortality from environmental health impacts, human rights infringements and displacement are potential source of distress and poverty (Cernea, 2000; IIED-WBCSD, 2002; McMohan, 1998; MERN Working Paper Series).

At the pre-mining stage, there could be displacement of people, clearing of forests, removal of vegetation and several other impacts due to acquisition of land. Apart from the mining activity, the large scale in migration of construction workers and the transport of heavy mining equipment for construction, trial shipment of mine products and bulk samples further aggravate these impacts. The existing infrastructure including roads is often not upgraded to cope with the heavy load. Vehicular emissions and dust contribute to air pollution even before active mining begins. The environmental impacts of mining during the operational phase are likely to be greater than those in the pre-mining phase. These range from the impact on land, ground water quality and levels, air and water pollution and solid waste generation. Cropland productivity loss is the outcome associated with the degradation of soil, either due to silting or due to desiccation. This leads to creeping expropriation and a marginalisation of farming communities.

The post-mining phase has long-term implications for the ecology of the area. Negligence in planning of long-term water management, safety and stability of mining voids, and final rehabilitation can render the mining area uninhabitable. Abandoned and closed mines are often associated with ongoing ground and surface water contamination, which may continue for a long period. The magnitude and significance of impact on the environment due to mining varies from mineral to mineral, the type of mining (e.g. underground vs open cast) and also on the potential of the surrounding environment to absorb the negative effects of mining, geographical disposition of mineral deposits and the size of mining operations.

Tribal and poor peasant women are specially affected through environmental degradation that accompanies development given their dependency on common grazing lands, fuel and fodder from forests or crop land for their subsistence needs (Agarwal, 1994). Loss of forests, common property resources and crop lands affect their lives and livelihoods in very material ways, often causing a movement into poverty. There is evidence of how their access to water is affected by development activity, for example mining, either through the pollution of surface water, which they may depend on for their daily needs, or increased depletion of ground water in regions of open cast mining. All these externalities add considerably to their hardships, prolonging their already long days and travel time, reducing the quality of their nutrition, affecting their health and lowering their income from common property resources (Agarwal, 1992).

Resource development projects use these common resources and disrupt the ecosystem through operations very often without paying for them. This may reduce the cost to the developer, but it poses a cost to the local community as they have to bear these costs either because they lose economically (e.g. farmers and other forest dependent communities) or through adverse health and reduced well being. The developer in this case just transfers these costs to the local community. Moreover, not all of the ecosystem disruption costs can be monetized, and be amenable to compensation payments. As Turner (1999) points out an ecosystem has a social value that may not be the same as the aggregate total private economic value of its components.

Legal and federal context of land acquisition and resource development

The right to seek compensation emanates from either principles such as Justice, polluter pays, resettlement and rehabilitation policies; or right over the resource itself, either of absolute ownership, control or usage. Compensation payments need to be supported by legislation or be based on general principles of law such as torts or those developed by judiciary as in the case of compensatory afforestation. Beside their treatment in the constitution and the laws, the nature of the resource also has an important role in determining any liability that arises for use or depletion of the resource and associated environmental and socio-economic externalities.

Payment to resource bearing regions and to people in the region needs to address four primary issues, viz, compensation, corrective (and distributional) justice and deterrence. The goal of achieving corrective justice is to redress a wrong; that of distributional justice is to ensure that proceeds are used to make the Project Affected Families (PAF) better off than before the project and to improve the lives of the least well-off; and that of achieving deterrence is to regulate future behaviour.

The exercise of the rights to own, control, use, levy a charge on a resource are all dependent on another right of the government that is to legislate on these matters. In India, the proprietary title to the minerals vests in the federating states. However, this ownership is subject to the legislation governing regulation and control of mining enacted by the Indian parliament. With respect to minor minerals, the situation is different as States can make their own rules and regulations.

Although the Union may be empowered by the constitution to take mines and minerals development under its control, the MMDR Act does not sufficiently recognise the ownership rights of the states. Despite states being the owner, important matters such as royalty fixation and revision are under the Union‘s control. This control is in place in order to ensure that mineral resources are used in the national interest. While this is reflected in the fact that regulation and control over the major minerals needs to be vested in the Centre, an independent body should undertake the control over decisions that relate to revenue augmentation for the states.

A central issue both from the point of the working of federalism and in terms of the impacts that resource development can have on local people is the monitoring, regulation and enforcement of laws and rules. It is evident that India has a clear framework for regulating the powers and responsibilities in the case of resource development and to address environmental (and some social) implications of resource development. Yet, poor environmental and social outcomes suggest that there is inadequate oversight by regulatory bodies at various levels of government, and poor enforcement of the laws. Evidence of this is unfair payment arrangements for land bought for resource development from the local people and complaints of human rights infringements (Noronha, 2005).

Multifunctional view of resources

The complexities for resource development policy, and consequently for compensation issues arises from the roles that resources perform, the values attached to them. Resources need to be seen not just as natural resources, but also as having cultural aspects; not just having material (use) values, but also non-use values. Use values refer to both actual (direct and indirect) use and option value, where direct refers to benefits derived from goods and services obtained, while indirect are those derived from ecosystem functioning, necessary for production and for living. Option value refers to the potential of using a resource or acquiring information about it. But resources can also have cultural value or an existence value, a – value within a larger economy of signification, which crucially shapes their modes of appropriation (Baviskar 2003). They sometimes are also seen as – resources for collective representations that exceed the concern with immediate material use (*ibid*). The nature of demands made by various stakeholder groups reflects the different meanings and values that are attached to the resources. So resources have multiple values and meanings in context of 'space' and 'place', and their development thus has different meanings and implications for different groups industry, government and community. In this context, whose interest should get priority and how, become key to the compensation debate.

'Space' and 'place' are key geographical concepts, which have different connotations. Literature suggests that scholars studying the relationship between people and physical landscape have used a variety of terms and different ontological and epistemological perspectives to describe this phenomenon. For instance, Low and Altman (1992) used the term place attachment to refer to the phenomena of human place bonding. While they stressed that affection, emotion and feeling are central to the concept, they also indicated that these emotional elements are often accompanied by cognition (thought, knowledge and belief) and practice (action and behaviour). Researchers working within a naturalistic paradigm have stressed the subjective nature of the sense of place construct. For example, Tuan (1977) distinguished between space and place by suggesting, What begins as undifferentiated space becomes place as we get to know it better and endow it with value. In describing his interpretation of sense of place, Steele (1981) also referred to people's subjective perceptions of their environments and their more or less conscious feelings about those environments.

This multi-functionality of resources creates three key policy issues: One, of balancing the interests of the wider constituency with that of the more vulnerable, regional groups that often have insufficient information and voice for representation; Two, of seeking to understand and include the interests of different stakeholder groups, and particularly of the marginalised, and three, of addressing the aspirations to modernity of adivasi groups while providing them with the option of remaining or being able to return to traditional ways of living, given that people have multiple affiliations that are intrinsic to people's lives and that create contradictions between what they want at different points of times.

Questions of who benefits and who loses, whose interests are being furthered, who is being marginalized are key to understanding current dissatisfaction in a number of states, which are involved in resource development, infrastructure projects and development of Special Economic Zone (SEZ), and require serious engagement at all levels.

Mineral bearing states

In India, the geographical distribution of minerals (mainly coal) and metallic mineral reserves is highly uneven. Coal and metallic mineral reserves are spread across central and eastern India along the states of Madhya Pradesh, Chhattisgarh, Jharkhand and Odisha, as well as some areas of Maharashtra (bordering Chhattisgarh and Madhya Pradesh) and Andhra Pradesh (bordering Chhattisgarh and Odisha). Coal is also found in Assam and Meghalaya, while lignite occurs along the Eastern Ghats in Tamil Nadu.

India's iron ore deposits are in Odisha, Chhattisgarh, Jharkhand, Karnataka and Goa. The deposits of copper, lead and zinc are mainly in Rajasthan, while the reserves of bauxite are concentrated in the states of Odisha, Chhattisgarh and Andhra Pradesh. Unlike coal and metallic minerals, non-metallic minerals show an even geographical spread across India. For instance, limestone deposits are spread from Himachal Pradesh in the north to Andhra Pradesh in the south and from Gujarat in the west to Meghalaya in the east (Bhushan, 2006).

With respect to concentration of mineral deposits, Jharkhand, Odisha and Madhya Pradesh and Chhattisgarh emerge as the top mineral-bearing states (Table 12.2). About 70 per cent of India's coal, 80 per cent of its hematite iron ore (high-grade ore), 60 per cent of bauxite, 40 per cent of manganese and almost all its chromite are found in these three states (Source: GSI, CSE) with strong overlap of resources with forests and indigenous populations. It is now well recognised across the world that wealth generated by the mining sector comes at a substantial development cost, along with environmental damages and economic exclusion of the marginalised. This has also been exhaustively documented in India. In fact, the major mining districts of India are among its poorest and most polluted. Considering the negative externalities of the mining sector, new policies and practices are being explored and implemented across the world to ensure that mineral wealth can be converted into sustainable development benefits for local communities. In fact, the famous 1997 Supreme Court judgment on this matter (also referred to as the Samata Judgement) directed that in Schedule V areas, where the state government is undertaking mining, at least 20 per cent of net profits would be set aside as a permanent fund for development needs. This will be in addition to reforestation and maintenance of ecology.

Mining and Mineral Development Bill (MMDR)

The government's proposal to replace the MMDR Act with the MMDR Bill 2011, to include a specific provision for sharing 26 per cent of the net profits with local communities is an important step ahead in building an inclusive growth model. This proposal is also in line with the best practices being followed in the world. The principles are not new and many mineral rich countries have been following it for years without impacting the genuine profitability of mining companies. The fund will be deposited annually to the DMF, an amount equal to 26 per cent of profit after tax or a sum equivalent to the royalty paid during the year, whichever is higher. The DMF will then distribute monetary benefits directly or indirectly to affected people. However, there are many ambiguities with regard to identification of beneficiaries, who will administer the fund, utilization of the funds etc. However, the Government has introduced mining ordinance in 2014 and since the legislation is still evolving so it's difficult to comment on the precise percentage of benefit sharing at this point of time. But major policy shift that is visible is the acceptance of benefit sharing as a fair principle in the resource development process.

The concentration of minerals in these districts clearly reflects the uneven distribution of natural resources and also reflects how much significant wealth they are generating for the country. The socio-economic status of the community in these districts raises a critical question: 'why rich land has poor people'? As almost in all of these districts more than 50 per cent of the population lives below the poverty line. All of these states are extremist affected regions as declared by the Government of India and has strong naxals presence. Undoubtedly, the naxalites gets tremendous support from the local community, which justify their presence and existence. The state needs to understand that why people depart from the state? And if there is dissent, there are significant reasons. The provisions of profit sharing as proposed in the MMDR bill will significantly address many of the socio-economic and governance issues of these states.

Case study: Singrauli

The Singrauli region spreads across the states of Madhya Pradesh (Sidhi and Singrauli districts) and Uttar Pradesh (Sonebhadra district) and has been for a long time promoted as India's energy capital. It continues to be considered as South Asia's biggest industrial area[1]. Literature suggests that ever since 1840, when coal was discovered in Singrauli, the area's development has revolved around exploiting this mineral resource[2]. Singrauli region hosts some of the oldest thermal power stations and operational coal mines in India, set up by the NTPC and NCL. It has a long story of displacement and deprivation, of neglect and underdevelopment. Loss of livelihood and displacement has become a recurring feature for the people of Singrauli due to dams, power and mining projects over the last five decades. Over the past decade the Government of Madhya Pradesh has received a large number of proposals by private companies to establish resource-based industries in Singrauli. It is the single district, which has more than one lakh crore private investments[3] in the region. Communities are again in the process of being displaced with private players setting up 5 mining and 5 super thermal power projects in the area.

Singrauli contributes for more than 13 per cent of the total thermal power generation in the country, providing electricity to some of the major states: Maharashtra, Punjab, Haryana, Himachal Pradesh, Uttaranchal, Gujarat, J&K, Delhi, Goa, Daman & Diu, Dadar Nagar Haveli and Madhya Pradesh (Source: singrauli.nic.in, ntpc.co.in). It is expected that by 2017, Singrauli will generate 35000MW of electrical power to the grid alone. Singrauli, has a major contribution in revenue generation to the state as well as central government in the form of royalty, cess and taxes. However, half of the population in this region is still living below the poverty line. Inaugurating the Rihand Dam, which was to herald all this 'development' in 1964, Nehru promised the

Singrauli would become the 'Switzerland of India'. While inaugurating the district Singrauli in the year 2008, the Chief Minister of the State Shivraj Singh Chauhan said, 'he wants to develop Singrauli into another Singapore'. The political leaders have been portraying different illusionary picture to the local populace. In 2008, the geographical boundaries of Singrauli were redrawn and a geographical space of around 5500 sq. km (out of which 2200 sq. km is demarcated for coal mining) was carved out of Sidhi district to provide a status of an independent district. It clearly reflects that the reason behind developing a separate administrative unit of Singrauli was to facilitate the entry of private capital into this region.

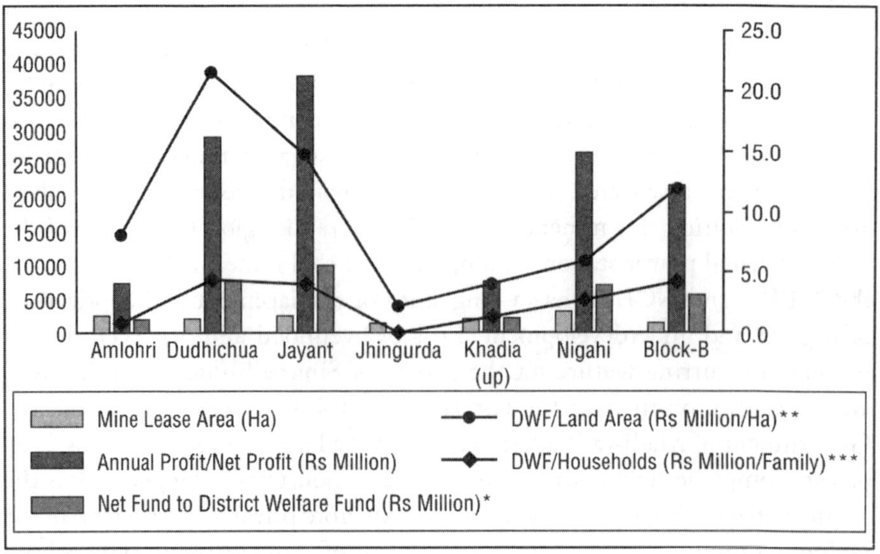

Figure 12.2 Revenue Generation and Profit Sharing for Mining Projects in Singrauli

The table 12.2 reflects that between 2008 and 2013 (after formation of the district) the operational coal mining projects have generated 131650 million rupees as net profit. Considering the proposed provisions of MMDR bill, 34229 million rupees (26 per cent of net profit) would have come to District Mineral Fund in the last 5 years as profit sharing mechanism. The allocation of such funds at district or local level can address many developmental challenges of these mineral rich districts. For a long period, the resource extraction process has been unfair to the local people and surrounding region. To address the increasing geographies of 'distributive in equality' in asymmetrical federalism in India, its high time the government start adopting localised development approach. The governance and distribution of such funds needs detailed analysis. The identification of beneficiaries in terms of directly or indirectly affected by project needs holistic approach. As mining activity involve large tracts of land acquisition (particularly forest land) and disrupts lives and livelihoods of large population. Some part of the fund must be set aside for improving the environment and local afforestation. The Singrauli region is still inhabited by some of the primitive tribes of the nation such as Baigas and Gonds along with other tribal groups. Undoubtedly, the region needs special focus in terms of resource allocation and localised development.

Benefit sharing: international experiences

Approach towards compensation and resource revenue distribution and management vary among nations, regions and resources. In the context of this study, the key questions that guided this review are to what extent other countries have systems of payment in place to address the various resource development issues and how have they engaged with the issue of compensation to resource bearing regions. Many mineral rich countries have enacted legislations in which provision of benefit sharing with the local communities is explicitly stipulated. Many of these legislations are built around a comprehensive framework in which compensation, benefit sharing and community development plans are integrated and the roles of local communities, governments and mining companies are clearly delineated.

Benefit sharing

In some of the resource rich countries like Canada and Australia, there are specific provisions in the legal framework to recognise the indigenous land claims and share a part of the profit from resource development activity in that particular region.

I. Canada

Impact Benefit Agreement (IBA) is legally- binding private contracts, which are voluntarily initiated by resource developers. They are used by aboriginals to influence decision-making in their lands and address concerns about mining impact on their environment, land, and their traditional way of life.

There are two types of agreements: One is legislative and the other is commercial. Legislative agreements are the ones that are entered into by particular aboriginals and federal government of Canada. Commercial ones

Table 12.2 Mineral Rich States and Benefit Sharing Provision

State	*District*	*Value of minerals (crore): 2010–11*	*Population 2011 (lakh)*	*Mine lease area (as of March 31.2008) in hectare #*	*Population affected**	*Profit sharing MMDR Bill*	*Profit sharing per Population affected**	*Profit Sharing for every household of the district (Rs./annum)****	*Literacy rate (%)*	*SC+ST population (%)*	*Area under forest (% of Total area)*
Madhya Pradesh	Chhindwara	1776	20.9	5359	18970	187	98694	4478	63.0	46.3	38.4
	Shahdol	1729	10.6	3291	11322	182	161002	8558	58.5	51.8	27.4
	Blalgahat	600	17.0	2282	8396	63	75306	1858	68.8	29.5	54.1
	Betul	395	15.8	1203	3777	42	110215	1321	60.9	50.0	35.6
	Umaria	294	6.4	464	1466	31	211538	2409	56.9	50.9	49.9
	Sidhi	3392	11.3	9563	44375	358	80567	15868	55.0	41.9	39.0
	Overall	8187	82.0	22162	88306	863	97716	5260	61.6	44.0	40.5
Chattisgarh	Korba	9121	12.1	13907	46966	961	204691	39839	63.0	51.5	50.8
	Dantewada	3961	5.3	2742	3230	417	1292417	39175	36.5	81.9	64.4
	Surguja	1081	23.6	6198	17893	114	63705	2414	51.5	59.4	45.6
	Koriya	778	6.6	1100	2425	82	338098	6221	61.3	52.6	62.3
	Raigarh	494	14.9	991	4533	52	114879	1743	64.3	49.6	36.2
	Durg	366	33.4	3860	30234	39	12762	577	69.7	25.2	9.0
	Overall	15801	96.0	28798	105282	1665	158190	8677	61.1	45.7	44.3

Contd.

Contd.

State	*District*	*Value of minerals (crore): 2010–11*	*Population 2011 (lakh)*	*Mine lease area (as of March 31.2008) in hectare #*	*Population affected**	*Profit sharing MMDR Bill*	*Profit sharing per Population affected**	*Profit Sharing for every household of the district (Rs./ annum)****	*Literacy rate (%)*	*SC+ST population (%)*	*Area under forest (% of Total area)*
Jharkhand	Dhanbad	3760	26.8	6362	163387	396	24256	7386	65.3	24.4	6.8
	Hazaribagh	1895	17.3	15075	120601	200	16563	5760	59.4	26.8	34.2
	Singhbhum	1195	15.0	16596	69371	126	18157	4194	49.5	58.2	38.7
	Chatra	1083	10.4	10321	56766	114	20109	5476	50.9	35.8	47.8
	Godda	1041	13.1	3909	48628	110	22563	4183	47.4	32.2	18.8
	Bokaro	953	20.6	7032	100698	100	9977	2436	63.4	25.6	29
	Ranchi	541	29.1	5828	64108	57	8895	979	66.9	47	24.7
	Palamau	250	19.4	1576	12009	26	21956	681	54.8	44.4	40.7
	Deogarh	202	14.9	518	6238	21	34139	714	54.7	24.8	6.8
	Overall	10921	166.7	67218	641806	1151	17934	3452	58.8	35.5	31.2
Odisha	Keonjhar	7370	18.0	28724	124661	777	62310	21544	59.3	56.1	38.9
	Angul	3049	12.7	13700	54526	321	58938	12635	69.9	28.9	41.9
	Sudergarh	2705	20.8	14604	62504	285	45614	6851	65.3	58.8	41.8
	Jharsuguda	1324	5.8	6491	35570	140	39233	12041	70.0	48.4	14.4
	Jajpur	1149	18.3	4195	52862	121	22915	3316	71.3	30.8	8.8
	Koraput	191	13.8	6565	20483	20	9841	732	42.1	62.7	19.1
	Overall	15788	89.4	74279	350607	1664	47463	9309	62.7	48.2	31.9

Source: CSE 2011, Census 2011 and Fieldwork Data.

Table 12.3 Operational Mining Projects and Revenue Generation in Singrauli between 2008–2013

Name of Project	*Mine Lease Area (Ha)*	*Total land acquired Private/ Govt/ Forest (Ha)*	*Project Affected Family (Nos)*	*Employment (Permanent Positions) (Nos)*	*Coal Production (MT)*	*Value of Mineral/Sale Value (Rs. Million)*	*Annual Profit/Net Profit (Rs. Million)*	*Net Fund to District Welfare Fund(Rs. Million)**	*DWF/Land Area(Rs. Million/ Ha)***	*DWF/ Households (Rs. Million/ Family)****
Amlohri	2383	2383	226	1471.8	30.87	30853.4	7104.7	1847.2	0.8	8.2
Dudhichua	1752	1752	353	2368	61.04	75261.0	29261.7	7608.0	4.3	21.6
Jayant	2480	2480	668	2534.8	68.69	72435.5	38276.5	9951.9	4.0	14.9
Jhingurda	1200	1200	57	921.4	9.83	9065.5	451.3	117.3	0.1	2.1
Khadia(up)	1640	1640	494	1428.2	20.82	24463.3	7644.2	1987.5	1.2	4.0
Nigahi	3036.4	2650.4	1178	2468	60.44	70748.9	26825.5	6974.6	2.6	5.9
Block-B	1339	1339	482	325.4	18.98	30973.4	22086.0	5742.4	4.3	11.9
Total	13830	13444	3458	11518	271	313801	131650	34229	17	69

Source: NCL Headquarter Singrauli, Revenue Department and Field Work 2013.

take place between mining companies and the aboriginals. IBAs are negotiable and are categorised as socio-economic agreements. These can include direct or indirect payments. Direct payments encompass profit sharing arrangements like cash or compensation funds. Indirect benefits may include employment, business opportunities and finance or equity provisions. As far as financial provisions are concerned, sometimes a fixed annual payment and subsequent payments based on value of minerals is made while sometimes royalty sharing is also considered. Agreements also make sure that business opportunities go to the affected sections by encouraging joint ventures between aboriginals and non-aboriginals. These agreements are thought to benefit those communities more who have some form of authority over traditional lands.

II. Australia

In Australia, revenue sharing mechanisms depend on the applicable act. Under the Land Rights Act, the mining royalties are given to the Australian Business Register (ABR) by the state government. It establishes the ABR, which has the responsibility to receive and disburse royalties to the aboriginal stakeholders. The funds are received in the form of 'mining royalty equivalents' (MREs) which is the sum of royalties paid to the central and the territory governments by mining companies for activity on aboriginal land. Under the Native Title Act, revenue sharing occurs through agreements between aboriginals and mining companies. Agreements are a central feature of the relationship between aboriginals and mining companies. Individual agreements are defined depending on goals pursued by particular indigenous groups.

There are six different types of financial sharing models:

Model 1 is a onetime upfront payment. Model 2 is a fixed annual payment. In this model, a particular amount is to be paid for some years and a different amount for the remaining years. It is advantageous because predictable amount each year will be paid to the community and it doesn't face all or nothing situation as in case of upfront payments. Model 3 is royalty based on output thus payments are linked to unit royalty. It is advantageous because as amount of production an increase so does the finance for people. The pitfall is that as production falls the money also reduces and even if the prices of minerals are high the advantage cannot be shared with the community. Model 4 is royalty based on value of mineral output 'thus royalty rates are based on production and prices. Model 5 is profit after tax.' Model 6 is equity participation.' The shares are obtained at substantial concession or for free for the indigenous groups. For the company it is beneficial to have an equity share of aboriginals as it increases their stake in making the project a success. In this case indigenous equity participation is more of cooperation rather than negotiation. Combination of different financial models is applied at different stages of project cycle for instance, a combination of upfront, annual payment and unit royalties.

Challenges before the state

The profit or benefit sharing provision in principle is well accepted across the world. The provisions in the MMDR bill will definitely improve the lives of the local affected community in particular and the mineral rich regions in general. This would also counter the argument behind resource curse that regions rich in mineral resources should not be deprived of development benefits. However, the experiences of the resource rich economies suggest that there are layers of complexities in implementing the profit sharing mechanism at project and regional level. As mining projects adversely affects large area including privately owned and common property resources, identification of directly and indirectly project affected people would be a major challenge. The role of Gram Panchayat would be critical in identification of affected families. The review of international experiences suggests that the list of directly mining affected families should be rational and selective. The list should not be broadened to an extent that profit sharing becomes meaningless and the money gets diverted for generic development activities of the district. The families losing land and primary source of livelihood should be given the first priority to be entitled for direct payment. Some part of the profit sharing fund can be utilised for general health care, education, rural infrastructure etc that can benefit the other indirectly affected families in the mining region.

Conclusion

Resource extraction process, by and large has been unfair for the local community and the surrounding region. There has been a policy shift in land and mining laws towards enhancing compensation and sharing project benefits with the local people. It is important to understand that there are layers of public in the bracket of 'public purpose' and the immediate public who loses his/her land and livelihood for such projects should be the first beneficiary of those projects. The loss of land and disruption of livelihood creates a sense of dissatisfaction among local community and creates reason for dissent. A large number of resource development projects in mineral rich states are held up due to land acquisition and environmental clearance issue. In fact, the momentum of economic reforms lies with the investments at state level. The growing demand for more compensation and resource revenue sharing indicates that both Project Developers and Central Government, can't ignore this fact and the fate of such projects are dependent on such policy change. Land is an important and unique factor of production due to its immobility, geostrategic value and so on. How much it actually constitutes of the total project investment and the amount of compensation from a rehabilitation point of view these are crucial questions and initiatives taken by UPA government in amending the Land Acquisition Act is highly appreciable but considering its special characteristics as factor of production there is need to go beyond this 'linear, technocratic, economistic (laws of production both Marxist and Neo-Liberals) and also reductionist view to a more expansive political view'. Anyone who is slightly familiar with the history of land struggles in the colonial India would stand for a more political view of land. Second, considering the relationships between land and the state; one cannot overlook the question of 'sovereign rights of state' over land especially regarding so-called public land.

Land has been and will continue to be a central fault line in near future more than the 'clash of civilization'; clashes of land have the potential to radically alter the existing fault lines in politics and also development policies. Let us not forget that almost all Maoist violence is sourced and concentrated in the land especially forest land mining land where compensation has become a dirty word and rehabilitation as slur! And the approach of providing 'development packages' from Centre to the mining districts at the time when there is a violence or crisis is highly absurd, why such spaces are kept deprived in very first place. On issue of compensation: no amount of compensation is enough when a robust and inalienable right to livelihood is not inbuilt in the quantified models of compensation. Some would prefer 'monetary compensation' based on 'informed consent' whereas many would still prefer to transvaluing the compensation in terms of 'who they are, where they are coming from and what they will be in future' the classical communitarian questions are not amenable to easy resolution. This shows why democracies are often vulnerable to pressures from land struggles whereas authoritarian political systems often offer swift answers. The classical political economy question of 'land' still remains unresolved; perhaps modernity's future rests on the resolution of this question, though the proponents of neo-age economy would not like to believe that land still matters!

Laws and Policies

- Australian Expropriation Law
- Constitution of the United States, Amendment V
- Constitution of the Philippines, Article III
- Constitution of Brazil, Article 153
- Constitution of Cambodia, Article 44
- Constitution of Japan, Article 49
- Expropriations Law, 1936, Mexico
- Land Administration Law, 1988, Peoples Republic of China
- The Singapore Land Acquisition Act, 1996
- The UK Town and Country Planning Act, 1990

List of Acts

Land Acquisition Act 1894
Mines and Mineral Development and Regulation Act
Mineral Concession Rules
Forest Conservation Act
Environment Protection Act
Coal Bearing Act
Constitution of the USA (5th Amendment)

Endnotes

1. For details, see: http://en.wikipedia.org/wiki/Singrauli
2. For details, see: http://www.blacksmithinstitute.org/projects/display/147
3. For details, see: www.singrauli.nic.in

References

2008. 'Seized: The 2008 Land Grab for Food and Financial Security.' *GRAIN.* Barcelona.

Cernea, M. M. 2000. 'Risks, Safeguards, and Reconstruction; A Model for Population Displacement and Resettlement.' In *Risks and Reconstruction: Experiences of Resettlers and Refugees*, edited by M. M. Cernea and C. McDowell. Washington D.C.: The World Bank.

Cernea, M. M. 2005. 'The 'Ripple Effect' in Social Policy and its Political Content: A Debate on Social Standards in Public and Private Development Projects.' In *Privatising Development: Transnational Law, Infrastructure and Human Rights*, edited by B. M. Likosky. Leiden: Martinus Nijhoff.

Cernea, M. 2007. 'Financing for Development: Benefit Sharing Mechanisms in Population Resettlement.' *Economic and Political Weekly*, 1033-1046, March.

Baviskar, A. 2003. 'For a Cultural Politics of Natural Resources.' *Economic and Political Weekly* 38 (48): 5051–5056.

Baxi, U. 1989. 'Notes on Constitutional and Legal Aspects of Rehabilitation and Displacement.' In *Development, Displacement and Rehabilitation: Issues for National Debate*. New Delhi: Indian Social Institute.

Balakrishnana, R. 2004. *Jharkhand Matters: Essays on Ethnicity Regionalism and Development*. Delhi: Konark Publishers.

Bhattacharya, H. 2005. 'Federalism and Regionalism in India: Institutional Strategies and Political Accommodation of Identity.' *Heidelberg Papers in South Asian and Comparative Politics, Working Paper No. 27.*

Bhushan, C. 2008. *Rich, Lands, Poor People: Is Sustainable Mining Possible*. Delhi: Centre for Science and Environment.

Billon, L. P. 2001. 'The Political Ecology of War: Natural Resources and Armed Conflicts.' *Political Geography* 20: 561–584.

Borras, S. M. Jr., P. Michael and I. Scones. 2010. 'The Politics of Biofuels, Land and Agrarian Change.' *The Journal of Peasant Studies* 37 (4): 575–592, October.

Clark, D. H. 1997. 'The Fiscal Transfer System in Canada.' In *Financing Decentralized Expenditures: An International Comparison of Grants*, edited by E. Ahmad. UK: Edward Elgar Publishing Ltd.

Chan, N. 2003. 'Land Acquisition Compensation in China – Problems and Answers.' *International Real Estate Review* 6 (1): 136–52.

Corbridge, S. 1987. 'Perversity and Ethno-Regionalism in Tribal India: The Politics of the Jharkhand.' *Political Geography Quarterly* 6 (3): 225–240, July.

Collier, P. and A. Hoeffler. 1998. 'On Economic Causes of Civil War.' *Oxford Economic Papers* 50: 563–573.

———. 2004. 'Greed and Grievance in Civil War.' *Oxford Economic Papers* 56: 563–595.

Dana, C. 2003. 'Singrauli: An Unfulfilled Struggle for Justice.' In *Demanding Accountability: Civil Society Claims and the World Bank Inspection Panel*, edited by C. Dana, J. Fox, T. Kay. USA: Rowman and Littlefield Publishers Inc.

Deininger, K. 2003. *Land Policies for Growth and Poverty Reduction (A World Bank Policy Research Report)*. Oxford: Oxford University Press.

De Soysa, I. 2000. 'The Resource Curse: Are Civil Wars Driven by Rapacity or Paucity?.' In *Economic Agendas in Civil Wars*, edited by M. Berdal and D. Malone. Colorado: Boulder, CO .

Fernandes, W. and G. E. Thukral. 1989. *Development, Displacement and Rehabilitation: Issues for National Debate*. Delhi: Indian Social Institute.

Gunton, T. 2003. 'Natural Resources and Regional Development: An Assessment of Dependency and Comparative Advantage Paradigms.' *Economic Geography* 79 (1): 67–94.

Mahalingam, A. and A. Vyas. 2011. 'Comparative Evaluation of Land Acquisition and Compensation Processes across the World.' *Economic and Political Weekly* 46 (32): Mumbai.

Noronha, L., N. Srivastava, D. Datt and P. V. Sridharan. 2009. 'Resource Federalism in India: The Case Minerals.' *Economic and Political Weekly* 8 (17). Mumbai.

Noronha, L. 2005. 'Assessing Quality of Life in the Mining Region.' *Economic and Political Weekly*, 72–78. January.

Pandey, B. 2000. 'Impoverishing Effects of Coal Mining Projects: A Case Study of Five Villages in Orissa.' In *Development Projects and Impoverishment Risk: Resettling Project Affected People,* edited by H. Mathur and D. Maesden. Oxford University Press.

Porwal, V. and Shashi Singh. 2011. 'Land Acquisition and Determination of Land Price: A Critical Appraisal of the Existing and Proposed Normative Framework as Applied in Singrauli District, Madhya Pradesh.' In *Development Induced Displacement, Rehabilitation and Resettlement in India: Current Issues and Challenges*, edited by S. Talwar and S. Saumyaji. London: Routledge Publication.

Ramanathan, S. 1996.'Displacement and the Law.' *Economic and Political Weekly* 31: 1486

Rao, G. and N. Singh. 2005. *Political Economy of Federalism in India.* New Delhi: Oxford University Press.

Rosser, A. 2006. 'The Political Economy of the Resource Curse: A Literature Survey.' *IDS Working Paper No. 268*. England.

Ross, M. 2004. 'What Do We Know about Natural Resources and Civil War?.' *Journal of Peace Research* 41: 337–356.

Ross, M. L. 1999. 'The Political Economy of the Resource Curse.' *World Politics* 51: 297–322.

Rost, R. O. and G. H. Collins. 1984. 'Land Valuation and Compensation in Australia.' *Australian Institute of Valuers,* 667.

Sachs, J. D. and A. M. Warner. 1995. 'Natural Resource Abundance and Economic Growth.' *NBER Working Paper No. 5398.* Cambridge: National Bureau of Economic Research.

Sharma, R. N. and S. Singh. 2009. 'Displacement in Singrauli Region: Entitlements and Rehabilitation.' *Economic and Political Weekly* 14 (51), December.

Singh, J. 2006. 'Separation of Powers and the Erosion of the Right to Property in India.' *Springer* 17: 303–324. Accessed October 14, 2010. Available at, http://rd.springer.com/article/10.1007/s10602-006-9008-7?state=cookieless.

Singh, M. P. 2004. 'Federal Division of Responsibilities in India.' *Indian Journal of Federal Studies* 1 (9).

Smith, N. 1984. *Uneven Development.* New York: Basil Blackwell.

Tuan, Y. F. 1977. *Space and Place: The Perspectives of Experience.* St. Paul, MN: University of Minnesota Press.

Turner, R. K. 1999. 'The Place of Economic Values in Environmental Valuation.' In *Valuing Environmental Preferences*, edited by I. J. Bateman and K. G. Willis, 17–41. Oxford University Press.

Upadhya, S. et al. 2006. 'Estimating the Economic Value of Forest Land: The Legal Perspective.' *Institute of Economic Growth.* Delhi.

13

Advice and Dissent

The Federal Politics of Reforming India's Land Acquisition Legislation

Rob Jenkins[1]

Introduction

The Right to Fair Compensation and Transparency in Land Acquisition, Rehabilitation and Resettlement Act 2013 (LARRA) was among the last major laws passed by the Congress-led United Progressive Alliance (UPA) government of Prime Minister Manmohan Singh, which governed India from 2004 to 2014. LARRA was passed just eight months prior to India's 2014 general election, in which the Bharatiya Janata Party (BJP) won enough seats to form a parliamentary majority under Prime Minister Narendra Modi, but also remained at the head of a coalition known as the National Democratic Alliance (NDA). Along with the National Food Security Act 2013 (NFSA), also passed during the UPA's final year in office, LARRA was one of the rights-based laws – including the Right to Information Act 2005 and the Right to Education Act 2010 – passed during Manmohan Singh's decade in power (Jenkins, 2013).

LARRA defines a set of rules, procedures, and oversight structures to govern the state's use of its power of 'eminent domain', as well as the responsibilities of state and private entities to individuals and groups adversely affected by the exercise of this power. This encompasses such issues as justifying the public purpose served by the acquisition (LARRA imposed higher standards), protecting certain categories of land (such as irrigated farmland), and assessing the likely social and economic impacts that would arise were land to be forcibly acquired. The politics surrounding LARRA's passage in late 2013 were complex and revealing about the character of the Indian state and the dynamics of India's policymaking processes (Jenkins, 2014), and are discussed briefly in the next section of this chapter. The strong cross-party support for LARRA also reflected the widespread feeling that the Land Acquisition Act 1894 (LAA), introduced by the British colonial government (though amended periodically after independence in 1947), was unable to afford the protections that a more aware and assertive public, operating in a modern democracy, increasingly demanded. Moreover, the protests were causing political instability and prompting potential investors to reassess the worth of the property rights they had negotiated with the state. A 2013–2014 study, which uncovered a total of 252 land-related conflicts, found that a quarter of India's districts experienced a significant level of land-related conflict, and that a majority of the most contentious cases involved the compulsory acquisition of land by state agencies (Society for Promotion of Wastelands Development and Rights and Resources Initiative, 2014). But even as LARRA came officially into force on 1 January 2014, the Act, and the model for extending rights that it represented, continued to be a point of intense public debate. Continued controversy over LARRA was partly the result of timing: the Act became law just as the country was gearing up for a general election – one in which the effectiveness of the UPA government's rights-based approach to addressing poverty was loudly being called into question.[2] Moreover, substantial overhaul, if not outright repeal, of LARRA was a major priority for business groups that had aligned themselves closely with the BJP. During the campaign, LARRA had been held up as a symbol of what business constituencies considered bureaucratic obstacles to investment, which the Modi-government promised, if elected, to remove.

This paper examines the successive political and institutional strategies adopted by the Modi government to advance its objective of amending LARRA in ways that would reduce the regulatory restraints on government and ease the process of acquiring land on behalf of private firms or public-private partnerships. Almost immediately upon taking office, the Modi government began acting on its promise to overhaul LARRA. Which considerations shaped the government's approach to reforming LARRA, given the available choices? How successful were its methods for overcoming political resistance to reform (which could be assumed to exist, given LARRA's recent vintage)? What role has India's federal system played in this process – whether through formal institutions or through the informal political leverage exercised by state governments and the parties that run them? And what implications does this process – including the federal politics of reform – have for the conditions under which the next phase of land-acquisition-law revision will take place? These are the key questions addressed in this chapter.

Background: The Politics of Passing LARRA 2013

The UPA government's commitment to introducing (and then steering through the parliamentary minefield) the LARR Bill 2011 (LARRB), which in 2013 was passed as LARRA, cannot be understood without also appreciating the complex and enduring effects of another law passed by the same government, eight years earlier – the Special Economic Zones Act (SEZA) 2005. The politically inflammatory process of implementing SEZA, which involved large-scale land acquisition to create low-tax, low-regulation industrial enclaves, had a major impact on the perceived need to develop a new legal framework for addressing the longstanding problem of development-induced displacement. SEZA, and the way in which state and central governments used it, created a political and institutional environment conducive to the framing of an integrated policy addressing both the compulsory acquisition of land for industrial or urbanization purposes and the needs of people affected by such actions (Jenkins, 2014). In the six and a half decades between India's independence and the passage of LARRA in 2013, efforts to bring the LAA 1894 into conformity with India's contemporary democratic ethos had been markedly unsuccessful. Amendments to the LAA introduced in the early 1960s were piecemeal, at best, and those of the 1980s not much more substantial. It was only in the wake of the UPA Government's SEZ policy that a comprehensive overhaul of land-acquisition legislation was pursued vigorously by a sitting government in New Delhi. The idea was to combine in one law provisions concerning the acquisition of land for industrial or infrastructural purposes and the obligations of both the state and private developers to people displaced by such projects. Serious efforts within government to promote such legislation came in the wake of land-related controversies associated with high-profile SEZs in several Indian states.

There were two key mechanisms through which SEZA helped to create conditions conducive to the formulation, in 2007, of the precursor bills that ultimately evolved into LARRA. The first was the political fallout from state governments' clumsy, and at times brutal, efforts to compulsorily acquire land for SEZ projects. Protests against large-scale land acquisition had occurred in different parts of India for decades. But SEZA provided a common – national – focus for complaint for activist groups waging otherwise isolated struggles in locations far from one another. Protests against SEZA's provisions, its underlying rationale, and the methods used to implement it brought together a wide range of constituencies dissatisfied with India's existing legal regime surrounding land acquisition and displacement. This combined with a powerful sense that it was morally unacceptable that property forcibly acquired would be transferred to private-sector industries rather than used for public roads, dams, or other conventional infrastructural purposes. This feature of SEZ land acquisition allowed local movements to draw in political actors and organizations that opposed pro-business economic reforms more broadly.

The second means by which SEZA (and its implementation) influenced the emergence of LARRA was through the creation of institutional structures whose operation catalyzed additional pressure for a comprehensive overhaul of the existing policy regime. These structures included the Board of Approvals (an inter-ministerial committee of senior civil servants that formulates rules for and gives clearances to SEZ projects) and (at the political level) the Empowered Group of Ministers (EGoM) on SEZs – one of many semi-executive cabinet subcommittees that both Congress- and BJP-led coalition governments have employed. The continuous deliberations and decisions of both the Board of Approvals and the EGoM attracted sustained media and political attention. This provided opportunities for opponents of specific SEZ projects to amplify their voices. It also reinforced, in political discussions, the need for a more thoroughgoing overhaul of land regulation.

In 2007, the UPA government introduced the Land Acquisition (Amendment) Bill, which called for, among other things, a Social Impact Assessment (SIA) to be conducted for any land-acquisition that would result in large-scale displacement. The Rehabilitation and Resettlement Bill 2007 was tabled in parliament around the same time. In February 2009, the Land Acquisition (Amendment) Bill 2007 and the Rehabilitation and Resettlement Bill 2007 were passed by the lower house of parliament. They remained pending in the upper house, and lapsed when parliament was dissolved ahead of the 2009 general election. Two years later, in May 2011, while a nationwide anti-corruption movement was in full swing, the Land Acquisition (Amendment) Bill and the Rehabilitation and Resettlement Bill were merged into the LARR Bill 2011 (Panel Suggests Changes to Land Acquisition and Rehabilitation Bills' *Business Today*, 2011; 'Sonia Council Seeks Land Bills' Merger' *The Telegraph*, 2011). The bill's passage required a two-year-long process of building consensus within both the civil service and among leading political parties, including the BJP.

LARRA is a complex piece of legislation. It is beyond the scope of this chapter to describe and analyse it in depth. But four features are worth noting in brief. First, the Act takes the unusual step of recognizing that state-facilitated development initiatives can deeply disrupt the basis of social, economic, and political life for entire communities. LARRA fundamentally changes the frame of reference used when considering effects: compensation was to be awarded not just to individual land-owners, but to stakeholders in the local economy more broadly, including those reliant for their well-being on the economic activities associated with existing land-use patterns. Second, LARRA acknowledged that 'public purpose' – the justification for the state's forcible acquisition of privately held land – must be defined more narrowly than it had been in recent decades, and that any purported social benefits must be carefully weighed against a more comprehensive accounting of social costs. Under LARRA, officials must attest that the 'land proposed to be acquired is the absolute bare-minimum extent needed' and that 'there are no other less displacing options available.' Third, LARRA spelled out a set of citizen-initiated procedural mechanisms through which the state, in theory, ensures the fulfillment of specified economic rights. The 'views of the affected families' must be included in the SIA, and non-governmental actors must be involved in appraising the SIA report. LARRA called for local 'consent' when land was to be acquired for private companies or public-private partnerships. Citizens would also participate in Rehabilitation and Resettlement Committees and in social audits. Fourth, LARRA created institutions to carry out functions identified in the Act: not only the local bodies mentioned above, but also a National Monitoring Committee for Rehabilitation and Resettlement and a Land Acquisition, Rehabilitation, and Resettlement Authority for each state.

These four features of LARRA are found, in one form or another, in almost every other piece of rights-related legislation enacted by the UPA government: the Right to Information Act 2005 (RTIA), the National Rural Employment Guarantee Act 2005 (NREGA), the Forest Rights Act 2006 (FRA),[3] the Right to Education Act 2010 (RTEA),[4] and the National Food Security Act 2013. These Acts, as well as a number of bills that never became law, represent a particular model of rights-based legislation. Its hallmark is the combination of specific social and economic entitlements with precise procedural mechanisms to involve people in overseeing their fulfillment – what James Manor and I have elsewhere termed 'governance rights' (Jenkins and Manor, 2016).

Federal Policymaking and National Reform

After taking power in May 2014, the BJP-led NDA government immediately began the process of making good on its promise to undo what it saw as LARRA's anti-business/anti-development bias. The options available included outright repeal of LARRA, national legislative amendment of provisions within the Act, the framing of regulations to counter the Act's effects, and/or having state governments take the initiative on reform, whether through regulation, legislation, or a combination of the two. Article 254 (2) of India's constitution leaves it in the hands of the President to determine whether, for subjects that the Constitution assigns jointly to the central and state governments, a state law that contradicts elements of a federal law may be enacted and upheld – a point made publicly by former BJP minister Arun Shourie (Jain, 2014; Verma, 2014).

That LARRA was a key target for much of India's business community, as well as many political leaders from within and beyond the BJP, was evident from the routinely harsh condemnation of the Act's structure, concept, and provisions. In November 2014, as the government's reform process gathered steam, one commentator dubbed LARRA 'The Law from Hell' (Nayyar, 2014). Having won a seemingly decisive electoral mandate, the Modi government felt no obligation to acknowledge the BJP's partial ownership of the Act. That LARRA, and its precursor Bills, went through two parliamentary committees, both chaired by BJP leaders (Kalyan Singh and Sumitra Mahajan) was considered insufficient to constrain the prime minister's reform agenda. More importantly, the Modi government rejected the idea that it would be politically strategic to divert responsibility for undercutting LARRA to India's state governments.[5]

Despite the Modi government's lack of a majority in parliament's upper chamber, the Rajya Sabha, the business constituency that helped to get the BJP elected (and the pro-business elements in the ruling party) pressed for bold action at the centre, rather than leaving the matter up to state governments. This meant amending (or even repealing) LARRA in parliament. There was considerable optimism in the BJP that passing a LARRA Amendment Bill was possible even without a BJP (or even an NDA) majority in the upper house. Votes, the prime minister was assured by at least two senior cabinet ministers, could be secured from discontented Congress members and MPs from smaller parties who might have their own reasons to fall in line with the policy agenda of a hugely popular new prime minister. Not only was LARRA cast as an obstacle to industrialization, BJP Finance Minister Arun Jaitley argued that reform of LARRA was essential to the Modi government's much-publicized objective of creating 'smart cities' across India ('Government Examining Land Act Provisions to Fix States' Concerns: Minister' Zee News, 2014).

The NDA government's approach to overhauling LARRA was a modified form of the strategy used by its predecessor to pass LARRA in the first place. The Congress-led UPA had implicated the BJP in LARRA's passage by addressing enough opposition concerns during the bill's mark-up stage that BJP MPs feared voting against an ostensibly pro-farmer policy in the run up to a general election. However, for the Modi government there was no impending election to scare opposition-party MPs in the Rajya Sabha into backing the overhaul of LARRA it was proposing. Instead, the NDA government began targeting a potentially more pliable element in the hierarchies of these parties: the state governments where they were in power. Chief Ministers do not always see eye to eye with their respective parties' national leaders, particularly when it comes to how state governments should go about striking a political balance between the demands of agricultural and industrial interests. Indeed, chief ministers typically view the process of land acquisition for industrial purposes as a key means of generating the illicit funds that allow them to operate their respective political machines – a stance which in this case puts many of them at odds with their parties' national policy agendas. Even within the highly centralized Congress, state-level elected officials are often more likely than the party's MPs to speak out publicly on issues that matter to them (in this case what they perceived as LARRA's deficiencies). A similar dynamic was at work in state governments ruled by regional parties (or *de facto* regional parties), whose leaders perceived the same threat to their political machines as Congress chief ministers did, but usually faced far fewer constraints from Delhi-based party executives. Regional parties – including 'national' parties whose electoral presence is confined to one or two states – had significant representation in the Rajya Sabha, and political strategists in the Modi government calculated that MPs from these parties might be more inclined to back an overhaul of LARRA if state governments they controlled were seen to be embracing much of this agenda.

Recognizing the divergent incentives between national party leaders (in Congress and other parties) and their respective counterparts in the states, the Modi government found it convenient to draw the resultant policy differences into the open. It did this, in part, by engaging in a form of 'cooperative federalism', a practice that the BJP claimed during the election campaign would characterize its approach to governance (Kailash, 2015). Cooperative federalism has a specific meaning in the academic literature on federal institutional relations, implying a system in which there exists not only a shared legal responsibility between central and state-level governments, but also the capacity to engage – through dedicated institutions – in joint endeavors to fulfill these mandates (Zimmerman, 2001). The concept emerged in the United States during the New Deal, when collaborative ventures between the federal and state governments were undertaken to counter the effects of the Great Depression (the Tennessee Valley Authority being a prime example). The Modi government deployed the idea of cooperative federalism to refer to mechanisms through which the central government would consult with state governments on proposed legal, institutional, and policy changes. Federal consultations on LARRA would be convened as a way of publicizing the concerns of state-level governments, which, in turn, might provide opposition Rajya Sabha MPs legitimate grounds for supporting the government's LARRA Amendment Bill: they would be acting in accordance with substantive criticisms voiced by their own party members at the state-level, to whom the indirectly elected members of the Rajya Sabha in fact largely owed their seats ('Government Examining Land Act Provisions to Fix States' Concerns: Minister' *Zee News*, 2014).

The perspectives of state-level governments offered in public statements, and the policy inputs they provided via the consultative process overseen by the central government's Ministry of Rural Development (MoRD), revealed a range of positions concerning LARRA. Some state governments emphasized idiosyncratic features of their environments. This was most evident in the claims advanced by small states (and Union Territories) that their distinct needs had not been taken into account when LARRA was originally framed. These included the Andaman and Nicobar Islands, Daman and Diu, Lakshwadeep, and certain northeastern states ('UPA's Land Acquisition Law Likely to be Overhauled with Many States Seeking Recast' *The Times Of India*, 2014). This position among small states was consistently held, regardless of which party held state-level power at the time the consultations were convened in mid 2014.

By contrast, BJP-run state governments mainly supported either outright repeal of LARRA, or else substantial legislative amendments to remedy what they saw as fundamental defects. This was the view held by state governments in Chhattisgarh, Goa, Gujarat, Rajasthan, and Madhya Pradesh. Some of these states were more full-throated in their principled opposition to LARRA, drawing attention to the flawed process by which the law was enacted ('MP Govt Still Adhering to Old Land Acquisition Rules' *Zee News*, 2014).

As for state governments ruled by regional parties, a similarly consistent pattern could be discerned: almost every one voiced complaints about particular aspects of the law. The government of West Bengal expressed serious reservations about the compensation norms. It claimed that the law's provisions did not reflect the reality of landholding patterns in West Bengal. Apart from this, however, West Bengal Chief Minister Mamata Banerjee of the Trinamool Congress (TMC) claimed to support LARRA. This was not surprising: the TMC's historic election in 2011 – it ousted a Communist-led coalition that had ruled the state for the previous 34 years – was in large part the result of Mamata's ability to capitalize politically on widespread and violent protests against two high-profile land acquisition cases during 2007–2010: the proposed Tata Motors project in Singur and the chemical-sector SEZ slated for Nandigram. In Uttar Pradesh, where the Samajwadi Party had been in power since 2012, and where, during the preceding BSP government, another set of politically charged protests against land acquisition took place, the government of Chief Minister Akhilesh Yadav announced that it too had objections only to certain elements of LARRA. In particular, the state government wanted more authority devolved to states to determine the conditions under which the "urgency" clause could be invoked – that is, the provision allowing certain landowner and community protections to be bypassed due to 'extraordinary circumstances'.

Because of the centralization associated with the Congress Party, one might expect Congress-run state governments to present the mirror image of the fairly uniform rejectionist stance adopted by BJP-run state governments. Yet, Congress governments in almost every state failed to follow the party line by embracing LARRA wholeheartedly. Every Congress-ruled state government submitted proposals to the centre-state consultative process to rectify one or more of what its leaders considered problematic aspects of LARRA ('Most Congress States had Doubts on Original Land Acquisition Act' *The Economic Times*, 2015). Doing so was considered within the bounds of acceptable party behaviour by the Congress high command – mainly because the party's disastrous electoral performance in 2014 put its national leadership, and especially the Gandhi family, in a poor position from which to impose loyalty tests. It was this contingent autonomy from party discipline, combined with state-level politicians' desire to operate relatively free of regulatory restrictions when acquiring land, that drove the positions taken by Congress-led state governments.

Congress-ruled Arunachal Pradesh, for instance, a somewhat idiosyncratic state in India's far northeast, voiced several complaints that were consistent with the BJP position: that the SIA process had to be excised entirely or else seriously scaled-back, and that provisions requiring the return of unused land to its original owners within a stipulated timeframe should be scrapped. The Arunachal Pradesh government also objected to the powers LARRA conferred on the central government to acquire land in cases of natural calamities ('Appeal for Amendment in Land Rehabilitation Bill' *The Times Of India*, 2014). The Kerala government, ruled by the Congress-dominated United Democratic Front (UDF) coalition, stressed another of the critical points raised by Arunachal Pradesh: the 'cumbersome' SIA process ('State moots radical changes in Land Acquisition Act', 2014). As with the Samajwadi Party-run government in UP, the Kerala government also had issues with the limited scope for state governments to acquire land under an 'urgency' clause. Another LARRA provision – the payment of retrospective compensation – was the focus of complaints voiced by the state government in Haryana, which at the time of the June 2014 centre–state consultations organized by the Modi government was still under Congress rule. (It would lose power to the BJP in state assembly elections held in October 2014.) The Congress-led coalition government in Maharashtra, too, strongly opposed the provision in LARRA that required retroactive compensation. (As in Haryana, Congress would cede power in Maharashtra to a BJP-led government in October 2014.) Himachal Pradesh, another Congress-ruled state, worried that the special situation of mountainous states had not been properly addressed in LARRA. As another mountainous state, Congress-ruled Uttarakhand agreed with this position. But Uttarakhand also opposed a part of LARRA that BJP leaders in Delhi were particularly eager to see excised, or at least significantly qualified – the provisions that restricted the ability of state governments to acquire 'cultivable, multi-cropped land'. Congress-ruled Karnataka and Meghalaya, too, opposed specific clauses in LARRA, though without fully specifying which ones ('UPA's Land Acquisition Law Likely to be Overhauled with Many States Seeking Recast' *The Times Of India*, 2014).

It was on the basis of these inputs from state governments that the Modi government claimed to have drafted its LARRA (Amendment) Bill. The key feature of the Amendment Bill was a series of exemptions from LARRA's two most important procedural requirements: that projects involving the acquisition of land be subjected to an SIA and that, under the conditions stipulated in the Act, public authorities seeking to acquire land must obtain local 'consent'. These exemptions were framed so broadly (applying to projects that sought to, among other things, promote 'rural infrastructure' or 'industrial corridors') that critics feared any project could conceivably evade these and other procedural protections under LARRA. While the federal consultations convened by the MoRD were successful in eliciting and highlighting the complaints of many state governments ruled by non-NDA parties, by late 2014 it was becoming clear that the BJP would be unable to translate the disaffection of state-level ruling parties into anything like the level of support from non-NDA parties that was needed in the Rajya Sabha. The NDA had just 60 seats in the 245-member body, and the rest of the seats were fairly widely dispersed across other parties, few of which were showing signs of flexibility for the reasons outlined above. The Modi government resorted to issuing an executive 'ordinance' to bring the LARRA Amendment Bill's provisions temporarily into effect. Such ordinances lapse if they are not followed by affirmative parliamentary action, according to a specified timeframe. Eventually, in August 2015, when the last of its three successive ordinances was due to expire, the Modi government announced that its efforts to pass the LARRA Amendment bill ('Land Ordinance Gets a Burial' *The Hindu*, 2015), to which it had made revisions in a failed effort to win over fence-sitters, had come to an end. It was increasingly apparent that it would take until at least 2017 for the Rajya Sabha's composition to become significantly more BJP-friendly (Albright Stonebridge Group, 2015).

By this point a full-fledged campaign to thwart the LARRA reform agenda had come into being. In fact, resistance to the Amendment Bill was one of the few issues that brought opposition parties together – divided as they were on many other economic policy issues (many regional parties being considerably to the left of Congress). The cross-party opposition to seriously scaling-back LARRA was aided by the Modi government's perceived role in either condoning or excusing acts which impinged on the rights of India's religious minorities, particularly Muslims, on whose support many of these parties – notably, the TMC in West Bengal and the Samajwadi Party in UP – relied for electoral support. The opposition was also emboldened by the resistance to amending LARRA expressed by organizations affiliated with the BJP – notably, groups closely linked to the Rashtriya Swayamsevak Sangh (RSS).[6] This was all against the backdrop of growing civil society activism that sought to associate the Modi government's attempted roll-back of community protections under LARRA with what movement leaders portrayed as the BJP's pro-corporate, anti-poor bias. As the difficulties facing the Modi government's reform effort began multiplying – including complaints from business leaders from India and abroad that it lacked the perseverance necessary to execute politically fraught reforms ('Modi Govt hasn't Delivered on Promised Reforms' *CNBC Money Control*, 2015) – Congress and regional party MPs (including their representatives in the Rajya Sabha) sensed an unparalleled opportunity to embarrass the new prime minister, who had publicly aligned himself with LARRA reform in high-profile public speeches in early 2015 ('BJP, Led by

PM Narendra Modi, to Clear the Air on Land Bill' *The Economic Times*, 2015). In short, opposition MPs, despite the interests their state governments might have in making LARRA less of an obstacle to their own land-acquisition projects, were in no mood to defect.

State-Level Adaptation to LARRA

This extremely unwelcome outcome for the Modi government – disenchanted investors, a united opposition, better-networked grassroots movements, division in the Hindu nationalist ranks – raises the question of whether an alternative strategy for achieving its LARRA reform agenda could have been pursued. A government that recognized the concerns many state-level ruling parties had with LARRA could have focused on helping states to adapt their laws and regulations in ways that would mitigate what many saw as LARRA's excesses. Doing so would not only have been consistent with the idea of cooperative federalism, but also would have avoided much of the adverse political fallout (from the Modi government's perspective) from the strategy of pushing LARRA amendments through the national parliament. Arguably, state governments are better positioned than authorities in Delhi to gauge the likelihood and severity of potential political discontent in their respective jurisdictions. This is something successive Indian governments have recognized, and used to their political advantage, since economic liberalization took off in the early 1990s (Jenkins, 1999). And by the time Modi assumed office, state governments were already demonstrating their ingenuity in devising methods for evading and bypassing LARRA's more restrictive elements. Rather than seeing this as a sign that a politically less costly means of overcoming resistance to reforming LARRA was available, the Modi government interpreted it as evidence that by appealing to state-level ruling parties it could overcome the majority enjoyed by non-NDA parties in the Rajya Sabha. By adopting a particular form of cooperative federalism, in other words, the Modi government forfeited an opportunity to draw on some of federalism's other beneficial properties – notably, the tendency for 'competitive federalism' to spur a dynamic in which state governments seek to attract private capital by establishing investment conditions that exceed those prevailing in other states. The central government's desire to signal to potential investors its capacity to carry out one of its flagship reform measures appears to have outweighed any possibility of pursuing a stealthier option – one that relied not only on the incentives state governments have to dilute LARRA, but also their skills in managing political conflict within their borders.

Since LARRA passed in late 2013, state governments had been devising means of preserving their capacities to acquire land for a variety of public purposes. The Congress-run Andhra Pradesh government remained surprisingly quiet on LARRA prior to the May 2014 state assembly elections that led to its replacement by the Telugu Desam Party (TDP). Chief Minister Chandrababu Naidu was among the loudest voices denouncing LARRA's highly detailed procedures – the cornerstone of protections for landowners and other affected people – as far too costly and time-consuming for entrepreneurs seeking to respond to market signals. After taking office, Naidu's government sought 'work-arounds' for LARRA strictures. When asked how it would go about implementing LARRA, state officials indicated that the government was formulating amendments to the state's Municipal Act that would allow 'land-pooling' – a method of 'voluntary' land aggregation pioneered in Gujarat when Narendra Modi was chief minister – to be used as a substitute for 'acquisition' ('Andhra Pradesh May Amend Municipal Act', 2014). Land pooling allows a state government to evade some of LARRA's more onerous provisions – particularly the requirement that 70%-80% of affected people consent to the acquisition of land for the purpose in question ('Andhra Pradesh Government Looking for Best Model' *The Times Of India*, 2014). In addition, in September 2014, the Andhra Pradesh government sent its draft rules regarding LARRA implementation to the MoRD in New Delhi. The rules were seemingly compliant with LARRA's rehabilitation and compensation mandates; arguably, however, the governance structures proposed would have allowed senior political leaders (the Chief Minister and key members of his cabinet, in particular) great influence over the decision-making bodies further down the administrative hierarchy ('Land Acquisition Act Finalized in AP' *The Siasat Daily*, 2014).

Similar patterns could be seen in other states, regardless of which party was in power. The Congress-ruled Haryana government adopted a position that resembled Andhra Pradesh's once LARRA came into force at the beginning of 2014 – and even more vigorously after the BJP came to power a few months later. Haryana sought to use land pooling to take forward a number of projects, while announcing its intention to hold off on new 'land acquisitions', as such, until the anomalies between central and state government regulations were ironed out. Some Congress state governments were able to frame rules that complied with LARRA's provisions, but permitted the state government to take actions that would erode landowner-protection provisions in practice (Government of Karnataka, 2014; 'Govt Notifies Rules for Land Acquisition' *The New Indian Express*, 2014). Other Congress-ruled governments, such as the UDF coalition in Kerala, found it convenient to take no immediate action in framing rules for the operation of LARRA in the state. In Kerala, the state government was preoccupied with facilitating land acquisition for a major highway project in the state ('Kerala to Speed Up Land Acquisition for NH Development' *The Economic Times*, 2014), and this influenced the government's approach. Both Bihar (ruled by the more-or-less regional Janata Dal-United) and BJP-governed Chhattisgarh were reported to have (informally) adopted state-specific rules on both acquisition and R&R that aligned closely with LARRA, while quietly continuing to use coercive tactics to evade these regulations on the ground. In Odisha, the regional Biju Janata Dal adopted a quiet approach as well, circulating with little fanfare draft state-level rules for LARRA implementation (Government of Odisha, 2014). While these rules do not appear to directly contradict LARRA, they are vague enough about the processes to be followed, the oversight mechanisms to be used, and the personnel to be involved that state government officials may have good reason to be confident that they will possess the means to evade crucial procedural protections. The method for operationalizing the rules regarding consent were particularly lacking in precision.

In the newly created state of Telangana, whose voters elected the regional Telangana Rashtra Samithi (TRS) to power in May 2014, the state government also sought to promote rules that would provide it with the maximum feasible autonomy in navigating the constraints imposed by LARRA. The Telangana government announced that it had created a body to establish rules for land acquisition (Kurmanath, 2014), and indicated that in the meantime the state government would 'seek cooperation from local public representatives for getting consent from land owners' ('Harish Rao Keen on Faster Land Acquisition' *The Times of India*, 2014). Who exactly these intermediaries would be, how they would perform these functions, and what safeguards would ensure that indirect coercion was not brought to bear were not specified. The prospects for abuse are non-trivial. The additional rules the state produced in draft form also appeared intended to evade parts of LARRA by according officials considerable latitude in granting exemptions and defining acceptable standards.

By the time the Modi government assumed office in mid 2014, the state government in Rajasthan had gone furthest in developing a state-specific strategy for adapting to life under LARRA. The BJP, which enjoyed a large majority in Rajasthan's legislature after coming to power in 2013, enacted legislation that 'expands the category of projects exempt from the consent clause' found in LARRA (Dhar, 2014). The Rajasthan legislation also attempted to weaken the SIA, remove the requirement that people be resettled close to their original homes, and increase penalties for obstructing land acquisition ('States Take Lead in Making India Land Acquisition Easier' *Monitor Global Outlook*, 2014). This agenda was consistent with the state government's other economic reform measures, such as making more than twenty amendments to four labour laws, all designed to reduce restraints on management decision-making and to rein in the effective power of unions ('After Rajasthan, Madhya Pradesh to Tweak Labor Laws' *Centinnial Asia Advisors*, 2014; 'Indian States may Lead Way into Labor Reform' *Monitor Global Outlook*, 2014). Goa, another BJP-controlled state, took similar early action. Though acting by ordinance instead of by legislative amendment, the Government of Goa announced in November 2014 a change to LARRA's applicability in the state: 'where an award has been made and the compensation has been deposited in the government treasury or with any financial institution...on account of any land acquisition proceedings, such land awards will not come under the ambit of the new act', ('Ordinance to Validate Land Acquisitions' *The Times Of India*, 2014). In Tamil Nadu, governed by another regional party – the AIADMK – the state government passed a law exempting various categories of industrial and infrastructure projects from LARRA compensation norms. The purpose of the law was to facilitate 'speedy land acquisition for many ongoing projects'. To make the amendments appear more politically palatable, the government highlighted the help this would provide to initiatives designed to promote Dalit welfare (Sivan, 2014).

Using administrative rather than legislative means, the Government of West Bengal, ruled by the regional Trinamool Congress, sought to redefine the content of LARRA in the guise of merely elaborating a set of state-level rules under which LARRA would be operationalized. The West Bengal government stated that it would apply the compensation norms relating to rural land-holdings only if the site in question was located at least 120 kilometers from a town (Basak, 2014). Madhya Pradesh, controlled by the BJP, has at times completely defied LARRA, openly admitting that for the Nauradehi Wildlife Sanctuary the state was carrying out land acquisition and rehabilitation as outlined by the 2008 land rules, not LARRA. The state's forest minister was reported to have called LARRA "too complex" ('MP Govt Still Adhering to Old Land Acquisition Rules' *Zee News*, 2014). All of these efforts could have been interpreted as indications that state governments of varying ideological persuasions possessed the motivation as well as the capacities needed to bring about the substance of the Modi government's LARRA reform agenda.

Conclusion

This chapter has been a preliminary analysis of the Modi government's efforts, soon after taking office in mid 2014, to bring about fundamental reforms on an issue that had been a matter of great political contention during the preceding government's decade in power. Taking the Modi government's deregulatory policy orientation on land-acquisition as a given, the chapter has argued that the ruling party's political strategists were nevertheless presented with a choice: to seek national legislative amendments to LARRA, or to rely instead on state governments to bypass, undercut, and dilute LARRA in ways suited to their respective subnational political contexts. The national route had the advantage of clarity and efficiency – requiring changes to just one law, covering the entire country – but at the cost of great political exposure for the BJP and its newly elected prime minister. The alternative approach, on the other hand, would have permitted the Modi government to risk less of its political capital, but would have required a more convoluted process – a series of state-by-state reforms – over which the central government would have much less control. The Modi government chose the national legislative reform route for a variety of reasons. Perhaps most importantly, it was a way of signaling to a domestic and international business constituency that the new prime minister would not, particularly during his government's 'honeymoon' phase (Williamson, 1994), shrink from the task of enacting bold economic reforms. The government also calculated that (a) the incentives facing (non-NDA) state-level ruling parties was sufficient to build the required parliamentary support in the Rajya Sabha, where the BJP was in a minority, and (b) that it could use a form of 'cooperative federalism' to facilitate this objective. Federal consultations can indeed be a useful means of forging a broader, cross-party consensus on the need to promote legislative and regulatory reforms. But the Modi government appears to have paid insufficient attention to the context in which this was being attempted. It was not merely passing economic legislation after winning an election; it was seeking to overturn a signature piece of rights-based legislation – one that in its final form enjoyed widespread support – just months after it came into force. This meant that a formidable array of recently mobilized groups was likely to offer fierce resistance to the government's efforts.

When its foray into cooperative federalism did not trigger the parliamentary realignment the Modi government sought, it turned to the second approach to centre-state relations, one in which the competitive instincts and political management skills of state governments are harnessed toward a centrally defined objective – what, in this case, could be classified as a form of 'market-preserving federalism' (Weingast, 1995). This approach made political sense, and leading spokespersons for the Modi government said as much. The finance minister pointed to Tamil Nadu as an example of how states could act on their own ('Centre Will Let States Amend Land Act: Finance Minister Arun Jaitley' *NDTV*, 2015), and at least some other states appeared to be following suit, including Goa ('State Prefers NGT's Delhi Bench' *Navhind Times*, 2015). Indeed, in certain policy domains, including land, industrialization, and urbanization – LARRA's core concerns – politics at the state and central levels of India's federal system have become so profoundly interrelated that neither can be considered in isolation from the other. This interrelationship can be seen clearly in the actions (and inactions) of state governments for most of the year following LARRA's passage. Recall that state governments knew at least since 2011, when the original LARR Bill was introduced, that legislation along these lines was coming – and yet, still, in mid 2014, had no functioning policy-implementation machineries in place. The lack of concerted effort to create such structures partly reflected how states perceived the national political climate. The distinct possibility that the 2014 general election would bring to power a party that favoured repealing – or at least substantially scaling back – LARRA acted as a deterrent to long-term regulatory planning by state governments. Why invest in the administrative infrastructure of a fully elaborated compliance machinery if the national legal framework was itself about to be dismantled?

The Modi government's resort to a state-by-state strategy as its 'Plan B' for effecting its LARRA overhaul – and its reliance on newly created institutions, such as the Niti Aayog, to facilitate this process ('Panagariya for Law Reform by Executive Measures' *The Hindu*, 2015) – raises an important question regarding the 'political sequencing' of reform (Roland, 2002). Attention to 'political sequencing' has typically involved a conscious effort to anticipate the effects that early reform measures might have on the capacity or incentive of various interest groups, within and outside the state, to either thwart or support subsequent rounds of reform. But rather than think of sequencing only in terms of the type of reform measures contemplated – and when they are introduced – it is also worth asking whether the techniques adopted to effect any given reform should also be subjected to the logic of politically optimal sequencing that underlies theories of policy change. In the case of the Modi government's approach to overhauling LARRA, the question is whether turning to a state-by-state approach as a fallback option – after first failing to overcome political resistance to its legislative reform proposals at the national level – will yield the hoped-for results. In other words, does the effectiveness of a political strategy depend on when in the sequence of reform politics it is pursued? There are reasonable grounds for concluding that, in the case of LARRA reform, it does.

By the time the Modi government turned to its state-by-state reform strategy it had already created political conditions that would likely be less advantageous than if the state-level reform strategy had been attempted initially. Opposition parties had become relatively unified, and discord in the Sangh Parivar deeper, thanks to the unsuccessful attempt to pass an Amendment bill through parliament. Most importantly, the civil society groups that fought to prevent dilution of LARRA during the Modi government's first year in power became battle-hardened. They became not only better networked – allowing regionally based movements to more easily support the struggles of like-minded groups in other states – but also more acutely aware of the legislative maneuvers that state governments are likely to use when seeking to undercut LARRA's rights-based procedural protections. Crucially, this was all taking place just as a decade-long trend toward more engagement by the Government of India with progressive NGOs was being reversed. During the UPA government, the National Advisory Council (NAC), chaired by Congress Party President Sonia Gandhi, was instrumental in framing a raft of rights-based legislation, including LARRA. That India possessed a small but influential cadre of bureaucrats-turned-activists – including NAC members Harsh Mander, Aruna Roy, and NC Saxena – increased the capacity of social movements to exploit these opportunities to participate in official processes. The state machinery (and access to policy-making process) that the NAC provided to civil society groups was remarkable. To protect key provisions in the bills that became NREGA, NFSA, and the RTEA, civil society organizations lobbied at the highest levels of bureaucratic and political decision-making.

To some social activists this level of 'civic incorporation' was nothing new. It was an extension of the situation that prevailed during the Janata government, from 1977–1980. During that period, progressive CSOs had an outsized voice in government policymaking – not only in social policy debates, but also in the creation of official forums and frameworks for government-NGO partnerships (Franda, 1983). During the UPA government, there was occasional sniping within the activist community against groups and individuals who had forged a relationship with Congress leaders. Critics claimed that some of the "anointed" members of civil society had failed to learn the lessons about cooptation that emerged in the post-Janata period, during which the "NGO-ization" of erstwhile social action groups had begun, allegedly extinguishing the independence and popular accountability of these once-vibrant movements (Kamat, 2002).

The People's Union for Civil Liberties has argued that, under the Modi government there has not merely been a narrowing of the channels through which progressive social activists can exert influence – the NAC and the Planning Commission were both abolished – but rather that NGOs and protest movements have been actively targeted ('PUCL Condemns IB Report' *India Resists*, 2014).[7] This perception, whatever its merits, has driven social movement activism increasingly toward targeting state-level political arenas. This shift in emphasis is occurring at the very moment when state governments have been tasked with the politically sensitive task of overhauling LARRA. Influencing these state-level policy processes, as well as the application of legislative and regulatory measures to individual cases, is something that movement organizations appear well positioned to pursue in the years ahead. If civil society and political parties prove themselves capable of derailing state-government led efforts to roll-back LARRA's procedural protections, this might indicate that the effectiveness of devolving economic reform challenges to sub-national units is influenced by the sequencing of political management techniques.

Endnotes

1. The author is grateful for the first-rate research assistance provided by Jonathan Eckman of Hunter College.
2. The contours of the debate over rights-based approaches are reflected in two competing assessments of the UPA's economic record: for the prosecution, Bhagwati and Panagariya (2013), and for the defense, Dreze and Sen (2013).
3. The official title is the Scheduled Tribes and Other Traditional Forest Dwellers (Recognition of Forest Rights) Act 2006.
4. The official title is the Right of Children to Free and Compulsory Education Act 2010.
5. A suggestion along these lines was reportedly made in May 2014 by the (BJP) chief minister of Madhya Pradesh at a meeting with a leading member of the prime minister's economic policy team. Interview with a retired civil servant, Mumbai, 17 November 2014.
6. This included both the Swadeshi Jagran Manch, an economic policy forum focused on preserving India's 'economic sovereignty', and the Bharatiya Kisan Sangh, the Sangh Parivar's official farmers' association ('RSS affiliates up in arms against Modi govt on Land Acquisition Bill', 2015).
7. The Intelligence Bureau report on civil society activism that was leaked in mid-2104 became a frequent talking point within the broad centre-left because it implied that the government would be acting to curb movement groups that slowed down industrial projects or other state initiatives that face organized (or even sporadic) resistance ('Modi Government's Message to NGOs in India: Big Brother is Watching You', 2014). That the report was initiated by the previous government, did not seem to matter to many activists.

References

'After Rajasthan, Madhya Pradesh to Tweak Labor Laws.' *Centennial Asia Advisors*, September 11, 2014. Available at, http://www.centennialasia.com/after-rajasthan-madhya-pradesh-to-tweak-labour-laws-11-september-2014/.

Albright Stonebridge Group. 'Modi's Rajya Sabha Conundrum.' *India Newsletter*, March 20, 2015. Available at, http://www.albrightstonebridge.com/news/modi%E2%80%99s-rajya-sabha-conundrum.

'Andhra CM Outlines Plan for Capital.' *The Indian Express*, October 12, 2014. Available at, http://indianexpress.com/article/india/india-others/andhra-cm-outlines-plan-for-capital/.

'Andhra Pradesh Government Looking for Best Model.' *The Times of India*, September 20, 2014. http://m.timesofindia.com/city/hyderabad/Andhra-Pradesh-government-looking-for-best-model/articleshow/42949613.cms.

'Andhra Pradesh May Amend Municipal Act.' *The Times of India*, September 7, 2014. Available at, http://timesofindia.indiatimes.com/City/Hyderabad/Andhra-Pradesh-may-amend-Municipal-Act/articleshow/41892155.cms.

'Andhra Pradesh Unveils Land Pooling Policy to Build New State Capital.' *Zee News*, December 8, 2014. Available at, http://zeenews.india.com/news/andhra-pradesh/andhra-pradesh-unveils-land-pooling-policy-to-build-new-state-capital_1511496.html.

Antony, M. J. 2014. 'Speeding Up Land Acquisition Payments.' *Business Standard*, November 30. Available at, http://www.business-standard.com/article/opinion/speeding-up-land-acquisition-payments-114113000728_1.html.

'Appeal for Amendment in Land Rehabilitation Bill.' *The Times of India*, July 22, 2014. Available at, http://timesofindia.indiatimes.com/city/hyderabad/Appeal-for-amendment-in-Land-rehabilitation-bill/articleshow/38822777.cms.

Asher, Manshi. 2014. 'Gujarat and Punjab: The Entrepreneur's Paradise and the Land of the Farmer.' In *Power, Policy and Protest: The Politics of India's Special Economic Zones*, edited by Rob Jenkins, Loraine Kennedy and Partha Mukhopadhyay, 147–150. New Delhi: Oxford University Press.

Banerjee, Partha Sarathi. 2014. 'Orissa and West Bengal: The SEZ Imbroglio.' In *Power, Policy and Protest: The Politics of India's Special Economic Zones*, edited by Rob Jenkins, Loraine Kennedy, and Partha Mukhopadhyay, 289–290. New Delhi: Oxford University Press.

Basak, Probal. 2014. 'Mamata Wants to Pay Less for Land Near Cities.' *Business Standard*, August 8. Available at, http://www.business-standard.com/article/economy-policy/mamata-wants-to-pay-less-for-land-near-cities-114080800033_1.html.

Bhagwati, Jagdish and Arvind Panagariya. 2013. *Why Growth Matters: How Economic Growth in India Reduced Poverty and the Lessons for Other Developing Countries*. New York: PublicAffairs.

'BJP, Led by PM Narendra Modi, to Clear the Air on Land Bill.' *The Economic Times*, April 5, 2015.

'Centre Hints at Continuing MGNREGS in All Districts.' *LiveMint/The Wall Street Journal*, November 12, 2014. Available at, http://www.livemint.com/Politics/BRzf85s3CxQ91doSxw1S2L/Centre-hints-at-continuing-MGNREGS-in-all-districts.html.

'Centre Will Let States Amend Land Act: Finance Minister Arun Jaitley.' *NDTV*, September 18, 2015. Available at, http://www.ndtv.com/india-news/centre-will-let-states-amend-land-act-finance-minister-arun-jaitley-1219216.

Dasgupta, Manas. 2010. 'New Land Acquisition Policy in Gujarat.' *The Hindu*, December 17. Available at, http://www.thehindu.com/news/national/other-states/new-land-acquisition-policy-in-gujarat/article956957.ece.

Dhar, Aarti. 2014. 'Rajasthan Cabinet Clears Land Acquisition Bill.' *The Hindu*, September 14. Available at, http://www.thehindu.com/news/national/other-states/rajasthan-cabinet-clears-land-acquisition-bill/article6410275.ece/.

Dreze, Jean and Amartya Sen. 2013. *An Uncertain Glory: India and Its Contradictions*, Princeton, NJ: Princeton University Press.

Franda, Marcus. 1983. *Voluntary Associations and Local Development in India*. Delhi: Young Asia Publications.

'Government Examining Land Act Provisions to Fix States' Concerns: Minister.' *Zee News*, December 1, 2014. Available at, http://zeenews.india.com/news/india/govt-examining-land-act-provisions-to-fix-states-concerns-minister_1507783.html.

'Govt Notifies Rules for Land Acquisition.' *The New Indian Express*, June 23, 2014. Available at, http://www.newindianexpress.com/states/karnataka/Govt-Notifies-Rules-for-Land-Acquisition/2014/06/23/article2295215.ece.

Government of the State of Haryana. 2012. 'Haryana Government Industries and Commerce Department Notification, the 14th August, 2012.' Available at, http://haryana.gov.in/misc/eng-final.pdf.

Government of the State of Himachal Pradesh, 1979. 'The Land Acquisition (Himachal Pradesh Amendment) Act, 1979.' Available at, http://www.prsindia.org/uploads/media/Land%20Acquisition/state/1980HP4.pdf.

Government of the State of Karnataka. 2014. 'Revenue Secretariat Notification.' June 21, 2014. Available at, http://rlarrdc.org.in/images/LA_Draft_Gazette_Copy.pdf.

Government of the State of Odisha. 2014. 'Draft Odisha Right to Fair Compensation and Transparency in Land Acquisition, Rehabilitation and Resettlement Rules, 2014.' http://www.orissa.gov.in/revenue/R_R_Policies/draft_RR.pdf.

Greater Mohali Area Development Authority. 2006. 'Land Acquisition Policy.' Available at, http://gmada.gov.in/category/land-owners/land-acquisition-policy/.

'Harish Rao Keen on Faster Land Acquisition.' *The Times of India*, October 15, 2014. Available at, http://timesofindia.indiatimes.com/city/hyderabad/Harish-Rao-keen-on-faster-land-acquisition/articleshow/44819215.cms.

'Indian States May Lead Way into Labor Reform.' *Monitor Global Outlook*, June 2014. Available at, http://www.monitorglobaloutlook.com/Briefings/2014/06/indian-states-may-lead-way-in-labor-reform.

Jain, Sreenivasan. 2014. 'Truth vs Hype: The Myth of Land Acquisition.' *NDTV*, November 30. Available at, http://www.ndtv.com/article/india/truth-vs-hype-the-myth-of-land-acquisition-627617.

Jain, Sunil. 2014. 'Modi Can Use Article 254 to Push State-Level Reforms: Shourie.' *The Indian Express*, April 24. Available at, http://indianexpress.com/article/business/business-others/modi-can-use-article-254-to-push-state-level-reforms-shourie/.

Jenkins, Rob. 1999. *Democratic Politics and Economic Reform in India*. Cambridge: Cambridge University Press.

Jenkins, Rob. 2013. 'Land, Rights, and Reform.' *Pacific Affairs* 86 (3): 591–612.

Jenkins, Rob. 2014. 'India's SEZ Policy: The Political Implications of "Permanent Reform."' In *Power, Policy and Protest: The Politics of Special Economic Zones in India*, edited by Rob Jenkins, Loraine Kennedy, and Partha Mukhopadhyay, 39–71. New Delhi: Oxford University Press.

Jenkins, Rob and James Manor. 2016. *Politics and the Right to Work: India's National Rural Employment Guarantee Ac*t. London/New York: Hurst/Oxford University Press.

Kailash, K. K. 2015. 'States of the Union: Now Ensconsed at the Centre, will BJP Fulfil its Promise of Cooperative Federalism?' *The Indian Express*, January 16. Available at, http://indianexpress.com/article/opinion/columns/states-of-the-union-2/.

Kamat, Sangeeta. 2002. *Development Hegemony: NGOs and the State in India*. Delhi: Oxford University Press.

Karnataka Industrial Areas Development Board. 1966. 'The Karnataka Industrial Areas Development Act, 1966.' Bangalore.

'Kerala to Speed Up Land Acquisition for NH Development.' *The Economic Times*. Accessed October 23, 2014. Available at, http://economictimes.indiatimes.com/news/economy/infrastructure/kerala-to-speed-up-land-acquisition-for-nh-development/articleshow/44916512.cms.

Kurmanath, K. V. 2014. 'Telangana Ministers Panel to Frame Rules for Land Acquisition.' *The Hindu*, July 3. Available at, http://www.thehindubusinessline.com/news/telangana-ministers-panel-to-frame-rules-for-land-acquisition/article6173658.ece.

'Land Acquisition Act Finalized in AP.' *The Siasat Daily*, September 9, 2014. Available at, http://www.siasat.com/english/news/land-acquisition-act-finalized-ap.

'Land Ordinance Gets a Burial.' *The Hindu*, August 31, 2015.

'Modi Government's Message to NGOs in India: Big Brother is Watching You.' *Forbes.com*. June 16, 2014. Available at, http://www.forbes.com/sites/meghabahree/2014/06/16/modi-governments-message-to-ngos-in-india-big-brother-is-watching-you/.

'Modi Govt hasn't Delivered on Promised Reforms'. *CNBC: Money Control*, July 31, 2015, Available at, http://www.moneycontrol.com/news/economy/modi-govt-hasnt-deliveredpromised-reforms-moodys_2241381.html.

Mody, Anjali. 2014. 'Karnataka: The Primacy of the Local.' In *Power, Policy and Protest: The Politics of India's Special Economic Zones*, edited by Rob Jenkins, Loraine Kennedy, and Partha Mukhopadhyay, 214–224. New Delhi: Oxford University Press.

'Most Congress States had Doubts on Original Land Acquisition Act'. *The Economic Times*. February 25, 2015. Available at, http://articles.economictimes.indiatimes.com/2015-02-25/news/59500123_1_land-acquisition-act-resettlement-act-land-amendment-bill.

'Most Land Conflicts in India Due to Acquisition by State: Study.' *Daijiworld.com*, November 27, 2014. Available at, http://www.daijiworld.com/news/news_disp.asp?n_id=279725.

'MP Govt still Adhering to Old Land Acquisition Rules.' *Zee News*, December 11, 2014. Available at, http://zeenews.india.com/news/madhya-pradesh/mp-govt-still-adhering-to-old-land-acquisition-rules_1513105.html.

Nayyar, Dhiraj. 2014. 'India's Law from Hell.' *BloombergView.com*. November 7. Available at, www.bloombergview.com/articles/2014-11-07/indias-law-from-hell.

'Ordinance to Validate Land Acquisitions.' *The Times of India*. November 25, 2014. Available at, http://m.timesofindia.com/city/goa/Ordinance-to-validate-land acquisitions/articleshow/45264892.cms.

'Panagariya for Law Reform by Executive Measures'. *The Hindu*, September 3, 2015.

'Panel Suggests Changes to Land Acquisition and Rehabilitation Bills.' *Business Today*, May 27, 2011. Available at, http://businesstoday.intoday.in/story/land-acquisition-%28amendment%29-bill--2009-and-resettlement-and-rehabilitation-bill-2009/1/15855.html.

'PUCL Condemns IB Report.' *India Resists*, June 13, 2014. Available at, http://www.indiaresists.com/puclcondemns-ib-report/.

Roland, Gérard. 2002. 'The Political Economy of Transition.' *Journal of Economic Perspectives* 16 (1): 29–50.

'RSS Affiliates Up in Arms against Modi Govt on Land Acquisition Bill'. *The Indian Express*, June 21, 2015. Available at, http://indianexpress.com/article/india/india-others/rss-affiliates-up-in-arms-against-modi-govt-on-land-acquisition-bill/.

Sivan, Jayaraj. 2014. 'In Bid to Push Industry, Tamil Nadu Breaks Hearts of Land-Losers.' *The Times of India*, February 21. Available at, http://timesofindia.indiatimes.com/city/chennai/In-bid-to-push-industry-Tamil-Nadu-breaks-hearts-of-land-losers/articleshow/30759970.cms.

Society for Promotion of Wastelands Development and the Rights and Resources Initiative. 2014. 'Land Acquisition Related Disputes.' Available at, http://www.rightsandresources.org/wp-content/uploads/Land-Conflicts-Map-updated-2013-14.pdf.

'Sonia Council Seeks Land Bills Merger.' *The Telegraph*. May 19, 2011. Available at, http://www.telegraphindia.com/1110519/jsp/nation/story_14001679.jsp.

'State Cabinet Okays Amendments to Rules.' *The Tribune*. July 27, 2011. Available at, http://www.tribuneindia.com/2011/20110728/himachal.htm#1.

'State Moots Radical Changes in Land Acquisition Act.' *The Times of India*. July 25, 2014. Available at, http://epaperbeta.timesofindia.com/Article.aspx?eid=31811&articlexml=State-moots-radical-changes-in-Land-Acquisition-Act-25072014002003.

'State Prefers NGT's Delhi Bench'. *Navhind Times*. Accessed October 23, 2015. Available at, http://www.goacom.com/test-1/29679-state-prefers-ngt-s-delhi-bench.

'States Take Lead in Making India Land Acquisition Easier.' *Monitor Global Outlook*. Accessed September 2014. Available at, http://www.monitorglobaloutlook.com/Briefings/2014/09/States-take-lead-making-India-land-acquisition-easier.

'TMC, CPI-M Converging against Land Law Changes: Arun Jaitley.' *India TV News*, December 12, 2014. Available at, http://www.indiatvnews.com/politics/national/tmc-cpi-m-converging-against-land-law-changes-arun-jaitley-23640.html.

'UPA's Land Acquisition Law Likely to be Overhauled with Many States Seeking Recast.' *The Times of India*, June 28, 2014. Available at, http://timesofindia.indiatimes.com/india/UPAs-land-acquisition-law-likely-to-be-overhauled-with-many-states-seeking-recast/articleshow/37346439.cms.

Verma, Suyash. 2014. 'Constitutional Law – Doctrine of Repugnancy and the Constitution of India (Centre-State Relations).' *Desi Kanoon*, May 26. Available at, http://www.desikanoon.co.in/2014/05/doctrine-of-repugnancy-and-constitution-of-india.html.

Vijayabaskar, M. 2014. 'Tamil Nadu: The Politics of Silence.' In *Power, Policy and Protest: The Politics of India's Special Economic Zones*, edited by Rob Jenkins, Loraine Kennedy, and Partha Mukhopadhyay, 312–318. New Delhi: Oxford University Press.

Weingast, Barry. 1995. 'The Economic Role of Political Institutions: Market-Preserving Federalism and Economic Development.' *Journal of Law, Economics, and Organization* 11 (1): 1–31.

Williamson, John. 1994. *The Political Economy of Policy Ref*orm. Washington, D. C.: Peterson Institute for International Economics.

Zimmerman. Joseph F. 2001. 'National-State Relations: Cooperative Federalism in the Twentieth Century.' *Publius* 31 (2): 15–30.

14

'Workers' or 'Beneficiaries'

The Varied Politics of NREGA Implementation in South-West Madhya Pradesh

Nandini Nayak

Introduction

The Mahatma Gandhi National Rural Employment Guarantee Act (NREGA hereafter) enacted by the Indian Parliament in 2005, created a legal, justiciable 'right to work' for all households in rural India. Adult members of all rural households were now eligible to 'demand' work on publicly funded worksites, for 'at least' a hundred days per household per financial year.

This chapter looks at how the text of rights defined under the NREGA interacts with a politics of claiming rights from the state. It draws on the work of the Jagrut Adivasi Dalit Sangathan (JADS), an indigenous people's collective working in Barwani district in south west Madhya Pradesh, examining the strategies adopted by members of the collective to seek work under the NREGA in the initial years after its implementation. Further, by using the example of Barwani district, the chapter highlights that NREGA implementation at the district level involves a varied set of institutional and civil society actors (Figure 14.1, annexed). It is suggested that novel rights defined under the NREGA can be drawn on for varied, and sometimes competing political agendas. It is argued, therefore, that the process of implementation of 'rights' under the NREGA is far from linear, and generates a new layer in the 'production' of local politics.

This chapter looks at the period between 2006 and 2009, i.e., the first three years of NREGA implementation. The empirical material presented in this paper draws on ethnographic field work, on letters and memoranda (or, *gyapan*) submitted by the JADS membership to the local state and other civil society organisations regarding implementation of public works programmes, and on secondary literature on the Government of Madhya Pradesh and the central government's role in NREGA implementation. The next section starts with a discussion on the Jagrut Adivasi Dalit Sangathan and strategies adopted by its members to claim work under NREGA. Section three discusses the engagement of the central government and the Government of Madhya Pradesh with NREGA implementation. Section four highlights the work of civil society actors other than JADS engaged in NREGA implementation in Barwani district, Madhya Pradesh, and section five is the concluding section.

Collective Action and the NREGA: The Work of Jagrut Adivasi Dalit Sangathan

The question of adivasi political mobilisation has formed the backdrop to a polarised debate in India in recent years.[1] The prominent focus of this debate has remained the nature of adivasi engagement with the Maoist movement in east-central India (Bhatia 2005; Harriss 2010; Kunnath 2006; Nilsen 2012). As highlighted by Nilsen (2012) west-central India, including south-west Madhya Pradesh has seen a trajectory of adivasi political mobilisation since the 1980s that is quite distinct from what has attracted mainstream attention in recent years. Baviskar (1997, 2001, 2004), Banerjee (n.d.), Godbole and Vira (2004), Nilsen (2010, 2012), Rahul (1998, 1999), amongst others discuss the work of diverse adivasi collectives that have engaged with questions of access to natural resources and livelihoods, adopting strategies of political resistance centred on asserting claims to local natural resources and 'reclaiming citizenship' .

In this backdrop, this chapter demonstrates how the NREGA, is used as an important tool for political mobilisation by the Jagrut Adivasi Dalit Sangathan (JADS). After it started working around 1999 in Pati block, Barwani district,[2] JADS expanded to a membership of about 4500 households in Pati, Pansemal, Barwani, Rajpur and Sendhwa blocks of Barwani district by late 2010. JADS membership is largely drawn from the Bhil, Bhilala and Barela adivasi communities. The collective is funded via a membership fees contributed by each household.

The NREGA effected the institution of a language of justiciable rights in relation to employment works that have been part of developmental

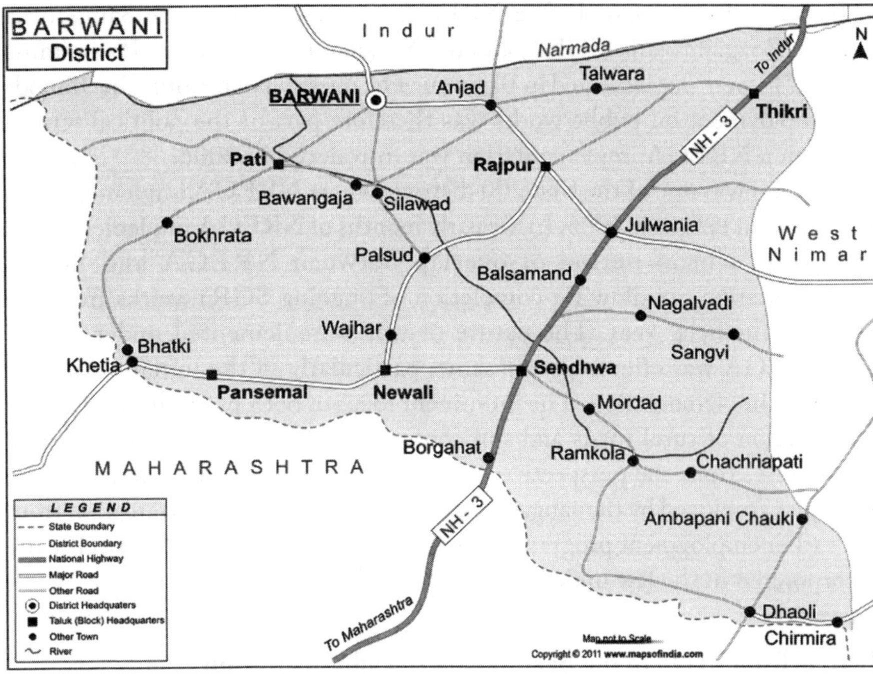

Map 14.1 Barwani District Map

Source: www.censusindia.gov.in/2011census/dchb/2324_PART_B_DCHB_BARWANI.pdf.

interventions of the Indian state since Independence. The NREGA created a specific legal tool of action with the enactment of the 'right to work', though this was not the first time that laws were used for the purpose of collective action by sangathans in west-central India. As highlighted by Banerjee (n.d.) and Nilsen (2012), sangathans such as the Khedut Mazdoor Chetana Sangathan (KMCS) and the Adivasi Mukti Sangathan (AMS) working in south-west Madhya Pradesh had in the past drawn on the Panchayat Extension to Scheduled Areas Act (PESA) for their work. The significance of the NREGA nonetheless lay in offering specifically defined universal claims against the state that were entirely new and unique. Thus while civil and political rights were expanded in earlier legislations, the NREGA expanded economic rights and a specific material claim against the state.

In the early 2000s prior to NREGA enactment, public works programmes of the Government of India were an important focus of the work of JADS not least because of recurrent droughts in the region and the precarious access to livelihood available to the Bhil, Bhilala and Barela adivasi communities in Barwani. In the years before NREGA enactment, both the Sampoorna Gramin Rozgar Yojana (SGRY) and the National Food for Work Programme (NFFWP) were implemented in Barwani. The question of claiming livelihoods and employment on public works was therefore part of the political terrain into which NREGA implementation was introduced in 2006.

Barwani was one of the first 200 districts where NREGA implementation was begun in February 2006. In the early months of NREGA implementation, there was a brief period of overlap between NREGA and SGRY implementation, to allow for completion of ongoing SGRY works from the previous financial year. The nature of works implemented under SGRY and NREGA was effectively the same, particularly in the initial months of NREGA implementation. The prominent focus of both programmes was the construction of rural roads and soil conservation works of various types. In some sense, from the perspective of the administration and in terms of the strategies employed by the sangathan, there was fluidity in the transition from the earlier employment programmes to the NREGA. This is also specifically incorporated in the law under Section 4, NREGA.

Letters from JADS to the Barwani district administration

An important 'tool of contention' (Tarrow, 1993; Tilly, 1978) adopted by JADS to demand probity in the implementation of public programmes was to submit letters to the district administration detailing problems with implementation of various government programmes. The content of these letters was compiled by sangathan members in village meetings. In the initial months after NREGA implementation commenced in February 2006, sangathan members continued to file letters with the administration in relation to SGRY implementation in Barwani district, for works that were ongoing.

One such letter, filed on 12 May 2006 by sangathan members from village Dervalia in Pati block, Barwani district, was about non-payment of wages under an SGRY work. The letter states that 600 workers employed on road works under SGRY in village Dervalia between 12 February and 19 April 2006, were not paid till May 2006. Further, it states that the 'Supreme Court has directed that payment for public works should be made within a week of work having been completed'.[3] The Barwani District Collector (DC) was asked by the sangathan to arrange to pay the workers *immediately*[4], and was asked to take action against the sarpanch and the secretary who had delayed the payments thus far.[5]

A second letter, submitted by sangathan members from village Pokhlya in Pati block on 12 May 2006, was about work being implemented under the NREGA. The letter stated that people employed on a small dam in the village from 1 May 2006 were told, on 7 May 2006, not to return to the site of work. On the night of 10 May 2006, an earth moving machine was used for doing work which could have been done by employing workers (in other words, a 'labour displacing machine' was used). 'Labour displacing machines' were banned from use in all government employment programmes, unless the work could not be done by human labour.[6] The reason for this is that the NREGA is envisaged as a programme to generate wage employment. Further, machines were typically owned by local contractors and businessmen, and their use allowed contractors to usurp money intended for payment as wages to labourers.

The letter went on to state that the owners of the machines were local businessmen from Pati town in Barwani district and Harda town in Harda district, Madhya Pradesh. Sangathan members asked the District Collector to take *disciplinary action* against the sarpanch and secretary of Pokhlya village and to re-employ the laid-off workers for the ongoing worksite.[7]

A third letter filed on 23 May 2006 from village Keli, Barwani block, Barwani district, reflected the beginnings of a change in dynamics between the sarpanch and secretary on the one hand and members of JADS on the other, in claiming work under the NREGA. In the two letters cited earlier, there was a 'demand' for wages and for 'disciplinary action' against erring and corrupt Panchayat functionaries. However, other than these specific demands and the call for public probity, the letters reflected a form of ordinary petitioning and did not reflect any changes in the dynamic of power between sangathan members and office bearers of the village panchayat.

As indicated in this third letter pertaining to village Keli, soon after enactment of the NREGA, sangathan members started demanding work by way of written applications that made it 'legally binding' on the local administration to provide work. While the local administration could dictate when a public work would be started under earlier wage employment programmes (including SGRY), the sangathan effectively wrested this power from the local state after NREGA implementation began, by making use of the provision to claim work on demand. This new assertion for work by sangathan members was viewed as a threat by constituents of the local state like the sarpanch and secretary, and in turn this led to instances of physical and verbal violence against sangathan members.[8]

The letter filed on 23 May 2006 from village Keli, Barwani block, Barwani district, states that on 14 April 2006 an (undisclosed number) of workers submitted a written application seeking NREGA work from 1 to 14 May 2006. Work had begun on 3 May 2006, but had stopped after half a day due to a death in the village. It was resumed on 8 May 2006, and stopped again after only eight days (on 15 May 2006) by the sarpanch and secretary of the village. Workers at the site sought to complete the 14 days of work for which they had originally applied. Signatories of the letter to the Barwani DC state, '*we were told we will not be employed, nor paid for the full fourteen days of work we had originally applied for. Later, when we questioned the sarpanch and sachiv, they came to blows with us. They said they will not 'employ' anyone who submits a written application for work. We have not been paid for the eight days of work done by us, neither have we got work for the full period for which we applied for work.*'[9]

The letter further states that on 18 May 2006 workers who had not applied for NREGA work were engaged by the sarpanch and the sachiv on the said worksite. The Barwani DC is informed that 'the sapanch and sachiv have since (15 May 2006) refused to employ workers who have submitted written applications for work.'

The suggestion here is that the sarpanch and sachiv associate a questioning of their authority, with giving work to those who have submitted a written application for work. There is therefore an effort on the part of these representatives of the local state to overtly resist this new form of power accorded to workers under the NREGA.

A copy of a letter filed with the Station House Officer (SHO) of the Silawad Police Station[10] on 16 May 2006 was also annexed along with the above letter submitted to the Barwani DC by sangathan members from village Keli.

The letter, addressed to the SHO of the Silawad Police Station on 16 May 2006, was filed a day after workers were removed from work in village Keli on 15 May 2006. This is a complaint with details of the fight with the sarpanch and sachiv referred to in the main text of the letter to the Barwani DC. The complainants state that they were 'walking towards their homes when an associate of the sarpanch approached them on a motorcycle. Referring to the written applications for work, and in the middle of a string of foul abuses and threats, he asked, "You think your father's the ruler around here? So you're going to dictate when work starts?" ("*Terebaapkaraajhai*? *Tukaamkarvaega*?") Getting more aggressive and abusive, he got off his motorcycle and slapped (IkkaKhajan) from the sangathan. As he left he said "Come to me tomorrow" … "I'll castrate you, turn you into a fly and swot you."'

The letter goes on to describe events on the next day when some sangathan members went to the village Patel's house.[11] The sarpanch came to the house while sangathan members were present there, and verbally abused and threatened them. The sarpanch caught Sardar Sutar[12] by his collar, used foul language and said "You think you're going to rule now? I rule around here, not you" ("*...turaajchlayga? Mera raj chalega, teranahi*"). Then the sarpanch turned to the women sangathan members who had also come to the Patel's house. He said to them, "...and you lot... just watch out, I'll add you to my harem..." ("*tumhe to main rakhunga*").'

Breaking away from the tone of the earlier letters that merely petitioned the state, this letter to the Barwani DC goes on to ask, '(S)o is this the law now? That the sarpanch keeps women after he is elected? If there is any such law, then all of us women will go to the sarpanch'. It is signed by 15 members of the sangathan.

This particular letter in effect seeks to shame the district administration. It is worth noting that the challenge posed to the administration in this letter nonetheless draws on the enabling legal rights detailed in the NREGA itself.

In addition to specific instances of delays in payment of wages, corruption by way of using machines and overt violence, letters detailing a wider list of problems with NREGA implementation were also submitted to the Barwani DC by JADS in the months after the legislation came into force in February 2006. The text of a fourth letter from the sangathan to the local state emphasises not only locationally specific collective action, i.e. from a particular village, but collective action that is spread wider, across several parts of Barwani district. It may be argued that this letter actively and overtly demonstrates the wider organisation of JADS, and highlights a wider assertion for the 'right to work' by the sangathan. One of the important outcomes of NREGA enactment commonly cited by JADS members is that the NREGA served as a tool for the collective to organise. The letter cited below provides evidence of this.

This particular letter details problems with NREGA implementation faced in villages spread across Pati, Pansemal and Barwani blocks of Barwani district and highlights problems common to several villages, including – (1) delays encountered in the receipt of job cards (JCs) after applications for job cards have been submitted; (2) non-payment and late payment of NREGA wages for work already completed; (3) work being denied to NREGA work applicants and being offered to those who have not applied for work; and, (4) the presence of private contractors in NREGA work implementation at some worksites.[13]

The contents of this fourth letter submitted three months after NREGA implementation commenced in February 2006, demonstrate a heightened sense of awareness about the enabling aspects of the NREGA. Where problems with implementation are cited, they are juxtaposed with a statement of formal rules as stated in law, to which the collective is asserting a claim. Rather than a form of ordinary petitioning, entrenched power hierarchies are challenged with an expansion of 'repertoires of contention' that draw on claims to 'rights' defined in law. The information presented in this letter was collated by sangathan activists in fortnightly sangathan meetings. The act of collation itself serves a political purpose. The text of rights under NREGA serves as a unifying thread and point of reference in spatially dispersed discussions. Thus, hurdles to claiming the right to work in specific locations are rendered 'commonplace' in sangathan meetings. As routinely experienced hurdles are listed, they are at the same time viewed as surmountable problems, due to the text of the law that supports these claims, and, more fundamentally, due to the commonly shared ethic of collective claim making that predates the NREGA itself. Within this setting, the prospect of claiming work under NREGA also serves as a useful rallying point around which people can organise and even expand the collective.

Claiming the unemployment allowance

The letters cited above aim to demonstrate an attempt by the sangathan to use the novel rights defined under the NREGA. Before moving to Section 3, the remainder of this section presents a discussion on efforts in Barwani in 2006 to claim the 'unemployment allowance' defined under the NREGA. It is worth noting that the provision for the unemployment allowance is an important section of the NREGA statute that specifies the penalty that must be paid by a state government if an application for work is not honoured. In December 2006, the unemployment allowance was paid to 1575 workers in Barwani district, after a protracted struggle that started in May 2006. The payment of the unemployment allowance was significant because this was the first time such a payment was made anywhere in the country after NREGA implementation commenced in February 2006. The payment of what was effectively a penalty imposed on the state government for not honouring the 'right to work' also set apart the NREGA from earlier public works programmes.

Section 7 of the NREGA defines the 'unemployment allowance' payable under the NREGA. As per the legal definition, if an applicant under the scheme is not provided employment within fifteen days of receipt of the application seeking employment *or* from the date on which employment has been sought in the case of advance applications then work applicants are entitled to a daily unemployment allowance.

In keeping with this section of the NREGA, 2877 sangathan members from 15 villages applied for the 'unemployment allowance' on 23 and 30 May 2006 and 6 June 2006, at sub-district or block level government offices in Barwani district (Khera, 2008; Nayak, 2008).[14]

These applications for unemployment allowance were initially rejected by the Pati Block Panchayat on 'technical grounds'. The 'grounds' for rejection of the application for unemployment allowance provided by the administration were: (a) that the applications had not been submitted on the right application form, (b) that the application was submitted as a collective application rather than as individual applications from individual workers and (c) that relevant work applications had not been attached with the application for unemployment allowance.

It could be argued that the Barwani district administration was using 'legal grounds' (Sundar, 2009) to challenge the sangathan's *legal* claim to the unemployment allowance. Here the text of the law itself became a site for contestation.

Under the NREGA, although there is a statutory provision for payment of the unemployment allowance, no specific procedure is laid out for claiming the allowance. Section 7(6) of the NREGA stipulates that State Governments should prescribe the procedure for payment of unemployment allowance. In the Madhya Pradesh Employment Guarantee Scheme issued in January 2006, however, no procedure for payment of the allowance was laid down. Thus, *any* proforma on which applications were submitted to the administration could potentially have been rejected, since specific procedural norms for claiming unemployment allowance did not exist.[15]

The rejection of unemployment allowance applications on 'technical grounds' was raised with the administration in two 'public hearings' in Pati. One of these meetings, on 16 June 2006, took a violent turn, when a scuffle broke out at the meeting between JADS activists and some elected panchayat heads from Pati block. This conflict was followed by the filing of criminal complaints both by and against JADS members. In the period following, letters were written by JADS members on the above incidents, including to the district administration, the central Ministry of Rural Development (MoRD), to Congress-(I) President Sonia Gandhi and to an electronic mailing list of the 'right to food campaign'. Since the letters to the district administration and the MoRD got no response, JADS members staged a sit-in at the Barwani

District Collectorate from 18 to 23 July 2006, to demand the unemployment allowance and protest the violent incidents of 16 June 2006.

The sit-in at the Barwani district collectorate was concluded on 23 July 2006, when the Collector gave a number of *written* assurances to JADS. Amongst other things, the Collector stated in a letter that (a) lists of job card holders would be displayed on Panchayat notice boards, (b) that 'social audits' of NREGA work would be conducted in the August 2006 gram sabha and (c) that work would be started in four villages where the administration had not started work till then. However, while the commitments mentioned above were recorded in *writing*, the Collector *verbally* conceded that the applications for unemployment allowance thus far summarily dismissed by sub-district level staff should, in fact, be considered favourably.

The conflicts highlighted above indicate that not only the village level bureaucracy but also the block and district level bureaucracy and local politicians viewed the sangathans' assertions for 'rights' under the NREGA with caution, or even as a threat. Further, in light of the above discussion, it is worth considering the question – 'what is significant about NREGA enactment?' or, 'what difference do rights make?' With NREGA enactment, claims for work could not be rejected outright as baseless or without 'legal grounds'. While earlier claims to work could be rejected on the grounds that there were no funds for implementation of a particular employment work, this was not tenable in the period after NREGA implementation. Following the sit-in at the Barwani DC's office in July 2006, a formal appeal was filed by the sangathan at the Collectors' office in response to the initially rejected applications for unemployment allowance. Later that month, the Barwani District Collector wrote a letter stating that as a result of the review on appeal, sub-district level authorities had been directed to pay unemployment allowance to applicants who had not exhausted a hundred days of work for the 2006–07 financial year.[16] Thus, the appeal filed by JADS was accepted by the district government. Between October and December 2006, Rs. 0.475 million was paid as unemployment allowance for 18 days of work to 1575 members of the sangathan.[17]

This chapter has so far described the strategies adopted by the Jagrut Adivasi Dalit Sangathan in Barwani, Madhya Pradesh, to claim work under the NREGA. Four letters submitted in quick succession by the sangathan to the 'local state', specifically, the block and district level administration were discussed, followed by a discussion on the events that led up to the payment of unemployment allowance in Barwani in 2006.

When NREGA implementation commenced in 2006, the strategy of writing to the local state, along with strategies of protest, to do marches and sit-ins were not novel for JADS. It could be argued that the tools of contention adopted by JADS substantively drew on the earlier engagements of the collective. At the same time, clauses within the NREGA offered opportunities for new forms of political action to emerge (Fox, 1996; Tarrow, 1993; Tilly, 1978).

Public works on private lands: initiatives of the central and state government

This section highlights some initiatives of the Central Government (GoI) and the Government of Madhya Pradesh (GoMP) with interpreting and implementing the NREGA. The NREGA was celebrated as an exceptionally progressive and 'radical' (Shah, 2008) legislation when it was enacted. However, it is highlighted below that the central and state governments' role in implementing specific sections of the NREGA contributed to subverting the 'right to work' itself.

Before going further, it is useful to review the 'statement of objects and reasons' mentioned in the NREGA statute. These are – '1) to provide minimum days of employment; 2) to provide guaranteed wage employment; 3) to enhance livelihood security for the poor'.

In a 'department order' issued on 9 September 2005, four days after the NREGA was enacted, the central government, with the Congress-(I)-led UPA at the helm, emphasised to all state governments, including GoMP that since this was 'the first time' the government would be implementing a programme with a 'time bound legal guarantee'.[18] It was stated that 'efficient and accountable delivery systems and processes' would have to be designed and put in place to honour the guarantee',[19] that in order for the 'right to work' to be honoured as per law, comprehensive planning would be required, including the development of a 'shelf of projects', or a list of works that could be used when demand for work was received.[20] Other aspects of implementation highlighted by the central government related to ensuring 'humane conditions for work' through the provision of drinking water, medical aid, and crèches for young children of workers, and ensuring that women workers were provided work and safeguards were put in place to ensure that there would be no discrimination against or harassment of women workers on work sites.

These and other letters from the MoRD repeatedly emphasised the novelty of the NREGA and that it was the first developmental programme in the country with a legal framework of rights, reflecting the high political interest in its implementation in the period following enactment of the NREGA.

While the message that enacted 'rights' should be widely publicised was made explicit, over time, some notable changes were also made to the NREGA statute by the central government. These changes were driven by the central Ministry of Rural Development, since the NREGA is a Parliamentary statute, implemented under the purview of the central government. Amendments to the NREGA statute were made by amending 'schedules' of the NREGA statute.[21]

Key changes were made to the *types of works* for which public funds routed through NREGA could be claimed. Permissible public works in the NREGA statute passed by Parliament included works for water conservation and water harvesting, drought-proofing, irrigation canals, etc. In addition to the implementation of these works on public lands, the original text of the NREGA also allowed works on private lands (vide Clause 1(iv) of Schedule I), for the provision of irrigation facilities for 'land owned by households belonging to the Scheduled Castes and Scheduled Tribes or to beneficiaries of land reforms or to beneficiaries of the Indira AwasYojana (IAY)'[22] implemented by the Government of India (GoI). Stated thus, Clause 1(iv), Schedule I, was a progressive clause that had the intent of encouraging publicly funded development of lands owned by arguably the poorest social groups in the country. The relevant clause under sub-paragraph 1(iv) of Schedule I, NREGA was amended by executive order in 2007, 2009, and in 2011.

In a notification issued on 6 March 2007, exactly one year after NREGA implementation began in February 2006, an amendment was made to allow for NREGA-funded works on private lands to be extended to families living 'below the poverty line' (BPL) as identified by the state governments.[23]

The expansion of NREGA works to lands privately owned by 'BPL' families effectively allowed the extension of publicly funded NREGA works to the vast and substantially flawed BPL category (Drèze and Khera 2010),[24] setting the stage for the use of NREGA funds for development of a much wider category of private lands rather than those owned only by SC and ST farmers.

On 22 July 2009, sub-paragraph 1(iv) of 'Schedule I' was further amended to include small and marginal farmers 'as defined in the Agriculture Debt Waiver and Debt Relief Scheme 2008', issued by the Congress-(I)-led central government. Given that eighty per cent of all farmers in India are small and marginal farmers (GoI, 2009) the July 2009 amendment was a further indication that public works funded under the NREGA were to be extended to a wide range of privately owned lands. The most recent amendment to clause 1(iv) of 'Schedule I' was made on 22 September 2011, to permit works on lands of beneficiaries under the Scheduled Tribes and Other Traditional Forest Dwellers (Recognition of Forest Rights) Act, 2006, an amendment that reiterated focus on the original intended beneficiaries of the clause.

Thus, from a provision within the law aimed specifically at offering state-funded land development to the poorest sections of the Indian population, sub-paragraph 1(iv) of Schedule I, NREGA was substantially expanded to include a wide range of social groups.

Some of these amendments were questioned in public forums. Nikhil Dey, who had been engaged in efforts to get the NREGA enacted, pointed out that the amendment to extend NREGA works to lands of small and marginal farmers was "not an obscure change," and that the amendment would "significantly change the focus of implementation" of the NREGA.[25]Aruna Roy and Nikhil Dey also voiced concerns that this amendment had been passed by the MoRD, GoI, without debate, and, further, that the nature of the changes envisaged could adversely impact transparency in programme implementation, since the focus of NREGA implementation would shift from work on community land to individual landholdings, that would make public scrutiny of the NREGA more difficult.[26] Others spoke out in support of the amendment to extend NREGA works to the private lands of all small and marginal farmers (Shah and Mohanty, 2010; Mihir Shah Committee Report, Government of India, 2012),[27] arguing that investment in privately owned lands would lead to an overall increase in agricultural productivity, and, therefore, should not be opposed.

The changes made to Schedule I, NREGA are an example of changes made to the original text of the law by the central executive in keeping with the provisions of Section 29 of the NREGA, that allows the central government the 'power to amend Schedules'. Thus while the enactment of the NREGA was celebrated as offering a secure right to work, the detail of the law itself was far from immutable. While the process of amending 'Schedule I' of the NREGA was legally sound, the amendments contributed to changes in program implementation at the level of the local state. Two points can be made in this regard. It could be argued that even if marginally, a politics of accommodation of landed classes was introduced into NREGA implementation. Further, in the process of implementation of works on private lands the ability of rural adults to claim 'work on demand' was potentially compromised.

In Madhya Pradesh, the state government (GoMP) placed significant emphasis on NREGA implementation on private lands as early as the 2007–08 financial year, the second year of NREGA implementation.[28] NREGA implementation on private lands was emphasised by the state government through the development of a wide array of 'sub-schemes' or sub-programmes that laid out detailed plans for NREGA implementation on privately owned lands. Some sub-schemes were targeted towards developing facilities for irrigation and land development, such as building wells,[29] or building 'bunds' or small embankments on private lands.[30] But other sub-schemes were aimed at developing small-scale commercial enterprises on private lands, funded by public money routed through the NREGA. Thus, under a Government of Madhya Pradesh NREGA 'sub-scheme', public money from NREGA was to be directed towards promoting silviculture[31] and to planting fruit trees on private lands,[32] with the intent that this would help NREGA workers move from wage employment to 'self-employment,'[33] and from 'unskilled' to 'skilled' work.[34]

It might be recalled that the NREGA statement of 'objects and reasons' passed by Parliament did not include promotion of 'self-employment' or 'skilled work' per se. Arguably, therefore, sub-schemes to promote self-employment and skilled work were part of specific initiatives taken by the state bureaucracy in the process of NREGA implementation, that went beyond the text of law. To some extent, it could be argued that these initiatives of the state bureaucracy were contingent on 'local' imperatives, which could be made to 'ride' on the NREGA. Senior bureaucrats in GoMP stated that, in Madhya Pradesh, 'NREGA was not seen as a wage employment scheme', but was seen as an 'opportunity to build assets and infrastructure' in order to have a 'long term impact on livelihood' and that implementing NREGA works on private lands was an important part of this strategy.[35]These initiatives had implications for the nature of implementation of the programme at the level of the local state, as discussed below.

The following paragraphs demonstrate that this 'strategy' for NREGA implementation adopted by GoMP adversely affected the possibility of claiming NREGA work as a matter of 'right' in some instances. Those seeking to get work sanctioned for their own land had to of course meet certain criteria, and the bureaucracy of the local state was to operate as a gate-keeper with the power to accept or reject an application for private land development, as is commonly the case for most beneficiary oriented programmes. Claimants of work, who were 'rights bearing workers' as per the NREGA, in some instances had to operate as 'beneficiaries' who could not always claim work as a 'right'. On paper, NREGA works on 'beneficiary' or privately owned rather than public lands were not viewed as contradicting the legal clauses of the NREGA itself.

As per law, a NREGA job card holder would be entitled to 'demand' work from the local administration. Further, the administration was to provide work within a period of fifteen days from the receipt of an application, as specified in law, irrespective of whether works in a village panchayat area at a given point in time, were being implemented on public or private land. If publicly funded work on private land was ongoing at the time when the application for work was received by the village panchayat, then work applicants would be assigned to the worksite/s on private land.

At the level of implementation in some places in Barwani and in East Nimar districts, a substantially different dynamic could be observed, where the original intended aims of enhancing wage employment and the emphasis on the 'rights based' implementation of the NREGA seemed to have dropped out of view.

The policy focus from the state bureaucracy for NREGA works on private lands influenced NREGA implementation in Village Panchayats (GPs). *Kapil dhara* wells were being constructed in villages across Barwani district in 2008–09 and 2009–10, including in areas where the above mentioned sangathan (JADS) was working. An inflated value for the kapildhara wells was often depicted in government records. In August 2009, for instance, twenty-four sangathan workers from Barwani block, Barwani district, wrote to the Barwani District Collector (DC) alerting him to corruption in the digging of kapildhara wells in their villages.[36]

In several sangathan meetings, other concerns were also voiced about works on private lands. Members of the sangathan were often concerned that the bureaucracy was disregarding the types of works being sought by the gram sabha, and deciding on works to be carried out in villages. In Ubdagarh Panchayat, (Pati Block, Barwani District) for instance, when more than 1000 sangathan members collectively applied for work in May 2008, they were asked to work on several *kapildhara* wells. Sangathan members refused to undertake this work, saying a large public pond was what the village needed, not wells on individual lands.[37] In a gram sabha meeting in Savariyapani village in Pati Block, Barwani District, the GP Secretary encouraged NREGA implementation on private lands, while gram sabha members, several of whom were sangathan members, asked instead for public water harvesting structures to be constructed under the NREGA.[38] In Roshani GP, in Khalwa Block, East Nimar district, Phulvatibai pointed out in April 2008 that she had managed to get some NREGA work in the past, but that since the GP was now exclusively implementing *kapildhara* wells on private land, only relatives of the respective landowners were being offered work, while others were being told that work was not available.[39] Ramsingh, a ward member from Roshani GP, corroborated this. On the *kapildhara* well on his land, he employed relatives and a few other people he knew who were not from his family, but were neighbours.[40]

It is worth emphasizing that the usefulness of NREGA works on privately owned land per se is not being questioned here. Indeed Ranaware et. al. (2015), highlight in relation to Maharashtra that such works can be of value. The preceding paragraphs highlight, however, that practices operative in NREGA implementation were on occasion contradictory to the stated intent and text of the law. This includes the intent of the NREGA to offer work as a 'right' and the legal provision to enable gram sabhas to decide on works to be implemented. The following section moves to a discussion on the 'web'[41] of actors engaged in the process of NREGA implementation in Barwani.

NREGA and the Web of Institutional Actors in Barwani, Madhya Pradesh

A complex institutional matrix related to NREGA implementation was observable at the level of the local state in Barwani in the first three years of NREGA implementation. At least fifty per cent of all NREGA works in a village are implemented by the Village Panchayat (or, Gram Panchayat, (GP)).[42] Works implemented by the GP include village ponds, roads, and soil conservation works on public lands. In addition, all works done on individual beneficiary lands come under the purview of the GP. The remainder of NREGA works (constituting 50% of the total value of works in a GP) are implemented by sub-district Panchayats (Janpad or Block Panchayats), District Panchayats (Zilla Panchayats), 'line departments' of GoMP, as well as NGOs engaged by the state and district administration.

The 'line' departments of GoMP acting as NREGA implementing agencies in 2009–10 in Barwani district Madhya Pradesh included the state Forest Department, the Public Works Department, the 'Narmada Valley Development Agency', the Directorate of Horticulture, Rural Engineering Services (RES), the Water Resources Department, and the Assistant Soil Conservation Officer.[43] Three NGOs, 'GraminVikas Trust' (GVT) (Village Development Trust), SarvodyaSamaajSevaSamiti, Sendhwa (Sarvodaya Social Service Committee, Sendhwa), and SarvodyaSamaajSevaSamiti, Niwali (Sarvodaya Social Service Committee, Niwali) were also appointed as implementing agencies by the state government. Of these, GVT worked in Pati block in Barwani district on watershed development projects.[44] In order to appoint these organisations, the state government published a commercial tender in national and regional newspapers seeking an 'expression of interest' from organisations willing to work with the government on specific aspects of the NREGA. Following this, several NGOs filed papers with the state government, providing details of work done by them in the past, as well as details of their finances. On this basis, organisations were shortlisted and 'allocated' by GoMP to the districts in which they were to work. The selected organisations, including GVT, were then directed to sign memoranda of agreement with the district government.[45] In addition to the abovementioned NGOs, 'Madhya Pradesh Rural Livelihood Project' (MPRLP) a project funded by the British Department for International Development (DfID),[46] was also appointed by the state government to work both with the GoMP bureaucracy and the Barwani district administration on NREGA implementation, specifically to promote NREGA sub-schemes of GoMP.[47]

In addition to the 'on site' supervision and carrying out of NREGA works, the district bureaucracies for all districts implementing the NREGA were required to organise a range of 'capacity building' activities in the district. These services were detailed in the Operational Guidelines for NREGA implementation issued by the MoRD, GoI, and not in the text of the NREGA itself.[48] These services related to 'training of personnel', 'communication' of legal provisions under the NREGA to create public awareness of the program, and 'training of key agencies and institutions' to carry out their 'responsibilities under the Act'.

In Madhya Pradesh, non-government and quasi-government organisations were appointed both as implementing agencies (as detailed above) and for 'capacity building' roles. The paragraphs that follow highlight the varied politics of claim-making that can be traced to actors engaged in NREGA implementation in Barwani.

Social audits, capacity building, and information-education-communication for NREGA implementation

This section highlights discussions with state and non-state institutional actors engaged with NREGA implementation in Barwani district, emphasizing the substantial difference in the politics of contention engaged in by these organisations, particularly when compared with JADS. It was argued earlier that JADS uses rights defined under NREGA as a tool in a wider politics of contention in relation to the state, thereby questioning extant hegemonies in relationships between state and non-state actors. The argument below demonstrates that while several NGOs engaged by the local state for NREGA implementation sought to work with an ethic of 'professionalism', they simultaneously served to reinforce existing power hierarchies in the course of NREGA implementation at the level of the local state. In other words, contra David Mosse (2004), who argues that managerial and professional cadres involved in implementing policy often take a 'simplistic' view of or act in ignorance of local social and political life, it is argued that several non-state actors engaged in NREGA implementation were aware of local politics but consciously acted to neutralise radical claim making and thereby 'depoliticised development'. Thus, a progressive text of law was co-opted to neutralise counter-hegemonic politics.[49]

As mentioned, MPRLP 'project facilitation staff' were accorded the task of promoting livelihoods, and implementing NREGA sub-schemes framed by the GoMP. MPRLP was also tasked by GoMPto train its staff to 'facilitate' gram sabhas, in Barwani, and several other districts in Madhya Pradesh. The rationale for engaging MPRLP staff to facilitate gram sabhas was rooted in the common observation that 'most gram sabhas do not meet,'[50] and that decisions related to local development are effectively taken by block and district level bureaucracies. MPRLP staff were therefore trained to ensure that gram sabhas meet regularly, and that matters related to livelihoods and village development are decided in these meetings at the level of the Village Panchayat.[51]

On the part of the state government in Madhya Pradesh, MPRLP 'cadres' were viewed as 'disciplined' and 'well trained,'[52] owing to which they would be able to act as neutral translating agents, making developmental programmes of GoI and GoMP intelligible in the villages where they work. On the part of GoMP bureaucrats, there seemed to be a ready acceptance of and resignation to the fact that the local level bureaucracy is not likely to perform the role of encouraging greater participation in gram sabhas.[53] However, narratives from within MPRLP revealed that while the organisation was able to train its staff to perform the role of managers and facilitators of gram sabhas, disturbing the societal status quo and the hegemonic position of those considered to be in positions of power within a village was actively discouraged.

The engagement of MPRLP cadres by GoMP, for 'village development' and NREGA implementation was in itself, not too different from the work of the 'village level worker' appointed for 'Community Development' (CD) by GoI in the years immediately after independence (Sinha, 2008). Subir Sinha points out that when Jawaharlal Nehru launched the CD programmes in 1952, 'planners were aware of deep disparities within rural communities, but... did not advocate using state power to radically alter rural power relations'. Sinha adds that in the view of planners, CD was 'avowedly 'apolitical'' (2008). Thus, 'structural reasons for inequality and poverty' remained outside the purview of CD, which 'merely provided an institutional framework for decreasing them' (2008).

In April 2008, the present author observed an MPRLP training programme on facilitating gram sabhas organised for new appointees to the MPRLP team in Barwani.[54] It was emphasised that the role of MPRLP was to 'encourage people to attend the gram sabha', to make Panchayat functionaries, including the sarpanch and sachiv, aware of their responsibilities, and to create a 'fear-free environment'[55] ('*bhaymukt maahaul*') in which gram sabhas could be held. To ensure the participation of gram sabha members[56] it was emphasised that small meetings with a few families at a time be held to encourage them to attend the gram sabha. This process of meeting people was aimed at 'educating' members of the gram sabha about their right to participate in this important village level meeting.

Training programmes of MPRLP staff were aimed at instilling 'community organiser' skills related to the facilitation of these meetings, and exploring the developmental role that gram sabhas are constitutionally required to play.[57] The prospect of MPRLP intervention to organise gram sabhas, however, was not welcomed in villages in Pati block with substantial JADS membership. I was told–

> 'An MPRLP team arrived in Kandra (village) to hold village meetings and organise gram sabhas. The people there asked them 'Who are you? We organise our own gram sabhas'. The next day, MPRLP staff came back with the Barwani Police, because apparently JADS members were obstructing the work of the MPRLP. We (JADS) filed a complaint with the Barwani Superintendent of Police, who admitted shamefacedly that the Barwani Police had asked to be involved in development projects, in an effort to build a relationship with 'the people'.[58]

At the MPRLP training in Barwani, it was emphasised that when gram sabhas are organised by MPRLP staff, the position of power held by dominant, landed groups should not be threatened or overtly challenged. One trainer cited his experience with attempting to intervene in a dispute related to construction of an NREGA funded village road ('*kutcha road*') in a village where MPRLP staff were already working.[59] A rich landlord had opposed the proposal to build the road in a poor hamlet in the village, where it would not be of use to him. Initial attempts by the said MPRLP employee to intervene in favour of allowing the road to be built in the poorer hamlet met with significant resistance from the wealthy landlord. In response, the MPRLP trainer was advised by his supervisors in the MPRLP Barwani District Office to meet the landlord. He subsequently met the landlord several times to assure him that MPRLP would 'not do anything to hurt his position' in the village. The road was built in the planned location, but only after the MPRLP employee stayed at the landlord's home as a house guest and won his support by assuring him that 'everyone could benefit from the NREGA'. The trainees in Barwani to whom this incident was being narrated were told, 'This is what we have to do. Our job is to go to the village, build trust, and get the job done'.[60] The message seemed to be that the implementation of a developmental initiative need not unsettle the societal status quo. The NREGA would thus need to be implemented in cognisance of local village dynamics. In contrast, NREGA implementation, as pursued by the membership of JADS was used to actively question those in positions of power within the state and within society itself.

The text below cites observations in relation to other NGOs engaged with the process of NREGA implementation in Barwani.

An important provision within the NREGA is the legal requirement that NREGA-related records and accounts be publicly disclosed and discussed on a regular basis in 'social audit' meetings. In the first three years of its implementation in Madhya Pradesh, NREGA-related 'social audits' were organised during gram sabha meetings in villages. However, soon after NREGA implementation started in 2006, GoMP made the decision to engage non-government and commercial organisations to facilitate social audits in GPs.[61] From the perspective of the state government, the logic behind engaging NGOs to facilitate social audits was similar to that of appointing the MPRLP to facilitate gram sabhas. This was part of government efforts to bypass potential hurdles in NREGA implementation due to inactive gram sabhas. In order to appoint NGOs to conduct social audits, a competitive bidding process was instated by GoMP. NGOs and commercial organisations were invited to submit bids in sealed envelopes, and the applicant with the lowest financial bid was to be selected to organise social audit meetings in villages in a specified district. This competitive bidding process was overruled by the Barwani District Collector, in order to appoint Asha Gram Trust (AGT), a long standing NGO established in Barwani in the 1980s.[62]

Importantly, it was not always the case that the organisations engaged to facilitate social audits adopted a position where they demanded full disclosure of public records related to NREGA implementation. This was also true of AGT, which sought to take a position of minimal confrontation with the district administration. Thus, in April 2008, while a social audit report for Savariyapani Panchayat, Pati Block, was submitted by AGT to the district administration, no discussion related to 'auditing' NREGA records had actually taken place in the gram sabha meeting.[63] In effect, in order to accommodate the hegemonic position of the district administration which implicitly discouraged reports that might indicate poor implementation of the NREGA, a radical provision within the NREGA to encourage transparency in government operations was effectively subverted. The provision was effectively implemented by AGT in a manner that entirely de-emphasized public accountability.

Since MPRLP was explicitly tasked by GoMP with facilitating gram sabhas as discussed above, the present author also asked MPRLP staff in Barwani about whether they had ever participated in and indeed facilitated disclosure of public records as required under the NREGA statute. Aware of the politically fraught terrain that would be encountered in seeking government financial records, those working within MPRLP were categorical in stating that 'arranging for disclosure of records' for the social audit process, 'is not what MPRLP does', and that asking for records 'is the responsibility of the gram sabha itself',[64] thus distancing MPRLP from a body (the gram sabha) that MPRLP was explicitly appointed to strengthen.

The Barwani district administration also appointed an NGO to conduct an 'Information Education Communication' (IEC) programme in villages, the stated aim of which was to ensure that people are made aware of their 'right to demand work' as defined under the NREGA statute. This contract was awarded to Samarpan Samaaj Sevi Sansthaan (Samarpan, hereafter) for Barwani District. Samarpan was also appointed by the district administrations of neighbouring Burhanpur and Jhabua districts to conduct social audits for NREGA implementation. Regarding social audits that Samarpan conducted, the organisational head candidly stated, 'the fact of the matter' was that 'the district administration only wanted good reports' (*'sach to yehhaikisarkarkosirfachchi report chahiye'*), so Samarpan staff 'made no effort to prove or disprove anything' (by way of seeking public disclosure of NREGA records). On asking for copies of the social audit reports which Samarpan submitted to the district administrations of Burhanpur and Jhabua, this researcher was informed that once submitted, the reports were the 'property of the district administration'. It was candidly pointed out that 'Samarpan' stood to lose if they challenged the district administration, since anything said against the district administration would have meant that they would get no other work from the government.[65]

The moot point being made here is that different actors engaged in the process of NREGA implementation draw on the law in vastly different ways. Not all engage in counter-hegemonic claim-making, and some actors engage with the rhetoric of rights in a manner that does not necessarily disturb the status quo ante, and, in fact even perpetuates it, in questionable ways.

Implications and conclusions

This chapter has discussed the engagement of a varied set of institutional and civil society actors with NREGA implementation, drawing substantially on examples from Barwani district, Madhya Pradesh. Rather than painting an exhaustive picture of implementation by each institutional actor, I have highlighted specific instances in their engagement with NREGA implementation.

A key point highlighted in this chapter is that the same text of law can be deployed in varied ways by both state and non-state actors. People's collectives such as JADS view rights defined under NREGA as offering a new set of tools to challenge the state, and in turn to challenge state-society relationships. It is possible this is the case because JADS as a sangathan was taking shape in the period when the NREGA was being debated and was later enacted. For JADS, then, the NREGA came into being at an important time in its own history. It is mentioned in this chapter that other people's collectives like the *Khedut Mazdoor Chetana Sangathan* (KMCS) on its part had attempted to draw on the law as a tool of social change especially after the enactment of panchayati raj related legislations. Having faced hurdles in the process of drawing on panchayati raj law, KMCS activists took a pessimistic view of 'rights' defined under the NREGA.[66]

It can be argued that different non-state actors can have different politics of engagement with the NREGA, and not all actors engaged in NREGA implementation seek 'emancipatory' (Santos, 2002) or 'counter-hegemonic' (Hunt, 1990) ends, where the prevalent subordination of social groups such as adivasis is challenged and questioned. To some non-state actors at the local level, the NREGA is a means to getting contractual work from the government and the reinforcement of existing societal hegemonies is an

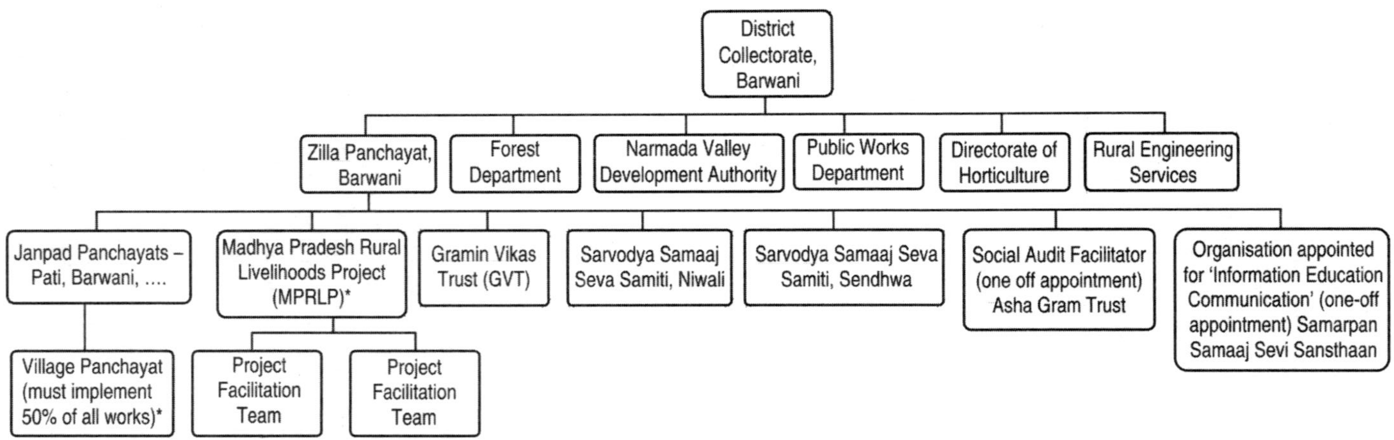

Figure 14.1 Web of Actors Involved in NREGA Implementation: Barwani District, Madhya Pradesh

Source: *Flexing legal Texts: The Politics of Claiming a Right to Work*, Unpublished PhD Thesis, SOAS, University of London (Nayak, 2012).

acceptable by-product in the pursuit of these contracts. To other non-state actors, the NREGA is a means to access funds to develop privately owned lands. To others still, including non-state actors such as JADS, the NREGA is a legislation that significantly changes their relationship with the local state.

Thus, civil society (viewed here as non-state actors outside the familial realm), is defined as much by a politics of power as by a politics of protest (Chandhoke, 2001). The politics of power operates when actors such as MPRLP agree that the societal status-quo must not be overtly challenged in the process of NREGA implementation. Other actors such as the organisations discussed above, that are contracted to conduct social audits, are complicit in obscuring state practice rather than strengthening transparency when they conduct 'social' audits without asking that books of accounts be made public, and when social audit reports are falsified or protected as 'secret' documents. As a result, state 'hegemony', understood in the Gramscian sense as a synthesis of coercion and consent (Anderson, 1976) is reinforced through a particular construction of participatory practice, carefully monitored and overseen by the local state. Here, institutional actors of the local state are closely invested in perpetuating a mode of implementation of the NREGA that is reminiscent of earlier developmental programmes where rights as defined under the NREGA were not available to citizens. The politics of protest on the other hand is geared towards a deepening of democracy (Harriss, 2001).

A second key point highlighted in this chapter is as follows. Varied ways of interpreting and implementing the NREGA lie at the heart of the journey traversed by citizens from being 'beneficiaries' of developmental programmes to 'rights bearing NREGA workers' and back to being 'beneficiaries' at the mercy of the local bureaucracy that may or may not sanction an NREGA funded work on private land or may fail to ensure that work from the NREGA continues to be provided to those who seek it.

It can be argued that the NREGA is being pulled in multiple directions, irrespective of the text of law. The NREGA can offer workers otherwise dependant on the informal economy an important means to resist underpaid and exploitative work (Drèze and Khera, 2011; Khera and Nayak, 2009), but where workers are unable to access work on demand and as a matter of right, the dominance of local landlords and contractors may continue. The case is not made here that self-employment programs per se are problematic, but rather, that making self-employment projects available under the NREGA tends to over-rule the 'rights' defined under the NREGA in the first place. As highlighted by Cornwall and Nyamu-Musembi, 'rights-based approaches to development' have been seen by some as the key to *re*-politicise development.

However, 'rights talk can function differently from different mouths' (Cornwall and Nyamu-Musembi, 2004), and indeed 'rights' too, can be de-politicised (Ferguson, 1990).

Further, it may also be noted here, that contra Corbridge et. al. (2005), who in their discussion of 'everyday state practice' in India, take the view that policies shaped by 'New Delhi' are often reinvented at the district and block levels; it can be argued that most 'reinvention' of policy at the level of implementation (district, block and village) is implicitly supported by the central and state governments and is carried out with their know-how and consent. Thus, arguably it is not simply the case that the central and state governments seek to implement the demand-driven-right-to-work in letter and spirit, which is, in turn, derailed by the local state. Rather, the local state draws on the reinvention of policy that is sanctioned by the central and state government; while also acting to emphasise its own authority and autonomy.

At this point we can come back to the question of the transformative potential that can be associated with a text of rights. As pointed out by Upendra Baxi, the 'universal' ideology of rights 'both' enables the 'legitimation of power and the *praxis* of emancipatory politics' (1998).[67] Further, as highlighted by Alan Hunt, legal and rights discourses offer discursive possibilities for subordinate groups to question their subordination and challenge dominant social groups, though these *possibilities* might not always be realised (Hunt, 1990). The real world of collective action and claim making as demonstrated by drawing on the case of JADS, requires a range of actions that include meetings, marches, demonstrations and the use of formal letters as a means of organising resistance. The 'right to work' under the NREGA injects an additional legal and radical tool that can be deployed to strengthen collective action in this arena. A text of rights might also create conditions for the seeds of radical politics to be sown anew, where a new set of rights is appropriated by new actors and deployed for progressive ends. However, what becomes clear is that the law does not settle politics as much as it contributes to creating a new layer in the 'production of politics' (Hall, 1999).

Endnotes

1. The 'Naxalite' movement itself dates back to the 1950s but reference is being made here to more recent revival of the debate related to the Maoist movement.
2. In the years before this, JADS worked as a 'sub-sangathan' of the Adivasi Mukti Sangathan (AMS), discussed by Banerjee (n.d.), Baviskar (2001) and Nilsen (2010, 2012). JADS started working independently of AMS in 2000 following differences with the AMS leadership.

3. Reference is being made here to Supreme Court orders under the 'Right to Food case', Civil Writ Petition 196/2001, People's Union of Civil Liberties v. Union of India, where the court issued orders related to SGRY.
4. Emphasis added.
5. Letter from JADS to Barwani District Collector (DC) submitted on May 12, 2006, signed by KS (name has been anonymized); translated from Hindi.
6. Specified in Paragraph 12 of Schedule I, NREGA, 2005.
7. Letter from JADS to Barwani DC, signed by TS (name has been anonymized), submitted on May 12, 2006; translated from Hindi.
8. As highlighted in Khera (2011), it is important to note that the practice of 'demanding' NREGA work by way of written applications was relatively rare in 2008 and continued to be so later (also see: Gaiha et. al., 2010)
9. Translated from Hindi.
10. This is the local police station for village Keli in Barwani block, Barwani district.
11. Regarded the head of the village as per Bhil custom, not the elected village head (*sarpanch*), as per constitutional law.
12. Member of JADS.
13. Letter from JADS to Barwani DC, Submitted on May 24, 2006, Signed by M. Krishnaswamy.
14. On May 23, 2006, 2508 workers filed applications for unemployment allowance (The number of applications from villages in Pati block were as follows: Kandra - 298; Kalmijhavar - 141, Ubadagad - 394, Limbi - 497, Borkhedi - 120, Kalakhet - 74, Ghatbara - 39, Tapar - 69, Ban - 87, Nalti - 50. The number of applications from villages in Pansemal block were as follows: Malgaon- 407, Karanpura - 144, Bhatki - 78, Umarbaida - 108. On 30 May 2006, 193 workers, and on 6 June 2006, 178 workers from Piparkund Panchayat also filed claims. (Source: Letter from JADS to Sonia Gandhi, President, Indian National Congress, dated on July 31, 2006).
15. In a conversation with Krishnaswamy on April 24, 2011.
16. Source: Letter number 427, dated July 21, 2006, from Barwani District Collector to Mihir Shah, Advisor to Office of the Commissioner of the Supreme Court (OCSC); translated from Hindi.
17. Source: Performance Audit Report 11 of 2008, CAG, GoI. Note that the unemployment allowance was not paid to workers whose households had completed 100 days of work by December 2006, the date when the allowance was finally paid.
18. Reference is made here to the legal requirement that work should be offered by the GP within 15 days of an application for work being received.
19. D.O.No.M.28012/2/04-SGSY (M) dated September 9, 2005 from Secretary Rural Development (RD), MoRD, GoI to all state governments.
20. Letter dated September 9, 2005, from MoRD, GoI to state governments, op. cit.
21. This is permitted u/s 29, NREGA, 2005. After NREGA enactment in 2005, the NREGA was amended primarily by executive orders later published in the Gazette of India. The only legislative amendment to the NREGA was made on December 12,

2009, when the name of the legislation was amended from 'National Rural Employment Guarantee Act' to 'Mahatma Gandhi National Rural Employment Guarantee Act', vide The National Rural Employment Guarantee (Amendment) Act, 2009.

22. Indira AwasYojana, IAY, is aGoI programme to provide housing to the rural poor.
23. Emphasis added
24. Drèze and Khera point out that based on 2004–05 National Sample Survey data for monthly per capita expenditure, only 53.1% rural households in the poorest quintile of households in India had a BPL card in 2004–05, while at the same time 17.8% households in the richest quintile had a BPL card (Drèze and Khera, 2010, 55).
25. Nikhil Dey, statement at press conference organised by 'People's Action for Employment Guarantee' (PAEG), Press Club of India, New Delhi, August 7, 2009.
26. See A. Roy and N. Dey, 'Dalits, the Poor and the NREGA', *The Hindu,* August 27, 2009.
27. Also see, MihirShah, 'Multiplier accelerator synergy in NREGA', *The Hindu,* May 30, 2009.
28. In 2006/07, Principal Secretary, Panchayati Raj, GoMP, issued orders that NREGA funded irrigation facilities should be provided to SC and ST families (letter number 6464, dated May 2, 2006).
29. Built under the *kapildhara*sub-scheme.
30. As per the *bhumishilp*sub-scheme.
31. As per the *resham*sub-scheme.
32. As per the *nandanphalodyan*sub-scheme.
33. GoMP, document on NREGA sub-schemes, 2009.
34. SP, Secretary GoI, Minutes of MoRD meeting, 2009, accessed online.
35. Interview with RS, CEO, MP State Employment Guarantee Council, GoMP, interviewed on September 1, 2009.
36. The letter was signed by sangathan members from Varalyapani, Vegalgaon, Mardai and Bori villages; letter submitted to Barwani DC, n.d.
37. Field work notes, Ubdagarh village, July 18, 2008.
38. Field work notes, Savariyapani village, August 16, 2009.
39. Phulvatibai, interviewed on April 10, 2008.
40. Ramsingh, interviewed on April 11, 2008.
41. The term 'web' rather than, say, 'network' of actors is used, since the different NGOs operate in relative isolation from each other. The organisations are nonetheless depicted in an indicative organogram in Figure 14.1, to indicate their relationship with the Barwani district administration.
42. In keeping with section 16, NREGA.
43. Barwani district, implementing agency wise expenditure statement, Audit no. 1742–0910, http://164.100.12.7/netnrega/impl_audit_report.aspx, accessed on 04/02/2011.
44. Source: Audit report op. cit. and interview with DA, GVT Project Officer, Barwani, interviewed on January 28, 2008.
45. DA, interviewed on January 28, 2008.

46. The nomenclature of 'UK Aid' was not yet in use.
47. The Madhya Pradesh Society for Rural Livelihood Promotion (MPSRLP) was appointed by GoMP, as an NREGA 'implementing agency' for Madhya Pradesh as a whole. MPSRLP was registered as a Society in July 2004, under the Madhya Pradesh Societies Registration Act, 1973, as the apex coordinating organisation for the 'Madhya Pradesh Rural Livelihood Project' (MPRLP). The registered Society, ie. MPSRLP was a collaborative initiative between GoMP and the UK Department for International Development (DfID).
48. MoRD, GoI, NREGA Operational Guidelines. (GoI, 2008).
49. This draws on analytical points made most prominently by Ferguson (1990), and more recently also by Sangeeta Kamat and Vasudha Chhotray about the possible depoliticising effect of 'development' (Chhotray, 2011; Ferguson and Lohmann, 1994; Kamat, 2002, 2004).
50. TR (name has been anonymized), Madhya Pradesh State Representative for DFID, UK. Interviewed on March 18, 2008, Bhopal.
51. TR, interview, op. cit.
52. RS (name has been anonymized), Interviewed on September 1, 2009.
53. RS, interview, op. cit.
54. These new appointees had been recruited for 'Phase II' of MPRLP (2008–12).
55. VR (name has been anonymized), Notes from MPRLP Staff Training Workshop, Barwani, April 6, 2008–April 7, 2008.
56. All voting age adults in the village.
57. Notes from MPRLP Staff Training Workshop, Barwani, April 6, 2008–April 7, 2008.
58. In a conversation with Krishnaswamy on April 5, 2008.
59. The road was to be built as a public work funded via the NREGA.
60. MJ (name has been anonymized), Notes from MPRLP training Barwani, April 7, 2008.
61. This practice was withdrawn by GoMP by 2009.
62. BS (name has been anonymized), Interviewed on February 16, 2008; and letter submitted by AGT to Barwani DC, dated January 19, 2007.
63. In April 2008, the GP Secretary of Savariyapani Panchayat gave the author a copy of a social audit report written by AGT staff. The report stated that a social audit exercise had been conducted in Savariyapani village on April 14, 2008. Fortuitously, I had attended this particular gram sabha meeting in Savariyapani village. Having witnessed the meeting itself, it was clear to me that the social audit related questions were not raised in the gram sabha meeting at all. The report had been written without any discussion, and was signed by five people allegedly from the gram sabha.
64. VR, Notes from MPRLP training Barwani, April 7, 2008.
65. DS, interviewed on September 5, 2009.
66. R. Banerjee, interview, September 6, 2009. Banerjee started the KMCS in Alirajpur, in south-west Madhya Pradesh in 1985. The Narmada BachaoAndolan later started around 1987. AmitaBaviskar (2001, 2004b), has written about KMCS.
67. Emphasis in original.

References

Anderson, Perry. 1976. The Antinomies of Antonio Gramsci. *New Left Review*.

Banerjee, Rahul. n.d. *Recovering the Lost Tongue: A Manifesto of Anarcho-Environmentalism*. Accessed March 1, 2011. Available at, http://sites.google.com/site/rahulindauri/recovering-the-lost-tongue-1.

Bagchee, Aruna. 2005. 'Political and Administrative Realities of Employment Guarantee Scheme.' *Economic and Political Weekly* 40 (42): 4531–4537.

Baviskar, Amita. 1997. 'Tribal Politics and Discourses of Environmentalism.' *Contributions to Indian Sociology* 31 (2): 195–223.

Baviskar, Amita. 2001. *Written on the Body, Written on the Land: Violence and Environmental Struggles in Central India*. Paper presented at the Berkeley Workshop on Environmental Politics, Institute of International Studies, University of California, Berkeley.

Baviskar, Amita. 2004. *In the Belly of the River, Second edition*. New Delhi: Oxford University Press.

Baxi, Upendra. 1992. 'The State's Emissary.': The Place of Law in Subaltern Studies.' In *Subaltern Studies 7: Writings on South Asian History and Society*, edited by P. Chatterjee and G. Pandey. New Delhi: Oxford University Press.

Baxi, Upendra. 1998. 'Voices of Suffering and the Future of Human Rights.' *Transnational Law and Contemporary Problems*, 8 (Fall): 125–169.

Bhatia, Bela. 2005. 'The Naxalite Movement in Central Bihar.' *Economic and Political Weekly* 40 (15): 1536–1549.

Chakrabarty, Dipesh. 2000. *Provincialising Europe: Postcolonial Thought and Historical Difference*. Princeton: Princeton University Press.

Chakrabarty, Dipesh. 2005. '"In the Name of Politics": Sovereignty, Democracy and the Multitude in India.' *Economic and Political Weekly* 40 (30): 3293–3301.

Chandhoke, Neera. 2001. 'The 'Civil' and the 'Political' in Civil Society.' *Democratization* 8 (2): 1–24.

Corbridge, Stuart, Glyn Williams, Manoj Srivastava and Rene Véron. 2005. *Seeing the State: Governance and Governmentality in India*. Cambridge: Cambridge University Press.

Cornwall, Andrea and Celestine Nyamu-Musembi. 2004. 'Putting the 'Rights-Based Approach' to Development into Perspective.' *Third World Quarterly* 25 (8): 1415–1437.

Drèze, Jean. 2002. 'On Research and Action.' *Economic and Political Weekly* 37 (9): 817–819.

Drèze, Jean, and Reetika Khera. 2010. 'The BPL Census and a Possible Alternative.' *Economic and Political Weekly* 45 (9): 54–63.

———. 2011. 'The Battle for Employment Guarantee.' In *The Battle for Employment Guarantee*, edited by R. Khera. New Delhi: Oxford University Press.

Drèze, Jean and Christian Oldiges. 2007. 'Commendable Act.' *Frontline* 24 (14).

———. 2009. 'Work in Progress.' *Frontline* 26 (4).

Ferguson, James. 1990. *The Anti-Politics Machine: Development, Depoliticisation, Bureaucratic Power in Lesotho*. Cambridge: Cambridge University Press.

Fox, James. 1996. 'How Does Civil Society Thicken? The Political Construction of Social Capital in Rural Mexico.' *World Development* 24 (6): 1089–1103.

Godbole, Girija and Bhaskar Vira. 2004. 'Towards an Alternative Politics: People's Movements Join the Electoral Process.' *Infochange India*. Accessed May 1, 2010. Available at, http://infochangeindia.org/governance/features/towards-an-alternative-politics-people-s-movements-join-the-electoral-process.html.

GoI. 2009. 'The Challenge of Employment in India: An Informal Economy Perspective.' National Council for Employment in the Unorganised Sector (NCEUS).

———. 2012. Report of the Committee for Revision of MGNREGA Operational Guidelines. Mihir Shah Committee Report.

Hall, Stuart. 1999. 'Reading Gramsci.' In *Gramsci's Political Thought: An Introduction,* edited by R. Simon. London: The Electric Book Company.

Harriss, John. 2001. 'Social Capital Construction and the Consolidation of Civil Society in Rural Areas.' *DESTIN Working Paper Series 01–16.*

———. 2010. 'The Naxalite/Maoist Movement in India: A Review of Recent Literature.' *Institute of South Asian Studies, Working Paper Series, Working Paper No. 109.* Singapore: National University of Singapore.

Harvey, Neil. 1998. *The Chiapas Rebellion: The Struggle for Land and Democracy*. Durham and London: Duke University Press.

Hunt, Alan. 1990. 'Rights and Social Movements: Counter-Hegemonic Strategies.' *Journal of Law and Society* 17 (3): 309–328.

Joshi, Anuradha. 2010. 'Do Rights Work? Law, Activism, and the Employment Guarantee Scheme.' *World Development* 38 (4): 620–630.

Kannabiran, K. G. 2004. *The Wages of Impunity: Power, Justice and Human Rights.* Hyderabad: Orient Longman.

Khera, Reetika. 2008. Empowerment Guarantee Act. *Economic and Political Weekly* 43 (35): 8–10.

———, ed. 2011. *The Battle for Employment Guarantee.* New Delhi: Oxford University Press.

Khera, Reetika and Nandini Nayak. 2009. 'Women Workers and Perceptions of the National Rural Employment Guarantee Act.' *Economic and Political Weekly* 44(43).

Kunnath, George. 2006. 'Becoming a Naxalite in Rural Bihar: Class Struggle and its Contradictions.' *Journal of Peasant Studies* 33 (1): 89–123.

Mosse, David. 2004. 'Is Good Policy Unimplementable? Reflections on the Ethnography of Aid Policy and Practice.' *Development and Change* 35 (4).

Nayak, Nandini. 2008. 'Songs of Hope'. *The Hindu Sunday Magazine*, September 14.

———. 2012. 'Flexing legal texts: The Politics of Claiming a 'Right to Work'.' Unpublished PhD Thesis, SOAS, University of London.

Nilsen, Alf. 2010. *Dispossession and Resistance in India: The River and the Rage*. New Delhi: Routledge.

———. 2012. 'Adivasis in and against the State.' *Critical Asian Studies* 44 (2): 251–282.

O'Brien, K. 1996. Rightful Resistance. *World Politics,* 49 (1): 31–55.

Rahul. 1998. 'Bhil Women of Nimad: Growing Assertion.' *Economic and Political Weekly* 33 (9): 445–446.

———. 1999. 'Grand Old Man of the Socialist Fringe.' *Economic and Political Weekly* 34 (16/17): 947–948.

Rajagopal, Balakrishnan. 2003. *International Law from Below: Development, Social Movements and Third World Resistance*. Cambridge: Cambridge University Press.

———. 2005. 'Limits of Law in Counter Hegemonic Globalisation: The Indian Supreme Court and the Narmada Valley Struggle.' *Law and Globalisation from Below: Towards a Cosmopolitan Legality*. Cambridge: Cambridge University Press.

Ranaware, Krushna et. al. 2015. 'MGNREGA Works and Their Impacts: A Study of Maharashtra.' *Economic and Political Weekly* 50 (13).

Roseberry, William. 1994. 'Hegemony and the Language of Contention.' In *Everyday Forms of State Formation: Revolution and the Negotiation of Rule in Modern Mexico*, edited by G. M. Joseph and D. Nugent. Durham: Duke University Press.

Samaddar, Ranabir. 2009. 'Prescribed, Tolerated and Forbidden Forms of Claim Making.' In *State of Justice in India: Issues of Social Justice* (*Vol. I: Social Justice and Enlightenment: West Bengal*), edited by P. K. Bose and S. K. Das. New Delhi: Sage Publications.

Santos, Boaventura de Sousa. 2002. *Toward a New Legal Common Sense: Law, Globalization and Emancipation, Second Edition*. London: Butterworths LexisNexis.

Santos, Boaventura de Sousa and C. Rodríguez-Garavito. 2005. 'Law, Politics and the Subaltern in Counter-Hegemonic Globalisation.' In *Law and Globalisation from Below*, edited by B. D. S. Santos and C. A. Rodríguez-Garavito. Cambridge: Cambridge University Press.

Shah, Mihir. 2008. 'Radicalism of NREGA [Letter to the Editor].' *Economic and Political Weekly* 43 (23).

Shah, D. and S. Mohanty. 2010. 'Implementation of NREGA during Eleventh Plan in Maharashtra: Experiences, Challenges and Ways Forward.' *Indian Journal of Agricultural Economics* 65 (3).

Sinha, Subir. 2008. 'Lineages of the Developmentalist State: Transnationality and Village India, 1900–1965.' *Comparative Studies in Society and History* 50 (1): 57–90.

———. 2011. 'The Long March from the Margins: Subaltern Politics, Justice and Nature in Postcolonial India.' In *The Borders of Justice*, edited by E. Balibar, S. Mezzadra and R. Samaddar. Philadelphia: Temple University Press.

Sundar, Nandini, ed. 2009. *Legal Grounds: Natural Resources, Identity, and the Law in Jhakhand*. Oxford: Oxford University Press.

Tarrow, Sidney. 1993. 'Cycles of Collective Action: Between Moments of Madness and the Repertoire of Contention.' *Social Science History* 17 (2): 281–307.

———. 2011. *Power in Movement: Social Movements and Contentious Politics*. Cambridge: Cambridge University Press.

Tilly, Charles. 1978. *From Mobilisation to Revolution*. New York: Random House.

———. 1979. 'Social Movements and National Politics.' Ann Arbor, Michigan: Center for Research on Social Organisation.

About the Contributors

Sai Balakrishnan, Assistant Professor in Urban Planning, Harvard University Graduate School of Design, Boston, MA.

Elizabeth Chatterjee, Postdoctoral Scholar, Department of Political Science, University of Chicago; Research Associate, Contemporary South Asian Studies Programme, University of Oxford.Rajeshwari Deshpande, Professor, Department of Politics and Public Administration, Savitribai Phule Pune University, Pune.

Rob Jenkins, Professor of Political Science, Hunter College & The Graduate Center, City University of New York, New York.

Kalaiyarasan A, Assistant Professor, Institute for Studies in Industrial Development, New Delhi

Ajit Menon, Professor, Madras Institute of Development Studies, Chennai.

Sripad Motiram, Indira Gandhi Institute of Development Research, Mumbai, and University of Massachusetts, Boston.

R Nagaraj, Professor, Indira Gandhi Institute of Development Research, Mumbai.

Nandini Nayak, Assistant Professor, School of Development Studies, Ambedkar University Delhi, Delhi.

Suhas Palshikar, Retired Professor, Department of Politics and Public Administration, Savitribai Phule Pune University, Pune.

Shashi Ratnakar Singh, Doctoral student, Department of Geography, Cambridge University, Cambridge, UK.

Partha Ray, Professor, Economics Area, Indian Institute of Management Calcutta, Kolkota.

Supriya Roy Chowdhury, Professor, Institute of Social and Economic Change, Bangalore.

Preeti Sampat, Assistant Professor, Sociology, School of Liberal Studies, Ambedkar University Delhi.

M Vijayabaskar, Associate Professor, Madras Institute of Development Studies, Chennai.

P. S. Vijayshankar, Founder Member, Samaj Pragati Sahayog, Bagli, Dewas district, Madhya Pradesh.

Index